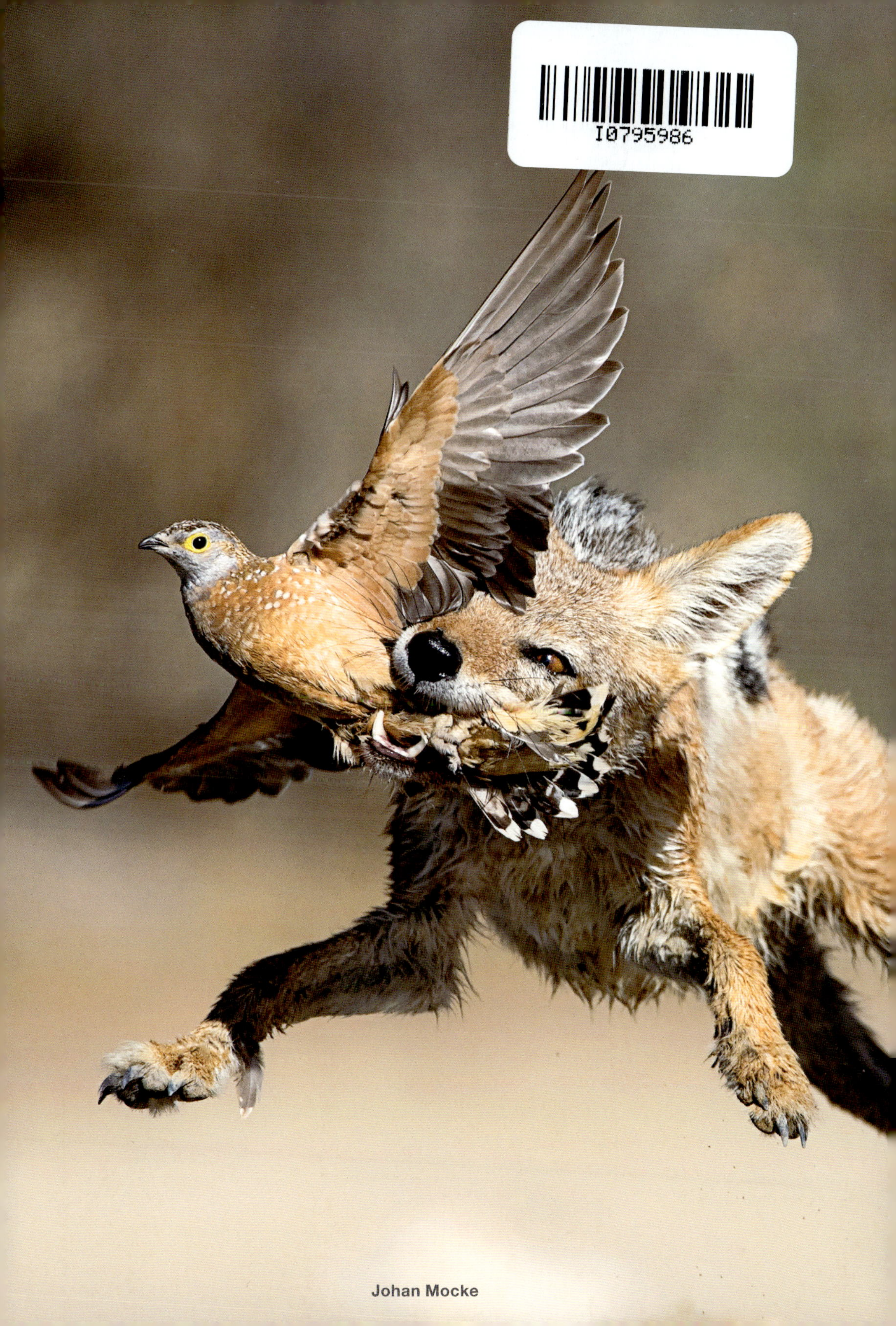

Johan Mocke

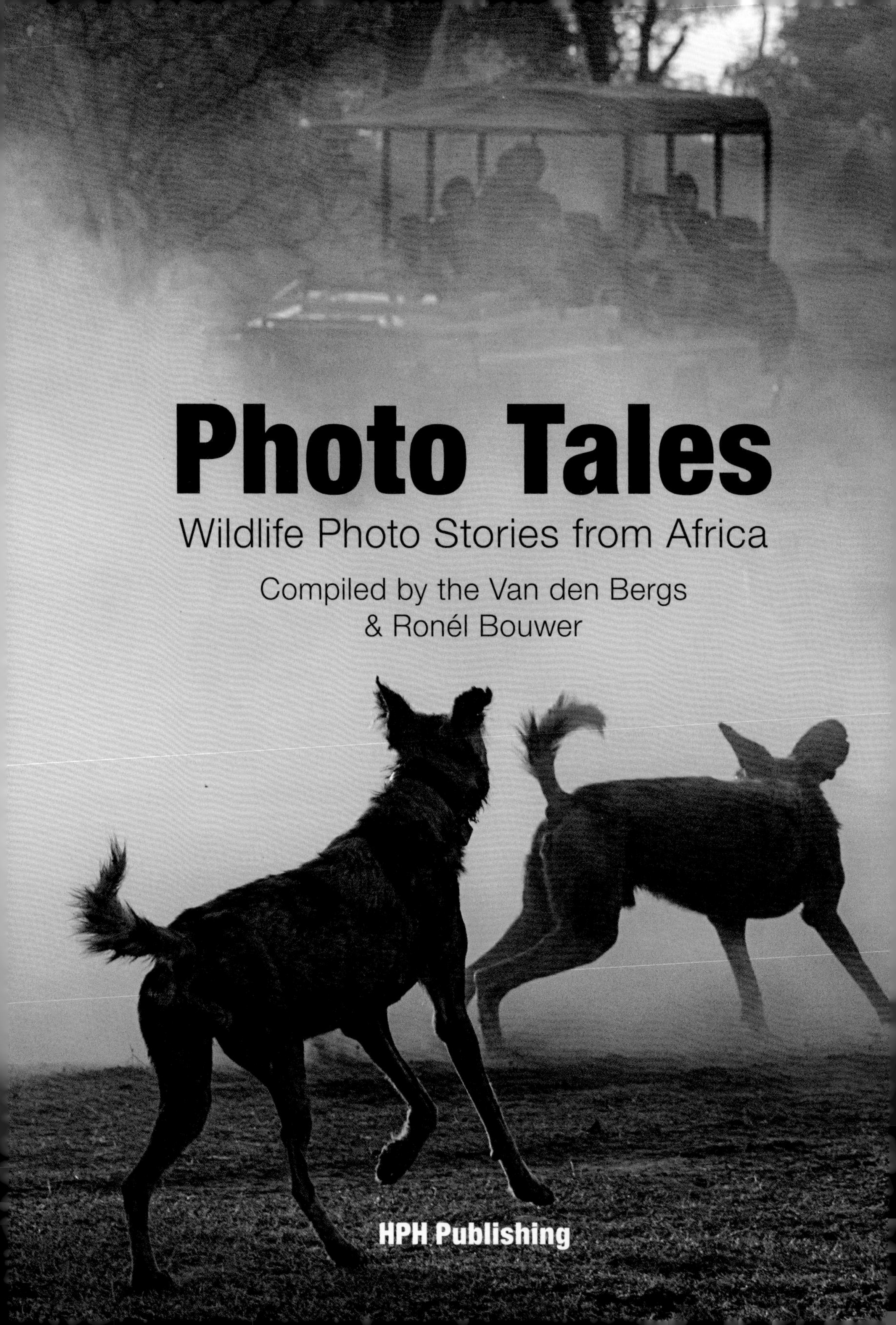

Photo Tales

Wildlife Photo Stories from Africa

Compiled by the Van den Bergs
& Ronél Bouwer

HPH Publishing

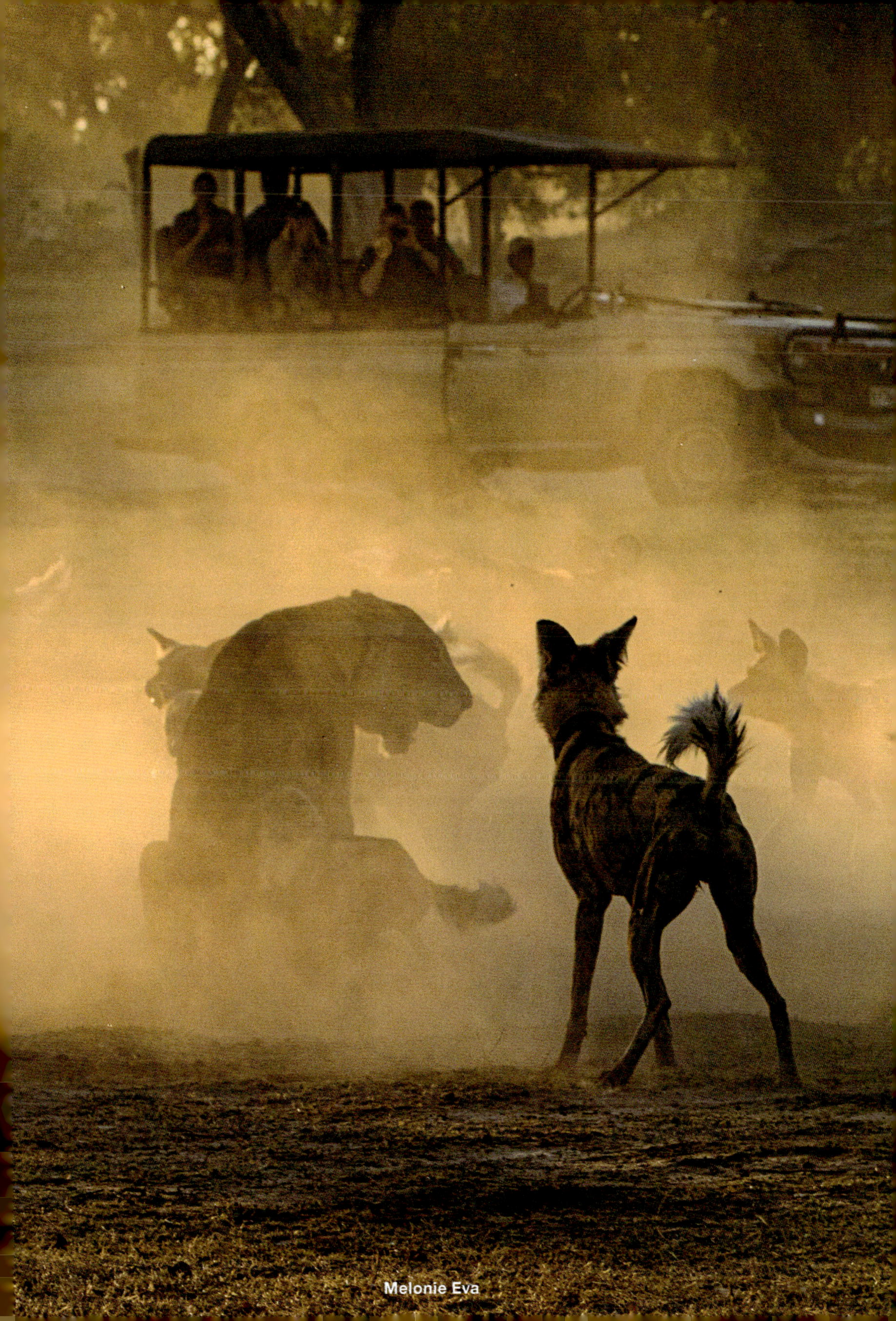

Melonie Eva

Contents

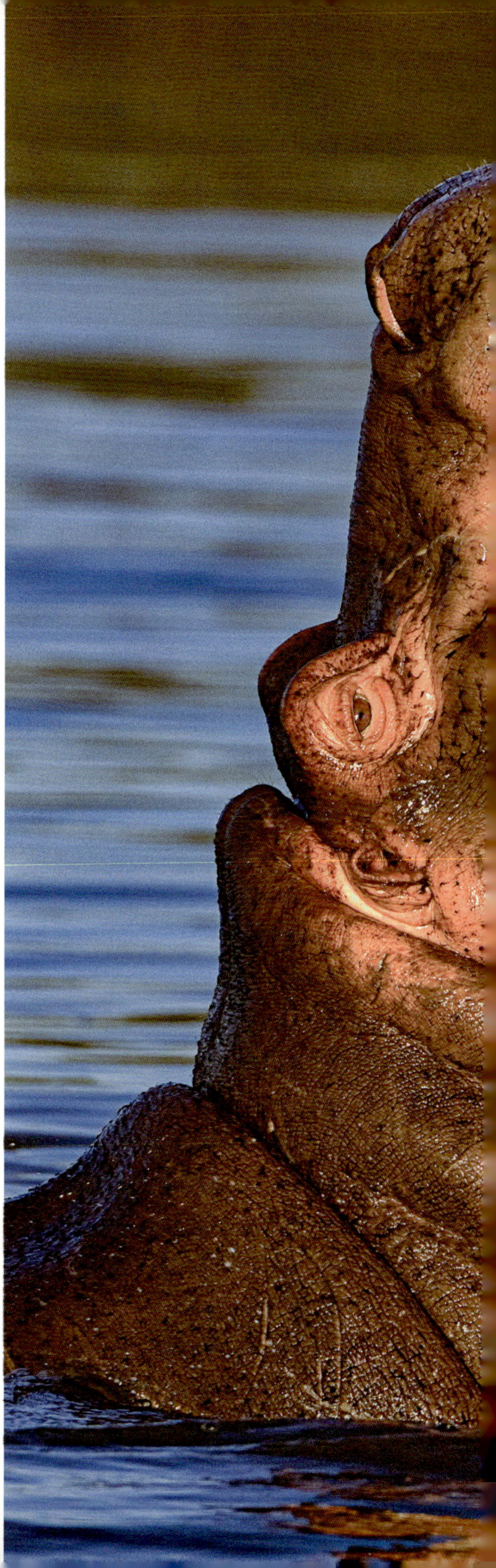

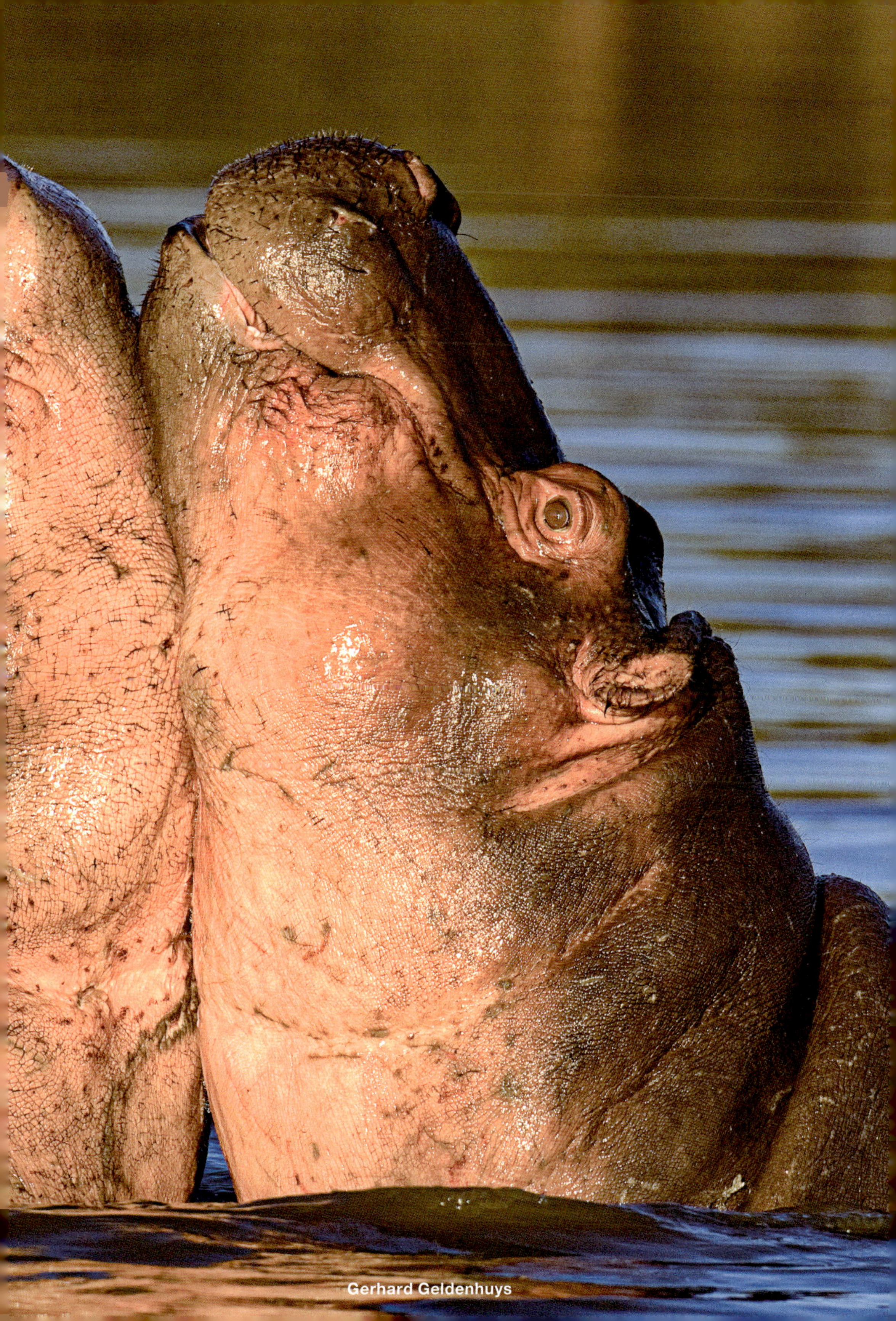

Gerhard Geldenhuys

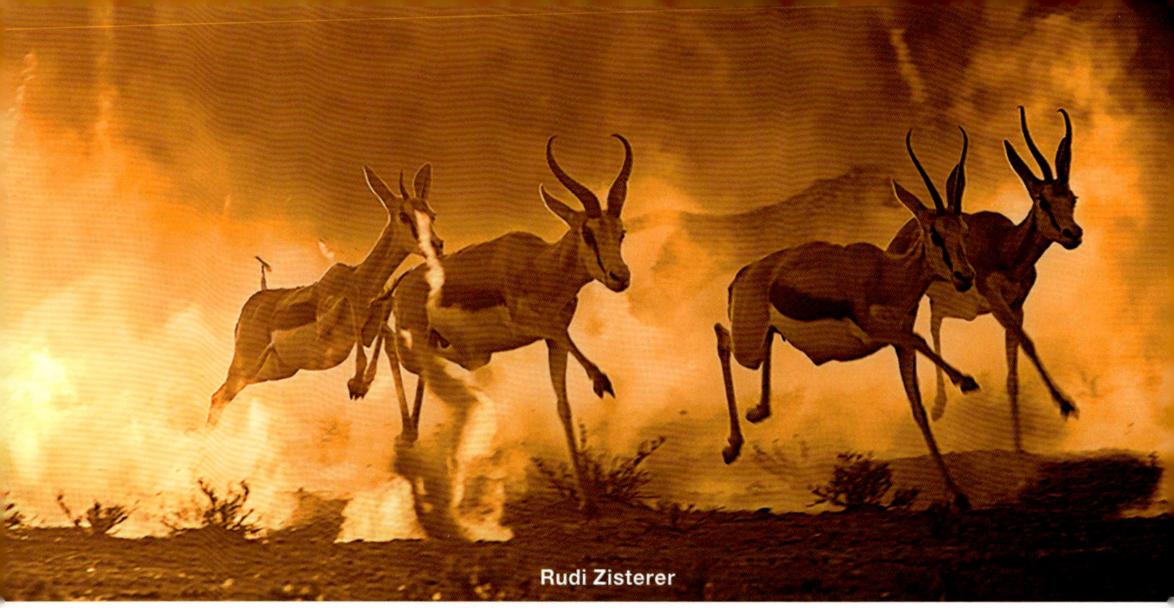

Rudi Zisterer

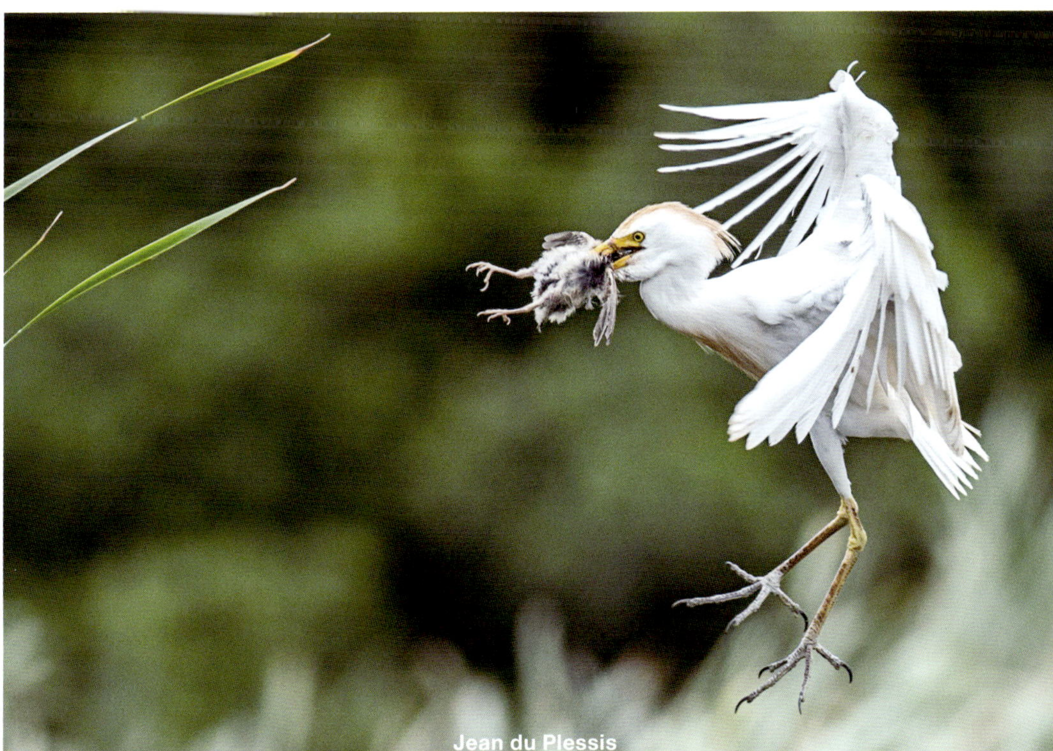

Jean du Plessis

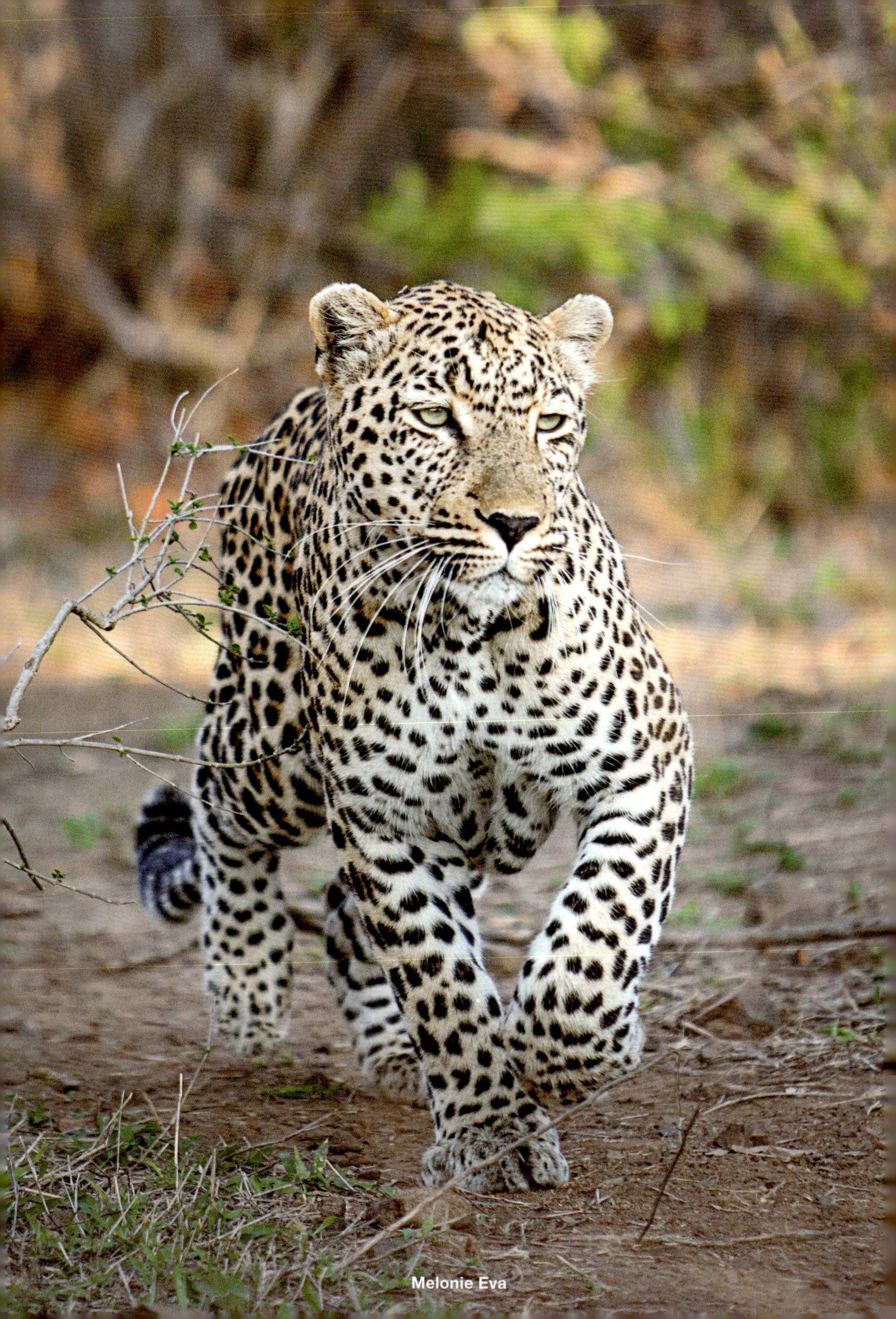

Melonie Eva

Introduction

At night, while we sit around camp fires in game reserves, the hands of Mother Nature wrap the wilderness in darkness, shake animals, and roll them out onto our game-drive board game, like dice. We never know what we will see in the morning.

But the thrill of going on a game drive is not only about what nature will show our eyes. Game drives are also about smelling the perfume of plants, hearing the voices of woodland kingfishers, feeling the howling wind of wild places, and following tracks crossing sandy roads that lead us into thickets of fantasy. Game drives are about the thrill of seeing dreams appear from nowhere, merge into reality, pass very close to our vehicles, and disappear again into our treasure chests.

Every game drive is a lottery, but even if we don't win the jackpot, we always win something. It is as if Mother Nature uses not only animals as dice, but human emotions and thoughts as well. Love and ideas are easy to spot while on a game drive, and we often drive into thoughts which would not have been possible in the smog of a city – epiphanies as clear as the morning sunlight, visions that flash over our heads like peregrine falcons.

With *Photo Tales*, **HPH Publishing** has tried to capture these visions. In its pages you will find tales of dreams that have come true as well as recipes for brewing wonder, tobacco for your pipe-dreams, and bait for luring fantasy from the thickets. This book is proof imagination can become reality if you are prepared to follow the tracks left by the dice in the soft sands of safari roads.

Heinrich van den Berg

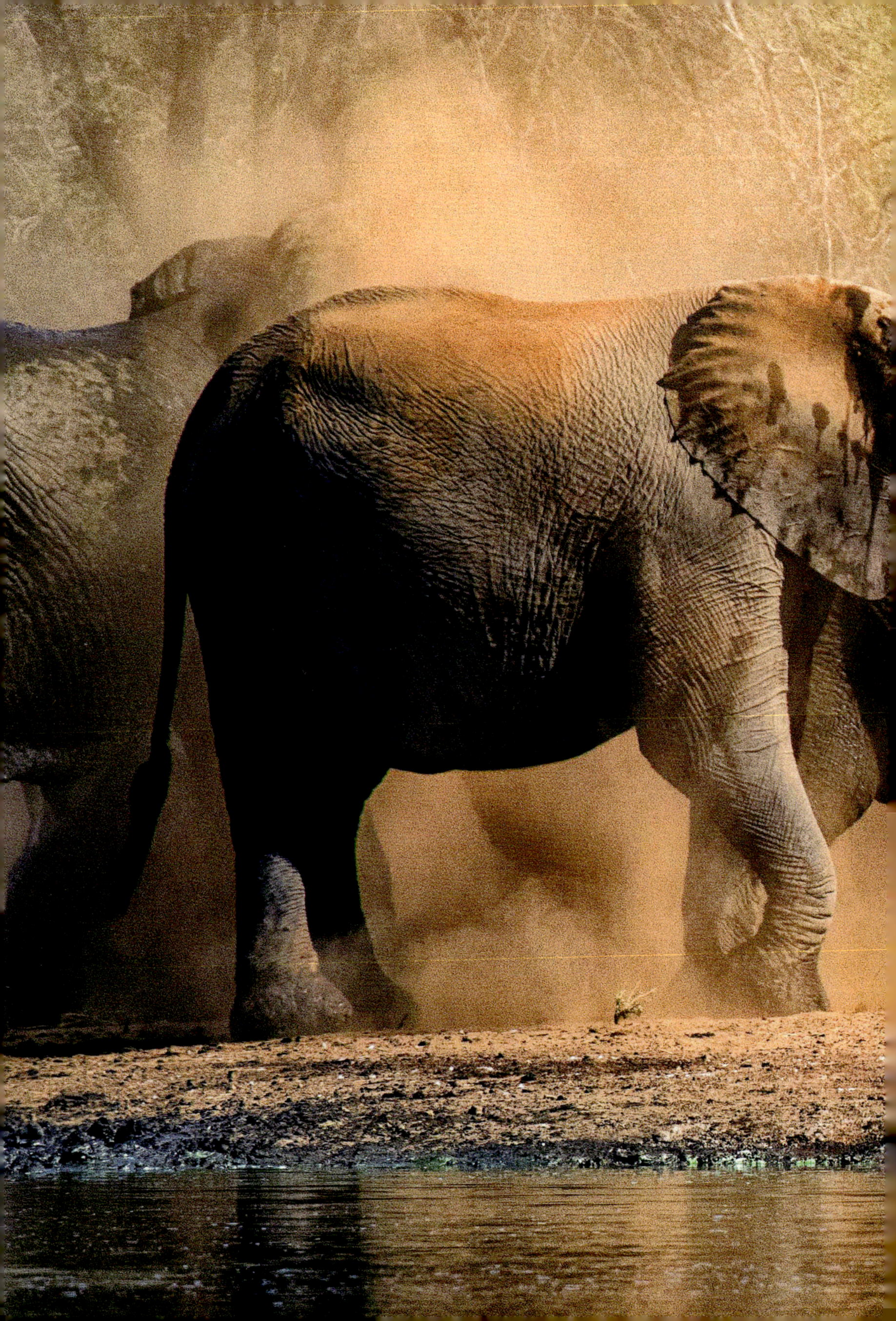

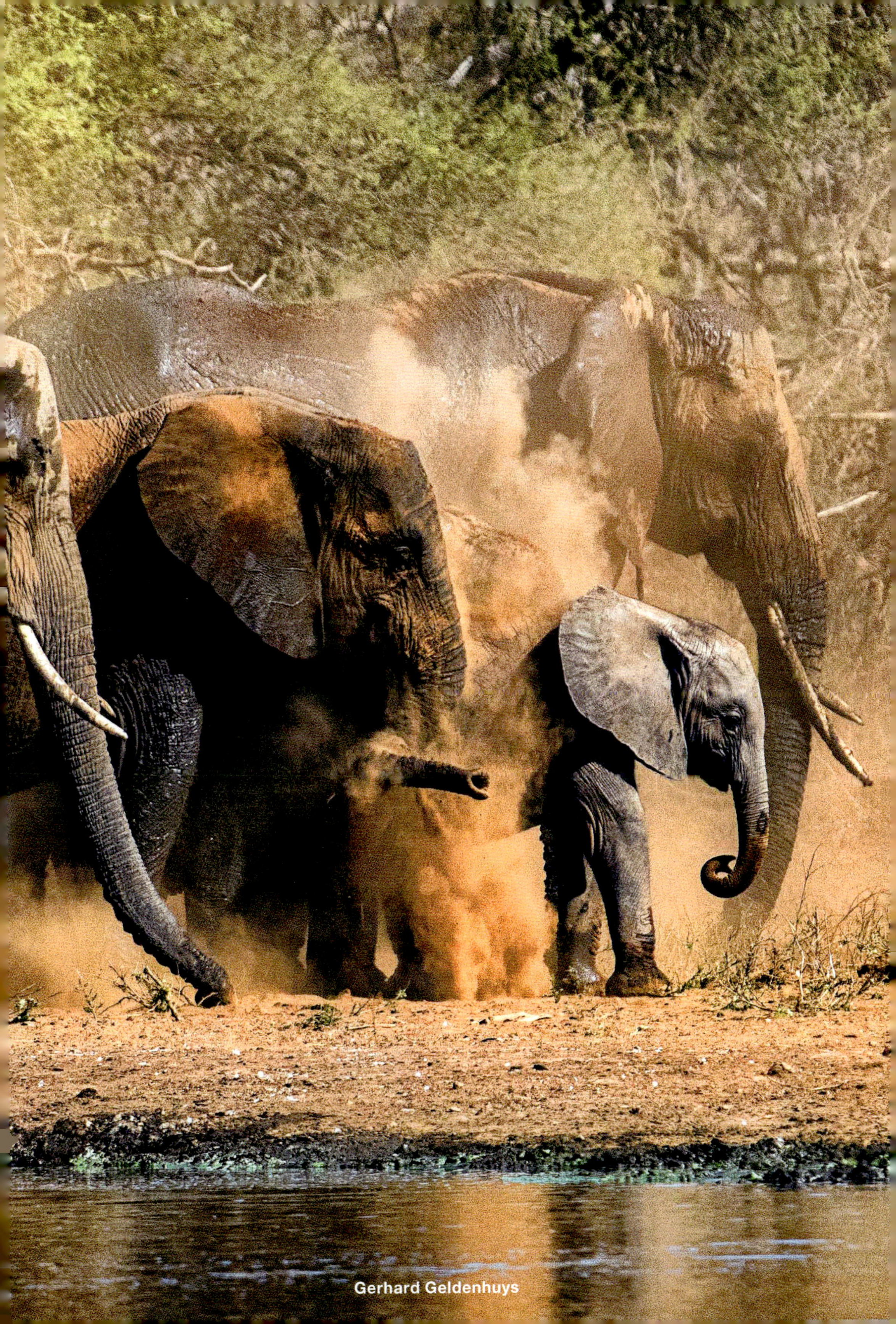

Gerhard Geldenhuys

A territorial battle

ARNOLD VAN DYK

Lake Panic, in the Kruger National Park, has often rewarded me with some exquisite sightings. Over the years, I've observed a resident pair of breeding fish eagles at the lake and have been treated to some beautiful and entertaining sights of these majestic birds of prey. Usually, there is a great variety of other waterbirds to be seen at the same time, so visits are always a pleasure.

One afternoon, I was keeping a watchful eye on a Goliath heron, which was casually scratching at the edge of the lake for something to feed on. Suddenly, I saw from the corner of my eye, and coming out of the blue, a fish eagle, diving like a kamikaze bomber. The heron ducked away, barely in time. Then the fish eagle's partner swooped in, from a slightly different angle but in rapid succession. For the next 90 minutes we were in awe, watching a type of territorial battle that I had never seen before. The heron used a thorn bush close behind it as a shelter to defend itself from the dive-bomb attacks of the two eagles. It was clear the strategy of the pair was to work together, attacking relentlessly without giving the heron sufficient time to recover from the first attack before the second attack followed. The heron, however, acted like a champion boxer: feathers standing upright, ducking and weaving, with wings wide apart, flapping and fending off the blows to its head and body. At times it went so low that it put its head in the water. In spite of eagle claws slamming into its body several times, the heron managed to stand its ground. After a gruelling fight, both eagles retreated to a nearby tree, leaving me, as the referee, to declare the fight a draw.

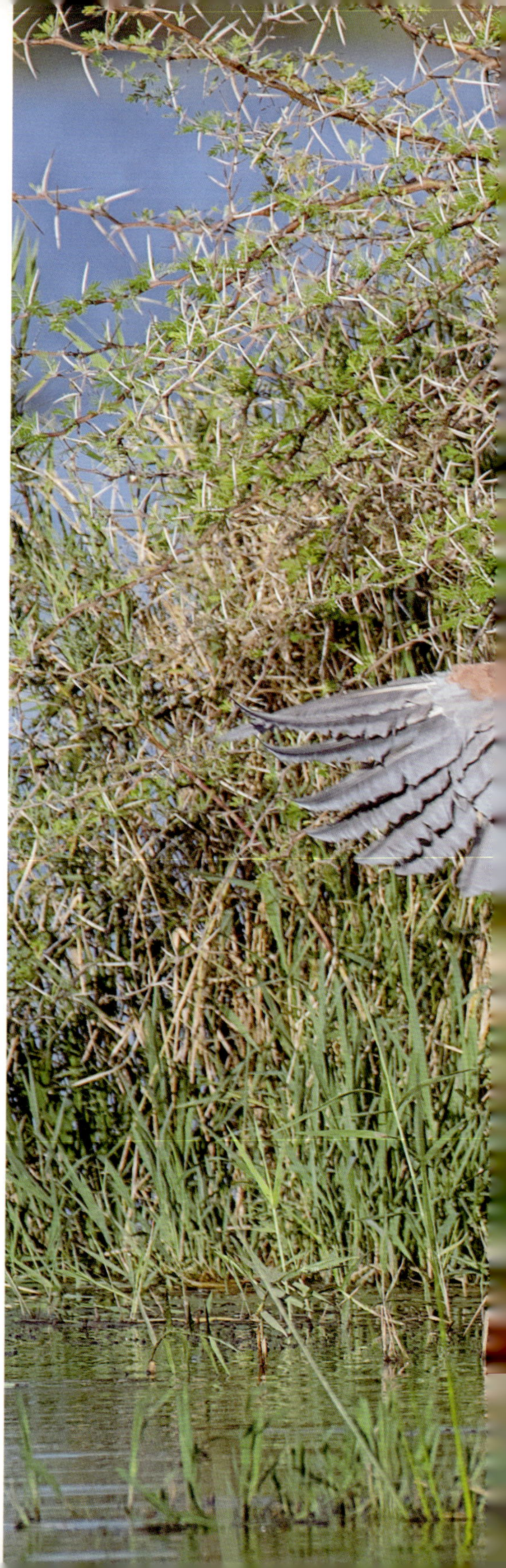

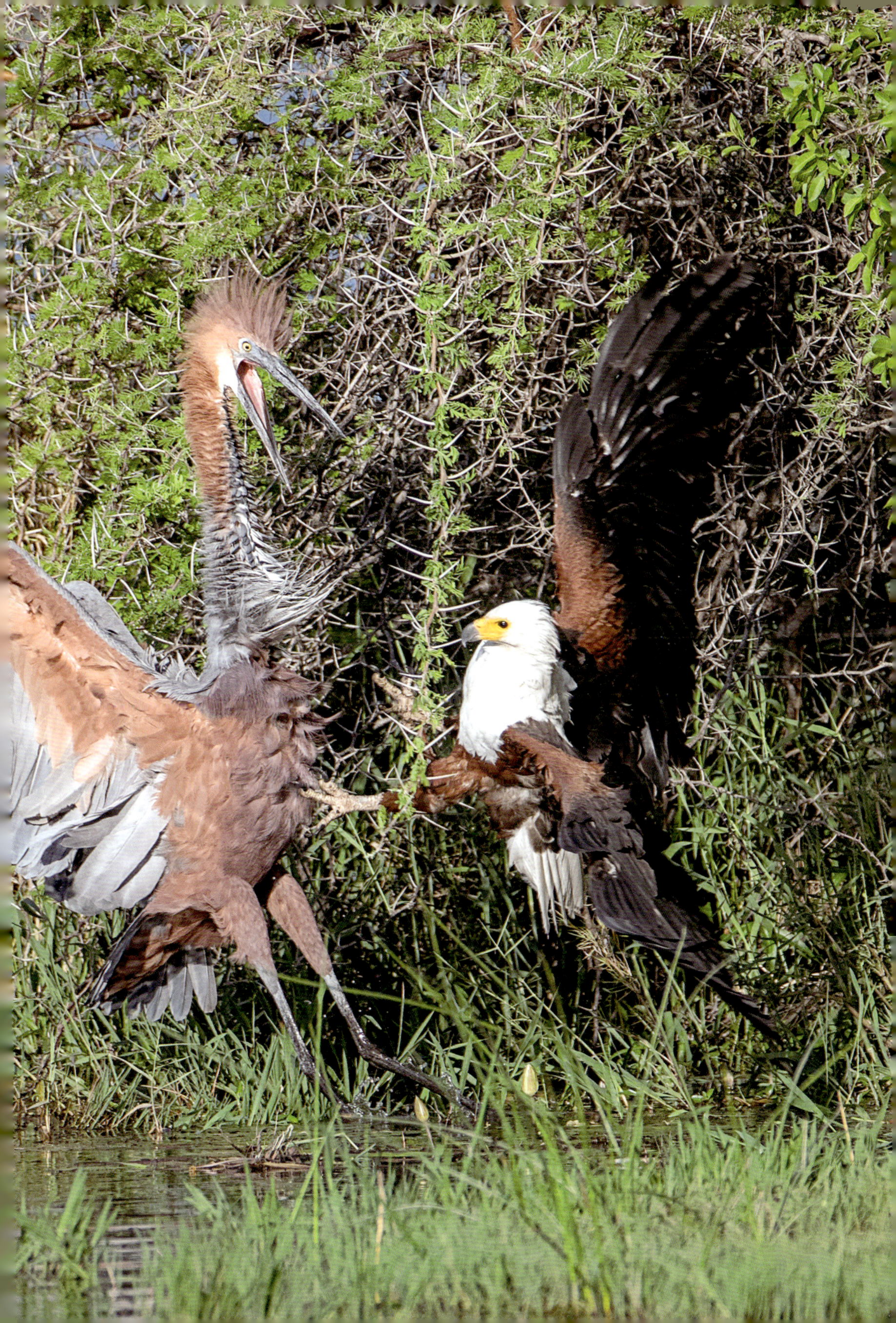

What is this hype about selfies?

BARBARA JENSEN VORSTER

As Dickens wrote, "It was the best of times, it was the worst of times…" It was an icy-cold afternoon in Mashatu Game Reserve in Botswana. We were on the Photo Mashatu open vehicle and I had a blanket over my knees. We stopped at a sighting of two lionesses with small cubs; one of them had two very small cubs. The interaction between them was fascinating, so I decided I should take a video on my iPhone X. I set my iPhone up on a small 'gorilla grip' tripod, started the video and then continued taking photos on my Canon 7D. After a while I noticed my iPhone was becoming unstable. I put my Canon down on my lap to remove the iPhone, and then, before I could stop it, the camera slipped off my lap and fell on the ground with a thud.

Without hesitation, the lioness with the bigger cubs approached, giving us no chance to retrieve the camera. It had fallen with the lens facing up. She gently flipped it over and grasped it by the barrel of the lens. After the initial shock of seeing my uninsured camera in a lioness's powerful jaws, I picked up my Canon 5D Mark IV and continued shooting. She carried her booty for quite a way while her cubs jumped up against her, keen to share in the fun. She eventually dropped it and the three cubs started playing with it and dragging it around in the dirt. Eventually, like all children, they grew tired of the new toy and we were able to rescue the camera.

Apart from two huge teeth marks on the focus ring and many small teeth marks on the plastic lens hood, there was nothing wrong with it, although, naturally, it was very dirty. You often see photos of cameras in the mouths of animals or – even worse – being eaten or trampled by them and you roll your eyes and think, "How stupid can a person be?" But I now know it can happen in a heartbeat. I regard myself as a seasoned wildlife photographer, but there I was staring at my camera held possessively in a lioness's mouth.

After I posted the photo on Facebook and Instagram it went viral. It was reposted more times than I can recall, sometimes credited, sometimes plagiarised. But 2018 ended well when the Modern Metropolitan chose the close-up of the lioness with the camera in her mouth as one of the top 36 photos of the year worldwide! I felt proud because the winner of the Wildlife Photographer of the Year was also one of the photos chosen. This more than made up for the momentary shock I'd experienced when the lioness decided to shoot some selfies with my camera.

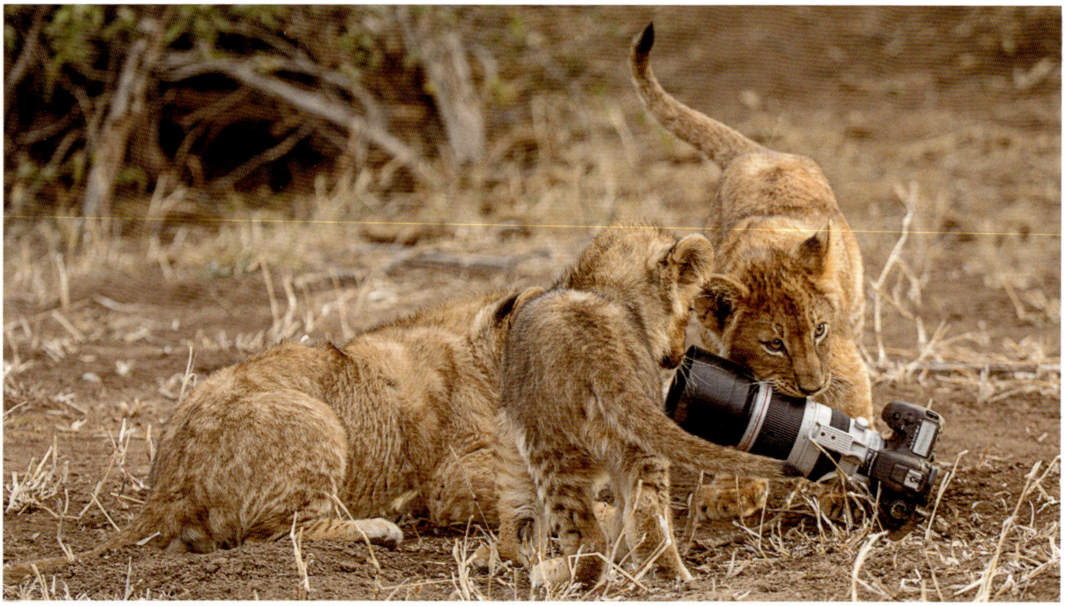

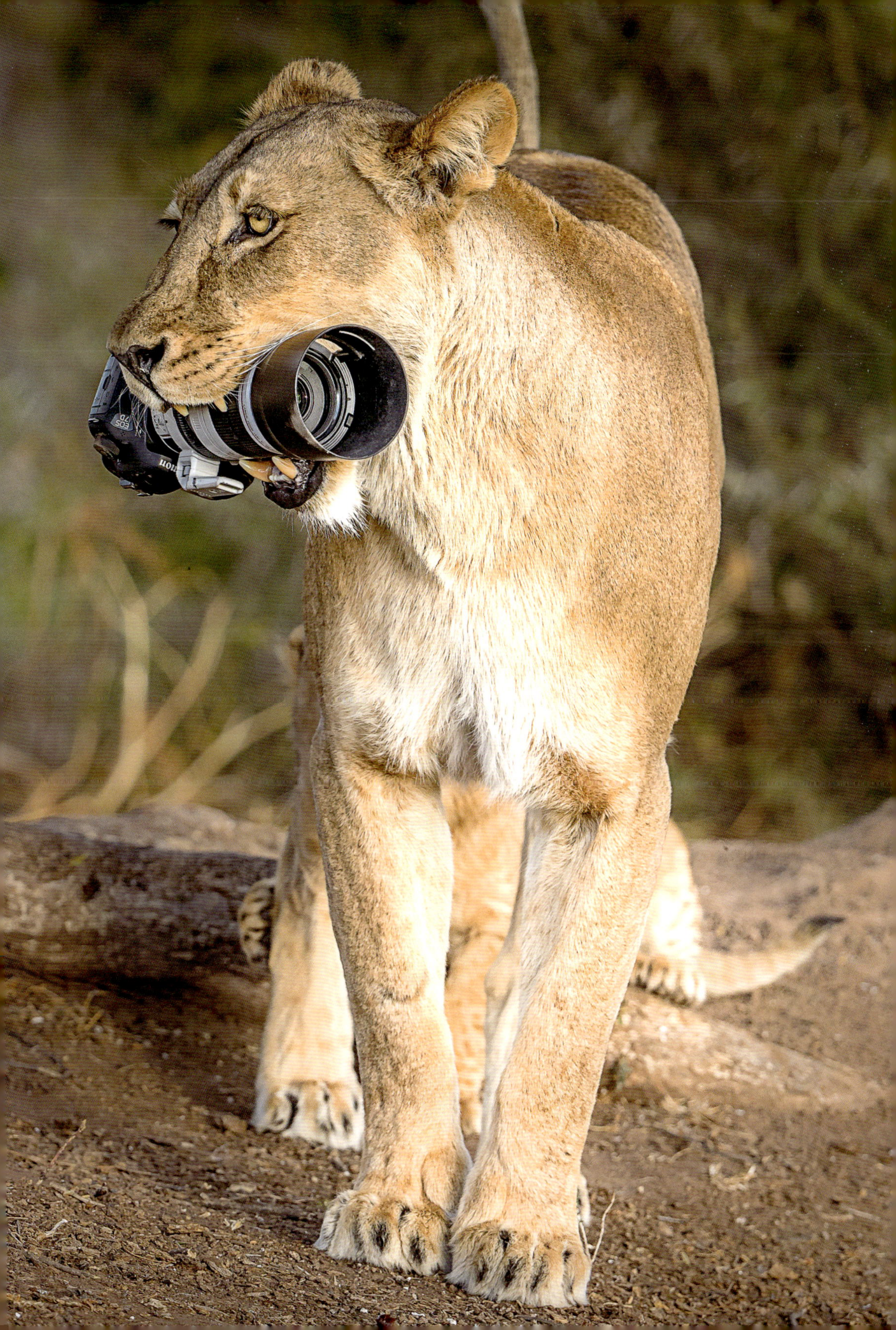
EOS 7D

A great disappointment and a greater blessing

ELMAR VENTER

Daybreak in the Kgalagadi Transfrontier Park presented the last full day of our May 2018 holiday. We all felt a little sad, knowing that tomorrow we would have to head home. But we chose not to dwell on these feelings because we intended to make the most of our final day under the open expanse of the desert sky.

As soon as the gates opened, we headed north, towards 13th Borehole. A magnificent male lion awaited us in the road but the sighting passed too quickly to get the shot. We recognised him at once by his one blind eye: the famous White Eye, ruler of the Auob riverbed. We had encountered him and his two brothers earlier in the week, but on this occasion his siblings were nowhere in sight. My photographic muse stirred, conjuring up visions of the three brothers lined up in exquisite golden light for a drink at the borehole. An unexpected roar from White Eye and a distant response from his two brothers caused more optimism. Knowing his brothers were in the area fuelled my photographic hopes.

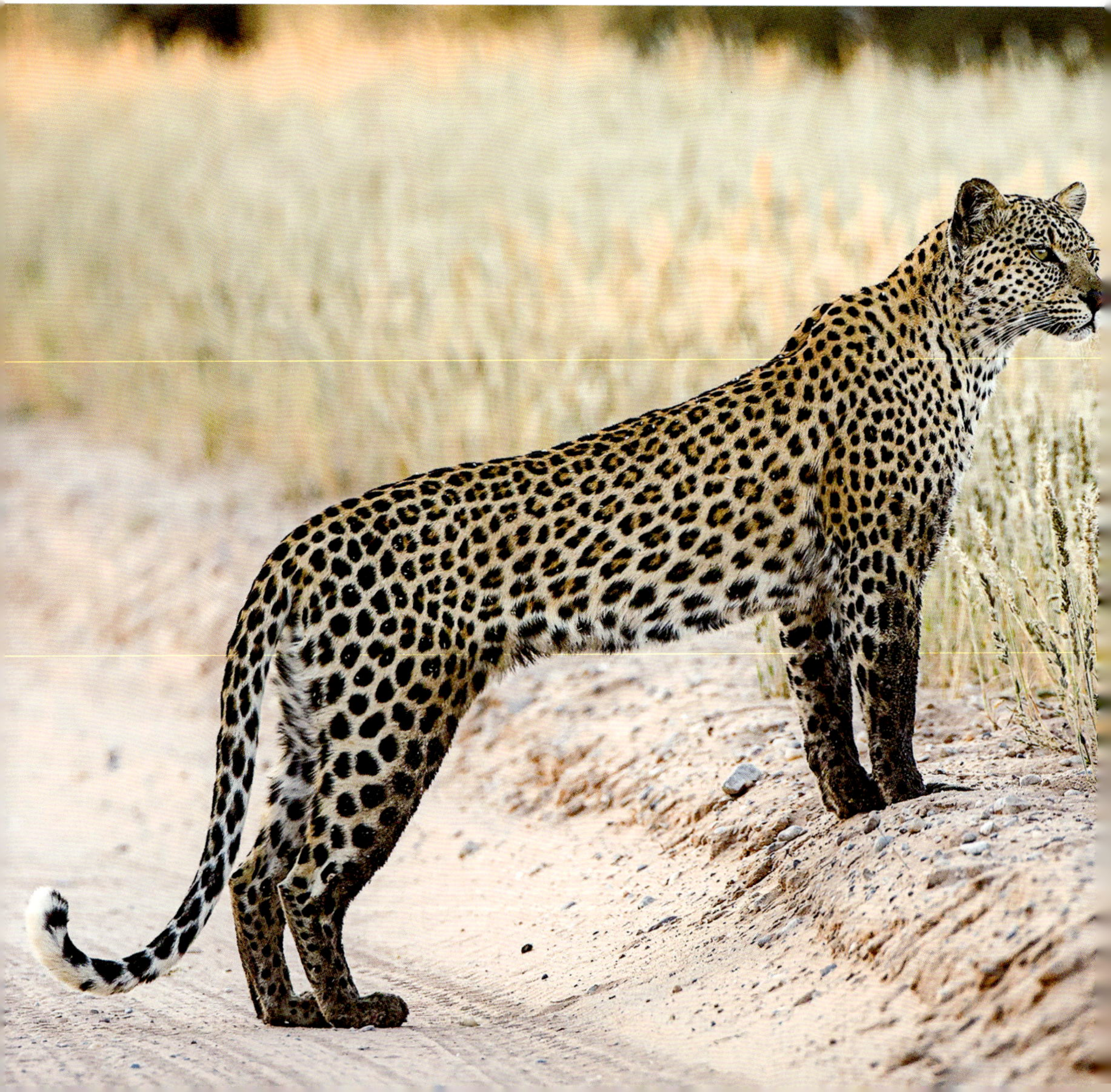

Without any regard for these dreams, White Eye rose and strolled away, disappearing over the nearest dune.

But I was not about to give up on the possibility of taking the ideal shot I'd envisioned. So, undeterred, I persuaded my parents, my patient travel partners, that we needed to return to 13th Borehole later and spend the afternoon there in the hope that the three brothers would show up for a drink.

We arrived back at the borehole around 15:00. I scanned the sand in the road for fresh tracks but there was no evidence the brothers had come for a drink since that morning. Curiosity and impatience got the better of me and I decided to drive around for a while to see whether we could find the brothers' shady hiding place. No luck. We returned to the borehole 20 minutes later. A vehicle was parked on the side of the road closest to the borehole. The man behind the wheel beckoned to me excitedly. He said, "You won't believe it – just a few minutes ago, three male lions were drinking at the borehole!" A quick glance at the sand in the road confirmed what he was saying: fresh lion tracks showed I had just missed out on what I'd been imagining since that morning. I'm usually a composed, even-tempered person, but now I felt overwhelming disbelief and disappointment, and a huge resentment. I almost flew into a tantrum. How could life be so unfair, so cruel? All I wanted to do was to head back to camp, pack up and go home. But a stern reprimand from my mother reminded me this was not the right way to deal with disappointment. So we decided to end the day with an unplanned drive south and then back to camp.

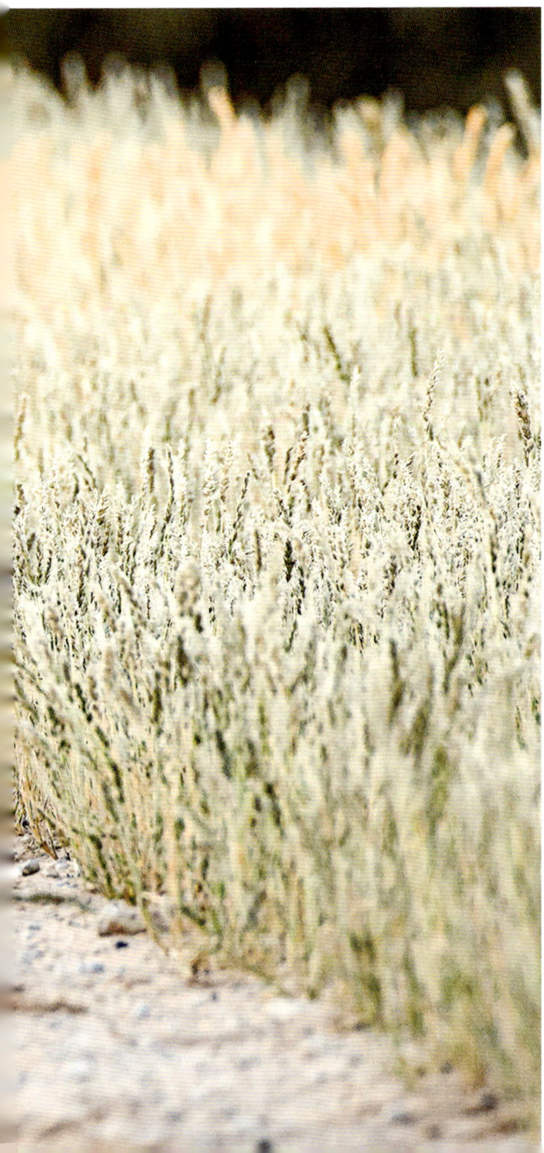

For endless kilometres it seemed that the Kalahari had nothing to offer to lift our spirits. We no longer noticed even the beautiful landscape in our emotional turmoil. We turned back to camp 20 minutes before the closing of the gates.

And then, we were granted a gift, in the torm of a most unexpected sighting. As we reached the turn-off to the upper dune road, close to Kamqua, a sleek, supple female leopard stepped into the road. She appeared like a ghost from the Kalahari sour grass, still tall after the late summer rains. She peered over the grass at a herd of springbok and then, without any hesitation, walked straight down the road, passing our vehicle. There were no other witnesses to this sighting. Ours was the only vehicle there, and we could watch her with bated breath, undisturbed. Oblivious to our heartache and longing, she lingered until she finally disappeared across a dune, and it was as if she had never been. With my heart racing, I flicked through the images on my camera, just to confirm this was not a dream.

Reflecting on it all later that evening, I realised there was a profound lesson in the day's events. Sometimes our greatest dreams are shattered and it seems impossible to progress beyond the disappointment. But if we can find the courage to journey on, who knows what greater blessing may be waiting down the road?

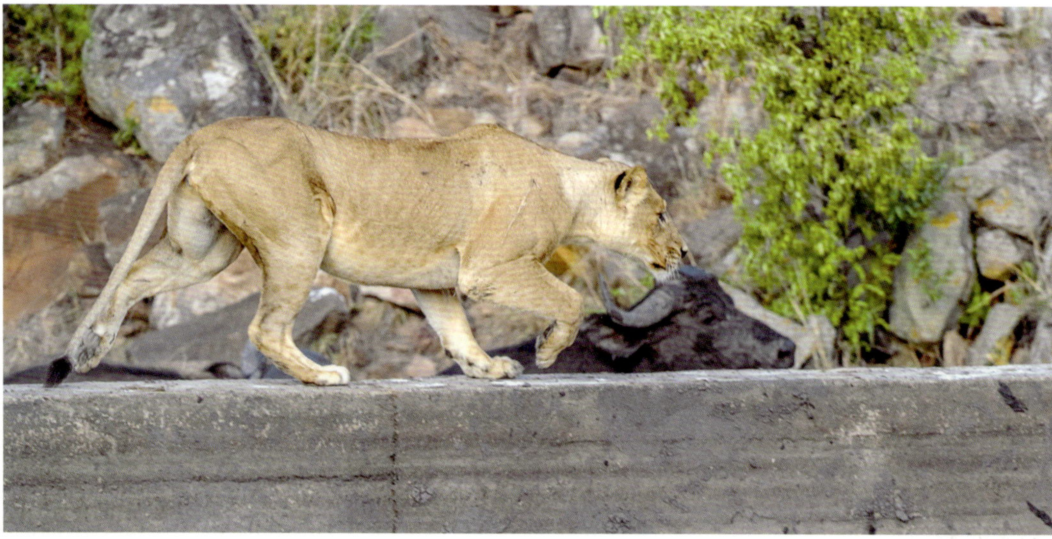

High noon at Klopperfontein

HENNIE BLIGNAUT

On the early morning drive from Punda Maria to Pafuri in the Kruger National Park, expectations were rising with the sun. It was late in December and there had been no rain. The Klopperfontein Dam on the S62 remained the one possible refuge for thirsty and hungry wildlife. In the distance we noticed a pride of eight lionesses, all very vigilant, staring intently, with twitching tails. This could mean only one thing: the hunt would soon be on.

Having stayed at Punda Maria for the last couple of days, I knew wildlife was abundant at the Klopperfontein Dam, especially the reliable meal of impala and buffalo. I backtracked to the dam and swung my Land Rover so that I had a view of the whole dam. The lionesses, I predicted, could only approach from my rear, scout the dam and follow the movements of the potential meal from the hiding place of a bush. At the same time, below the dam wall, part of a herd of buffalo moved up the river, towards the ravine and up towards the section where the wall and hilly outcrop joined. This route was an easier walk compared to going around the dam wall. What the buffalo did not know was that this offered a perfect place for an attack from a predator; they had to move more or less in single file up the hill so the narrow path gave them almost no chance to manoeuvre. The lionesses were watching the movement of the buffalo intently; they, too, had done the calculations and knew the best spot to attack was where the river, hill and dam wall met, exactly where the buffalo would be heading.

As it turned out, I was spot-on with my thinking because the lionesses did attack from the rear. But what caught me completely off-guard was the speed with which one lioness reacted. Having jumped onto the wall, she was in a perfect position to see the buffalo walking up the side of the river. With the element of surprise on her side, she jumped down. She got her claws embedded into the buffalo's side and grabbed its throat. This is it, I thought. High noon at Klopperfontein!

But it didn't work out the way I expected. Somehow the lioness's hold on her quarry was not as secure as she thought, and she was thrown off by the startled buffalo. By this time the lioness was in the same confluence of the hill, river and dam, right in the path of several disgruntled buffalo clan members. The buffalo promptly turned the tables on the lionesses, and it was an incredible sight. I'd heard stories of this happening but had never witnessed it. For the next hour, the buffalo, clearly aggravated by this attack, chased the lionesses all over the hill, venturing very close, and determined to show them who was boss of the muddy pool at Klopperfontein. Buffalo 1 Lion 0

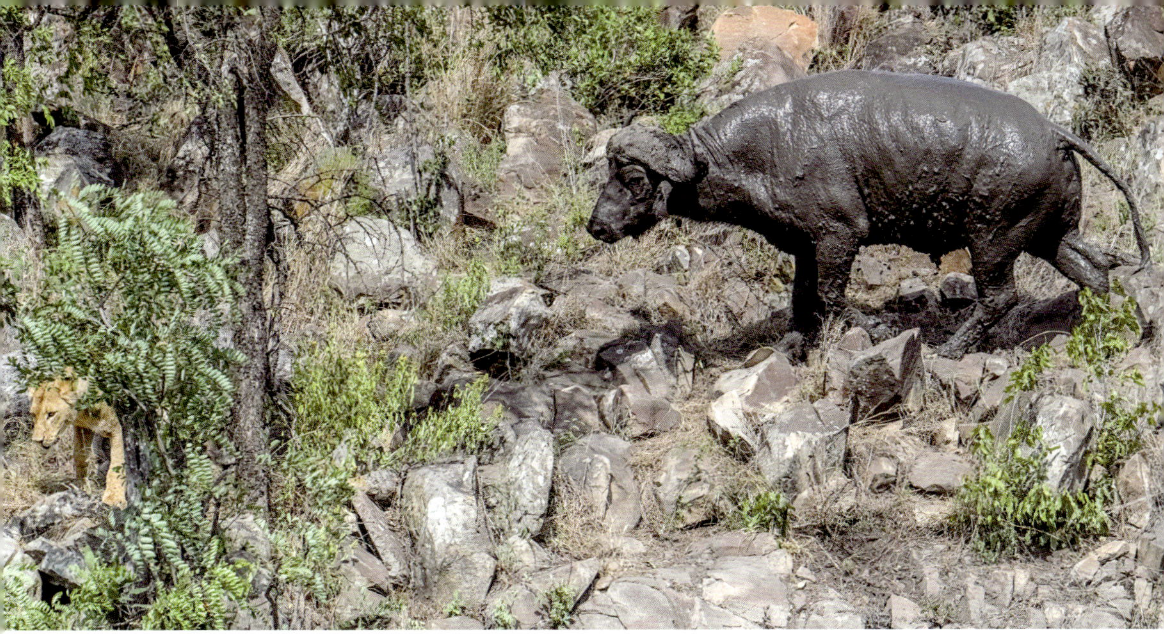

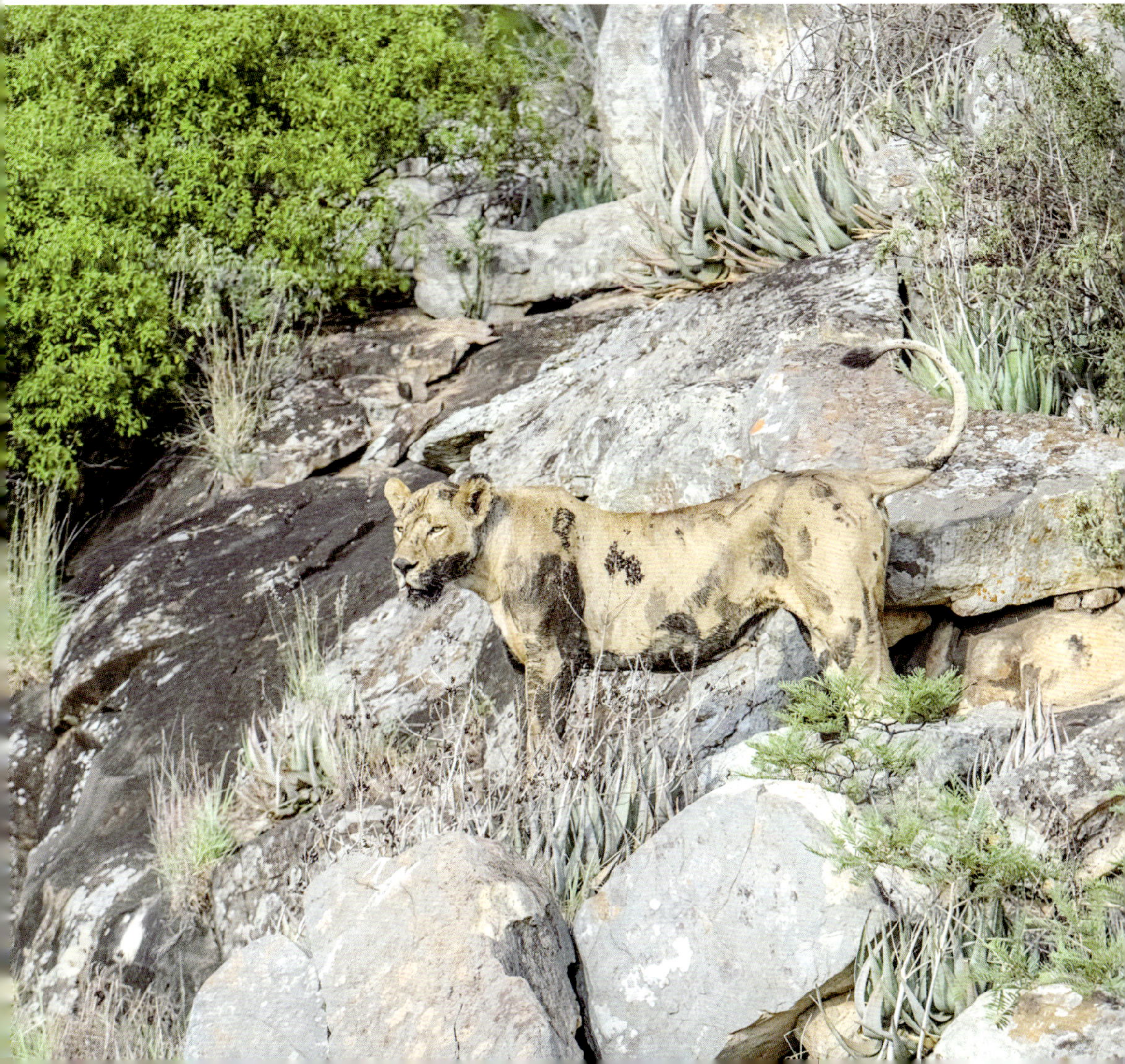

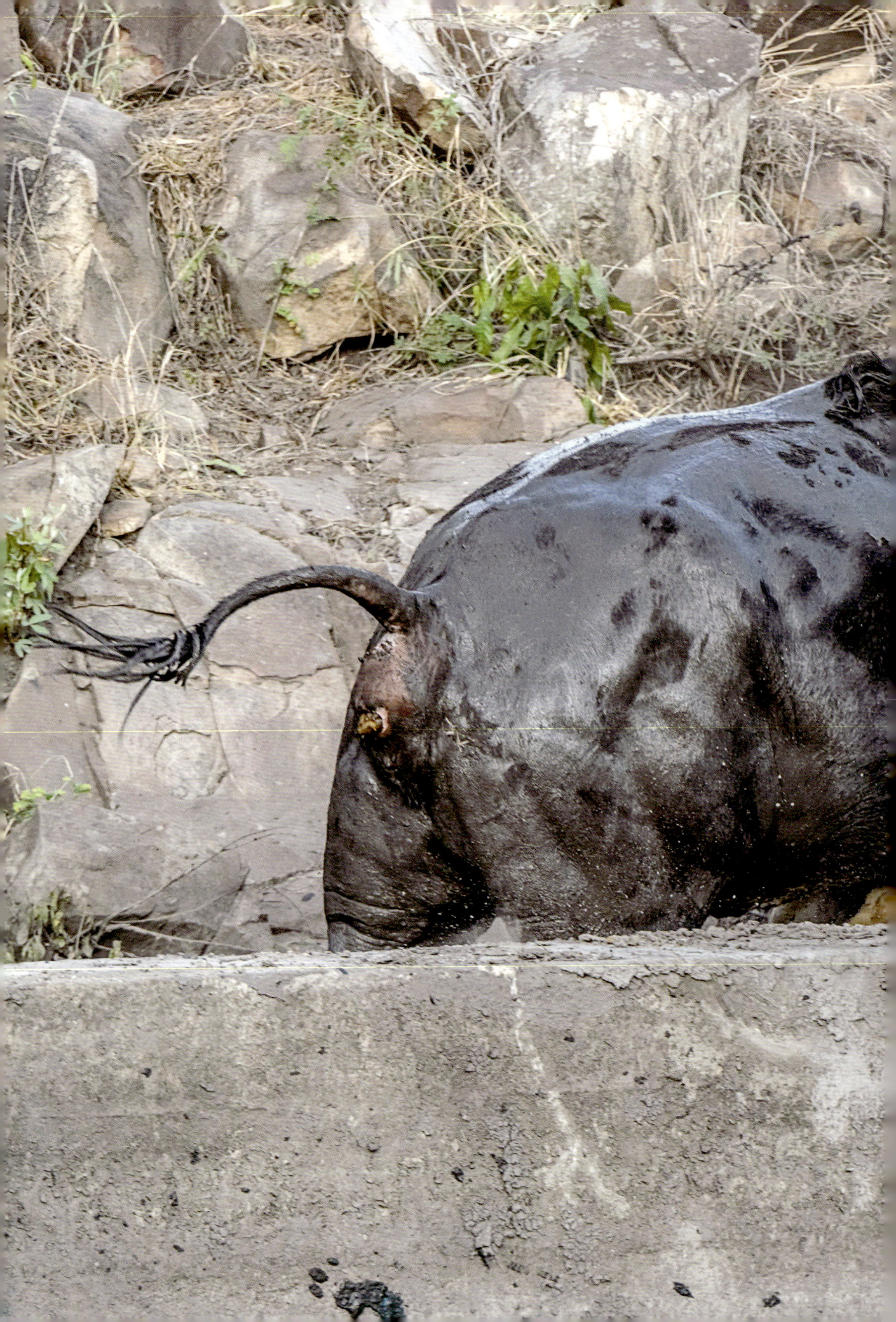

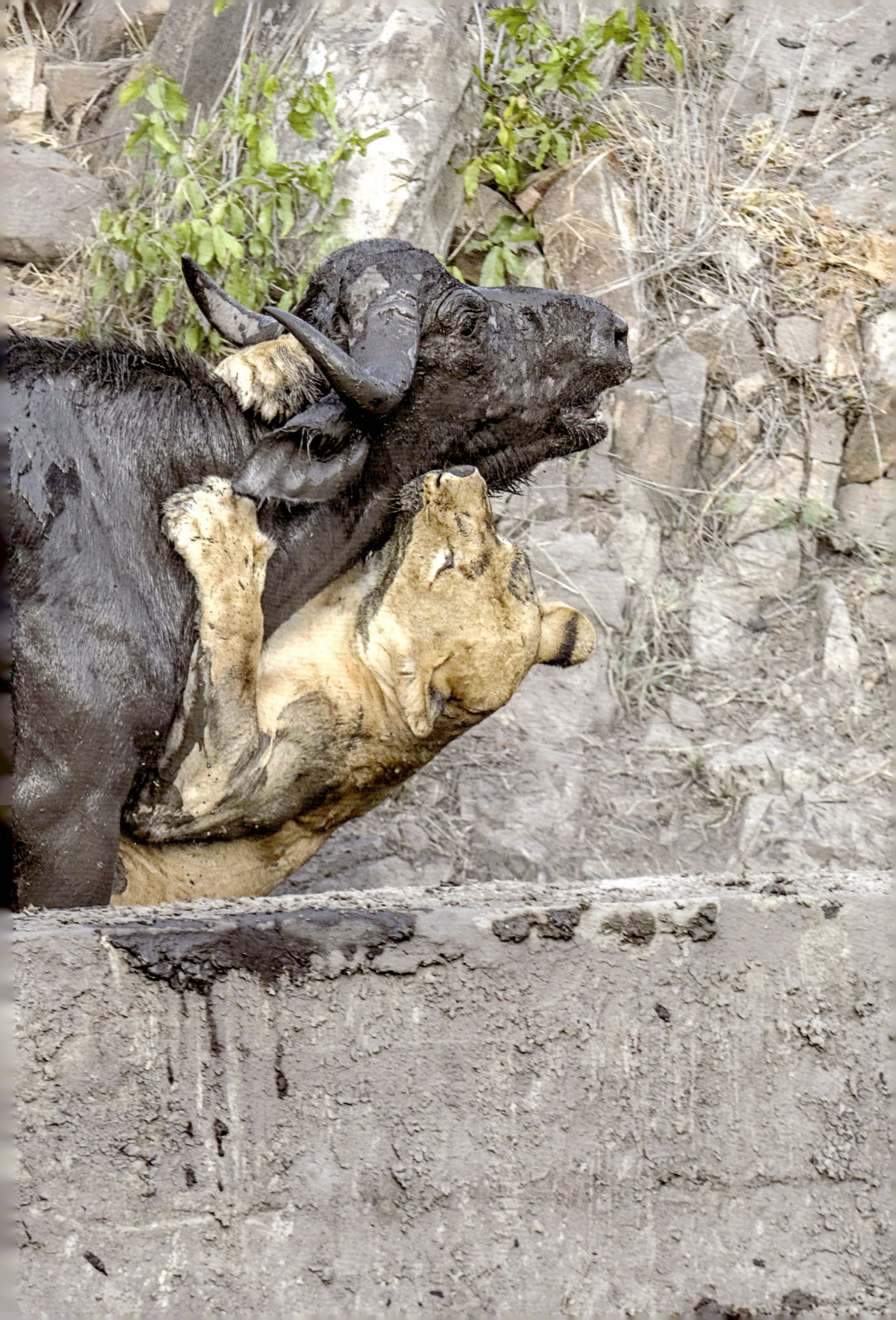

Caught in the act

JOHAN MOCKE

Stories about jackals catching doves and sandgrouse at certain waterholes in the Kgalagadi Transfrontier Park are well known. I had seen some pictures by other photographers and even taken a few myself. But on this particular occasion I managed to capture proof of a rather specialised hunting strategy.

We left north from Nossob Campsite to go to Cubitje Quap Waterhole, hoping to see some more examples of jackal-bird interaction. But the waterhole was quiet, with not much animal or bird activity. After sitting for a while, my wife and I decided to move further north to other waterholes. There was little action all over that morning, so we turned back to camp, now without any expectations. But when passing Cubitje Quap Waterhole again on our way back, we spotted flocks of sandgrouse coming in to land. There were also two young jackals sniffing around, though they didn't look as if they were serious hunters.

Suddenly, out of nowhere, a third jackal appeared. This was action! It instantly went into hunting mode – and what a mode it was. In about 15 minutes, it had caught and devoured five birds; then, just as suddenly, it left and ran off as if nothing had happened. The two other young ones, who were lying in the shade, got up and disconsolately sniffed some leftover feathers.

The jackal's first move was to take position in the shade of a tree about eight metres from the waterhole, and wait for the birds to move over its head before landing. As soon as the flock had passed, the jackal ran after them and caught one just as the birds were about to land. It rapidly ate the bird on the spot, and immediately returned to its waiting place under the tree, poised to take advantage of the next flight of birds.

I got the opportunity to take several photos, and managed to focus on single birds. This made the pictures different from others which are usually cluttered: lots of birds, with the jackal pretty much lost in the middle. We were all on our own. The next car arrived when the drama was over and the hunter jackal was already on its way with a full belly, so this experience was reserved for us alone.

Though we revisited the Kgalagadi regularly after that, I never saw this type of behaviour again. It truly was a one-off sighting.

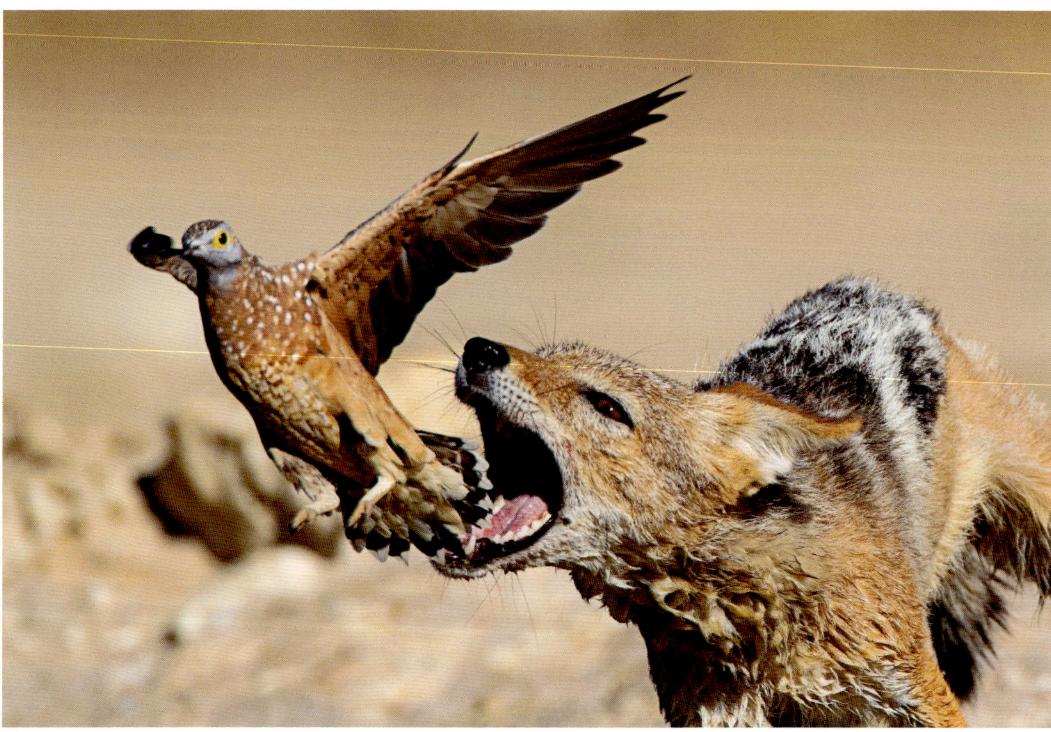

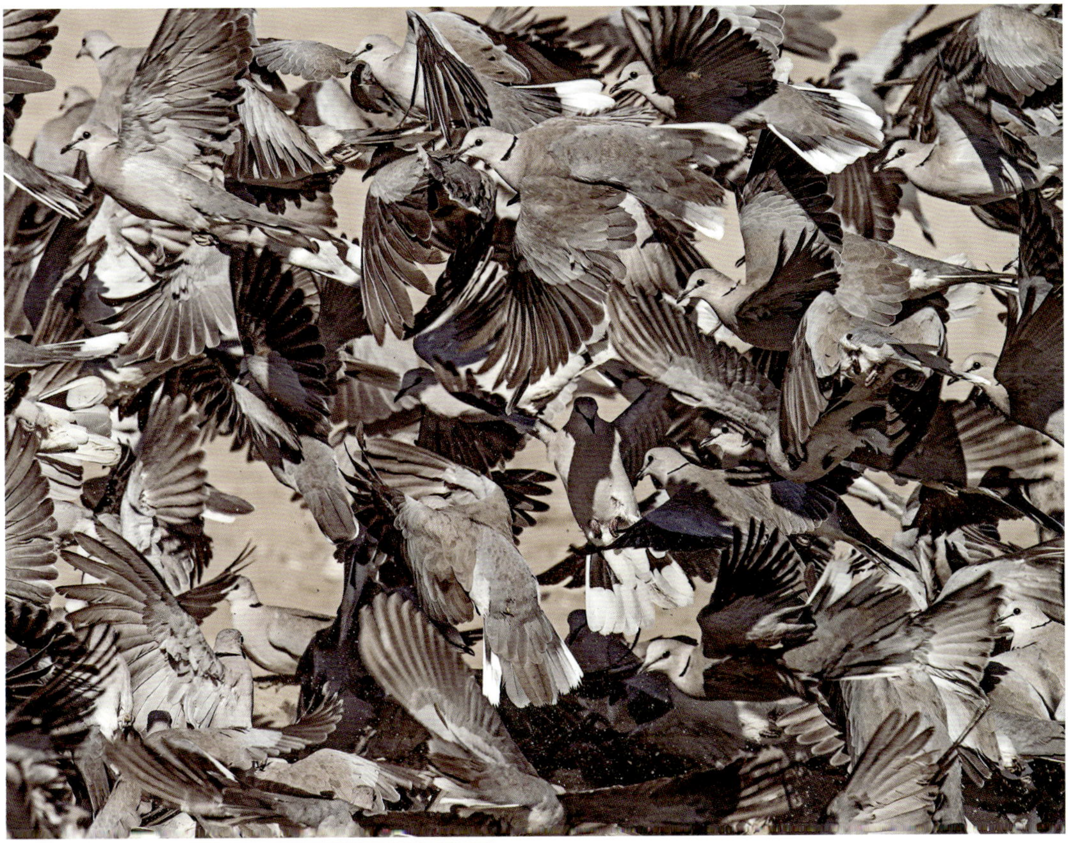

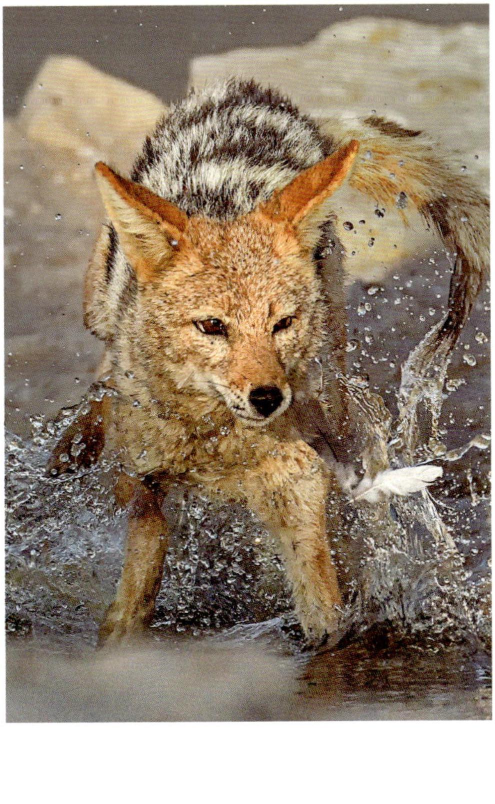

Waterhole chaos

JOHAN BOTHA

Cape turtle-doves arrive in their hundreds, in the early morning, for a drink at some waterholes in the Kgalagadi Transfrontier Park. The doves are a good food-source for lanner falcons and black-backed jackals. They are, however, difficult to catch, and there is chaos while the doves are trying to escape the predators' attacks. I'm always amazed there are no dove collisions. The falcons make many attempts but their success rate might be one dove per day.

The jackals, of course, do things differently. This one pretended to be sunning himself while the doves arrived. Then, using the waterhole rocks as a shield, he stalked. Summoning all his energy and focus, he accelerated over the rocks and flew into the air, hoping for an airborne catch. But success for the jackals remains rare; perhaps one or two catches a day, and sometimes the flying hunter lands in the water himself.

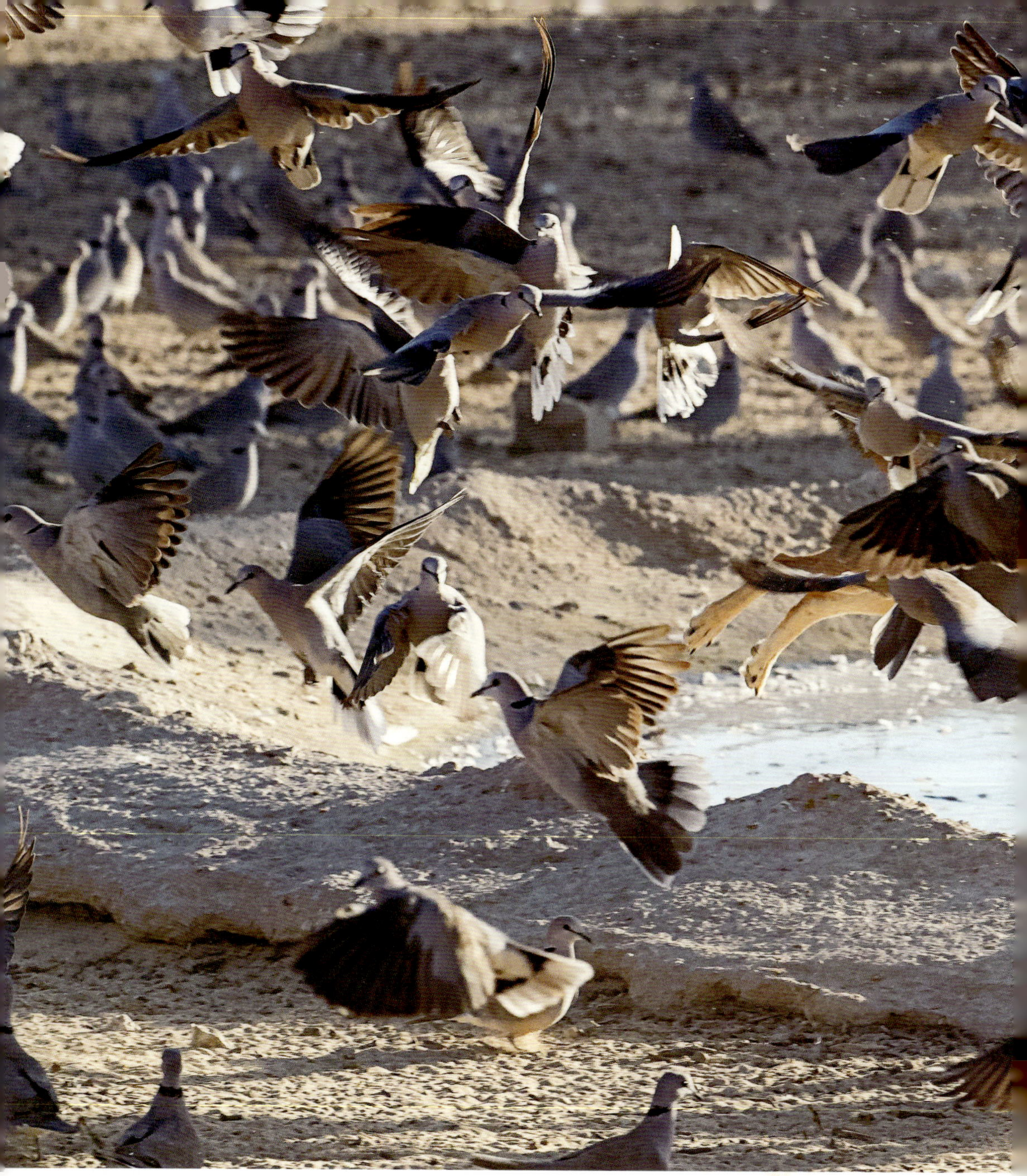

It's just not my day

STEPHAN SWANEPOEL

My favourite place in the world must be the Kgalagadi Transfrontier Park because in my opinion it has no equal for a keen wildlife photographer. The diverse nature of the different seasons means you need to experience all of them to really appreciate the ecosystem. That's why, in 2018, we found ourselves in the Nossob Camp in January, one of the hottest months in the park.

I headed off to the camp waterhole early in the morning. It was a sight to behold with hundreds (if not thousands) of Cape turtle-doves covering the trees like feathery Christmas decorations. Cape turtle-doves, like most granivores, derive almost no water from their food and in arid areas

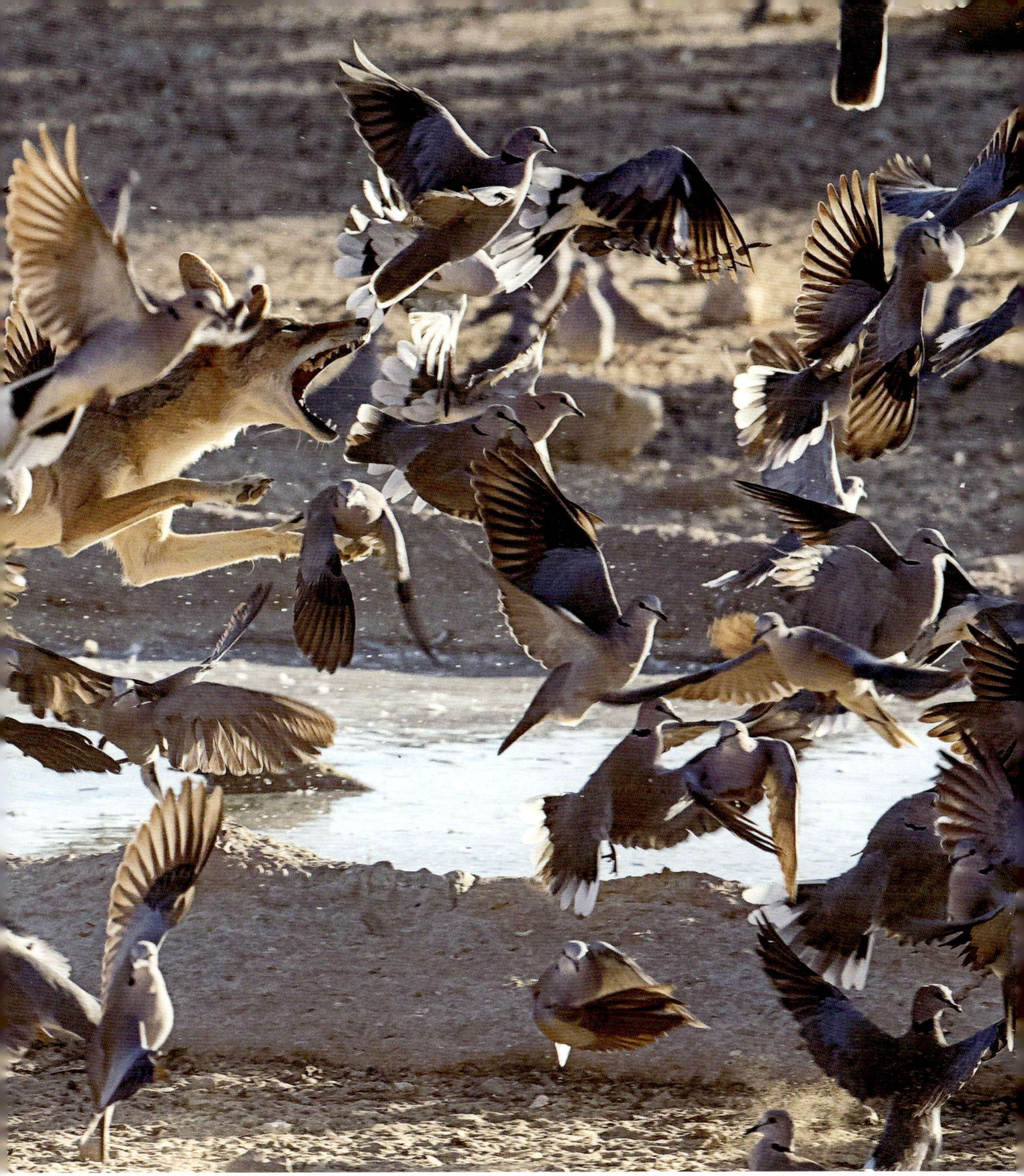

are dependent on waterholes. The black-backed jackals that congregate around the waterholes are well aware of this, of course.

One jackal in particular seemed overwhelmed by the abundance of potential food. He first tried to stalk the doves as they came down to drink and then leapt forward among them as they scattered. He almost succeeded a couple of times, but finally realised his strategy wasn't working. The doves would fly off in an explosion of feathers, just to come down again a few minutes later. So he decided to wait behind the waterhole in an ambush position and tried pouncing on the unsuspecting doves. The closest he got was a mouthful of feathers. The jackal eventually gave up, with no prize for his pains, but he had given me an entertaining morning, and a chance to get some special shots.

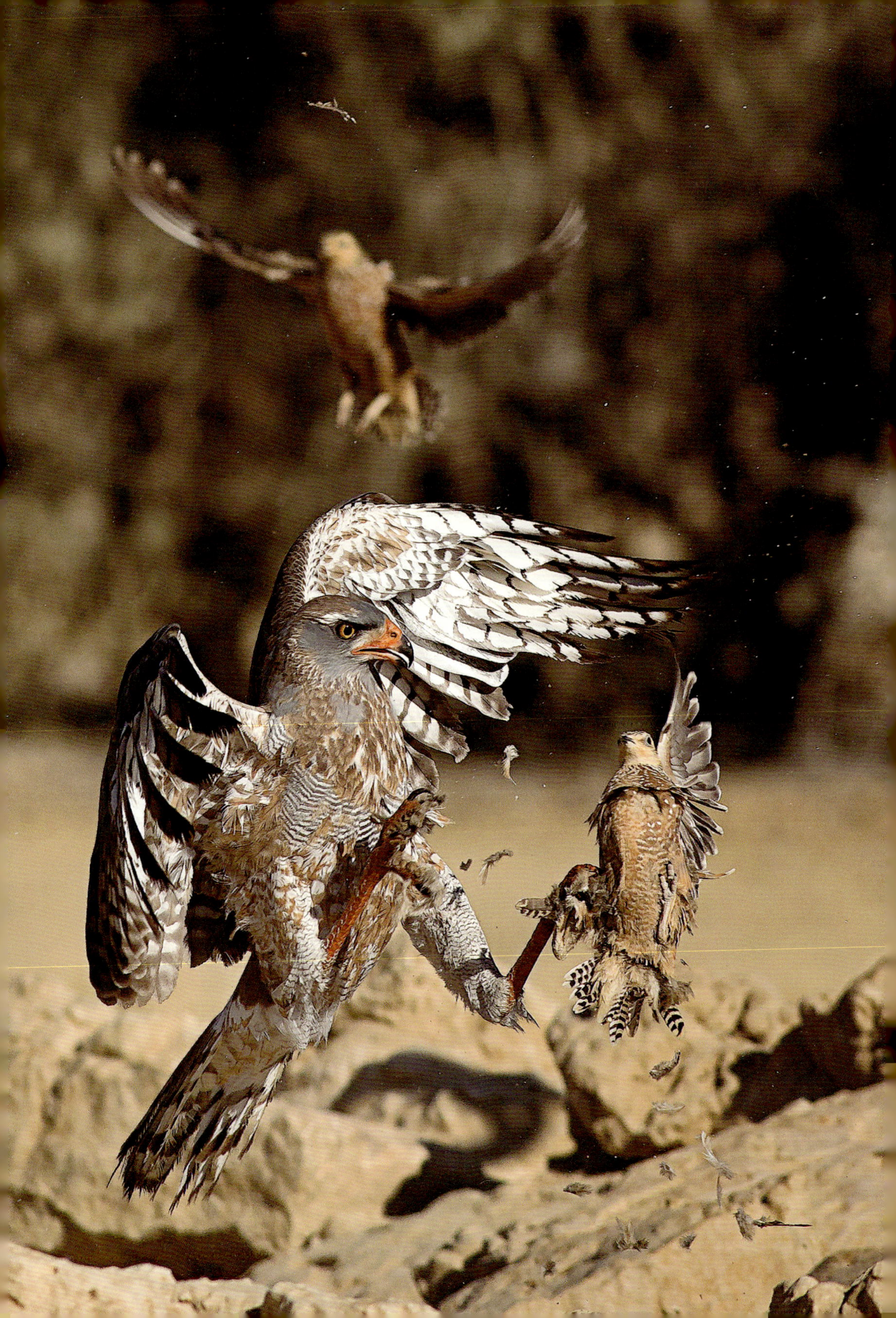

The final moment

ARNO ELLMER

It was mid-morning at the Cubitje Quap waterhole in the Kgalagadi Transfrontier Park. Namaqua sandgrouse and Burchell's sandgrouse, interspersed by hordes of Cape turtle-doves and the occasional sparrow and canary arrived for a break and a brief drink. I positioned myself at a suitable distance and surveyed the scene.

At the edge of my vision, I noticed an immature southern pale chanting goshawk that had just arrived. It stood frozen while unsuspecting sandgrouse and doves approached the water, but they rose and passed at close range when they noticed the would-be assassin. The goshawk suddenly assumed a crouching posture, gazing intensely at the delicacies flying past in tantalising proximity. Then, consternation followed. The goshawk launched a breathtakingly rapid attack on the nervous sandgrouse. In an explosion of feathers, the birds dispersed in panic and the goshawk landed again on the edge of the waterhole, ruffling its feathers. It had missed its target.

An eerie silence descended on the scene. However, within minutes, a new flock of sandgrouse arrived, desperate to land for a brief drink, and the routine was repeated. The goshawk readied itself again for the next attack. More unsuspecting sandgrouse and doves came in. Again there was a flurry of feathers and total panic reigned.

This fortunate group had also averted certain death by centimetres. The goshawk settled down with nothing more to show for its efforts than a bunch of feathers clasped firmly in its claws. But this hunter would not give up.

By now, I could anticipate the goshawk's moves and I was prepared for the next round. The subsequent attack was breathtakingly clinical and ruthless in its execution. The goshawk launched itself onto an unsuspecting sandgrouse side-on and, with outstretched claws, struck at its prey. Amid a frenzy of scattering birds and flying feathers, it pinned the unfortunate bird to the ground with ferocious intent, and administered the *coup de grâce*. It then paused briefly to recover and consolidate its murderous grip on its fluttering victim. With its quarry firmly gripped in one claw the goshawk shuffled off to some nearby bushes where it could hide from other aerial predators and peacefully devour its catch.

During my session at this waterhole I had to focus on the goshawk alone to capture its hunting process. Simultaneously, though, I was aware of several lanner falcons launching missile-like attacks on the same birds, and all around me there were waves of frantic birds. I felt as if I was living in nature's pillow fight. But the goshawk held my attention, resulting in these photos of its hunting technique.

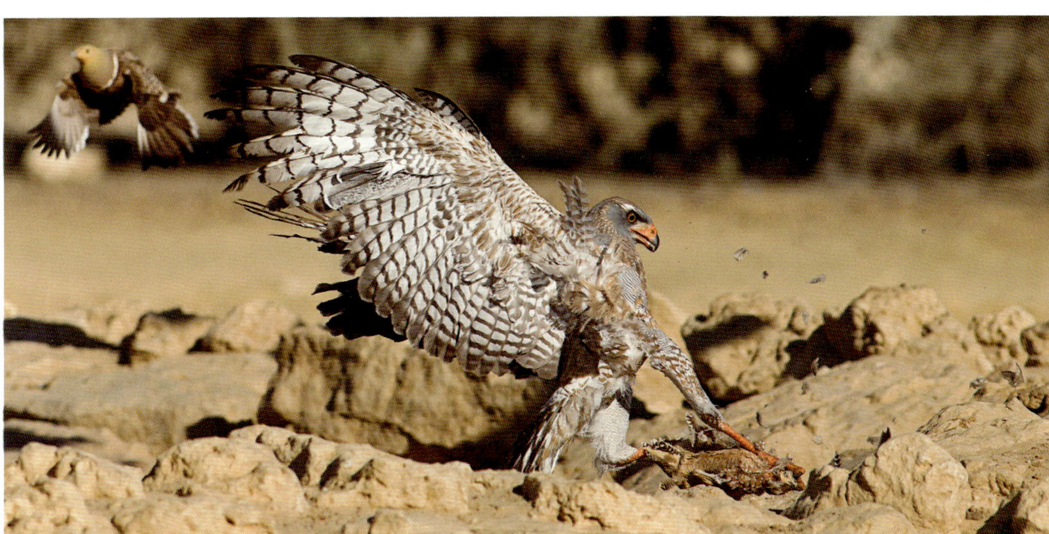

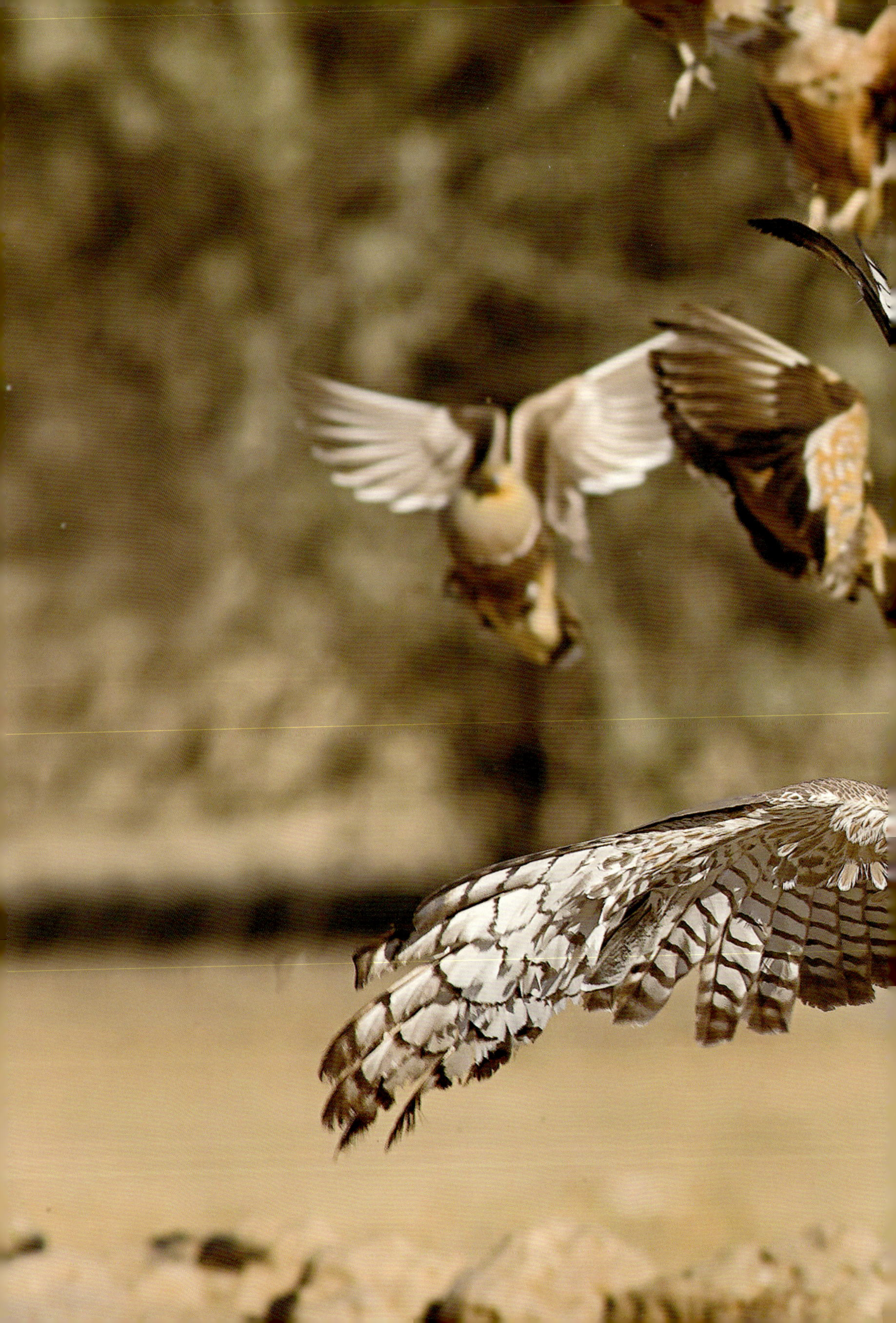

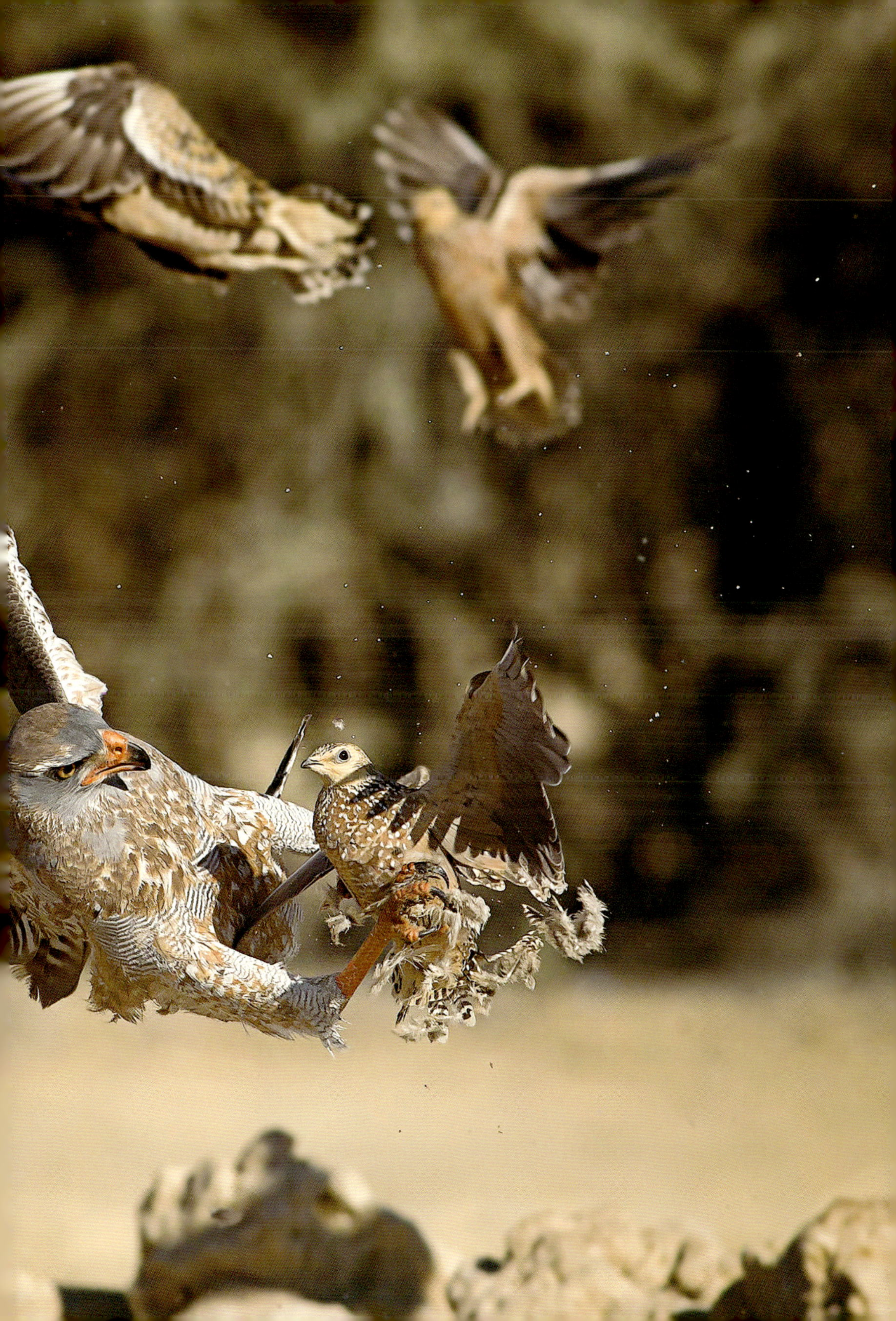

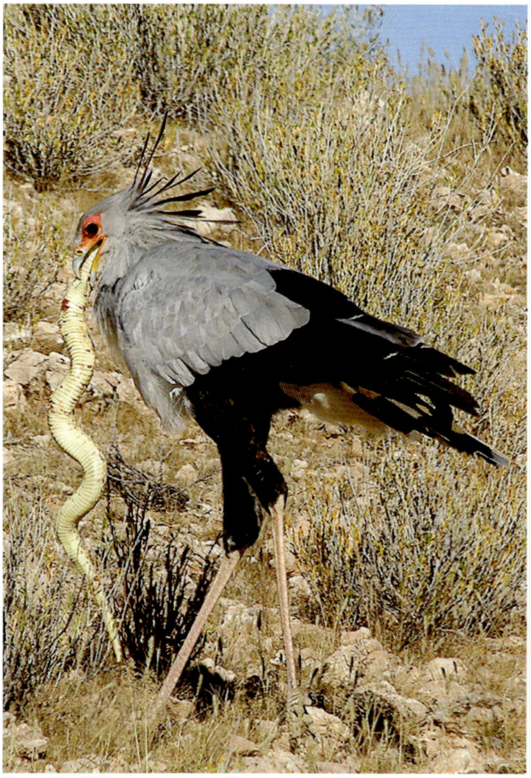

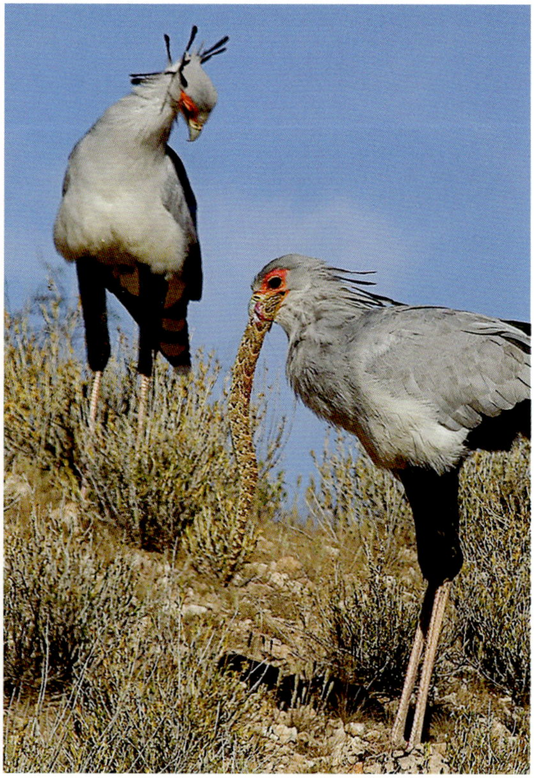

Biting off more than you can chew

MARIUS KRITZINGER

On our 21st visit to the Kgalagadi Transfrontier Park we were returning to Urikaruus Bush Camp after a braai with friends at the Auchterlonie Picnic Spot. Driving north up the Auob Valley, we noticed a pair of fully grown secretarybirds walking in their formal, stately manner about 50 metres from the road on a hill.

One of them suddenly stopped, and with its familiar war dance, attacked something on the ground, stamping its feet and flapping its wings. Both my wife and I thought that it must be a mouse or a locust, but we were wrong. We couldn't quite believe what happened next. The secretarybird straightened up with a large adult puff adder in its mouth, which it had grabbed by its head. We could see the snake had only one wound, which didn't look serious enough to be fatal. We assumed the adder had been surprised by the secretarybird and was probably slithering away into the undergrowth when the bird pulled it out. The snake wriggled wildly. When it stopped for a moment, we could see just how large this puff adder was. The height of an adult secretarybird is approximately 1.4 metres and, comparing the two, it seemed this adder easily measured 1.5 metres.

After the bird had swallowed the entire snake, we observed that the wriggling continued in the bird's crop. This was no doubt very uncomfortable for the bird and perhaps caused nausea. It promptly regurgitated the whole snake while we watched in astonishment. Then the bird started to trample on the snake, and kicked it vigorously, wounding it fatally this time, ready to be consumed. The process of gulping down the snake started all over again, and this time it was successful. Throughout the drama, the hunter was watched intently and with hungry eyes by its mate, but alas, not even a morsel was offered.

After the snake disappeared for a second time down the secretarybird's gullet, the pair continued on their leisurely stroll as if nothing exciting had happened during the last 40 minutes.

Who's afraid of the big bad snake?

MARIÉ JOEY DU TOIT

A pleasant morning drive in March 2017 in the Kruger National Park turned spectacular when we came upon a Burchell's coucal and a boomslang in a bush next to the road near the Skukuza Rest Camp. At first glance we thought the snake was attacking the coucal. But then we saw it was the other way around – the snake was defending itself. The coucal had the snake cornered at the top of the tree. We witnessed four minutes of the battle before the snake managed to escape out of the tree into the long grass surrounding the bush. The coucal immediately darted after it but our vision was blocked, so we were deprived of seeing who the final victor was.

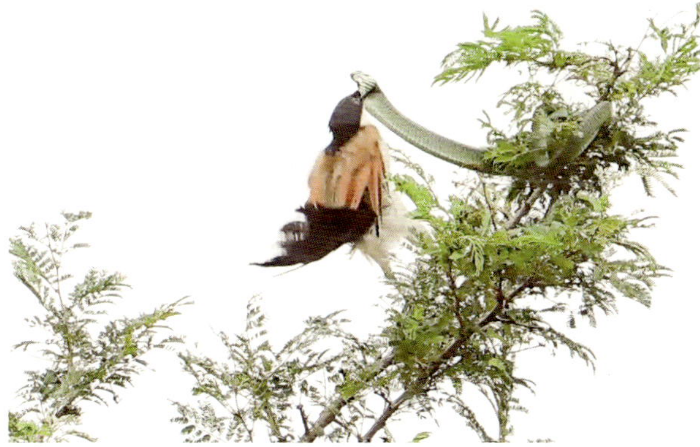

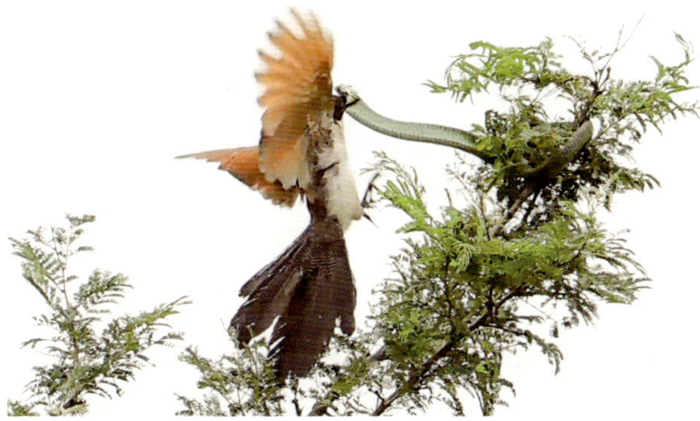

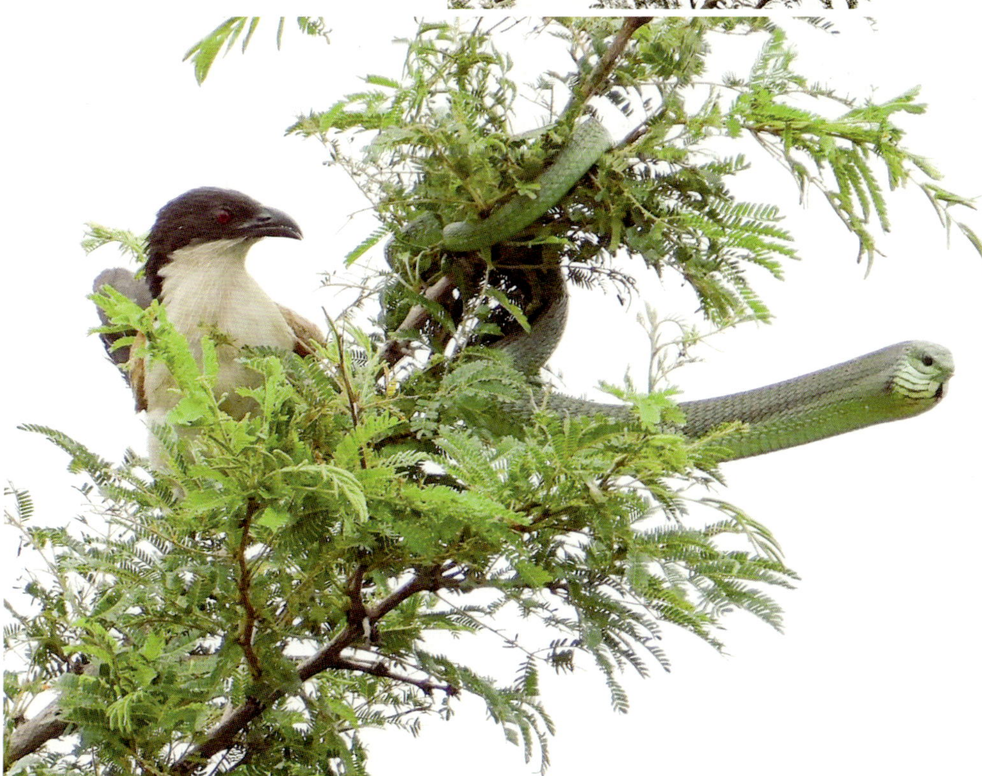

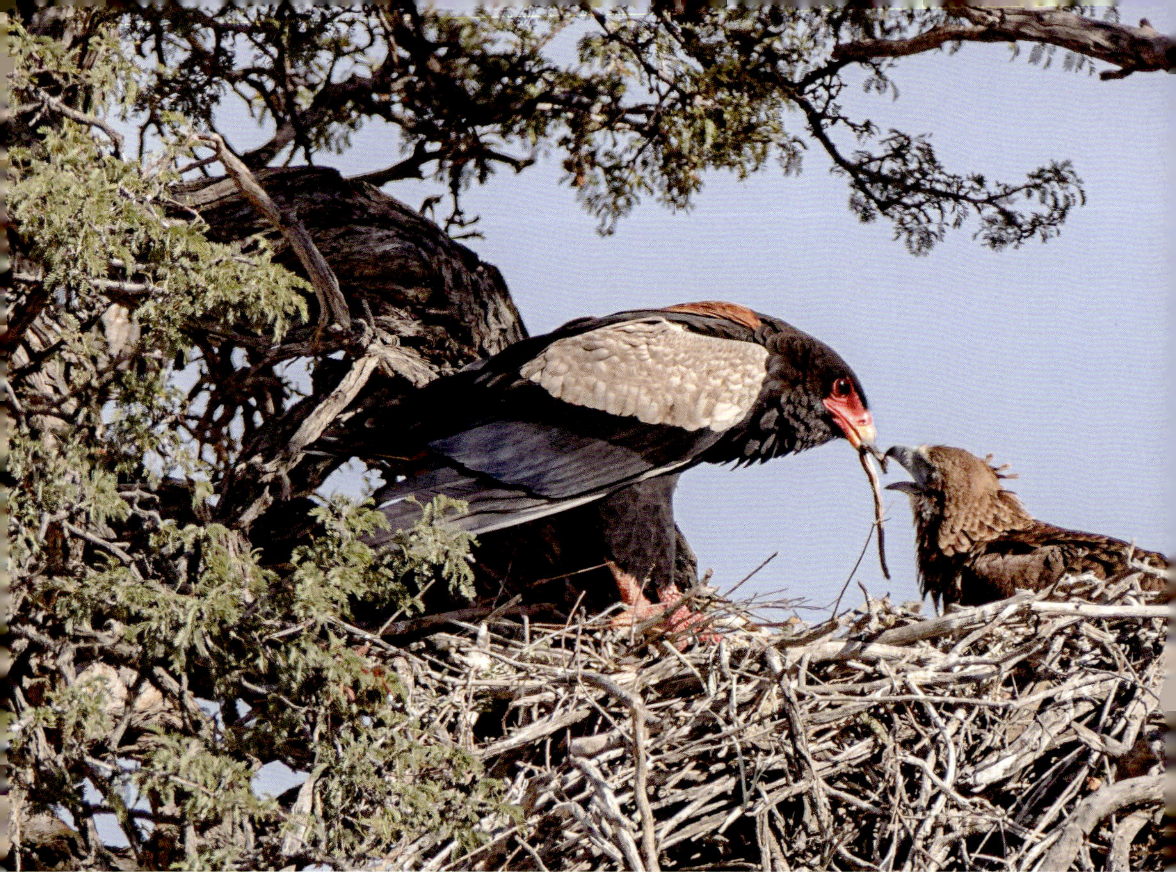

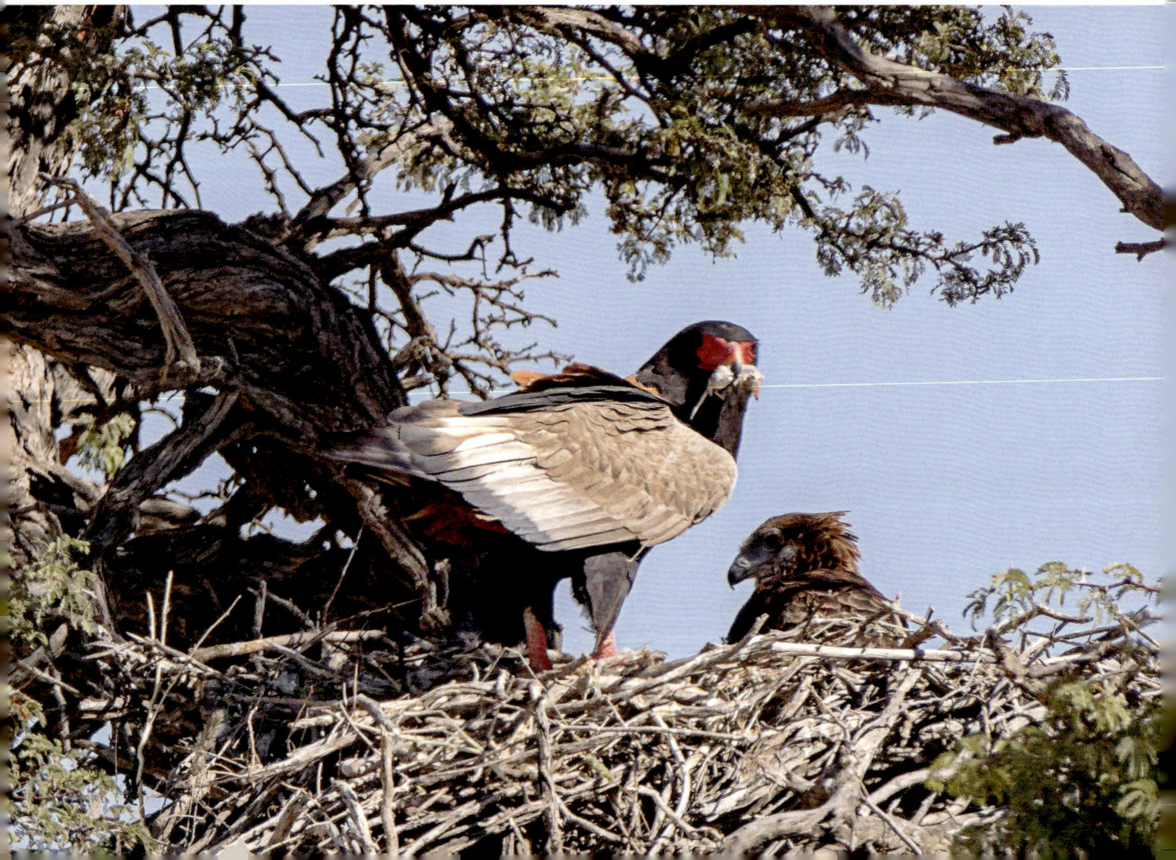

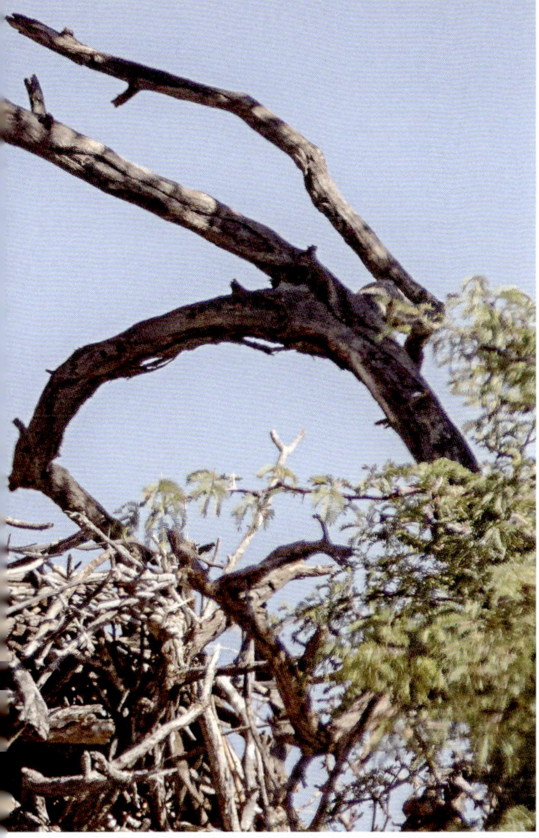

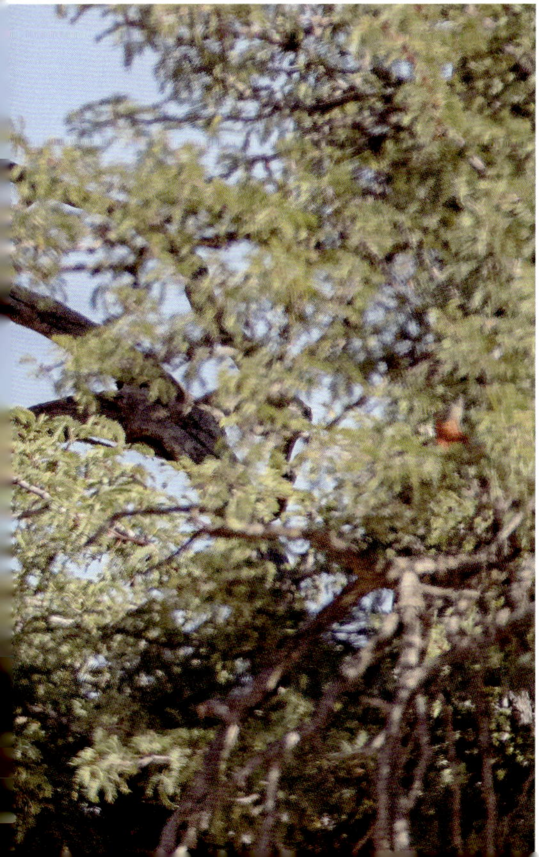

Caring bateleur parents

ARNOLD VAN DYK

While driving north in the Nossob riverbed of the Kgalagadi Transfrontier Park, I noticed a large nest in a camelthorn, quite a distance from the road. Through my binoculars it seemed the nest was empty, but then the head of a chick appeared. After a while, the chick sat straight up and with its feathers ruffled by the wind, it was clear it was a young bateleur chick. I decided to wait for the parents to return to the nest. From time to time I could make out the parents flying overhead, high up in the sky. Finally, after about 90 minutes, I was rewarded when one of them returned to the nest, carrying a mouse in its beak.

Over the next few days I was treated to a fascinating display of the bateleur pair caring for their young one. This was my first in-depth encounter with the parenting and nesting behaviour of a bateleur family. I tried to keep a record of their feeding habits; the intervals in between feeding sessions; the cleaning and rearrangement of branches in the nest; their preparation of the chick's food; periods when one parent would guard the young one as well as the chick exercising while the parents were off hunting. The particular manner of feeding, caring and interaction of the youngster and the parents was most interesting and gave me valuable clues to the behavioural habits of these magnificent birds of prey.

I was able to photograph different feeding sessions: the food mostly comprising mice and snakes. The adult usually tore apart the prey and fed it to the chick in small pieces, while clutching the food firmly in its claws. On another occasion, I was quite amazed to see large pieces of a snake were given virtually whole. A section of snake protruded from the chick's mouth as it battled to swallow this offering. It was fascinating to watch how the chick spent its time alone, walking around in the nest, at times patiently watching its parents flying by or searching to see whether they were bringing food. At regular intervals it would stand up, flapping and exercising its wings, well aware of where the boundaries of the nest ended. For me as a human observer it was a learning experience, valuable and unique, granting me rare insight into the early life of a bateleur chick.

The ground hornbill and the barn owl

ARNOLD VAN DYK

I have always been interested in the behaviour of animals and birds. During a visit to Khwai in Botswana, I was privileged to witness a strange encounter between a southern ground hornbill and a barn owl. The southern ground hornbill is non-migratory, and being territorial they mostly stick to their habitat throughout the year.

I noticed the hornbill in a tree from quite a distance and was curious about its antics. In a nearby tree there was a second hornbill partially hidden by branches and leaves. I immediately assumed it was a dominant breeding pair but at that distance was unable to establish sex. I also couldn't determine whether there was a larger family group nearby or on the ground. The more visible individual was sitting in the fork of a tree, striking away with its large beak which seemed to disappear into a hole in the trunk where it forked. A bit later, it pecked at the wood on the other side of the tree. Obviously it was impossible to say whether these holes were connected. We observed this strange behaviour for some time.

Most of my fellow photographers became bored after about 20 minutes. But I thought this occurrence was unusual enough to be interesting, so I waited patiently. I kept my camera focused because the combination of my Canon 5DS R with its high resolution and crop factor, together with my 600 millimetre lens gave me some leverage at this distance. This paid off, as, to my astonishment, a barn owl flew out of its hiding place from the hole in the fork of the tree. The hornbill tried to attack it but was too slow and the owl escaped unharmed. Even after the owl flew away, the hornbill kept on pecking at the opening of the side hole.

I am certainly not an expert on behavioural patterns of the species, but my assumption was that this was either a hunting expedition, or an attempt by a mating pair to secure a suitable nesting place. However, some questions remain unanswered. Did the pair perhaps use the specific tree as a breeding nest before? Was this a deliberate attempt to chase an intruder away or were the hornbills after chicks belonging to the owl in the nest? Whatever the answer, it was certainly worth the wait to be witness to such uncommon and rare bird behaviour.

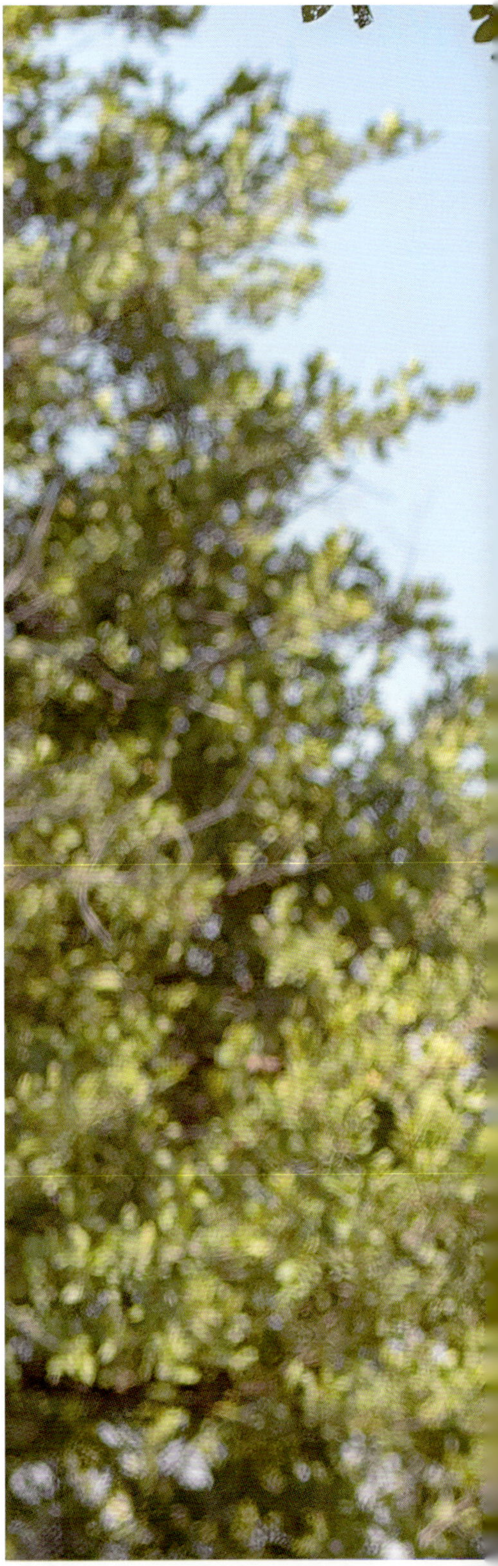

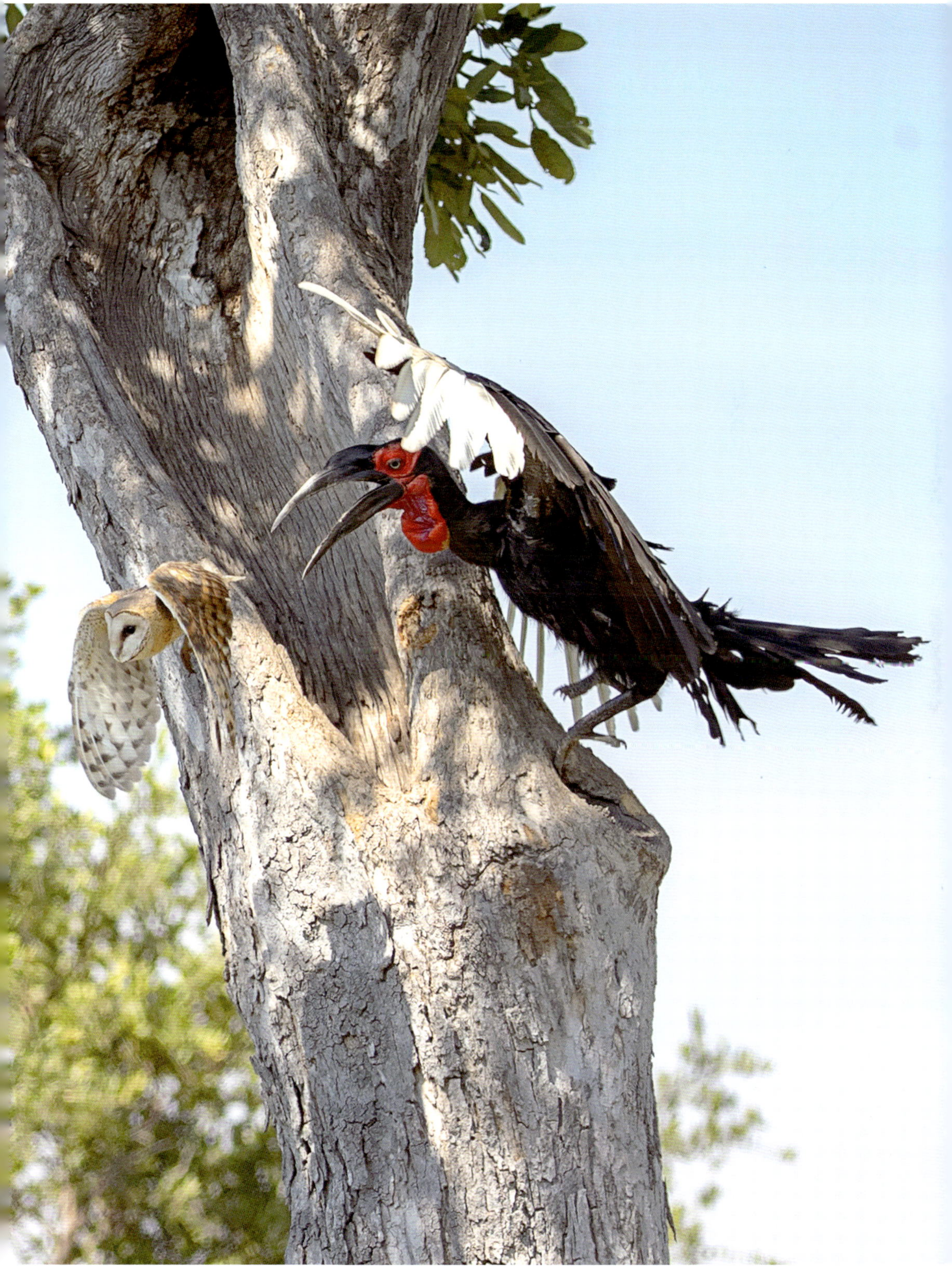

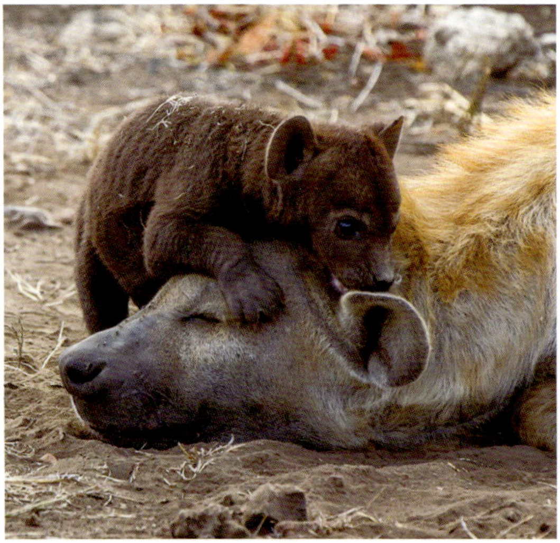

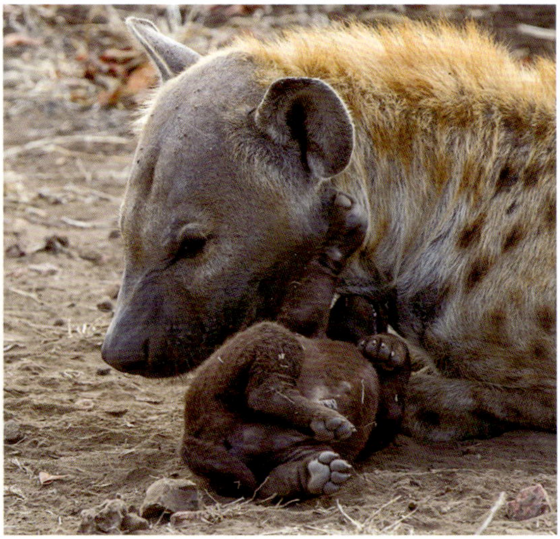

Please notice me!

BRIAN STRATTON

We were on the H1-6 en route to Shingwedzi in the Kruger National Park when we spotted a lone hyena next to the road. A little head popped out of a culvert that ran under the road and looked at us with some interest. Deciding we weren't a threat, it ventured out and busied itself with a nearby plant. It kept this up for a while before it spotted the adult and endeavoured to draw its attention. The adult's ear took its fancy and much biting and pulling ensued. The older hyena took this in good spirit, more or less ignoring the juvenile. However, determined to get the adult's full attention, the younger one rolled onto its back and wiggled under the adult's throat. Finally the playful young got the reaction it craved as the adult's irritated expression clearly indicates.

We would have loved to continue watching their interaction but as a large number of cars had gathered, we moved on so others could have a good view of this charming scene.

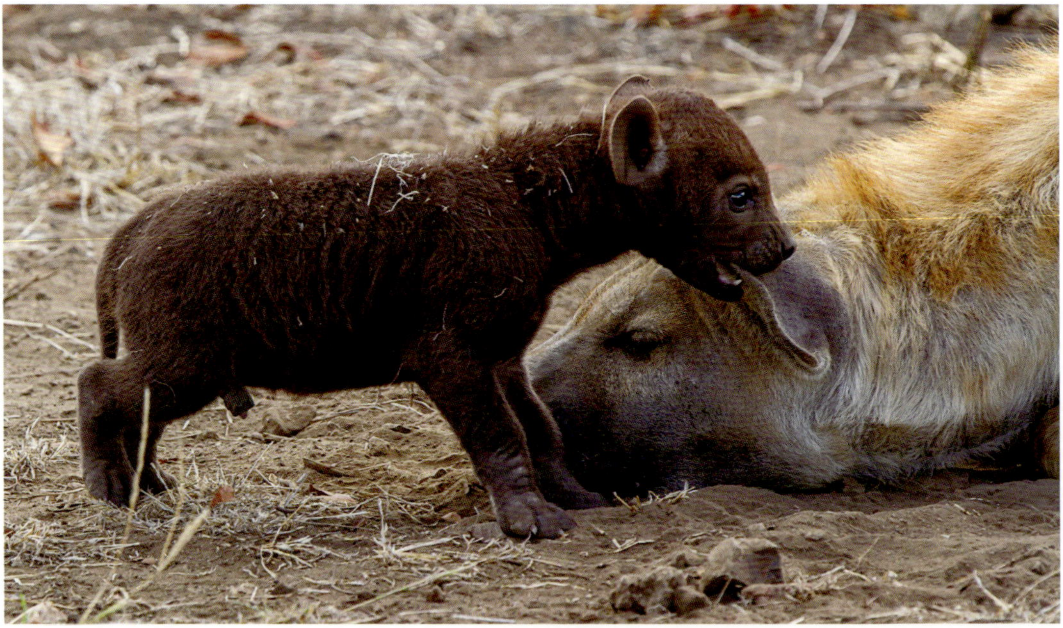

The playful caracal

ARNOLD VAN DYK

The caracal is, in general, a shy and reclusive animal and since they are mainly nocturnal, good daytime sightings are rare. Therefore, I regarded myself as extremely fortunate to encounter the elusive cat on an early morning drive in the Kgalagadi Transfrontier Park.

During May 2017, while driving from Twee Rivieren to Nossob I saw to my surprise, a caracal lying in full view about 20 to 30 metres from the edge of the road in the golden morning rays. I could immediately feel the adrenaline pumping, wondering which camera and settings would be best in these circumstances. I realised that to photograph this animal in its natural environment would be the opportunity of a lifetime. It astonished me that the cat seemed so relaxed and I was fortunate enough to get a few shots while it was at rest.

To my amazement, it jumped into the air and started to play with an object on the ground. At first I couldn't make out what it was, but after a while I was able to identify it as a tree-pod. This behaviour reminded me of the actions of a domestic cat: running, chasing, twirling, jumping, playing with and gnawing on the object while carrying it

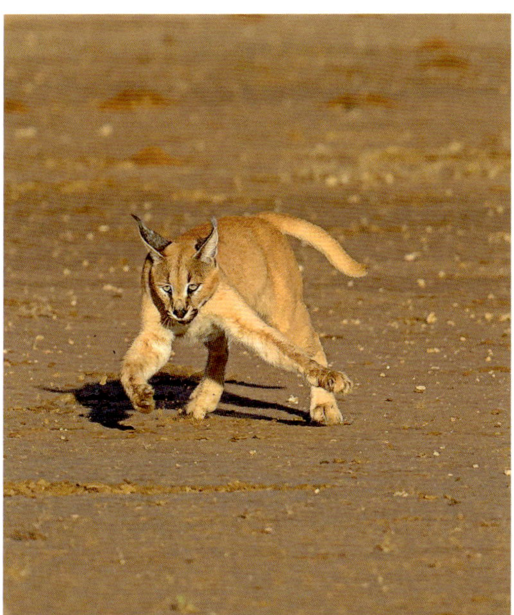

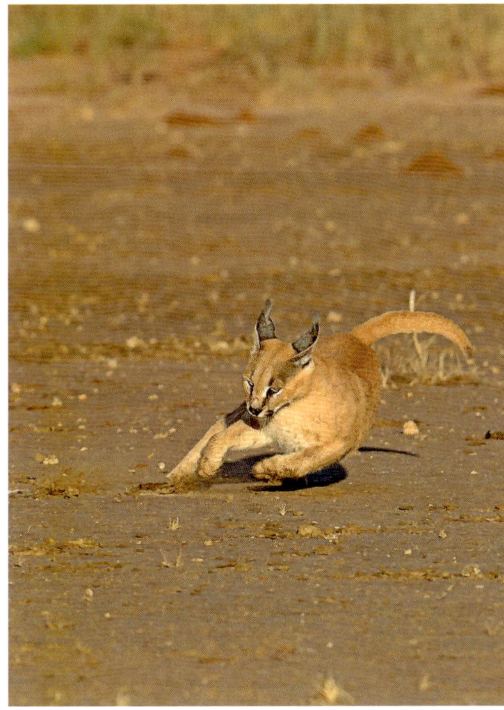

around – made evident by the reddish colour of the Kalahari sand around its mouth. What struck me particularly was its agility, as I witnessed it turning almost 180° at full speed. I know these cats can cause havoc for a sheep farmer, but right then it seemed unimaginable that anyone would kill such a magnificent specimen of nature.

In hindsight, I realised I ought to have taken some video footage but I was just so caught up in the moment and grateful to get a few pictures that I could share. The colours of the earth, the cat and the sun formed a perfect unit and I was treated to one of the most spectacular natural displays I had ever seen in almost 35 years of visiting nature parks in South Africa. I felt that the mere sighting of the caracal was special but to also view it caught up for some moments in the sheer abandonment of play, was a gift. For five minutes I gloried in its display but the episode ended abruptly when the cat, without warning, started running towards the nearest dune. On the top of the dune, it paused for a moment, looking back towards us as if to say goodbye. I sat in awe for a while, unable to say a word, and thanking the good Lord and nature for what I had been blessed enough to witness.

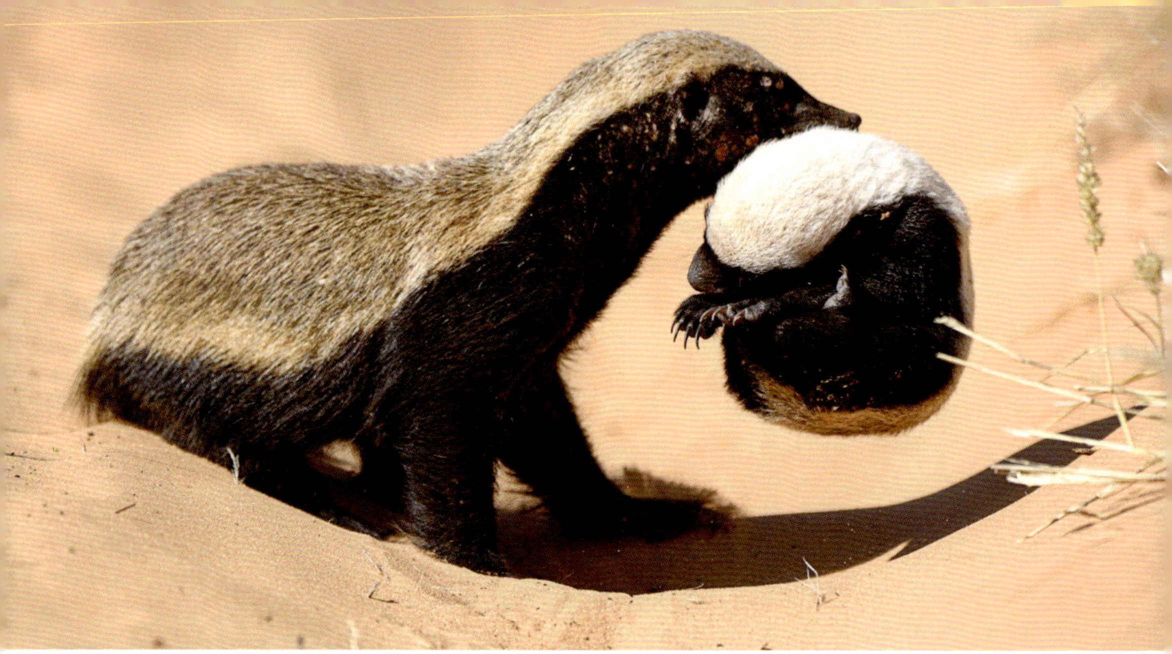

The long walk

HENNIE PRINSLOO

An early start on a mild winter's day in Mabuasehube Game Reserve. I crossed the two-spoor track roads of the Kalahari dunes, with the morning colours of the desert guiding me towards the Mabuasehube Pans, my next destination during this winter visit. The roads were patterned with lion, eland, hyena and gemsbok tracks. Kori bustards hid in the long yellow Kalahari grass and in contrast, the pale chanting goshawks were ever-present. I noticed four striped mice playing kamikaze with the Land Cruiser and the remains of tsammas next to the road.

Suddenly fresh honey badger tracks appeared in the right-hand lane of the sandy road. The imprint of the animal tracks seemed awkward. Every 100 metres or so there was an imprint in front of the honey badger's track, almost as if it was carrying something, but putting it down periodically and resting before continuing. The progress of the tracks excited me: perhaps the badger had harvested some honeycombs, found some scavenged food or even hunted something.

The morning sharpened and changed from just driving the dune road to actual wildlife tracking in the Kalahari, making me feel part of conservation. This new focus became intense curiosity about what might be around the corner. Often you follow a track, only to discover the animal has veered off the road and disappeared into the bushes, never to be seen. Usually, of course, the animals are hiding from the blistering heat of the Kalahari. However, this wasn't so likely on a mild day. As I continued to track the invisible honey badger my excitement and anticipation were building. I followed the tracks for over four kilometres, becoming more and more intrigued.

Around the next twist in the soft red sandy path, I saw something that brought me up short. All my expectations were exceeded, and it was difficult to contain my excitement. It was even harder to find my camera and decide how to document this marvellous sight. The moment was almost too stupendous to be true. There she was, the indomitable mother badger with her young in her mouth. She had been carrying her baby for the past five kilometres. The fresh lion's tracks surrounding her trail explained her urgency. The mother badger paused a while and allowed us to have a good view before she decided to take a left turn across the dunes, hopefully towards a new den and safety.

The incredible experience of tracking the badger, locating and documenting her, became one of my most memorable wildlife experiences within the Kalahari.

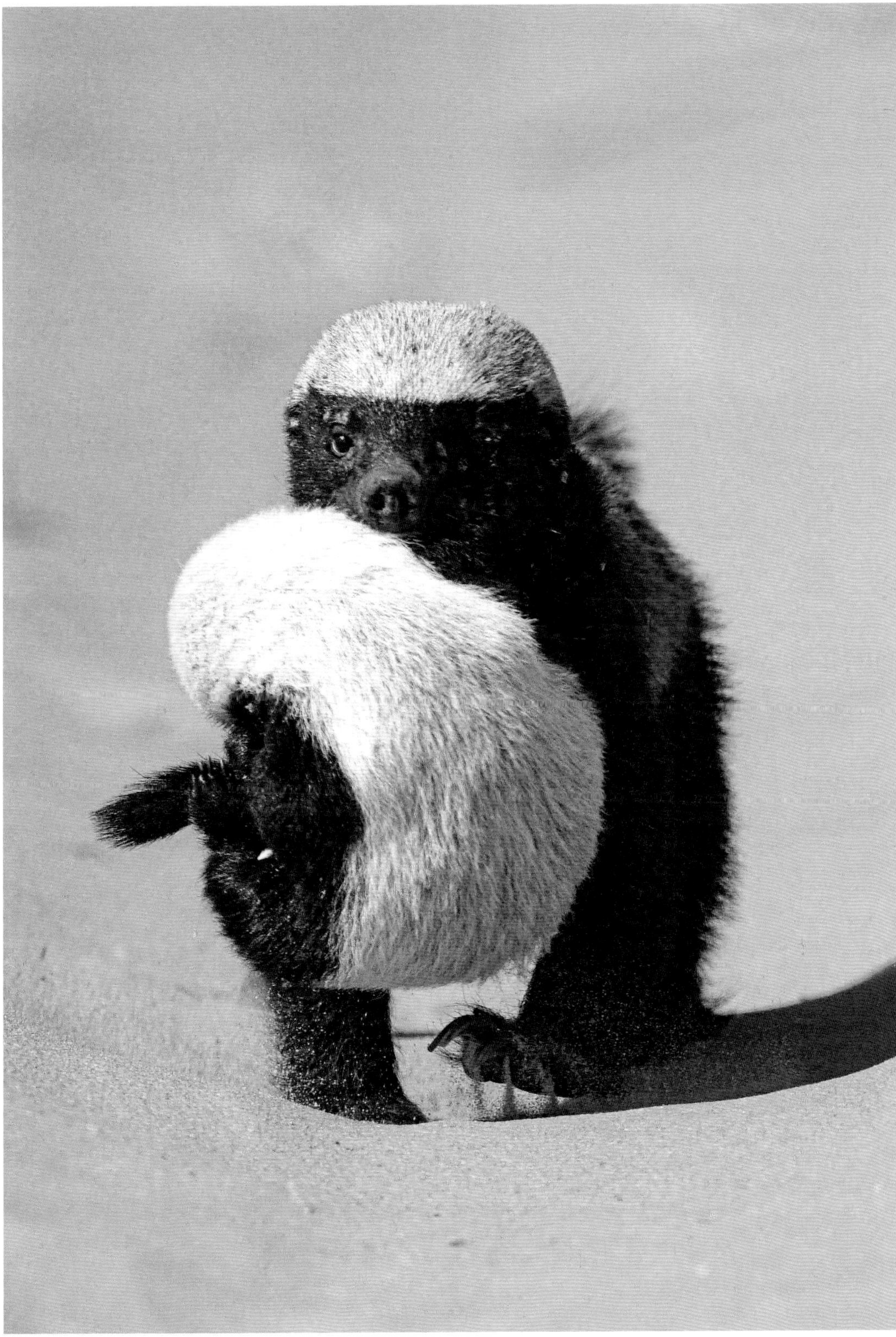

The honey badger thief

JACQUES BLIGNAUT

You can never dictate what you want to see in the bush. You might have a wish list but there is no guarantee your wishes will be granted. I have learnt this over many years going into the wild, so I always arrive with the attitude that anything I see is a boon. I've had many special sightings over the years: from elephants to the smallest insects, they have all been marvellous. Then there is the experience which truly stands out, and that probably no one else has had. But I have photographic proof of this unique sighting, so special you wouldn't even think to put it on your wish list.

During one of our visits to the Kgalagadi Transfrontier Park, a martial eagle and its chick were spotted close to Veertiende Boorgat. On the morning of 15 August 2018, another visitor told me where the nest was located. We'd already passed the location and so decided to visit the nest in the evening.

We arrived at the spot but could see neither the mother nor the chick. Off we drove all the way to Dertiende Boorgat and back. On the return journey I spotted the martial eagle in the nest and then I saw the chick. I was most excited as I have never seen a martial eagle chick before. The next moment I saw a honey badger in the nest and wondered what it could possibly be doing there. Before we could quite take it in, the intruder had snatched the chick. It was like a kidnapping in the movies.

We drove away five minutes later in disbelief. I had never seen anything like it. Not even the black-maned lion of the Kalahari could quite beat this. Looking back, I rate it as our most memorable sighting, despite the sorrow we felt, knowing as we did that the martial eagle lays only one egg every two years.

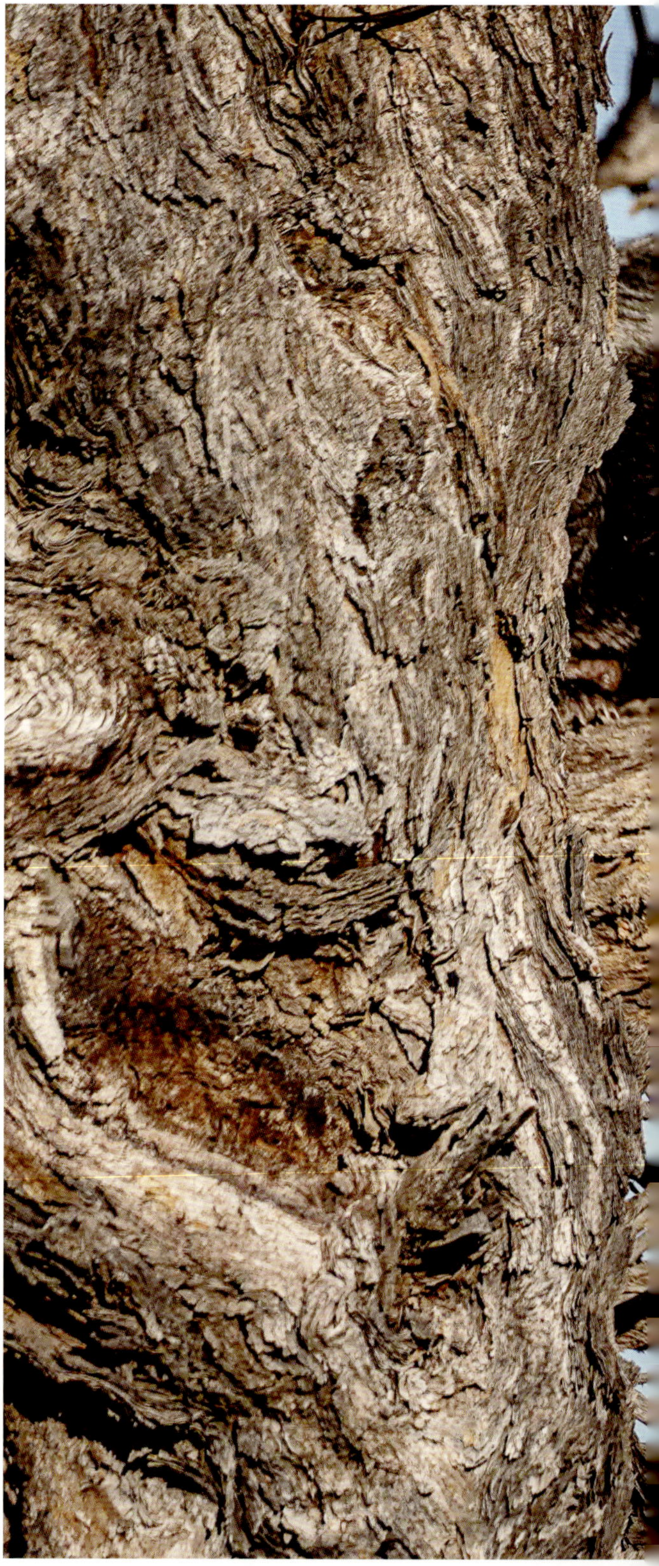

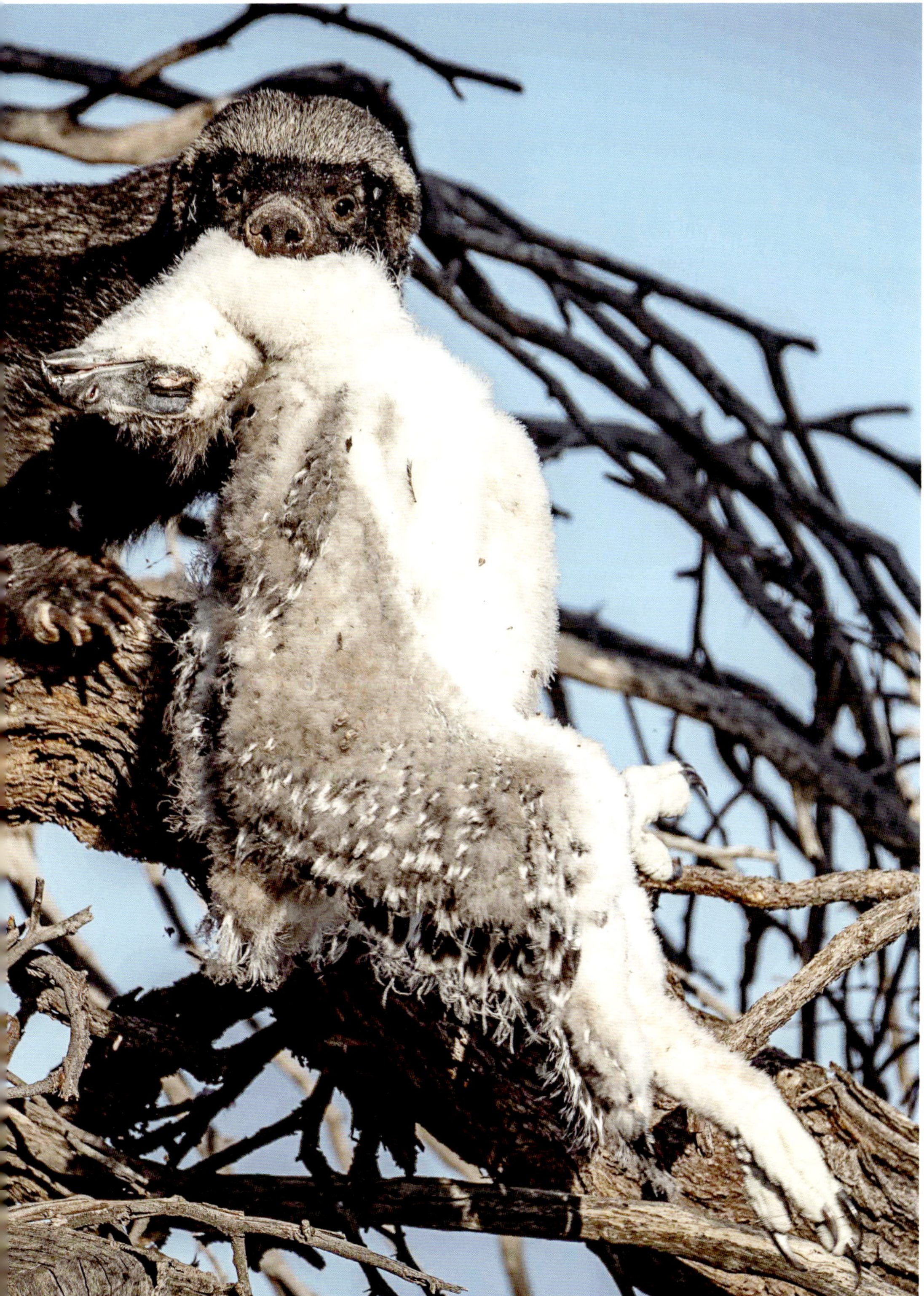

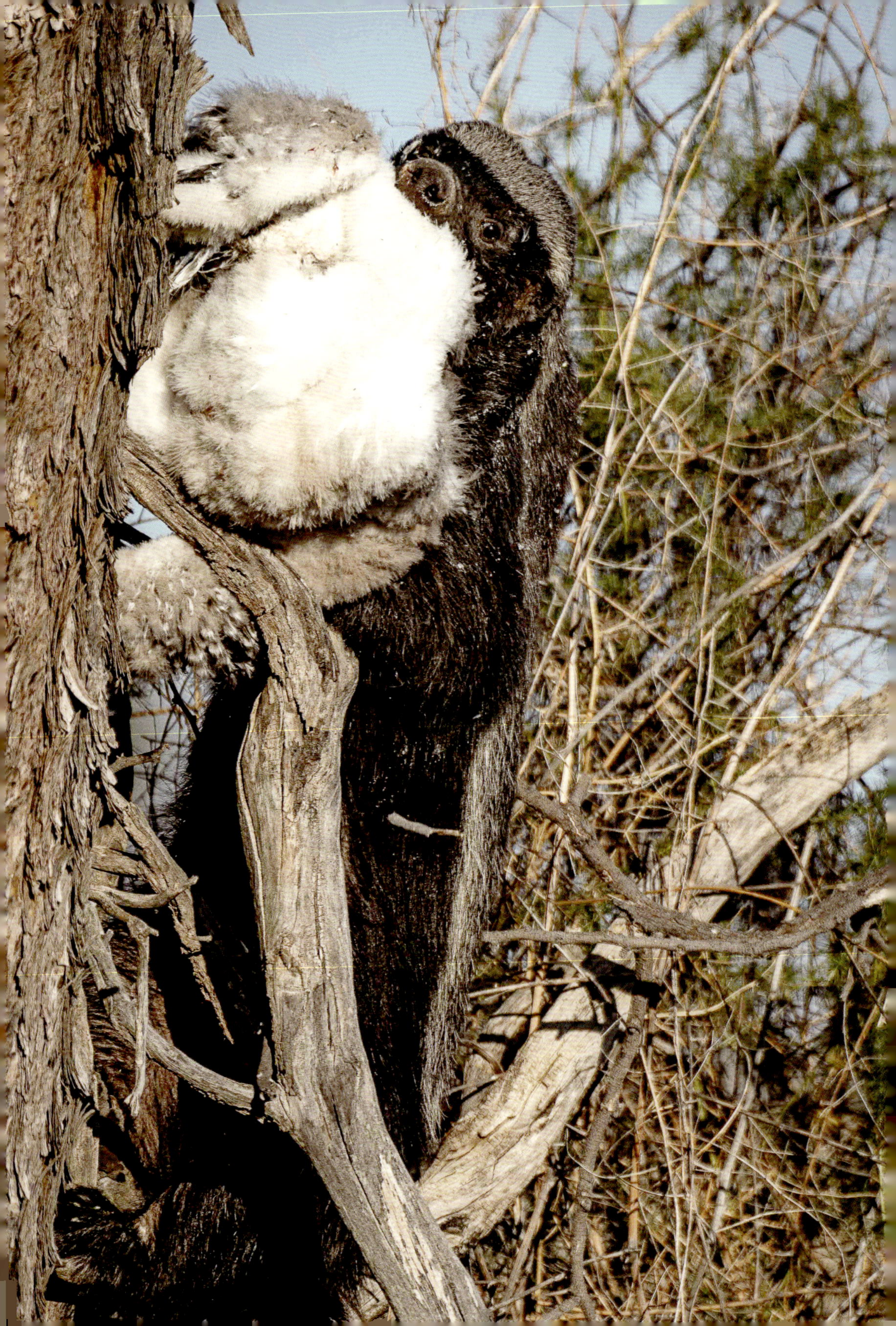

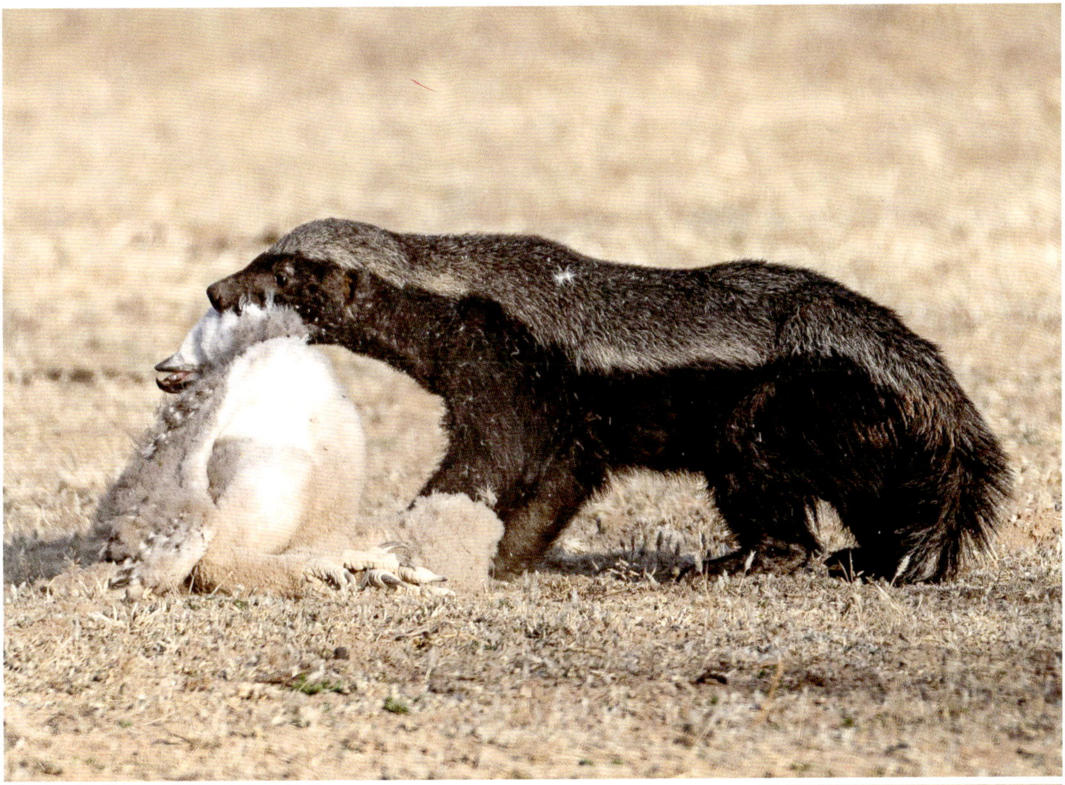

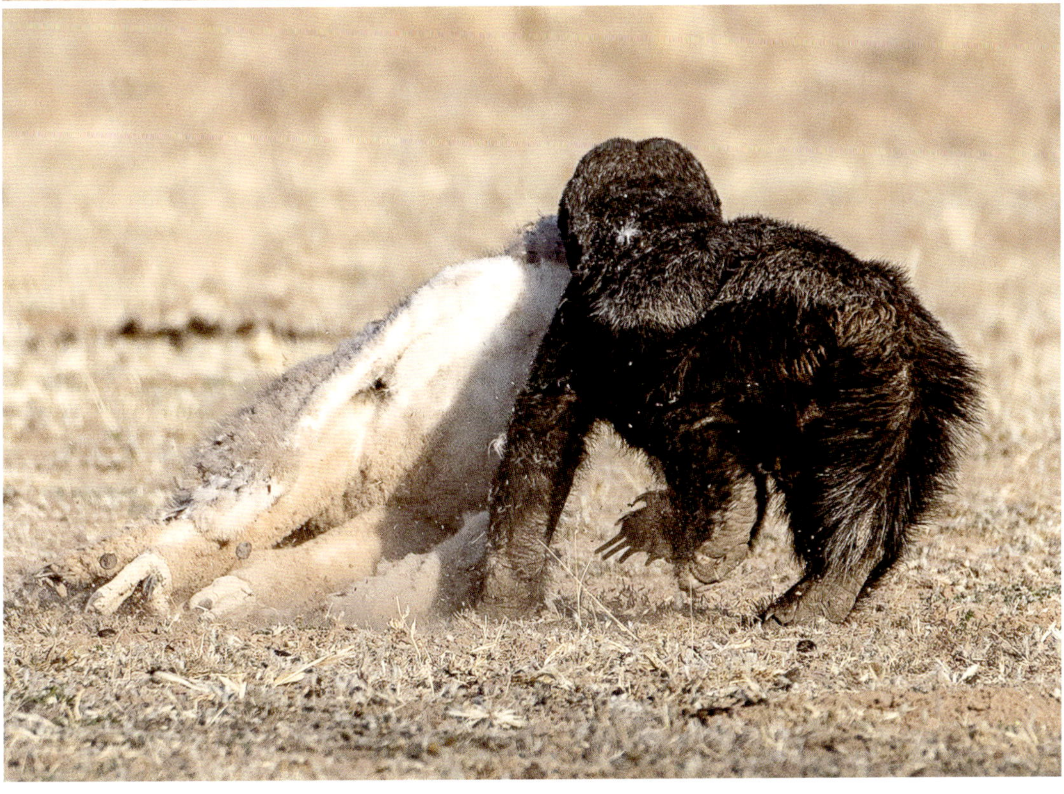

Honey badger secrets

JOHAN BOTHA

We were driving past a waterhole on the way to Mata-Mata in the Kgalagadi Transfrontier Park in November 2017 when I registered something from the corner of my eye. I reversed and closer inspection with binoculars confirmed I'd glimpsed the eyes and upper body of a honey badger, just visible above the water.

Then, much to our surprise we saw another face, completely covered in mud, appearing next to the honey badger. Was it a second honey badger? We couldn't be sure.

The honey badger I'd noticed got out of the waterhole, partially covered in mud. It started cleaning itself next to the waterhole and then came running directly towards us. It leant its back against a bush and cleaned itself vigorously. After a while it returned to the waterhole and ran around it several times as if looking for something. There was, however, no sign of the animal that had been covered in mud.

What happened? Did it drown? Had it been attacked by bees and dived into the mud for safety or relief? Was it smothered by the mud? Was it, in fact, another honey badger or perhaps another creature?

We waited for an hour but saw no further sign of it. Finally, we had to leave but we still wonder what happened to the other 'honey badger'.

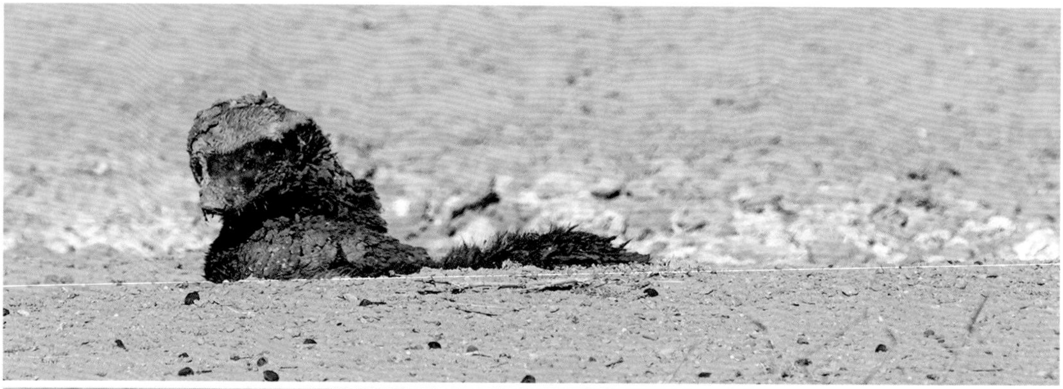

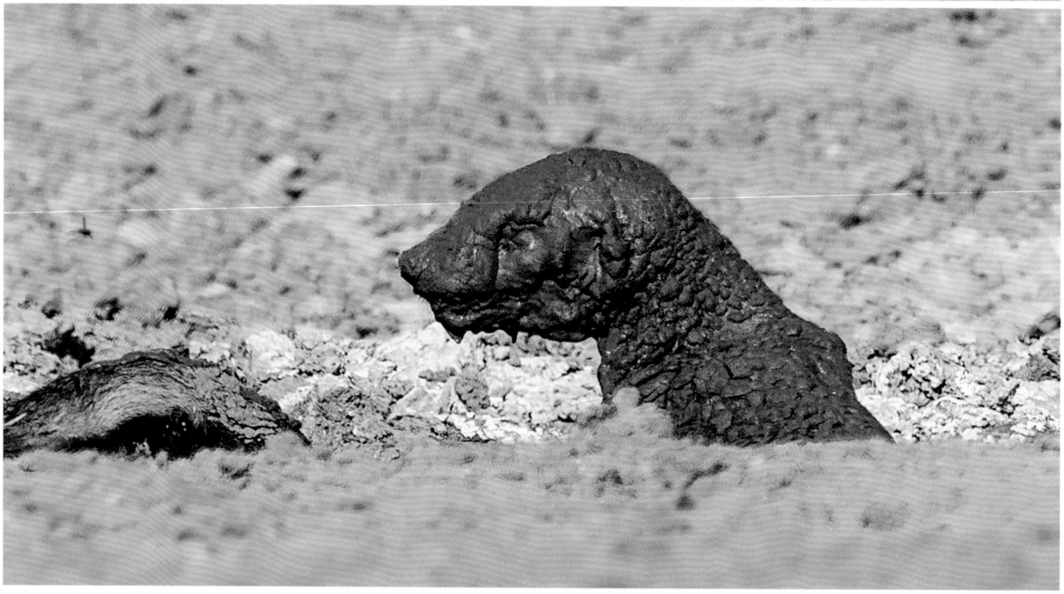

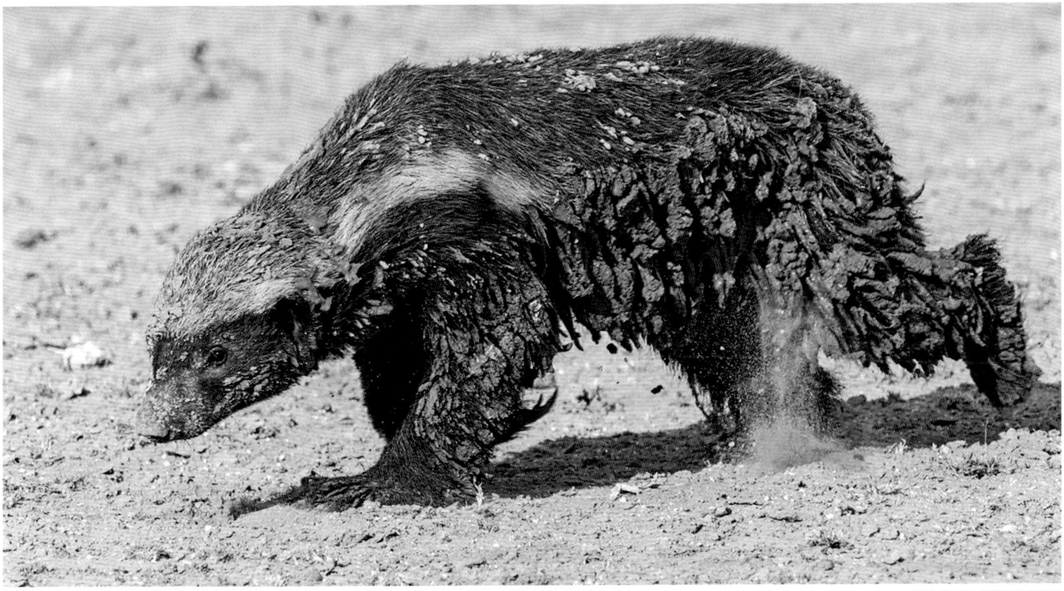

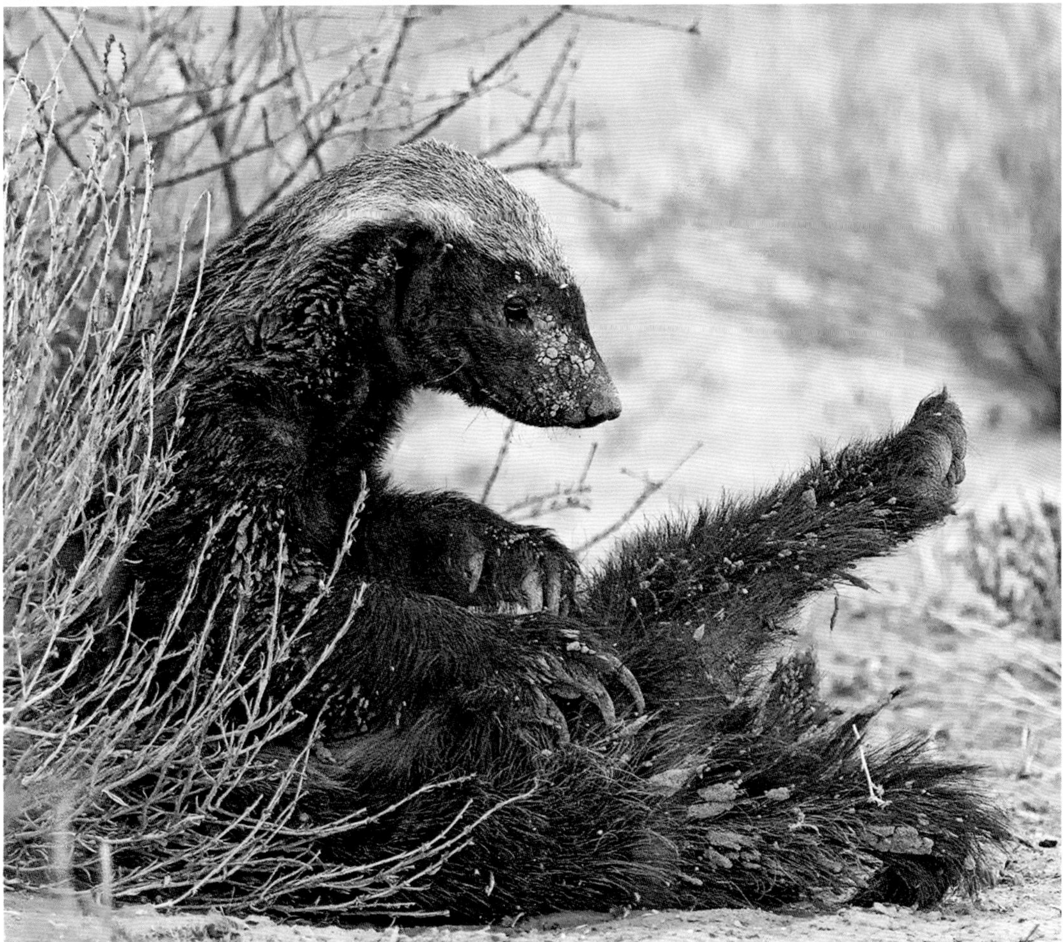

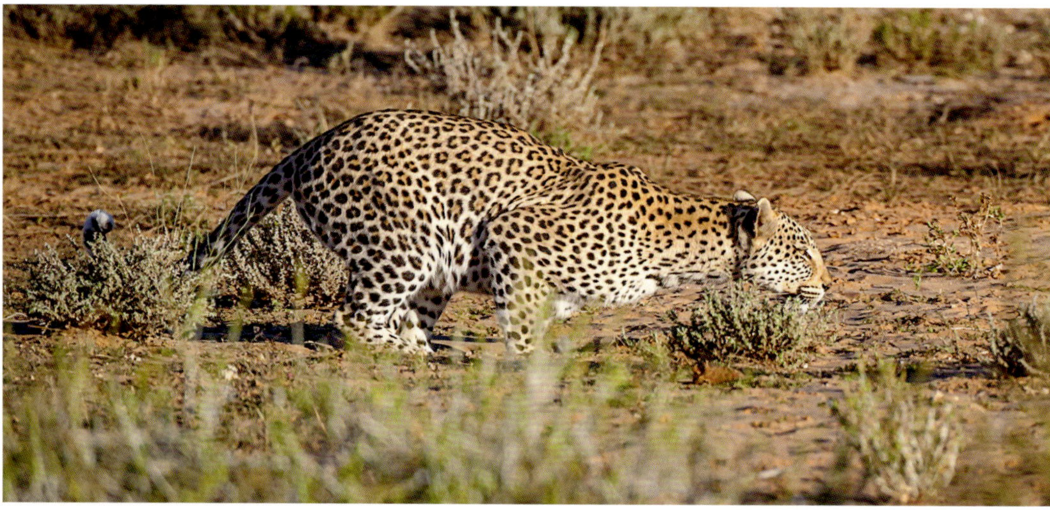

Wannabe photographer

JOHAN MOCKE

In May 2010, we accompanied friends to the Kgalagadi Transfrontier Park for the first time. I was a rookie photographer, keen to test my new camera and 200–400 millimetre lens. The first morning our experienced friends set off in the direction of Twee Rivieren on the then-Botswana Road, which has since become inaccessible. My wife and I followed closely, as we started learning how to 'do' the Kgalagadi.

When we spotted a leopard, the excitement was palpable. The magnificent animal was on the move, however, and although I was a wannabe photographer, I was also the driver of the vehicle. Trying to get my camera with the long lens ready to capture something worthwhile was no small feat. I had no fancy stabiliser or platform. Instead, a small window bean bag had to do the trick.

Everything happened at once… fiddling with the camera, manoeuvring the car and the leopard going into stalking mode. I couldn't see what she was after and desperately tried to get her into focus. Then it happened – she jumped! I sent my shutter into overdrive, in the hopes of catching the action. She flew through the air… what was she attacking? Had she succeeded? Had I even captured any of this? I was too scared to check the camera screen or the settings for fear of missing the action. Then came the delightful realisation; she was not attacking anything but mock-stalking and charging her cub! The excitement in the car grew in leaps and bounds, but there was more to come.

Out of nowhere a second cub popped up. I continued shooting – still unsure whether I was handling the new equipment to best effect – trying to determine where to focus and praying I wasn't ruining a very special moment.

The cubs played together for a while and then their mother tenderly groomed one of them, before moving away from the little ones and lying down under a bush. One of the cubs followed her and our memorable sighting ended with more bonding between leopard mother and cub.

As I lowered my lens, I looked at the clock. While it felt longer, I'd just experienced a full three minutes of Kgalagadi-rookie-photographer bliss.

A first with my camera equipment, our first time at Kgalagadi, a first morning scouting, a first sighting of a leopard and her cubs – all astonishing events, never to be repeated.

Needless to say, we were hooked, and we've visited the park about 14 times since then. This leopard sighting was a life-changing event for me. My photography skills may have improved, but those awe-inspiring three minutes marked my photographer soul like the birth of a firstborn child. I don't believe any other sighting has ever elicited the same depths of awareness in me.

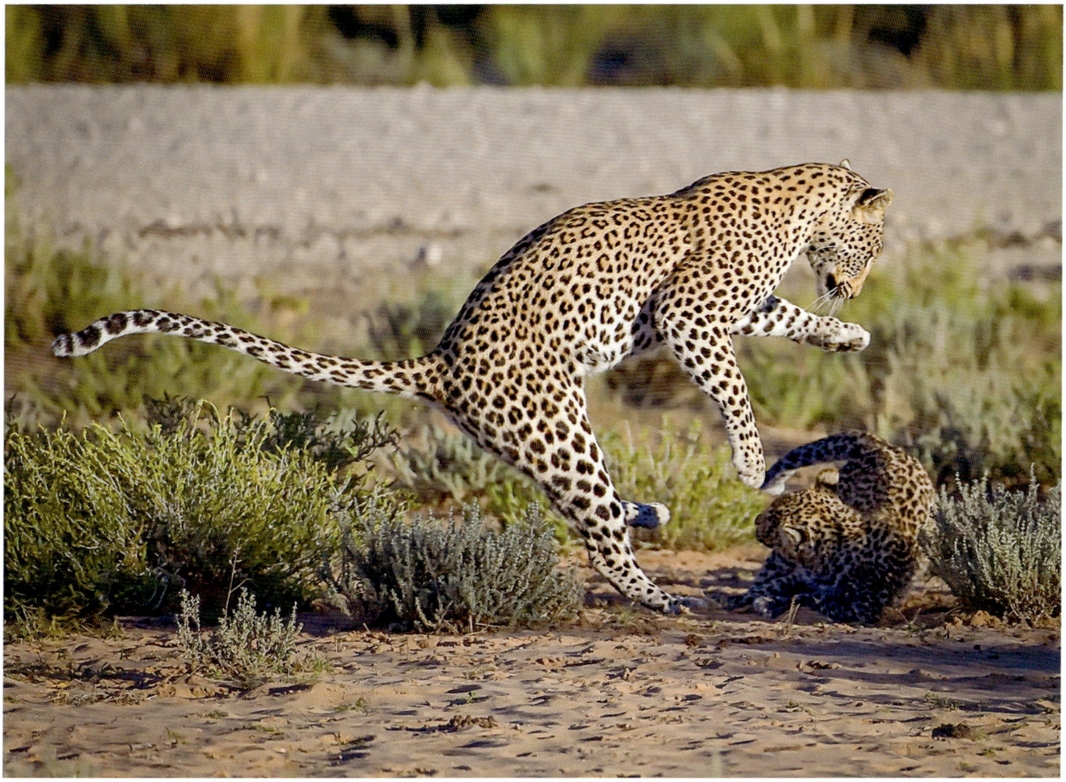

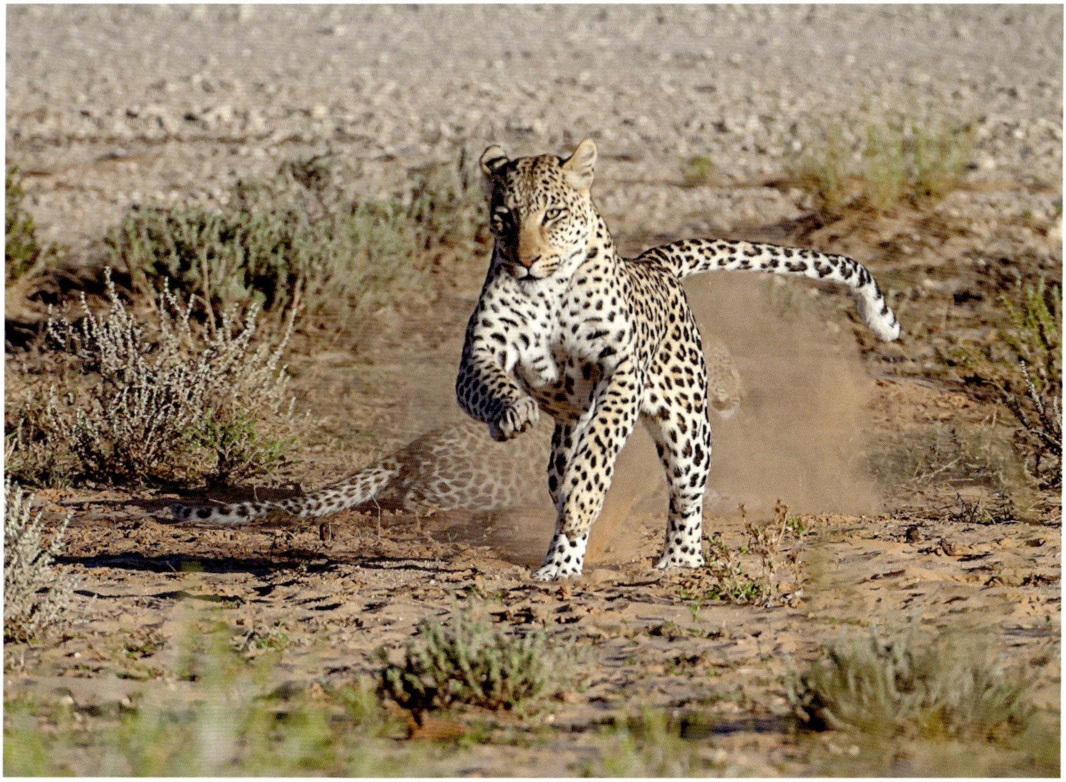

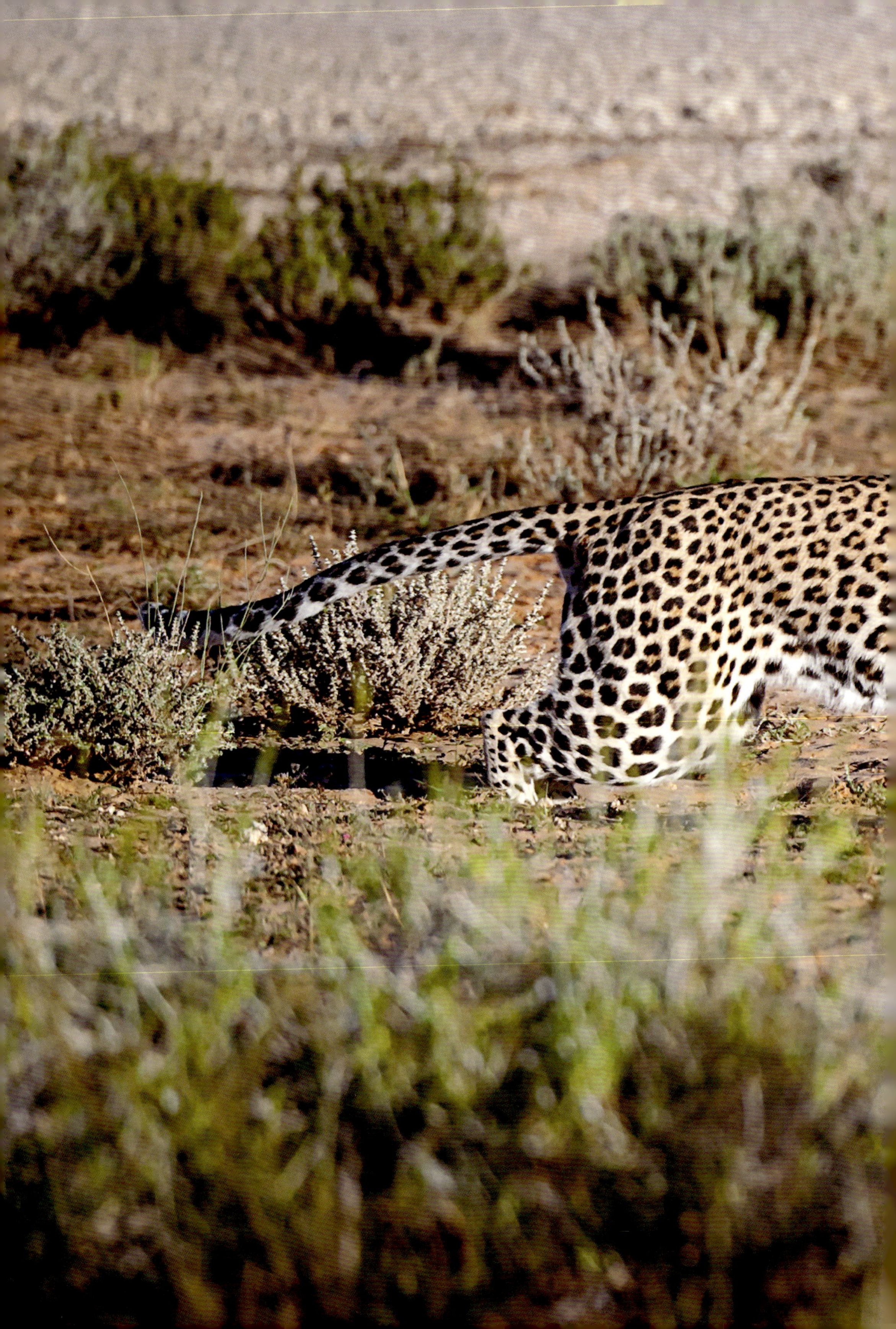

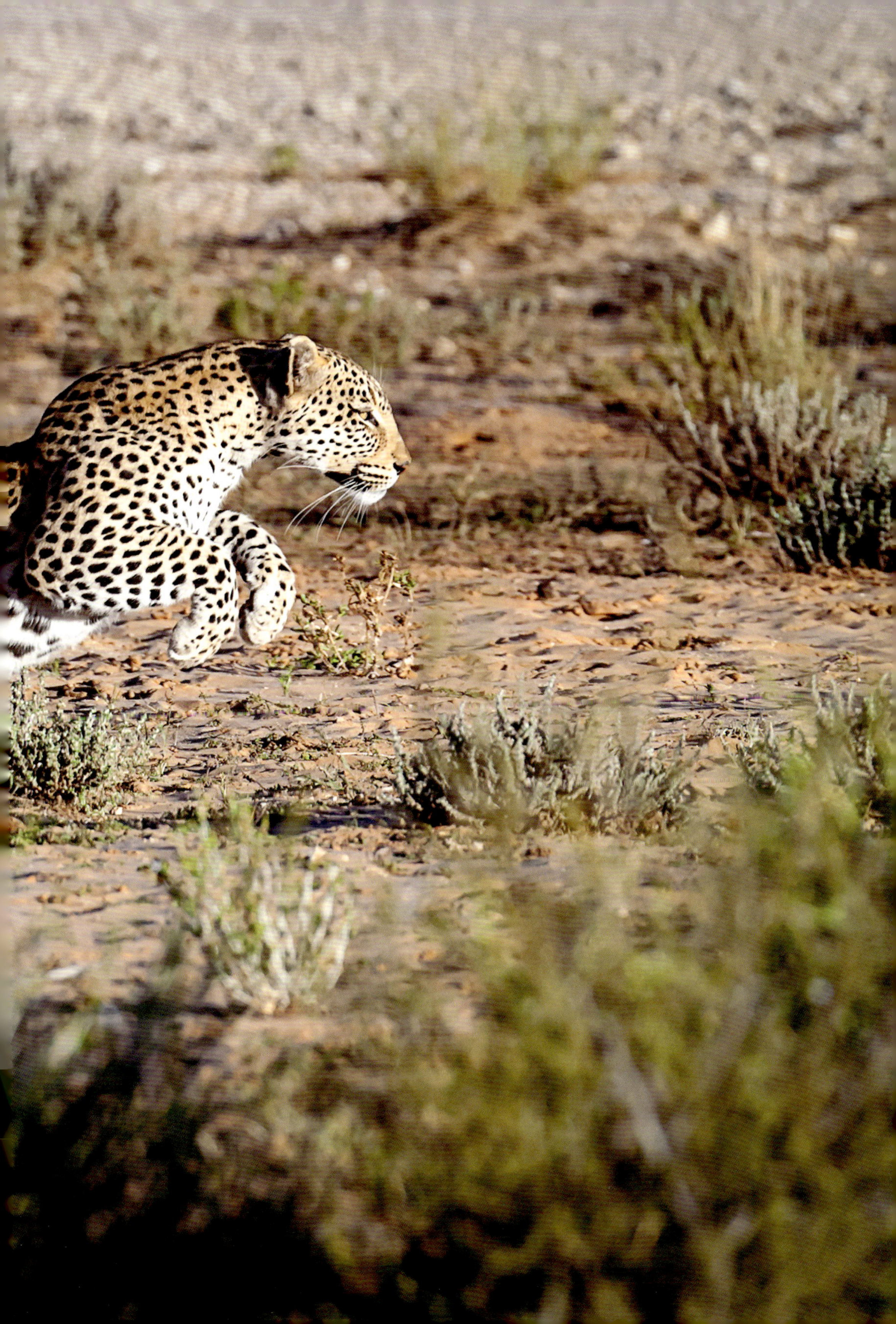

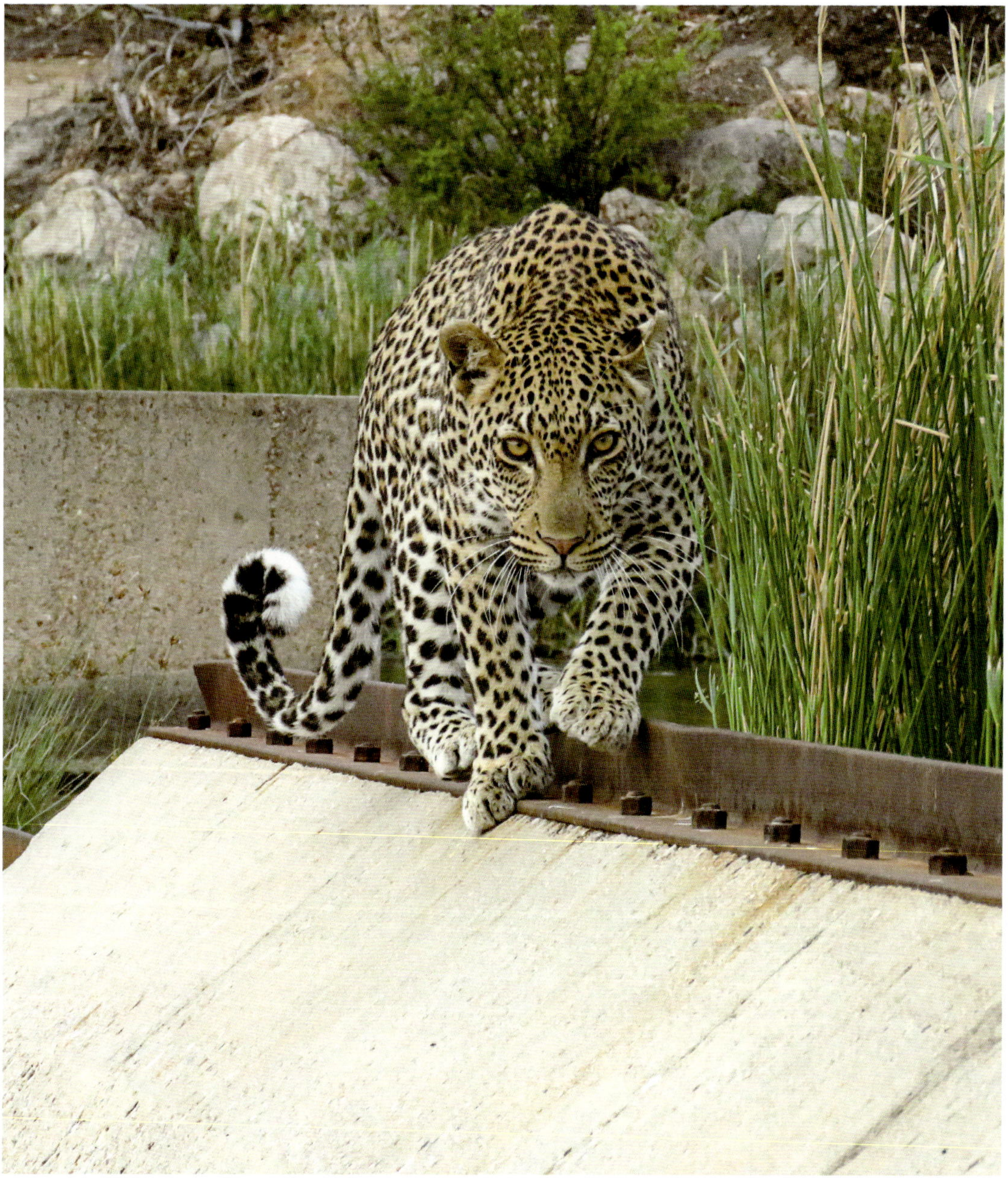

A leopard encounter at Biyamiti Weir

GRAEME MITCHLEY

Biyamiti Weir on the S114 between Skukuza and Malelane in the Kruger National Park has always been special. Besides the area being peaceful and beautiful, there is always a lot of animal and birdlife to admire. There is the resident bull hippo, massive crocodiles and a pair of fish eagles. We have been lucky enough to see wild dogs, leopards and the resident Eastern Bank Pride males. Lionesses and cubs are often seen in the area.

But in October 2016, I had a once-in-a-lifetime leopard sighting. My friend, Grant and I arrived at the weir from the north side just before 7:30. We had enjoyed a beautiful morning drive up to

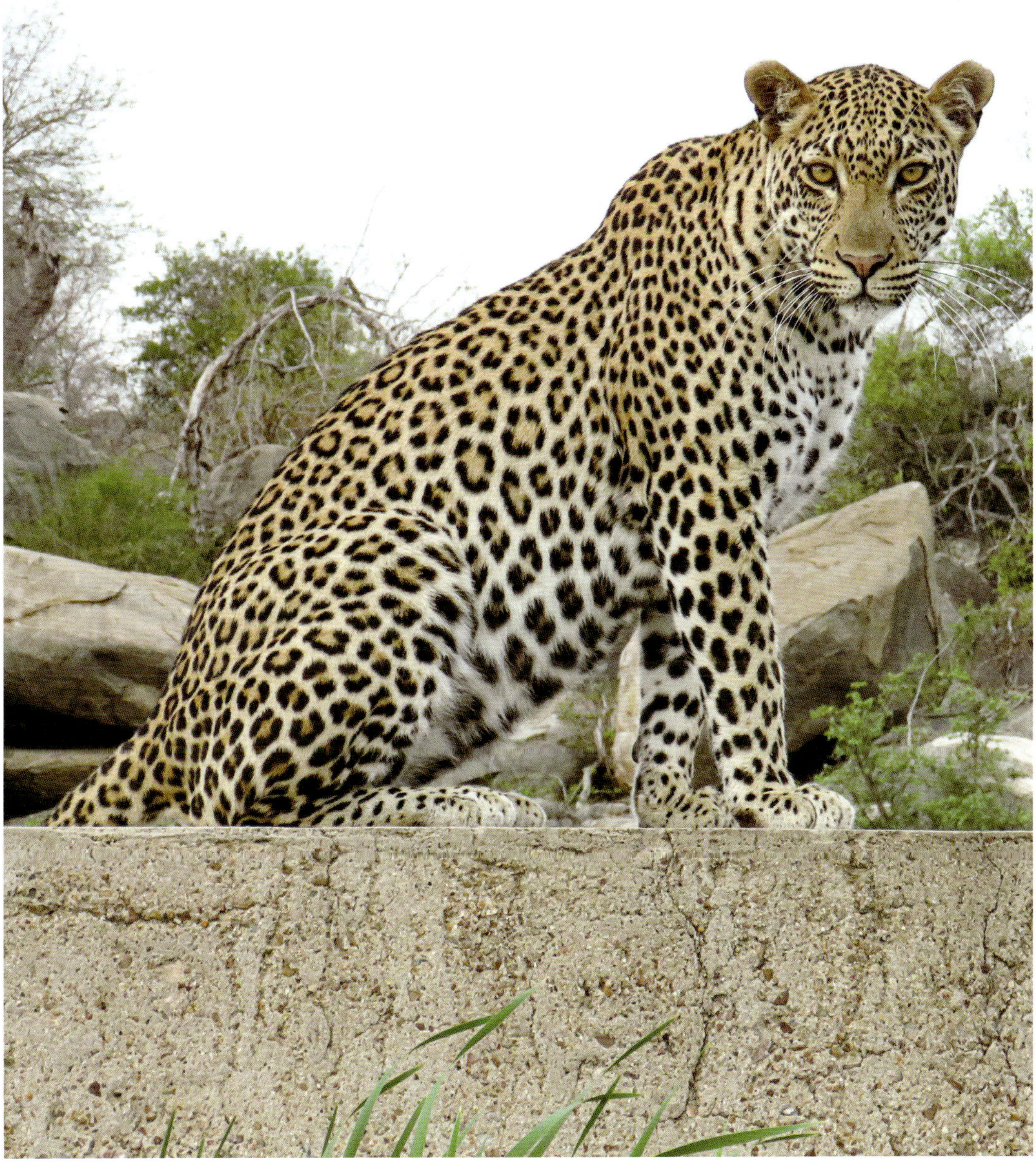

then but nothing could prepare us for what was to follow. The next 30 minutes was a total blur and adrenaline rush.

When we arrived at the weir, there was one other vehicle. The driver was friendly and casually asked us if we would like to see a leopard. Silly question: of course we would! A male leopard was lying on the rocks to the east about 40 metres away. After a while he started to walk towards the weir but was in no hurry. He was very confident and relaxed. This was his territory. He alternated between walking, sitting and lying down. All the time the cameras were firing away. We inched towards the concrete weir as the leopard moved in that direction. He walked straight towards us, looking us directly in the eyes, nearer and nearer until he was about five metres from the car. He walked in front of the car and was so close

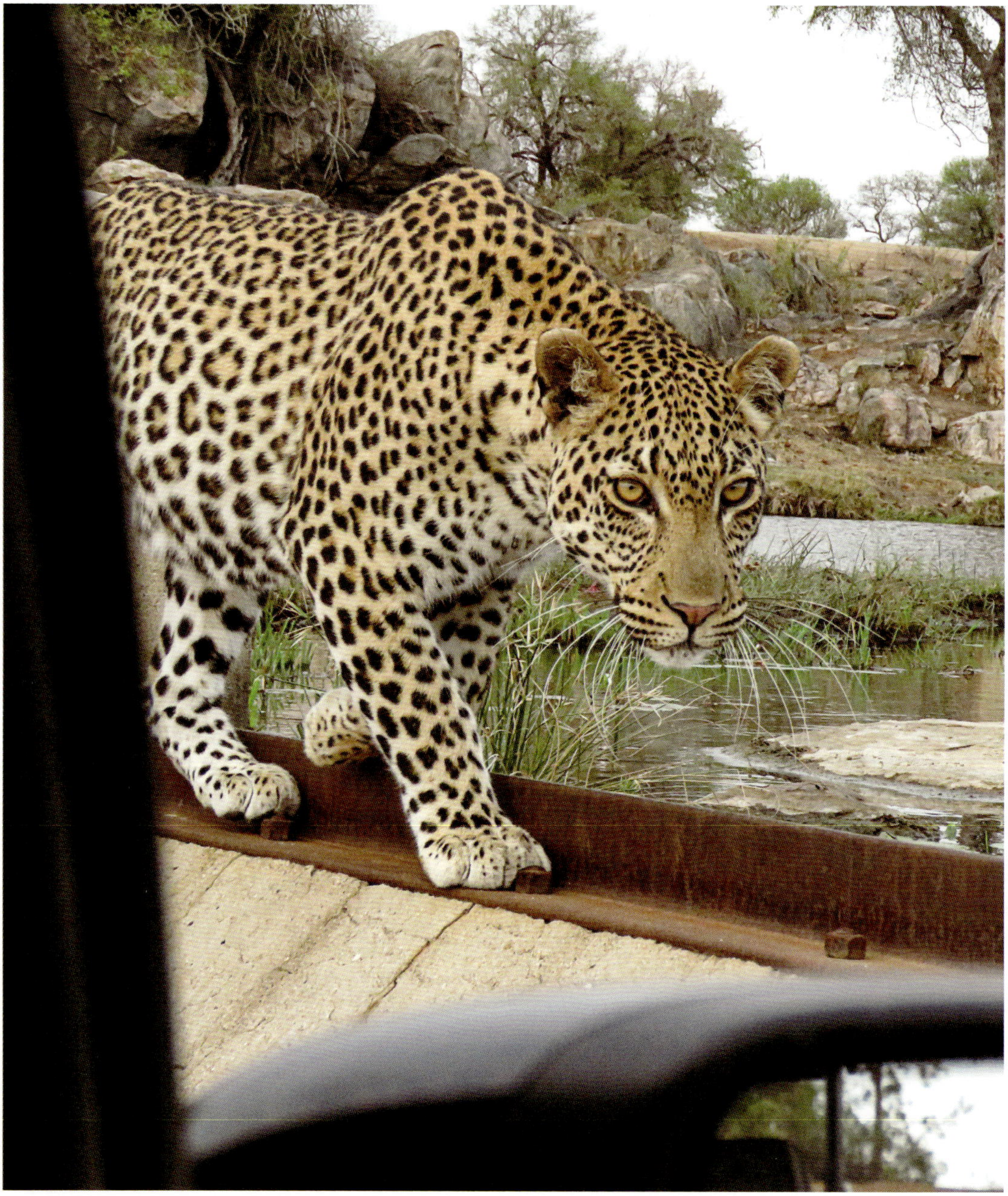

I could have sworn he brushed it. The leopard then moved away, towards the south entrance. I thought the sighting was over and that he was headed for the bush. I was over the moon to have experienced this and had no complaints.

But then, out of the blue, he turned around, jumped onto the weir and walked towards us again, this time at eye level. My heart was thumping! I managed to keep the camera clicking. I was in leopard heaven. He jumped up onto the concrete block and looked directly at us again. The look he gave seemed to go right through me. I held my breath. He wasn't finished yet – but he was thoroughly enjoying this catwalk. He didn't care that I thought I might have a heart attack. Although at that point I hardly cared myself. He jumped off the concrete block and headed straight for us. He got to less than two metres away, looked me in

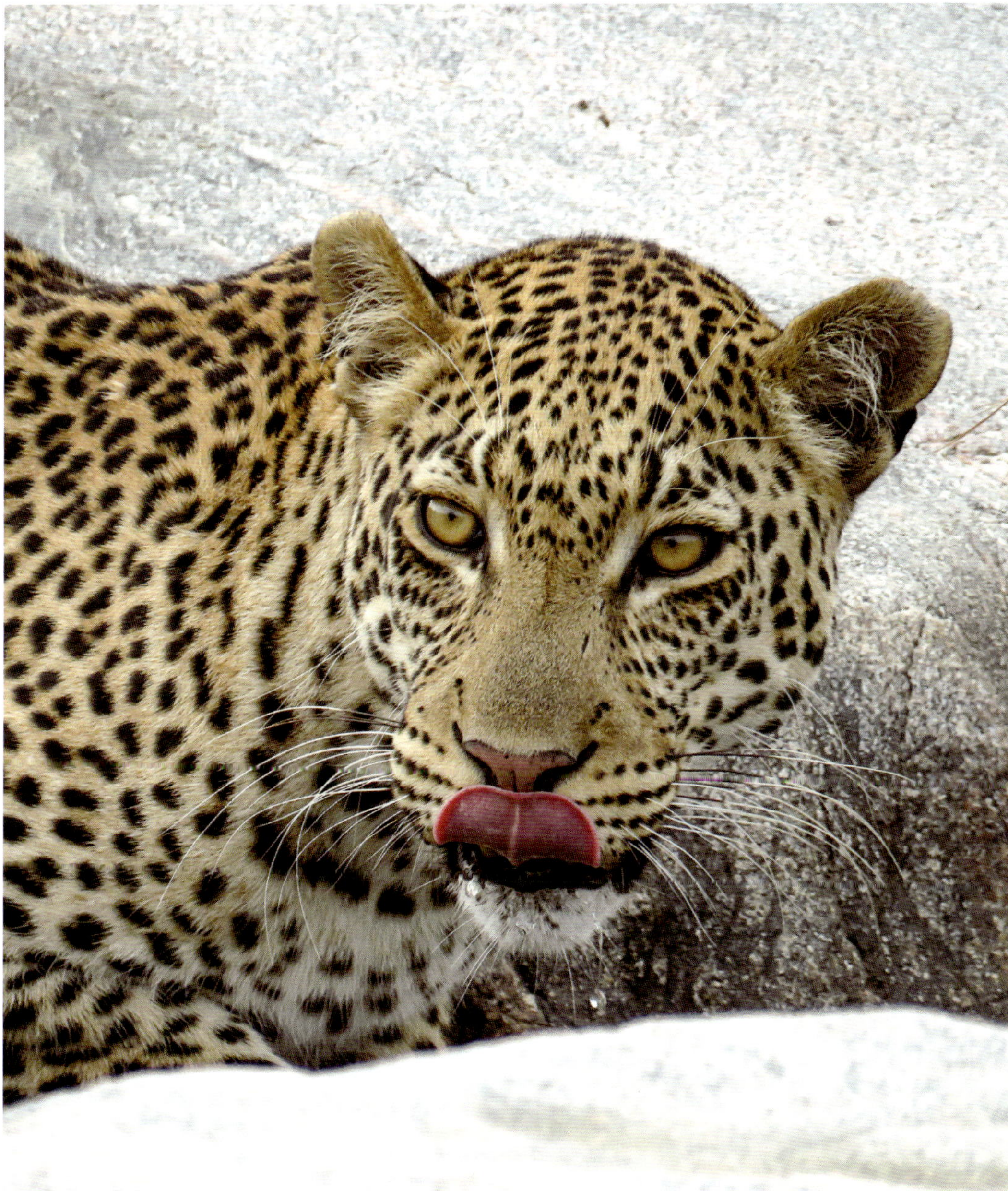

the eye and jumped down. This time he headed purposefully to the south entrance, drank some water and went up on to the rocks where he lay down while we were still able to photograph him. Other vehicles arrived and we let them have our spot to take their own photos. They had missed this spectacle by only a few minutes. We'd had the most amazing experience. There never was a better case of right time, right place.

As you can imagine, it took a few hours for the adrenaline rush to subside. We could barely contain ourselves the whole way home. We had to pinch ourselves to make sure it wasn't a dream. This was 20 leopard sightings all rolled into one. Even now, I still get goosebumps when I look at the photos. My up-close-and-personal encounter with the Biyamiti Weir leopard will live in my memory forever.

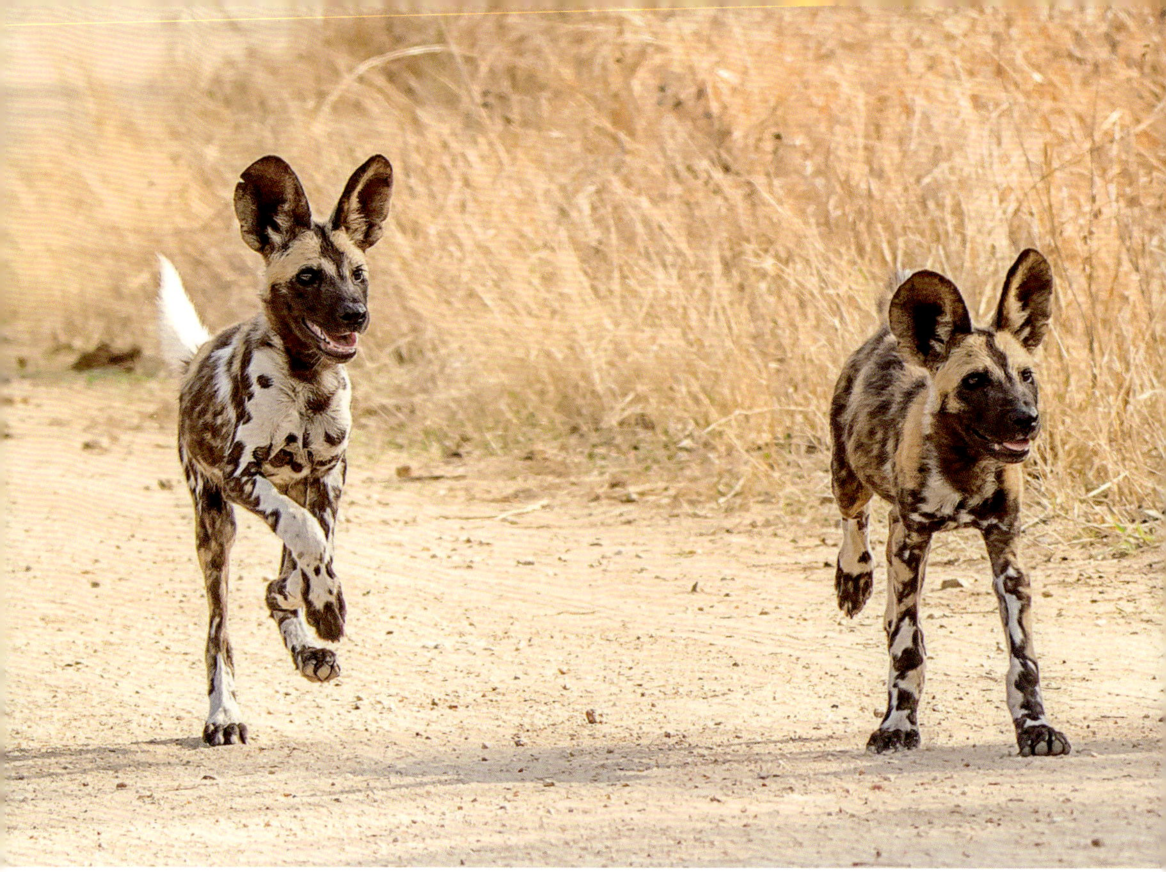

A golden morning with painted dogs

BILAL MOSAM & SAFIYYA LAHER

There was a time when we thought we'd only get to see wild dogs in the company of David Attenborough, on our couch. On a trip to Sabi Sands in August 2018, we counted ourselves lucky when we ran into three of them hunting in a riverbed. Because the bush was new to us, we thought this might be the first and last time we'd get a good view of them.

But the bar would be raised during our stay in the Kruger National Park in October 2018. It was the first time we had really explored the south of the park and we fell in love with Biyamiti Loop and the weir that welcomes you to it. It was our last morning in the park and we wanted nothing else but to enjoy the environment of the weir.

After spending a couple of hours watching giraffe and elephant drinking at the weir, we decided to take a drive up Biyamiti Loop. A kilometre in, as we came around a bend, we abruptly halted in disbelief when we were met by four adult wild dogs and five extremely excitable pups. In an instant, the adults were almost upon us, the look on their faces signalling their intent. They were on a hunt! We doubled back and tracked them as they traversed the road before disappearing into the riverbed below. We had a decision to make: stick around or go back to the pups. The latter seemed to be a sure thing and so we backtracked. A reward lay in wait for us.

Not even five minutes later, the pointed ears of the pups alerted us to the alpha male arriving with spoils from the hunt.

They greeted him hysterically before digging into their share. One of the pups managed to get a chunk out for itself, which led to an entertaining chase. We spent a good hour with them as they fed, played and found a place to rest, without another vehicle in sight. We couldn't believe our luck. Biyamiti will always hold a special place in our hearts.

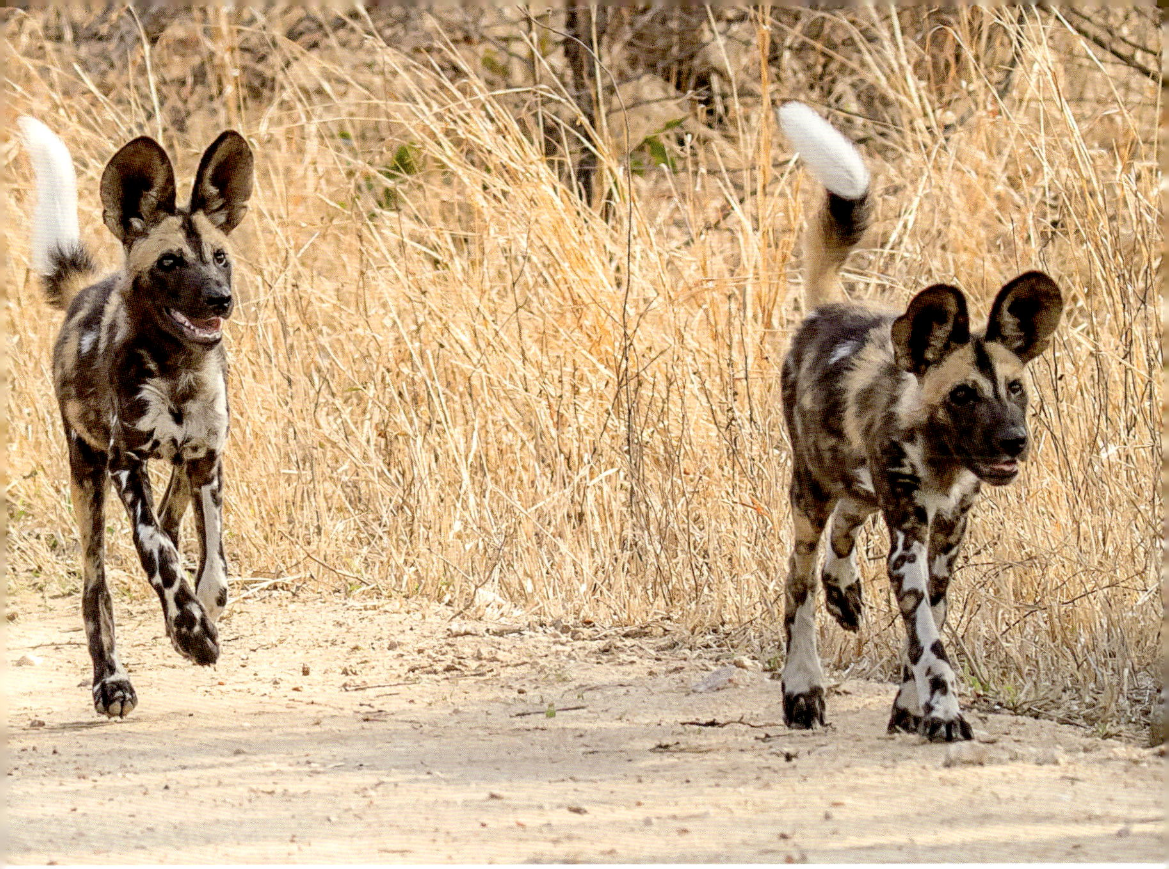

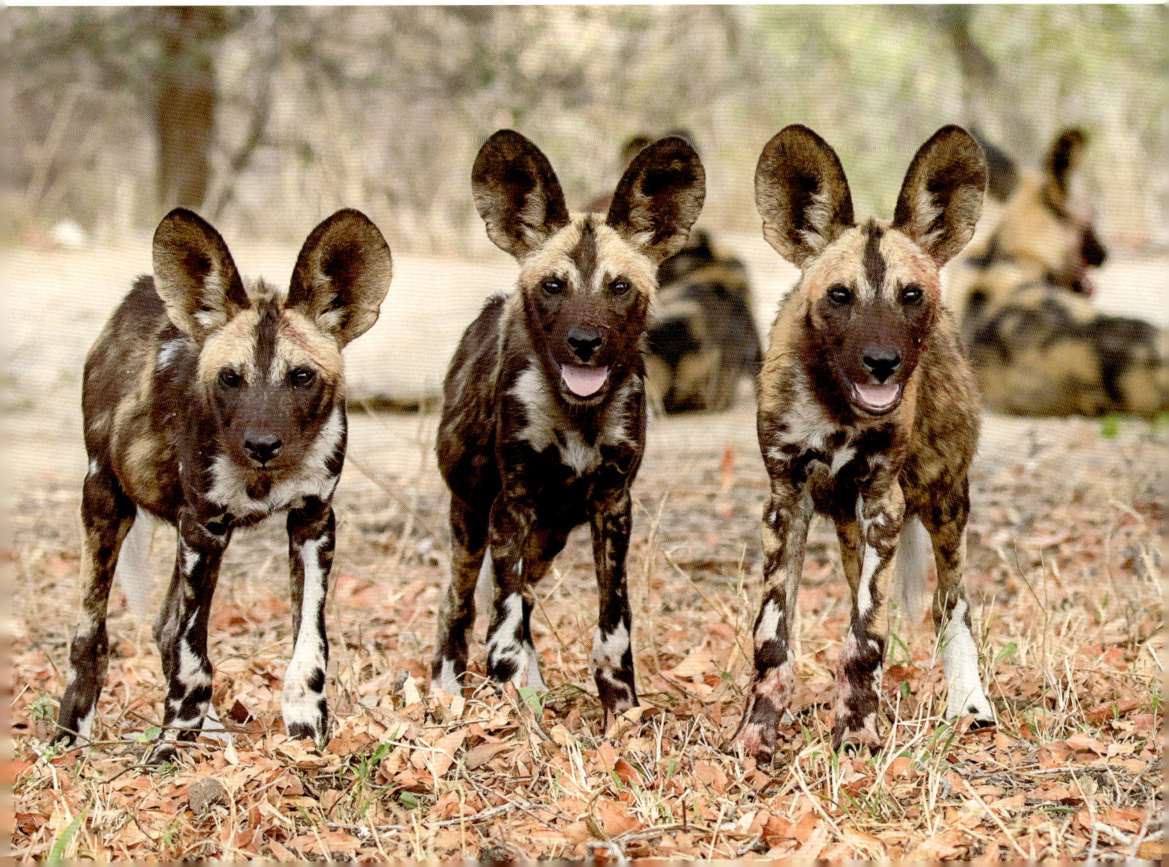

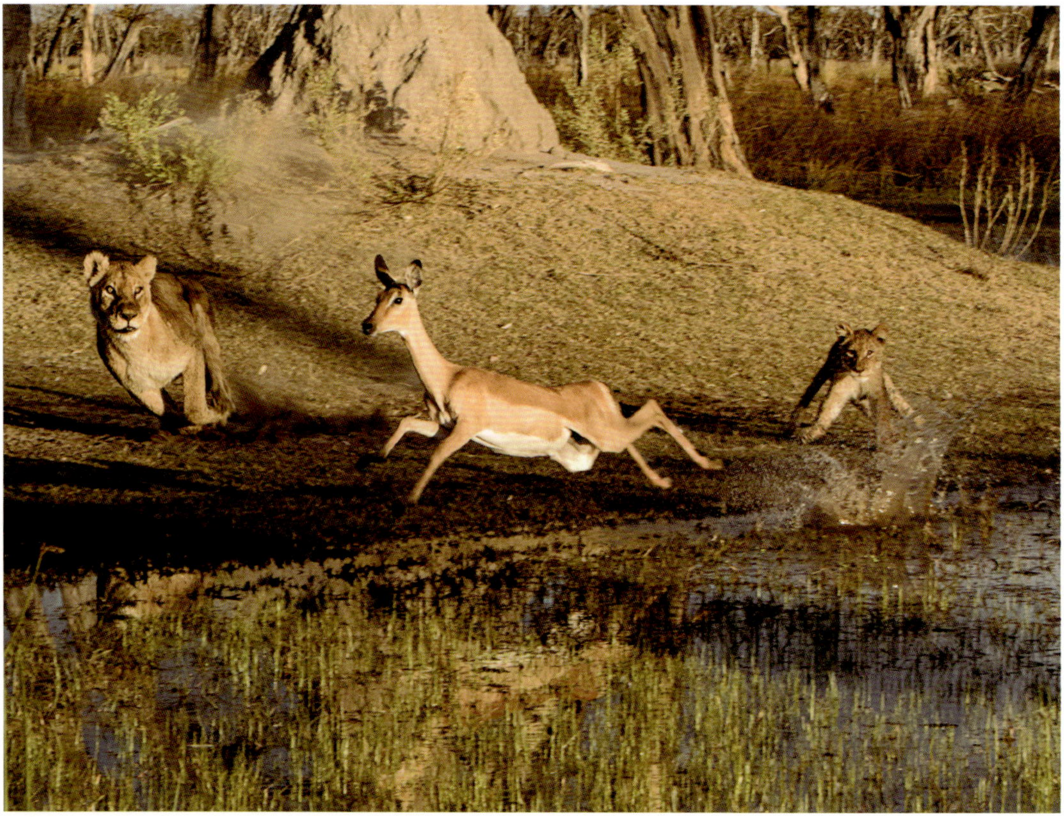

The great lion and African wild dog showdown

MELONIE EVA

It all started when we were scouting for a spot to have sundowners and photograph the sunset in Botswana's Moremi Game Reserve. Instead, we noticed a lioness and her cub basking in golden light on an ant hill, minding their own business.

Suddenly, 24 African wild dogs disrupted the scene. Chasing an impala, they raced straight towards us. The impala swerved behind us, to be met with the lioness and her cub. Instinct kicked in as quick as a flash and the lions joined in the hunt, pursuing a much-needed meal. The impala managed to get away by darting close to a safari vehicle behind us. Hot on its heels, the lioness was not so agile, however, and propelled by her own weight, collided into the back tyre of the vehicle.

But the chase was not over: the hunter became the hunted when the wild dogs turned on the lioness and her cub, and the fight of their lives began. Although I'd grown up in the African bush and experienced many amazing animal interactions, this was one of the most emotional sightings of my life. The dogs fought ferociously with the advantage of numbers, while the lioness was determined to defend her cub to the death. The tears streamed down my face with a desperate desire for the lioness and cub to make it. And then it was over. The dogs slunk off, scratched and bruised, with the fight lost. The battle-weary lioness found her cub hiding in a bush and they were reunited. The cub snuggled close to its mother while she fed it a reassuring drink.

The entire episode took 38 minutes from the sighting of the first dog, to the moment mother and cub lay exhausted together.

We followed the dogs only to be sidetracked by a leopard silhouetted in a tree, and on closer inspection spotted two cubs accompanying this female feline. What a day!

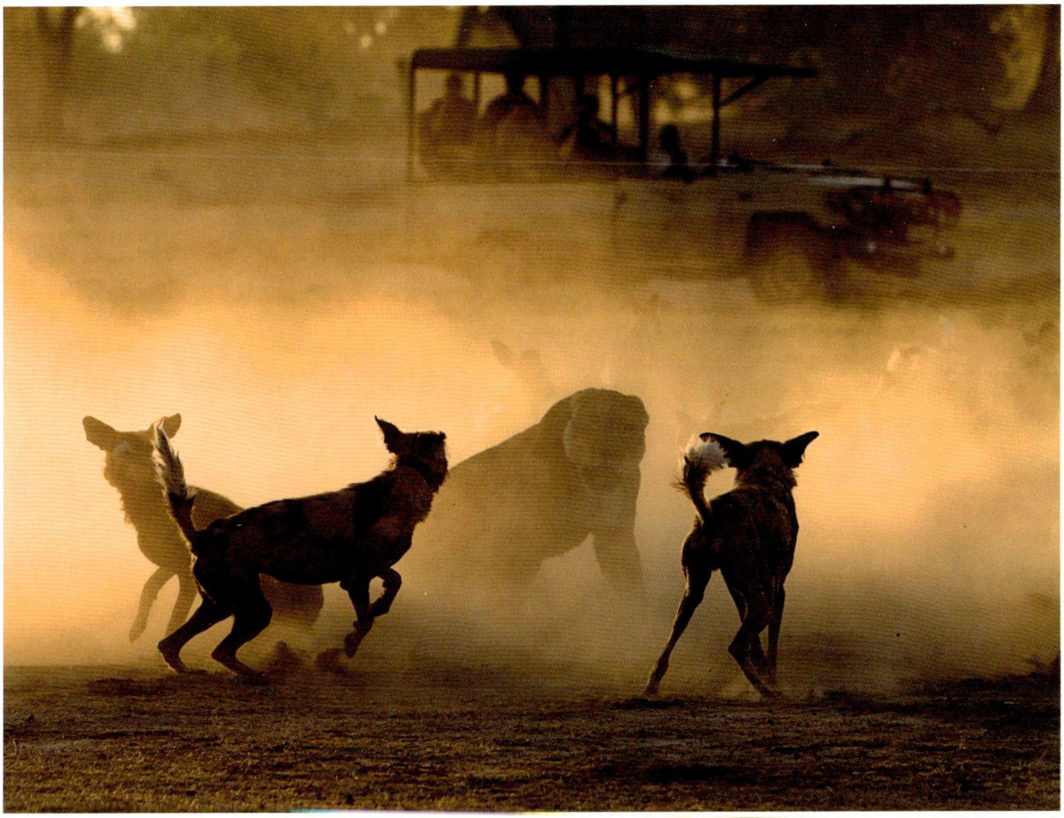

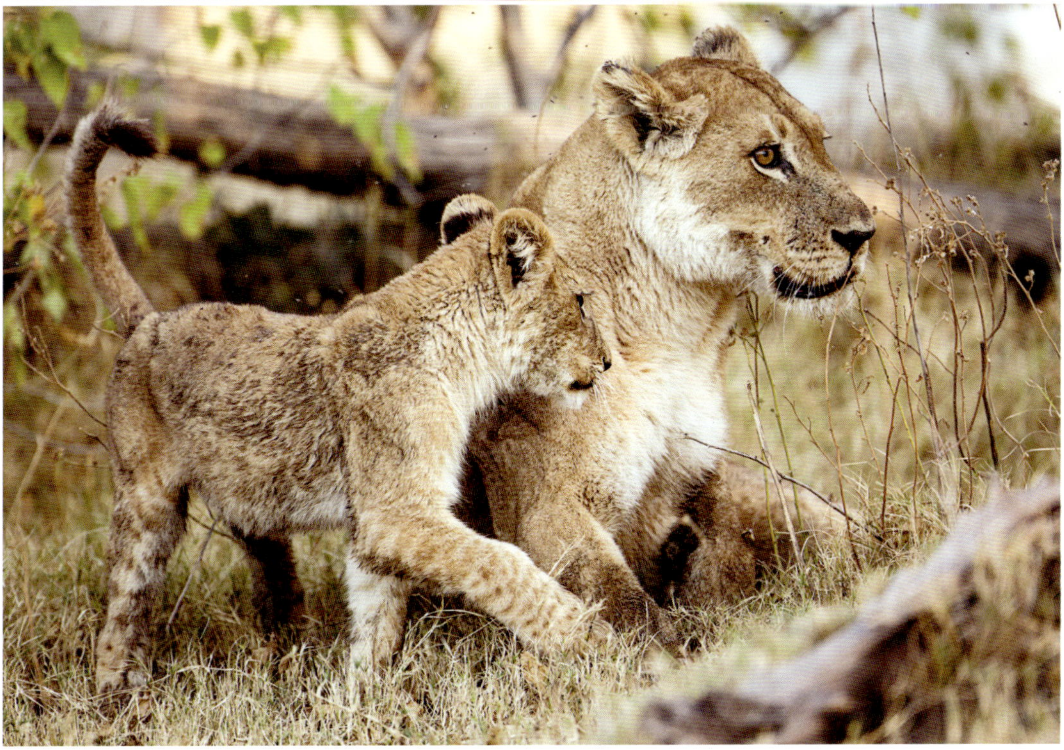

Catch us if you can

PHIL MULLER

Despite the congestion in and around Skukuza, my wife and I have had many wonderful Kruger sightings on the roads that lead from the camp. In November 2017, we were very fortunate to have had a good number of sightings of different packs of wild dogs.

One morning a pack of them came to drink at the dam on the S65. The resident hippo wasn't prepared to share his dam with the wild dogs so he came out to chase them away. Thirst was stronger than fear, however, and they wouldn't be scared away.

The hippo sank back into the water and gave a big yawn, as hippos do when they want to display their dominance. Having quenched their thirst, the dogs became playful, chasing one another around the edge of the dam. The hippo put up with this for a while, but then it came closer to the water's edge and tried to scare them away again. The wild dogs were enjoying their game and although they didn't make a sound, they seemed to be teasing him by going closer and then backing off when he approached. Eventually he lumbered out of the water and started chasing the wild dogs all over the area. I alternated between photos and videos and captured the comedy of this large, clumsy animal trying to keep up with the nimble-footed dogs.

At last they left the dam and the hippo, finally satisfied, returned to the water. We, in turn, were left with our digital memories to remind us of an exceptional sighting.

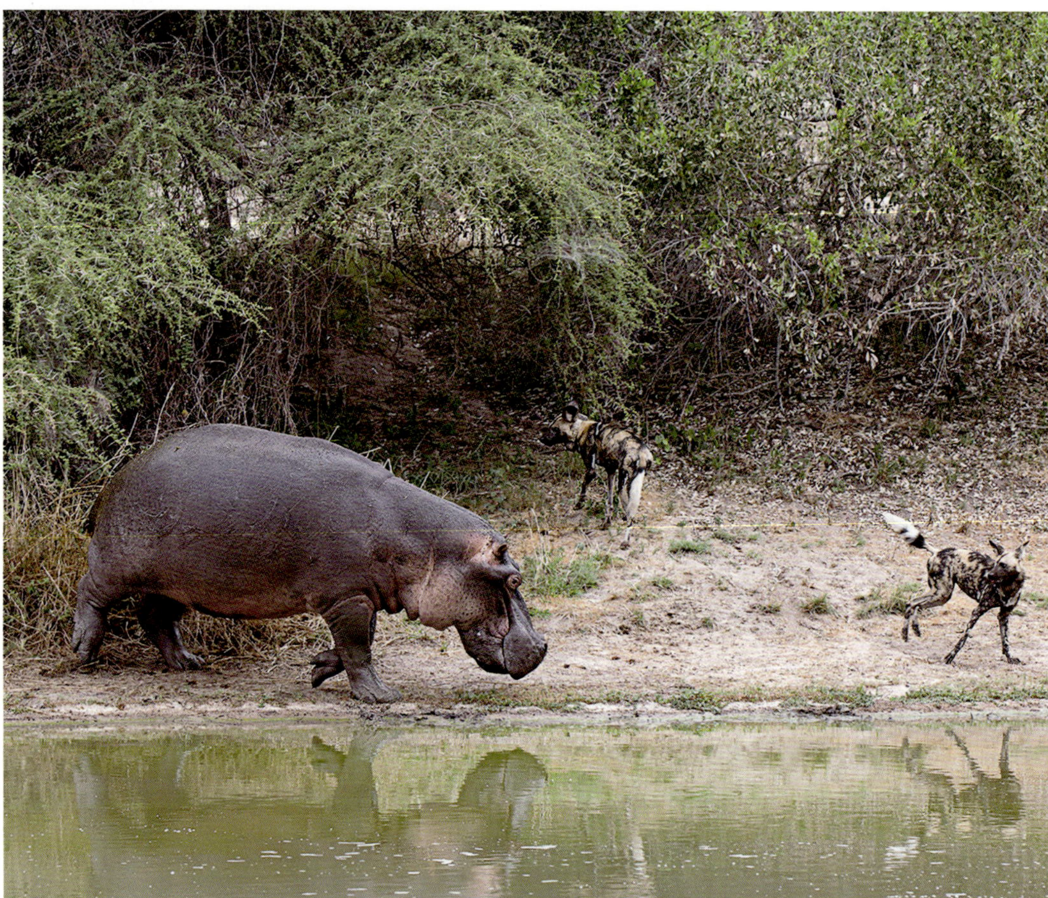

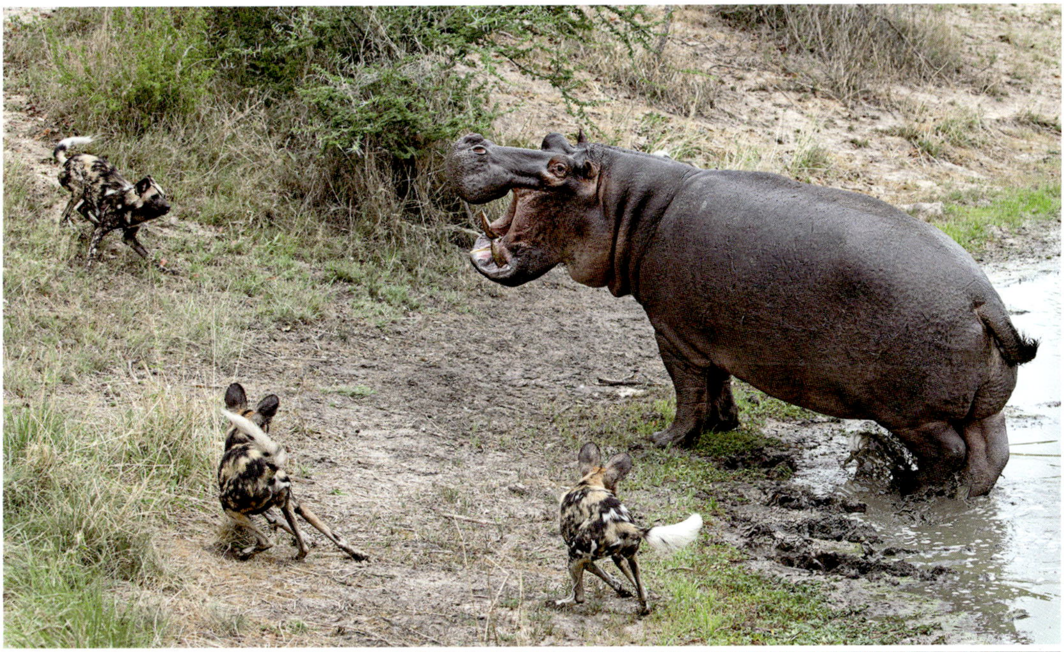

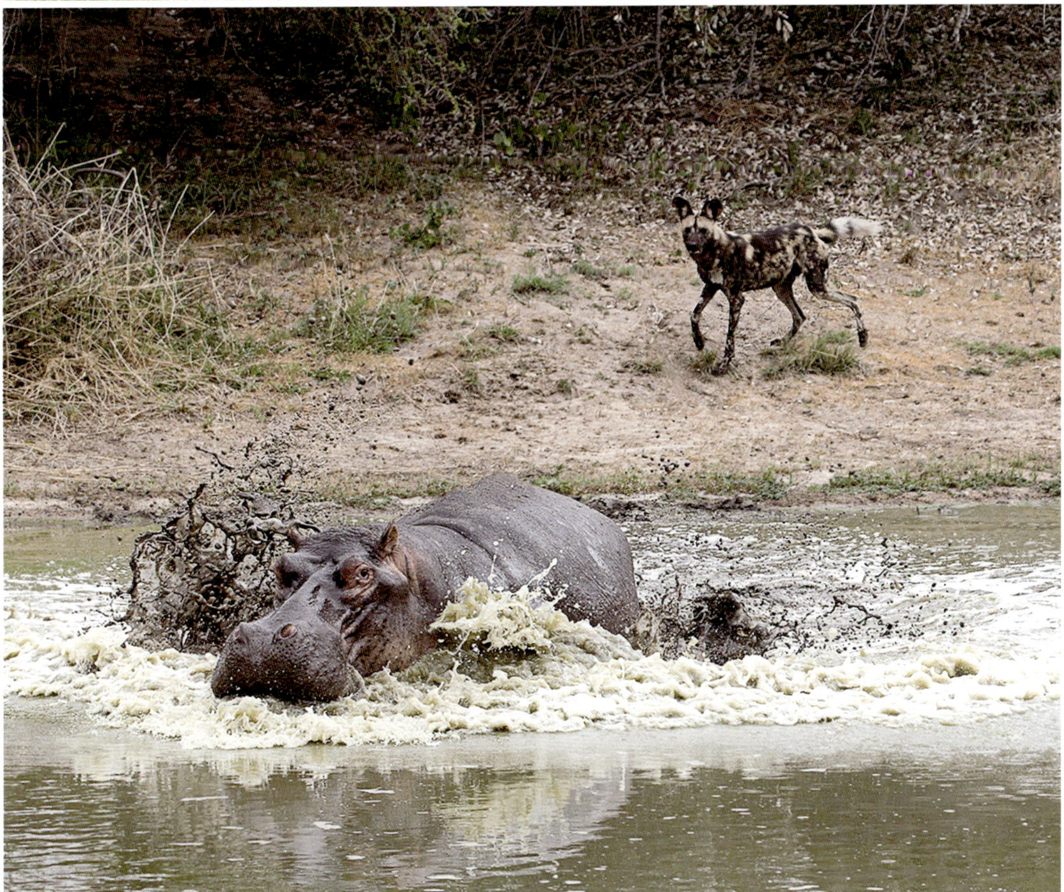

The hippo and the impala

TODD & MEGAN SHAND

Megan: It was the start of 2018 and we were driving from Shingwedzi up to Punda Maria. We debated whether to head straight up on the tar but our offspring voted to do the S56 Mphongolo Loop one more time, as we'd seen two lionesses there the day before. There wasn't a lot to see for the first 12 kilometres but we enjoyed the slow early-morning drive. We reached the junction of the S56, a short 1.2 kilometre road to the tar and decided to continue on the dirt. We cruised along, enjoying the smells of the bush and sounds of bird calls until, about five kilometres further down the S56, we came around a bend and heard the snorts of alarmed impalas. We stopped and looked down into the riverbed below the road, and there the impalas were, still snorting and staring at the pool of water they had been drinking from. We couldn't see any cats, so we were wondering whether there was a crocodile in the pool when a huge hippo rose up out of the water with an impala in its mouth.

You can imagine the exclamations and scrambling for cameras that ensued; we couldn't believe what we had just seen. In the seconds it took for Todd to grab his camera, the hippo went back under water and somehow the impala escaped, frantically swimming towards the sand as Todd started shooting. Unfortunately for the impala, the hippo resurfaced and grabbed it again, just as Todd snapped this photo. For several minutes the hippo alternated between holding its victim under the water and mouthing it, until the impala drowned. We were amazed by what we were witnessing.

Todd: I shoot predominantly with a large telephoto lens mounted on the car for stability, but the riverbank was so steep and the waterhole so close to the bank that I couldn't get a clear shot. While the hippo was holding the impala under water, I quickly switched to a more manoeuvrable combination of a back-up body with a mid-range compact telephoto zoom and set a forgiving aperture and an ISO that would give me a fast shutter speed, with the hope of freezing any action. Seconds later, the hippo reared out of the water with the impala in its mouth and I was able to capture this image.

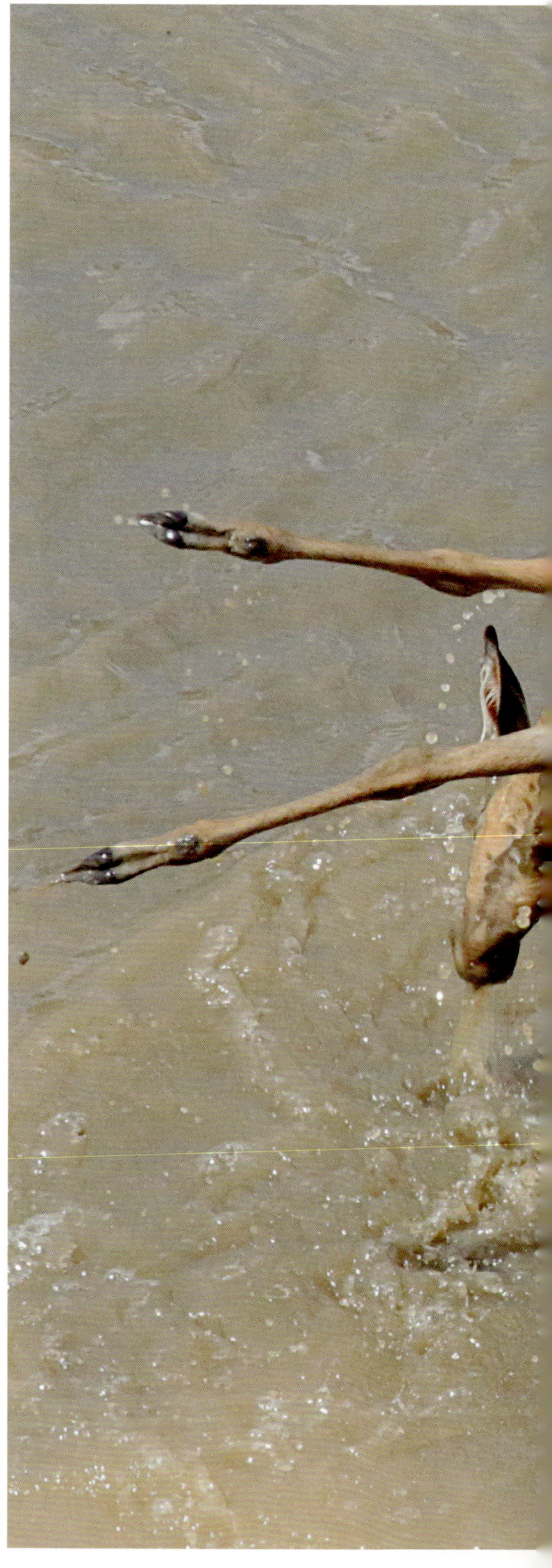

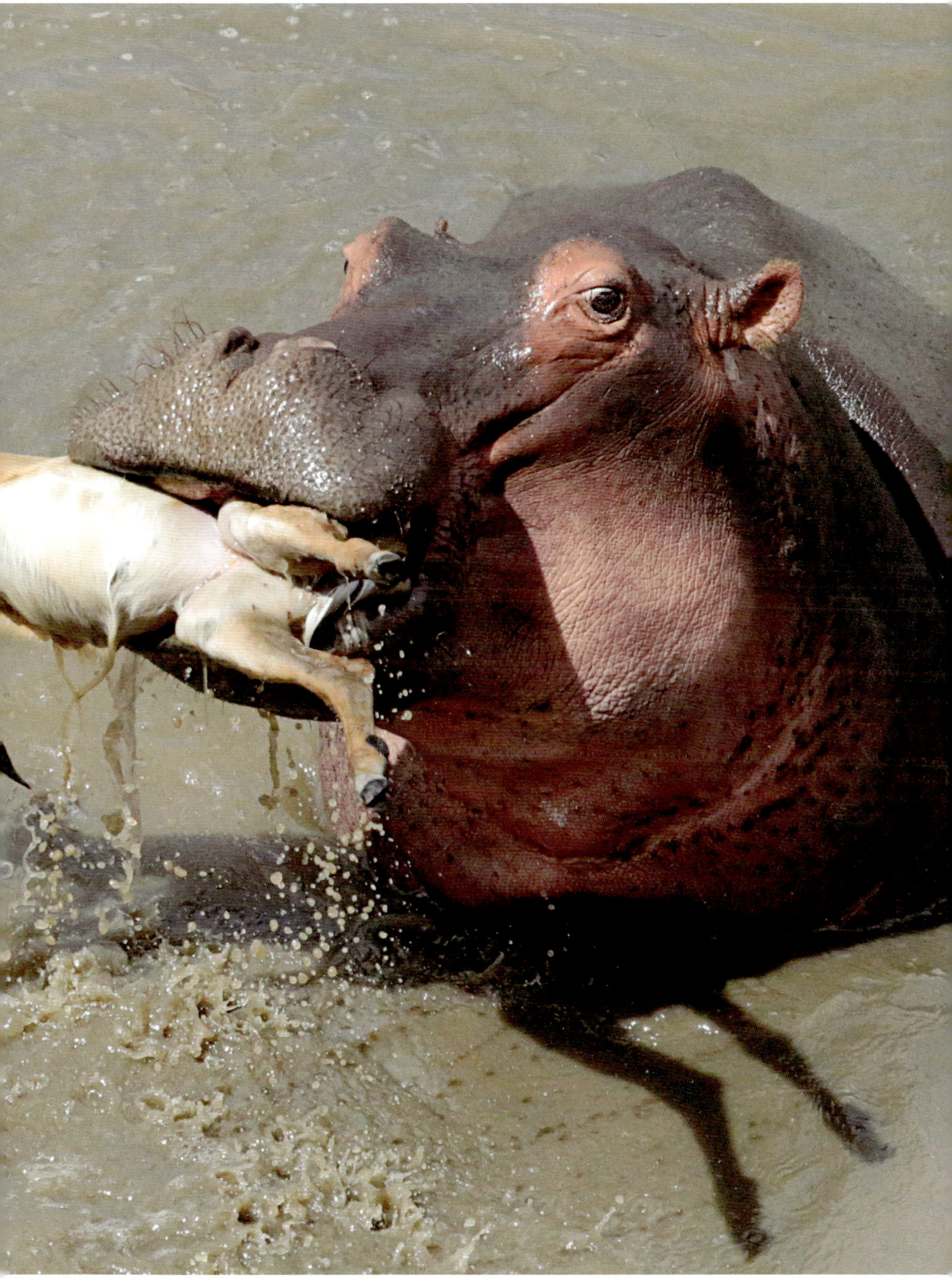

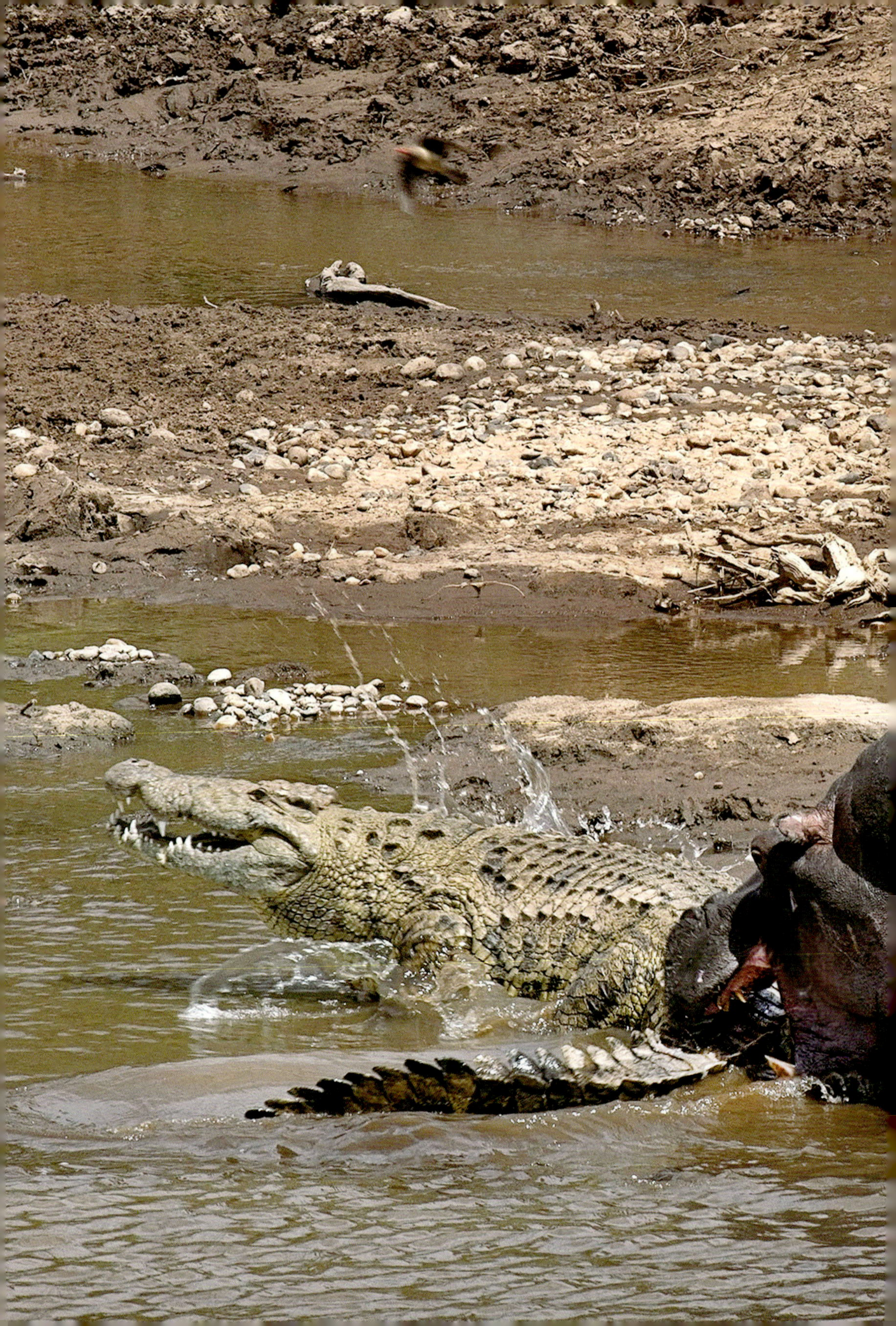

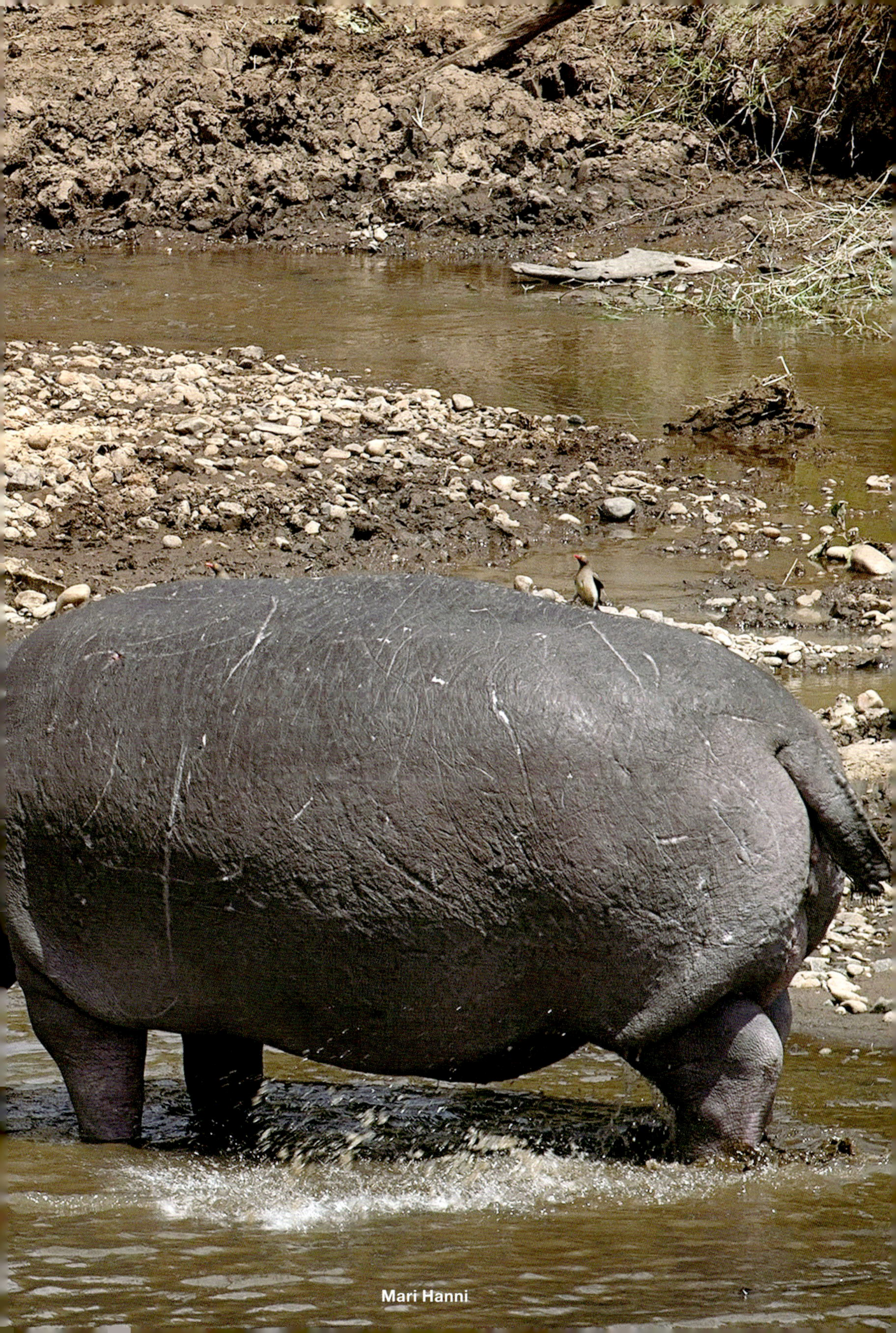

Mari Hanni

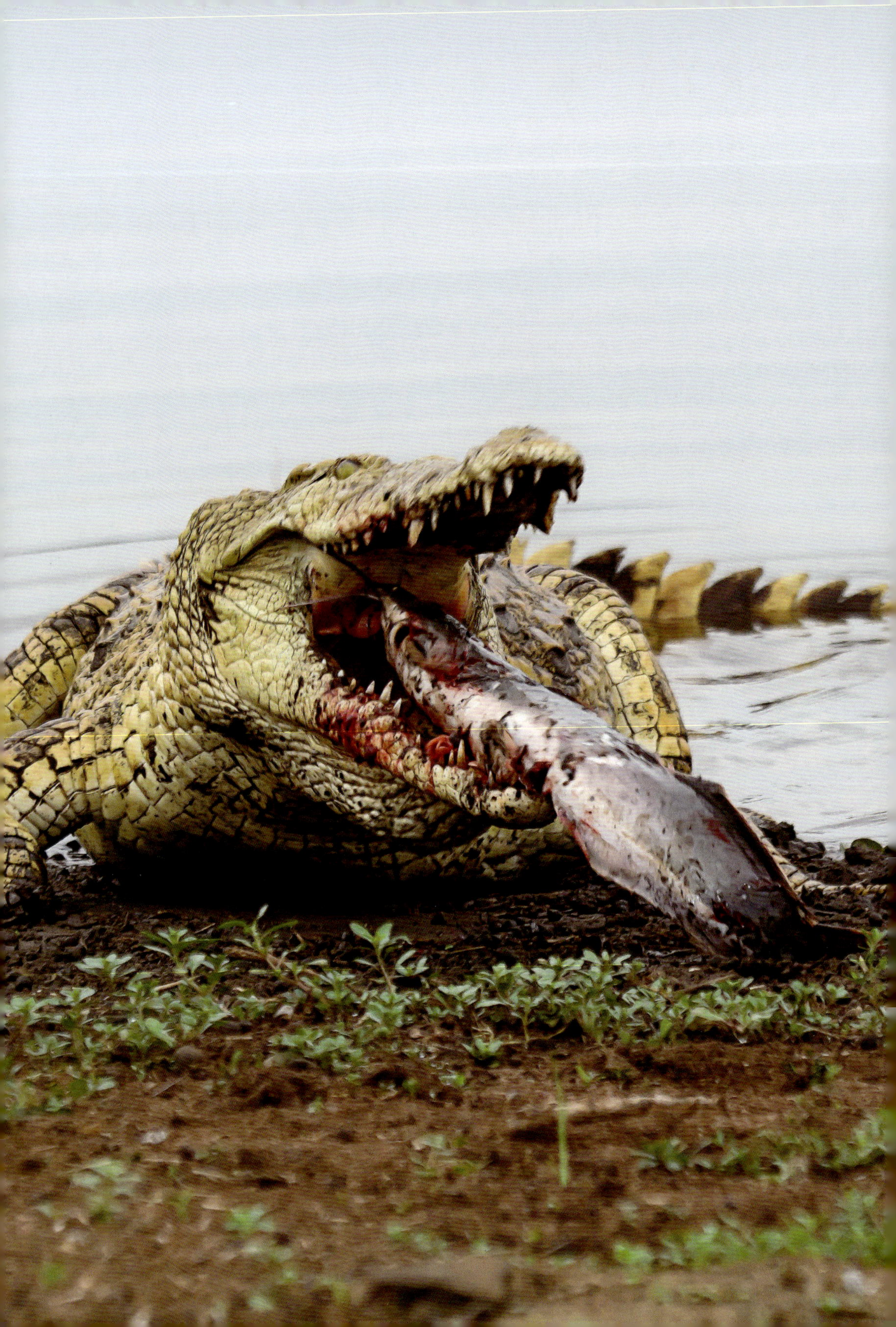

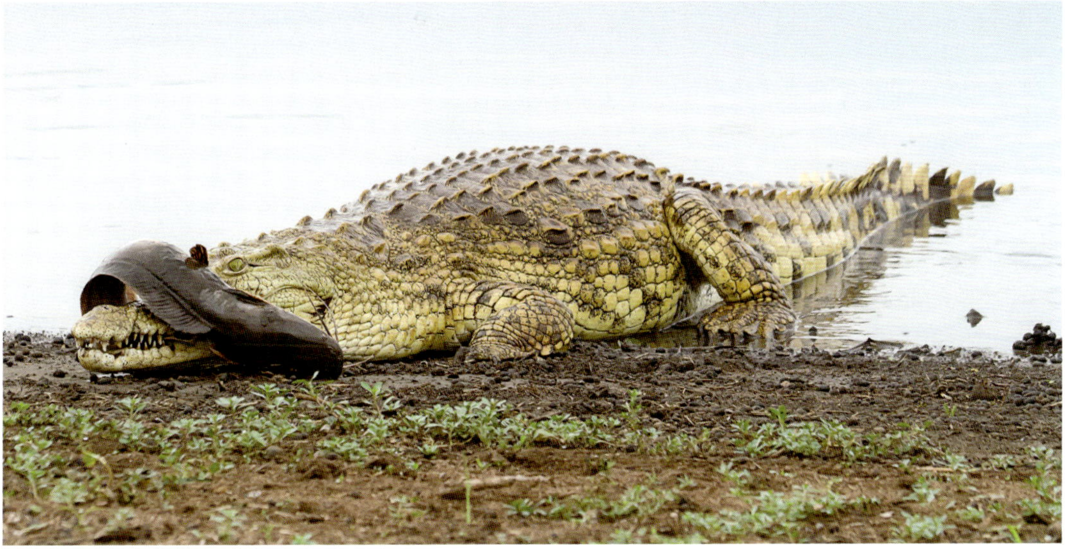

Fishy breakfast

BRIAN STRATTON

Early one morning, in October 2016, my partner and I parked at Sunset Dam in the Kruger National Park. It was a particularly dull morning and deadly quiet. Nobody else was present and no animals or birds were in sight.

After some time, as if from nowhere, a crocodile surfaced with a fish in its mouth. Slowly it crept onto the bank and then proceeded to open its mouth and toss its head back and forth while attempting to get the fish in a suitable position to swallow. After several side-to-side tosses of the head and plenty of noisy snatching with its jaws, the crocodile managed to grab the fish lengthwise and promptly swallowed it whole. As it walked past us, before sliding back into the water with its mouth all bloody, it appeared to grin, as if it was particularly pleased with the meal it had just enjoyed.

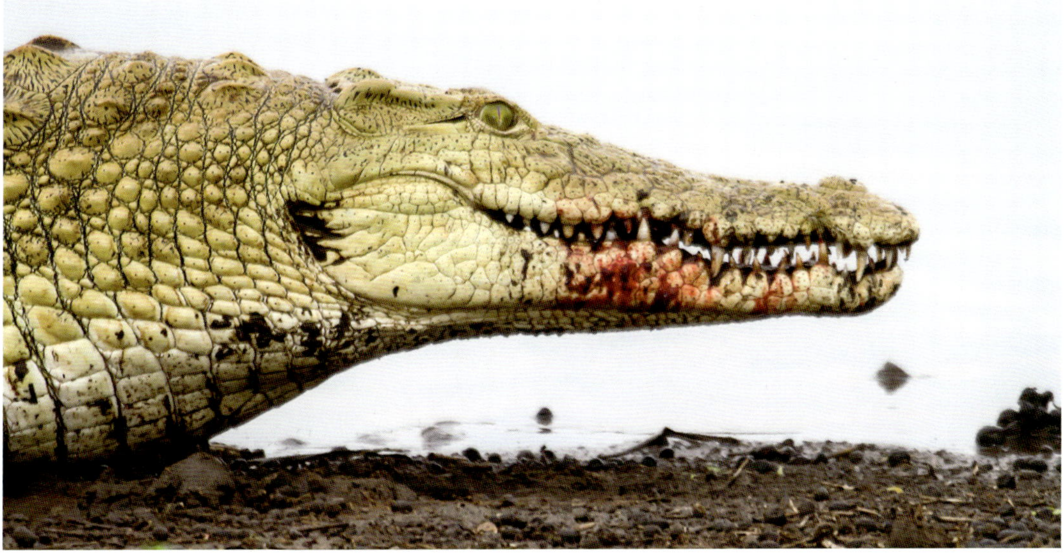

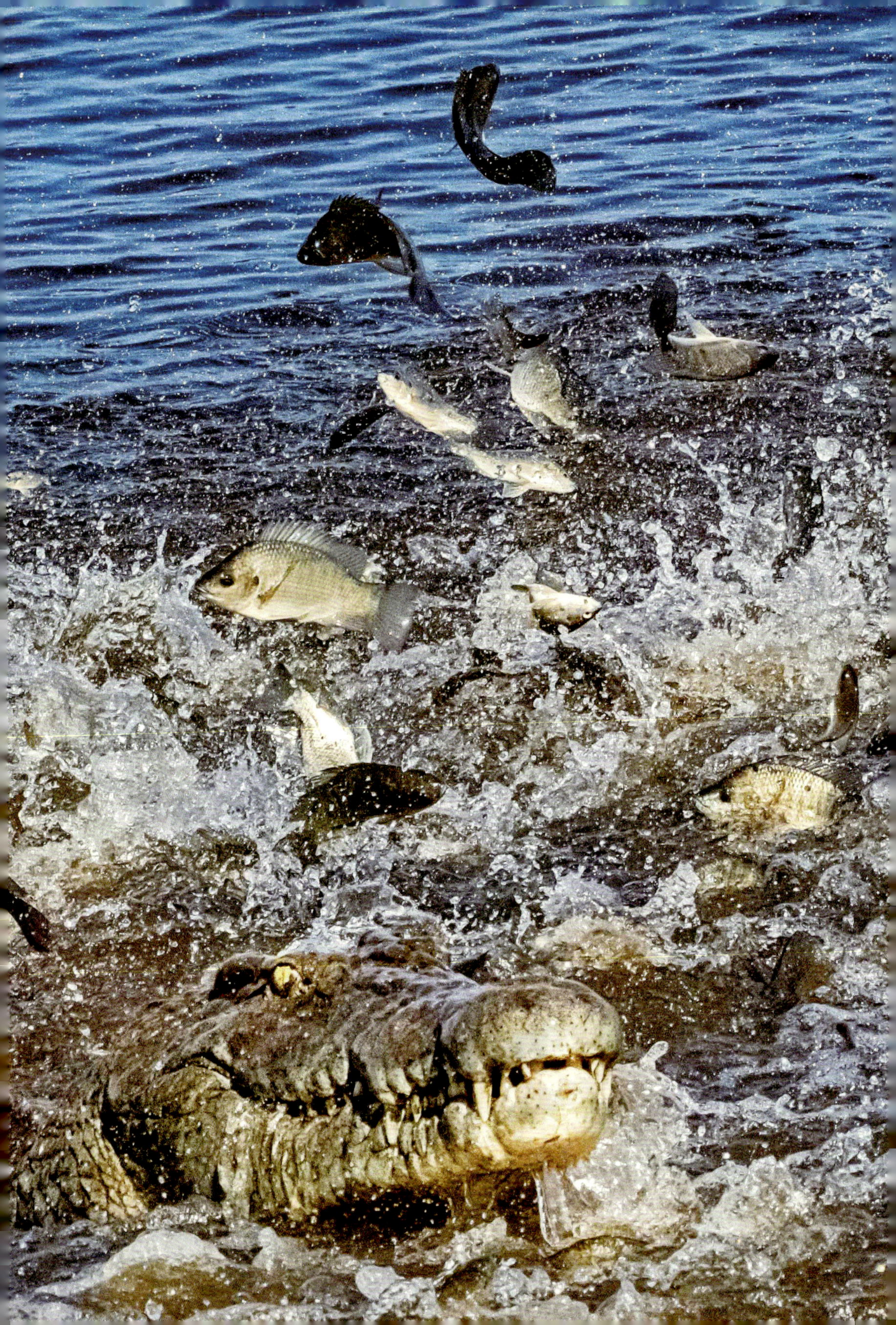

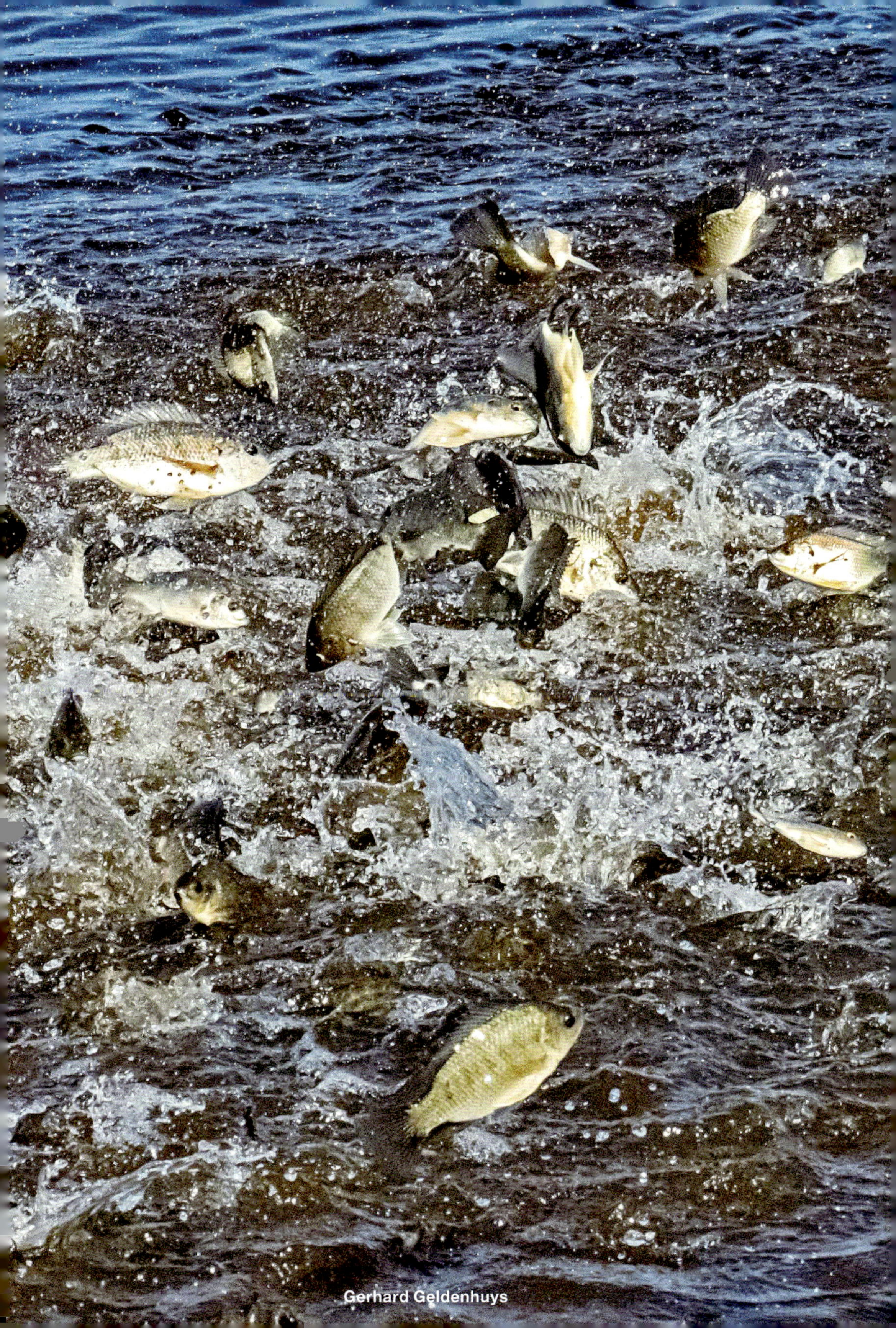

Gerhard Geldenhuys

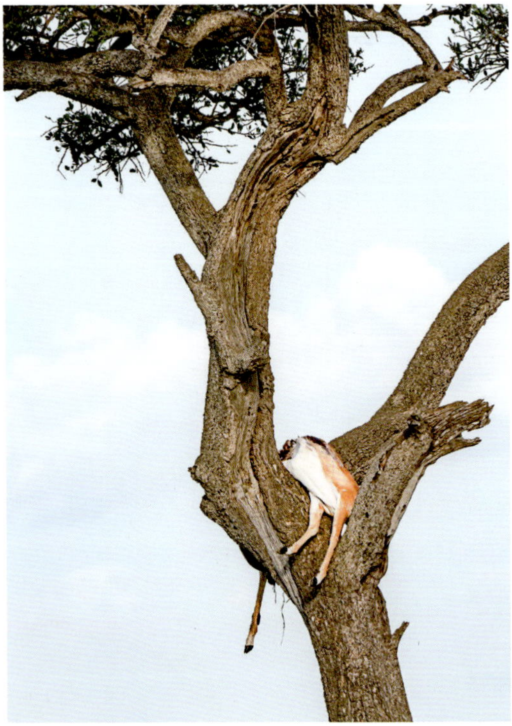

The heist

BARBARA HOLLWEG

The white underbelly of the lifeless young impala draped in the crook of the lone balanite tree was like a beacon guiding us as we searched for the elusive leopard. Approaching the tree, we noticed a female leopard resting at the base. Further inspection of the scene revealed the leopard had already gorged herself on her kill, leaving much of the impala's neck hanging from the carcass and exposing a large opening into its body. Assured that the leopard would climb the tree to resume her meal after resting, we settled down to wait for the action to begin.

After about two hours, as the sun was beginning to set, we were surprised to see a smaller leopard appear from the bush behind us: a young male leopard, approximately one year old, cautiously and deliberately headed towards the tree where his mother was waiting. The two greeted each other and the young cat headed up the tree for his portion of the bounty. The adolescent was enthusiastic, inept and awkward in his approach to positioning, repositioning and devouring the meal before him. After a while he lost control of the remains, the entrails were torn by their own weight dangling from the body and fell to the ground. Now the youngster was left with only the head and the eviscerated, skin-draped skeleton of the impala. Seemingly undaunted, the young male continued in his clumsy efforts to keep the bulk of the kill in the tree. Eventually, the prize slipped from his grasp and fell to the ground where the female leopard was feasting on the most coveted, nutritious parts of any kill.

Having lost his meal, the young leopard quickly descended and joined his mother in her orgy. We leaned back, revelling in our perfect timing and good fortune, satisfied with unexpectedly witnessing a unique scene. Our soft chatter was interrupted by the swift movement of our spotter, pointing in the distance to a dark figure slowly moving towards the cats under the tree.

With our mouths open in dismay, we watched as an adult hyena stealthily made its way to the cats' party. The leopards, distracted by their feast, were unaware of the newcomer on the scene. Once close enough to make its move, the hyena snatched one end of the impala while the female leopard promptly reacted by holding tightly to another part of the carcass. The adolescent leopard swiftly escaped up the tree to watch from above. A fierce tug of war between the possessive adult leopard and the scavenger hyena ensued. To no one's surprise, the hyena prevailed and ran off into the darkness with his scraggy prize. Completely speechless at the turn of events, we once again slumped back, trying to process our day's unparalleled experience.

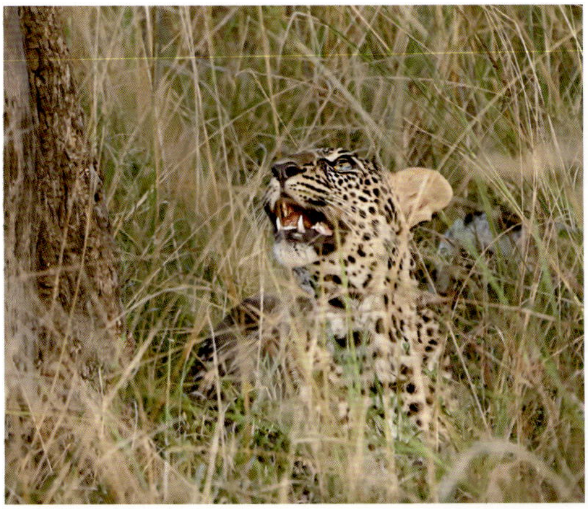

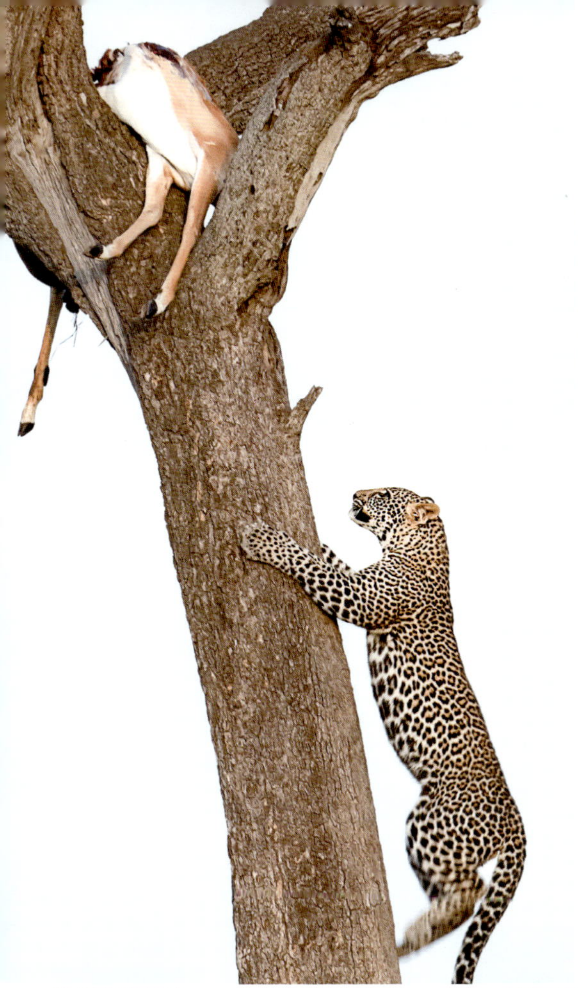

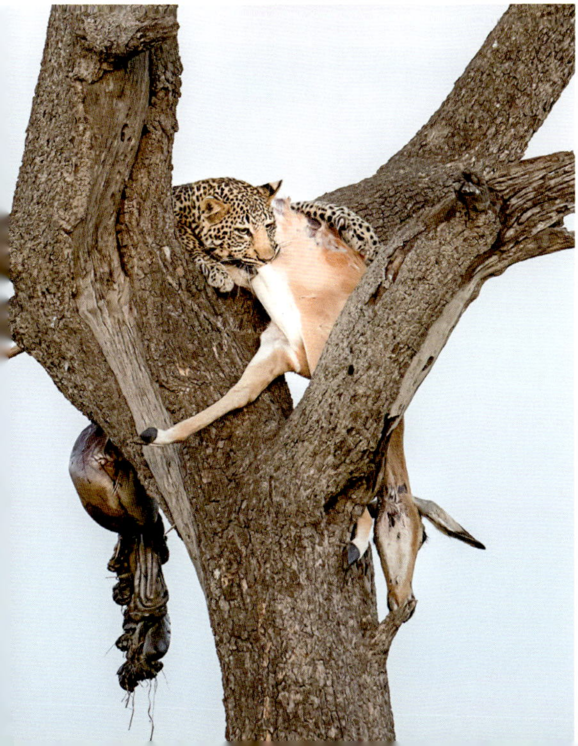

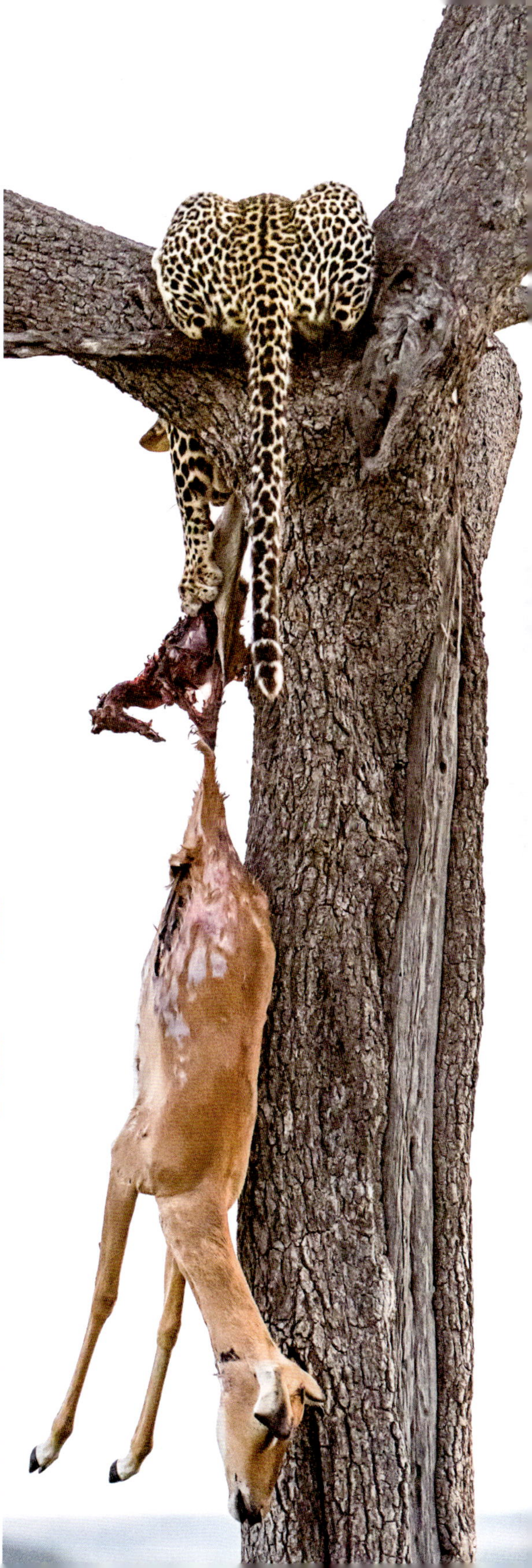

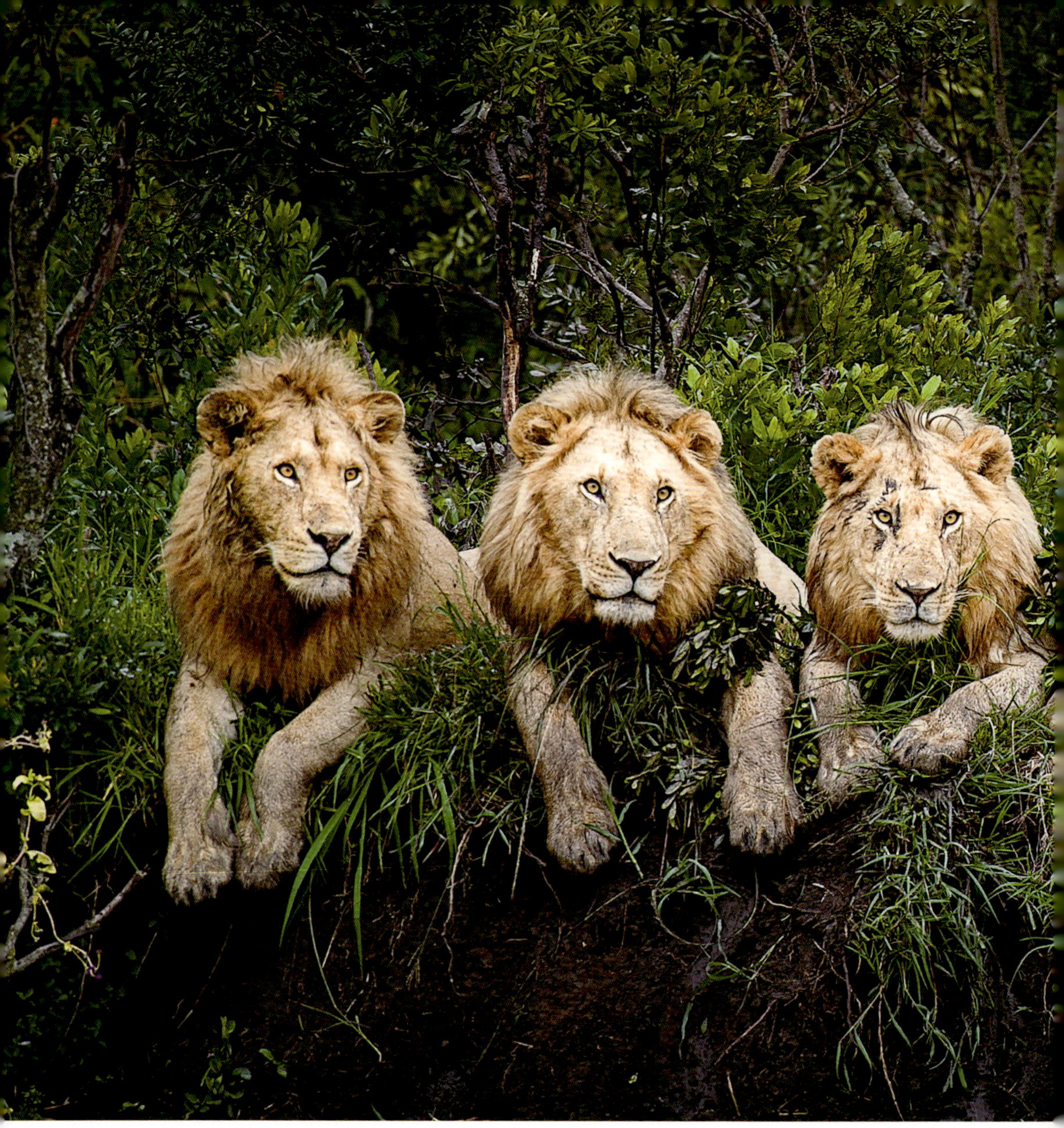

Almost too good to be true

DANIEL DOLPIRE

I took this once-in-a-lifetime shot at &Beyond Klein's Camp, a remote and exclusive camp set on a 10 000 hectare concession leased from Maasai landlords, in the corner of Tanzania's Serengeti National Park. The camp lies in the path of the Great Migration but there is also ample resident game and morning game drives begin at sunrise, with guides often on the lookout for lions resting from the previous night's hunt. Out on a drive, accompanied by a guide and tracker team, we came upon these lions on the edge of the Silio Stream – a tributary of the Grumeti River – at 7:17 in the morning. I scrambled for my camera and got the shot!

Exactly six minutes later the first lion got up and, within another five minutes, two others had also gone off into the bush, while the remaining three were sleeping. The &Beyond guides consistently monitor the animals in the region and their movements, so they were able to tell us

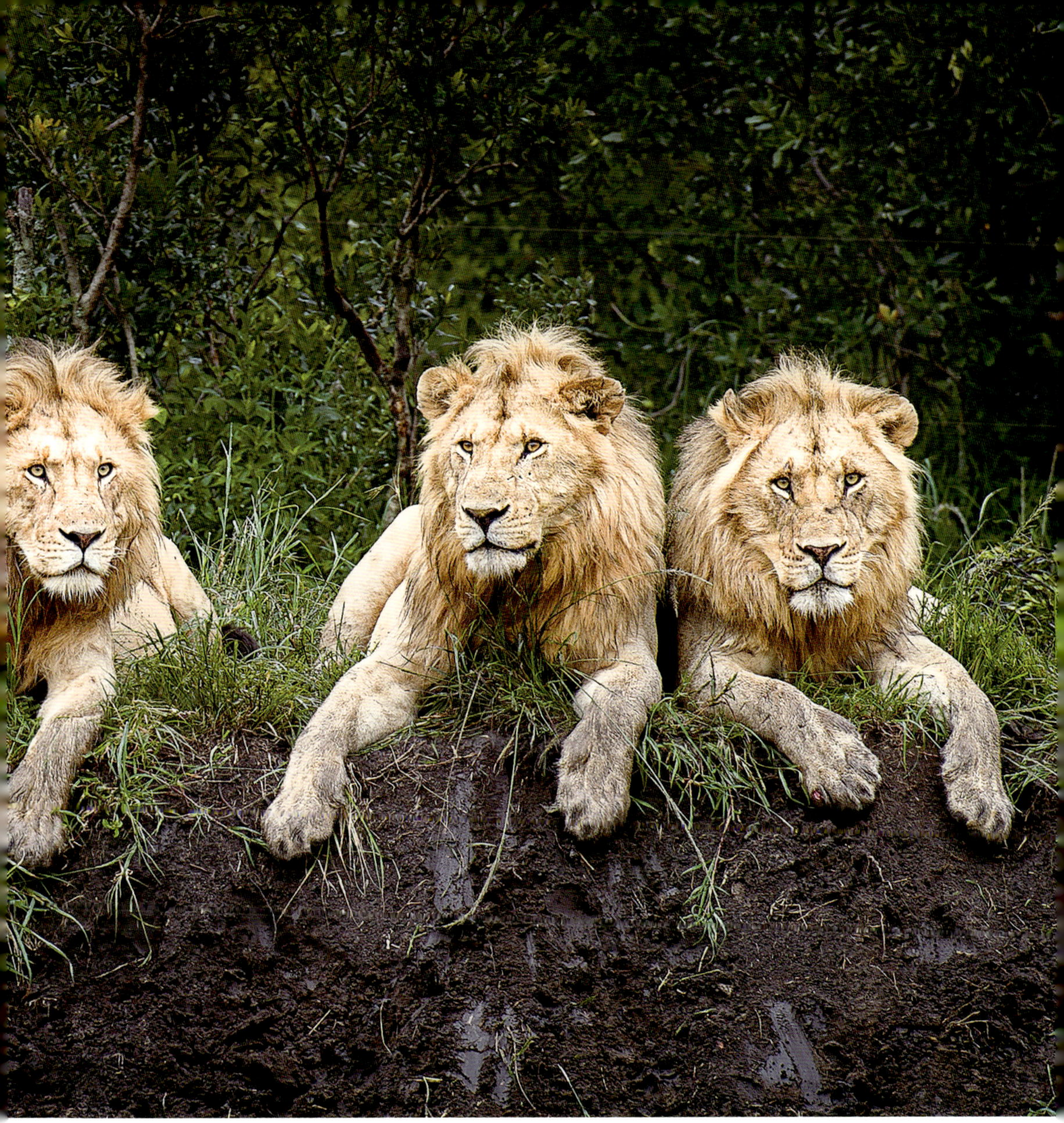

these six young males were part of the Black Rock Pride, the biggest pride in the reserve which frequents the northwest region. The pride consists of eight adult females, two dominant males, four sub-adult females, three sub-adult males, five cubs of approximately seven months old and eight young males, six of whom I managed to photograph. The six brothers were all sired by the same dominant male in the pride, although they have different mothers and came from different litters. All six are just over three years old.

I have been taking wildlife photos for over 20 years but this had to be my most special moment. When I followed up on news of the lions with &Beyond Klein's Camp, I learnt they had split up and are now only seen in pairs, so the timing for getting this exceptional shot proved to be extremely fortunate. There I was, in the unique position of being able to capture the six half-brothers all at once. So unlikely did this seem, that I was accused of Photoshopping the picture. But it was nature that Photoshopped this for me, and I count myself extremely lucky.

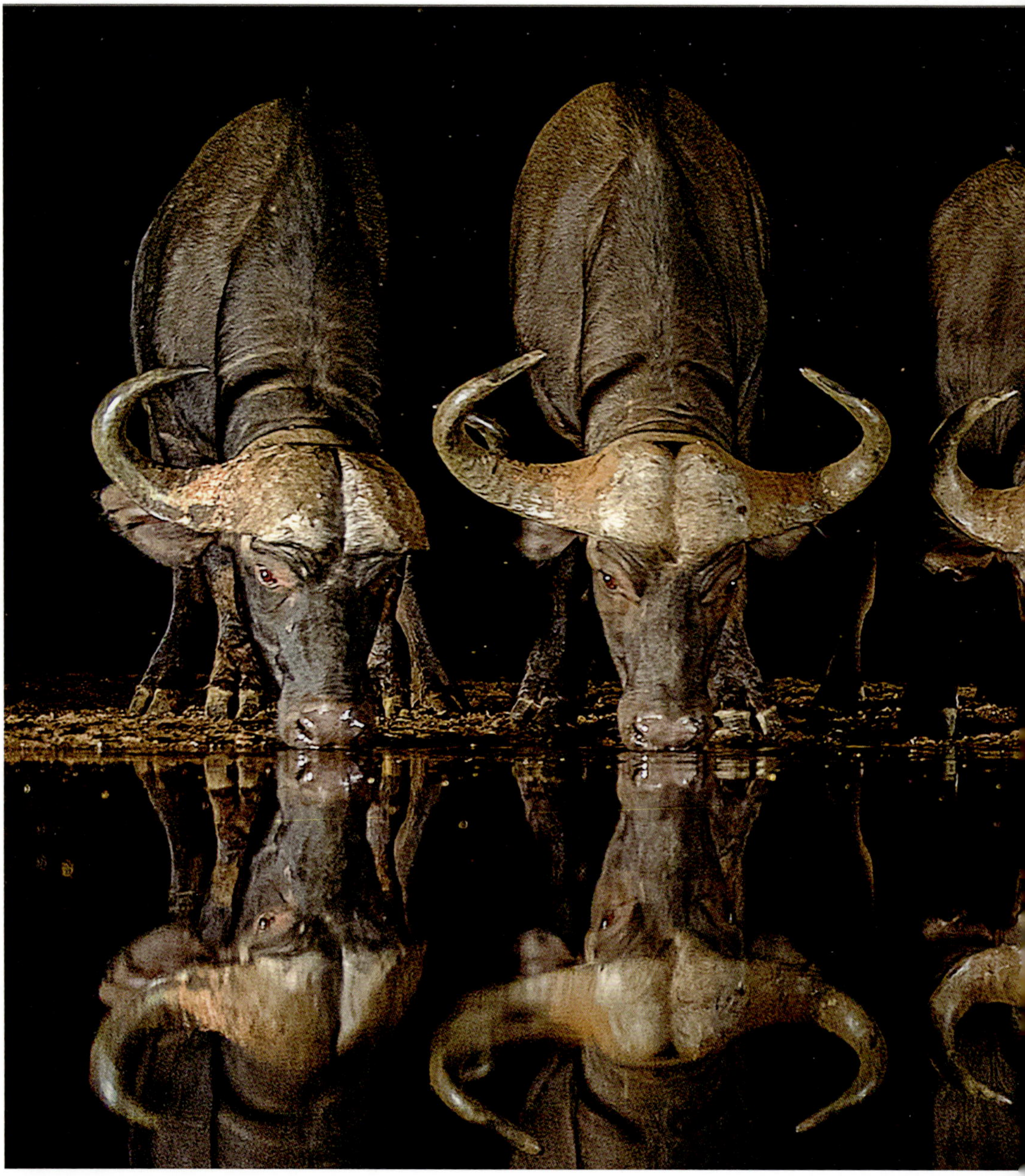

Five becomes ten

KATHY KAY

Buffalo often drink twice a day, so it is not unusual to see them quenching their thirst at a waterhole. However, the symmetry of this image appealed enormously to me. The bulky shapes of these buffaloes became statuesque, and were turned into an almost architectural pattern by the reflections in the water. Not only are they all drinking at the same time, but they are also watching the viewer, and simultaneously protecting the younger one placed in the middle.

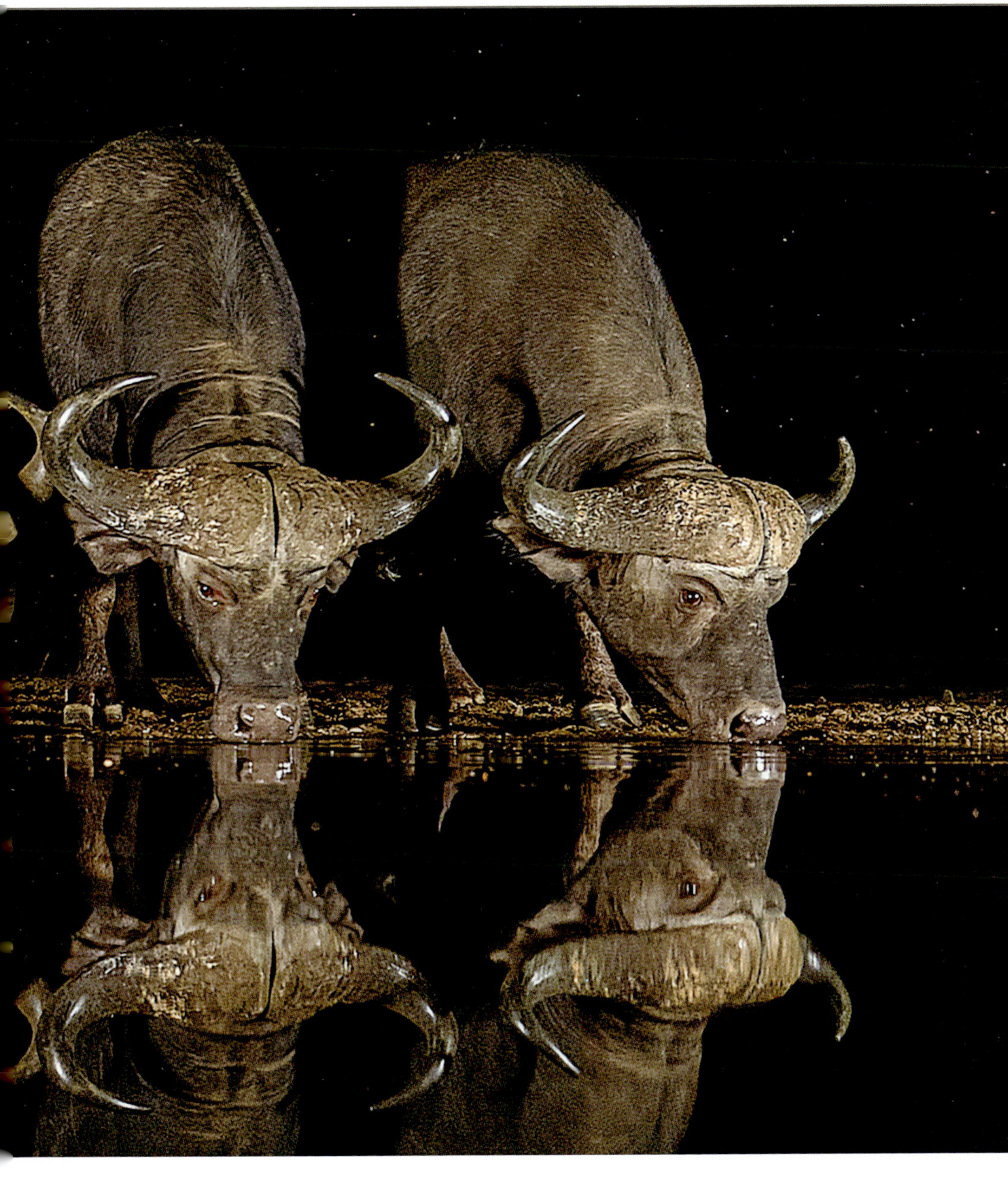

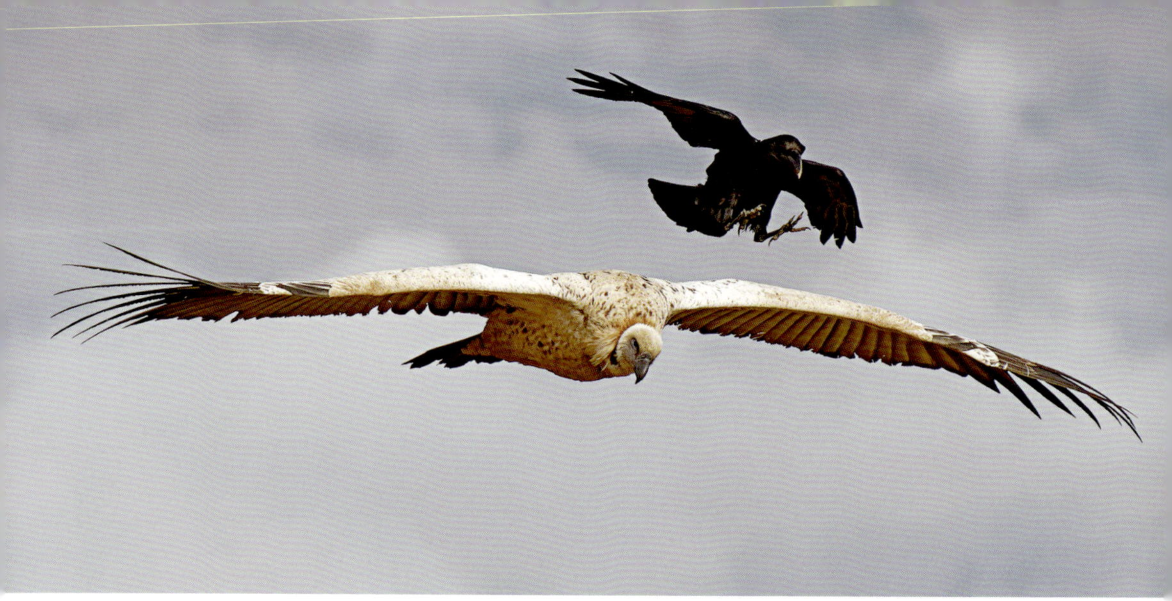

Catching a ride

BURKHARD SCHLOSSER

I got up at the crack of dawn to make my way up to Giant's Castle in the Ukhahlamba Drakensberg. We saw the occasional Cape vulture flying overhead on arrival at the hide. In the distance a black-backed jackal surveyed the scene, its fur glowing golden in the early rays of the morning sun. It was a wonderful start to the day. Then the bearded vultures started flying by, looking at the bones which were laid out to entice the birds to land and feast. The camera shutters clicked away as the vultures flew in to land and settle down for a snack.

With my camera zoomed in on a vulture nearing the hide, a raven unexpectedly approached from behind the vulture and raced after it. What happened next had me spellbound and open-mouthed in disbelief. The raven landed on the vulture's wing and stayed there for several seconds before the vulture dived down, which forced the raven off its wing. Never had I witnessed anything like this, although if I didn't have my photos to back up this sight, I'm not sure I'd have believed what I'd seen. That day is etched in my memory.

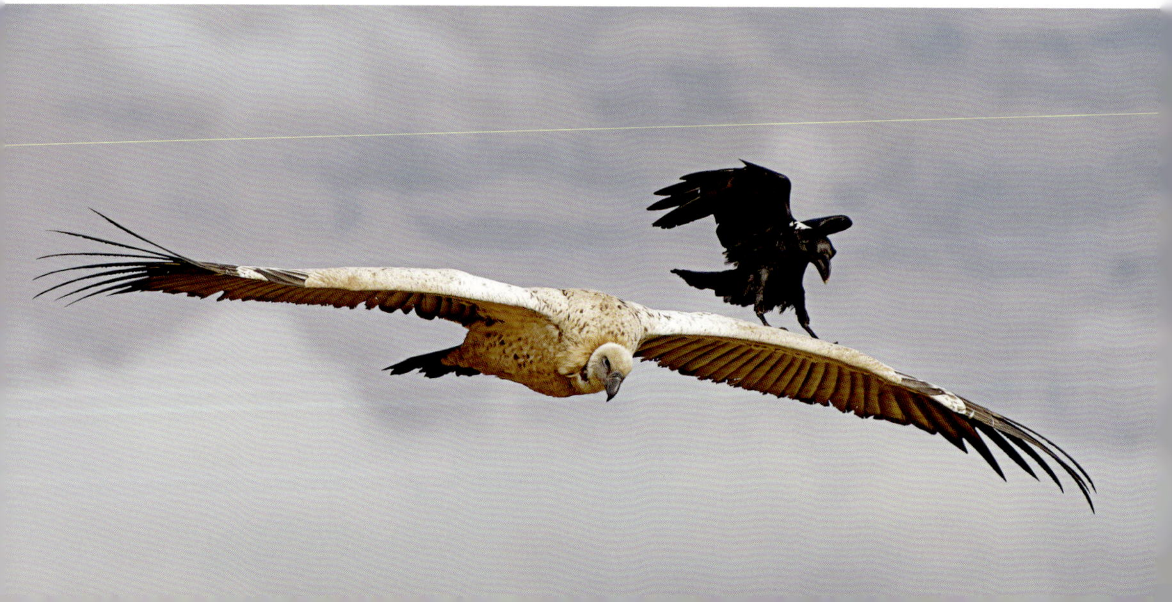

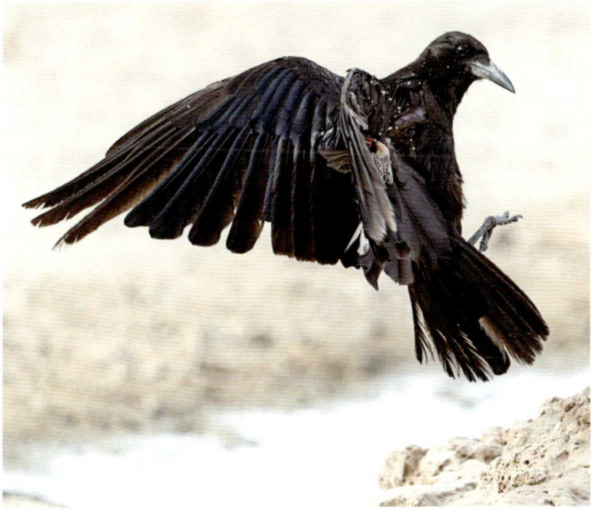

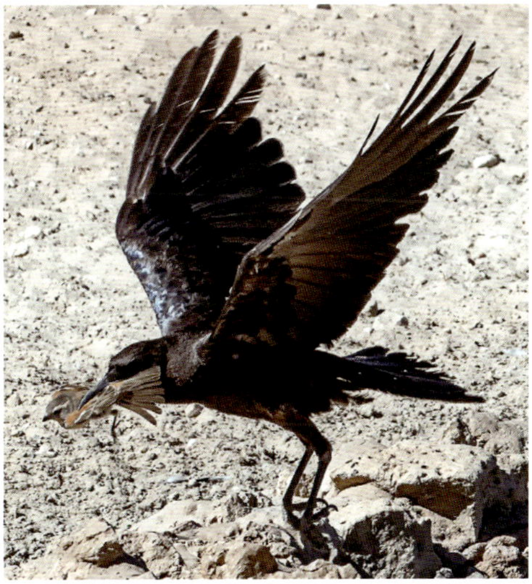

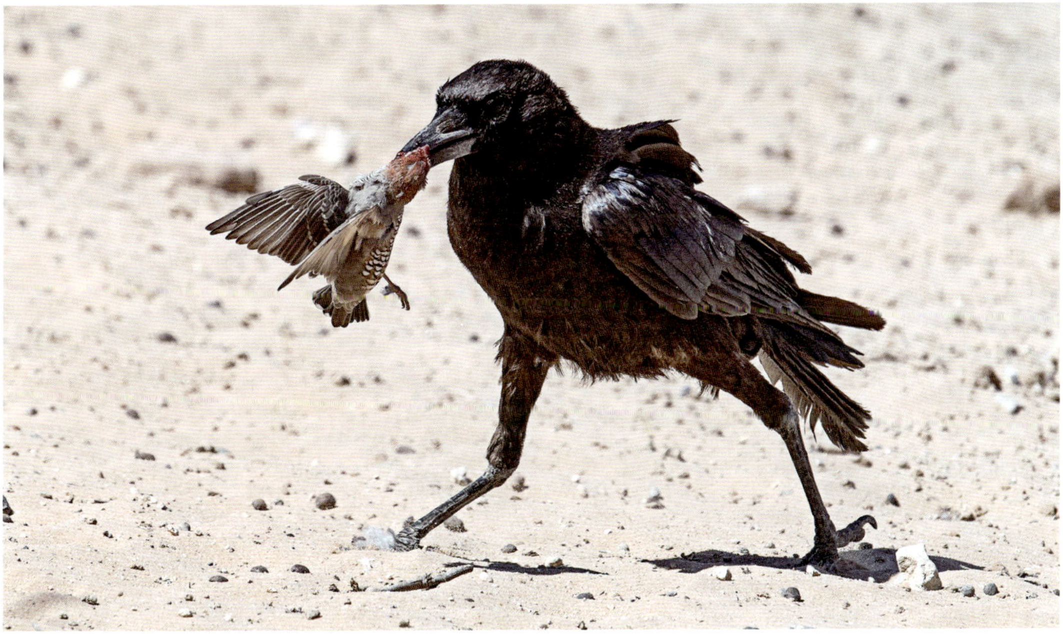

Cape crows' hunting strategies

JOHAN BOTHA

The Cape crow or black crow is a very common species in South Africa. Two of them are resident at the 14th Borehole drinking spot in the Kgalagadi Transfrontier Park. They often beg motorists for scraps by sitting on their cars, or more specifically, the mirrors. Margie, my wife and I observed this behaviour when we were there in January 2019. But we also saw some rather different behaviour: the crows were catching small birds coming down to drink. They either stabbed the birds with their beaks in flight, surprised them at the side of the waterhole, or caught them when they deliberately collided with an individual in mid-air. All in all, we saw them catching three different species of small birds and marvelled at how creatures devise cunning strategies for survival.

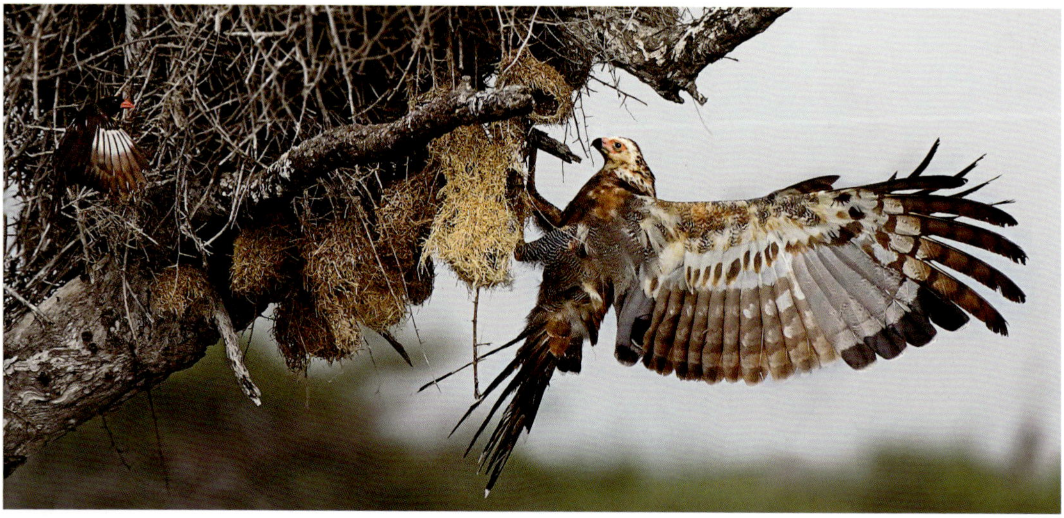

Empty nest

LEON PELSER

It was March 2018 around 16:00 at Sunset Dam near Lower Sabie in the Kruger National Park, when I spotted a young African harrier-hawk through my 500 millimetre lens in the big tree-skeleton in the dam. He was trying to steal a chick from a nest in the tree. A red-billed buffalo weaver was desperately trying to scare off the hawk without success. The hawk got one chick from the nest and gobbled it down while on the branch. Then it calmly repeated the process. Needless to say, the next day, there was no sign of the African harrier-hawk. It had emptied the nest and moved on.

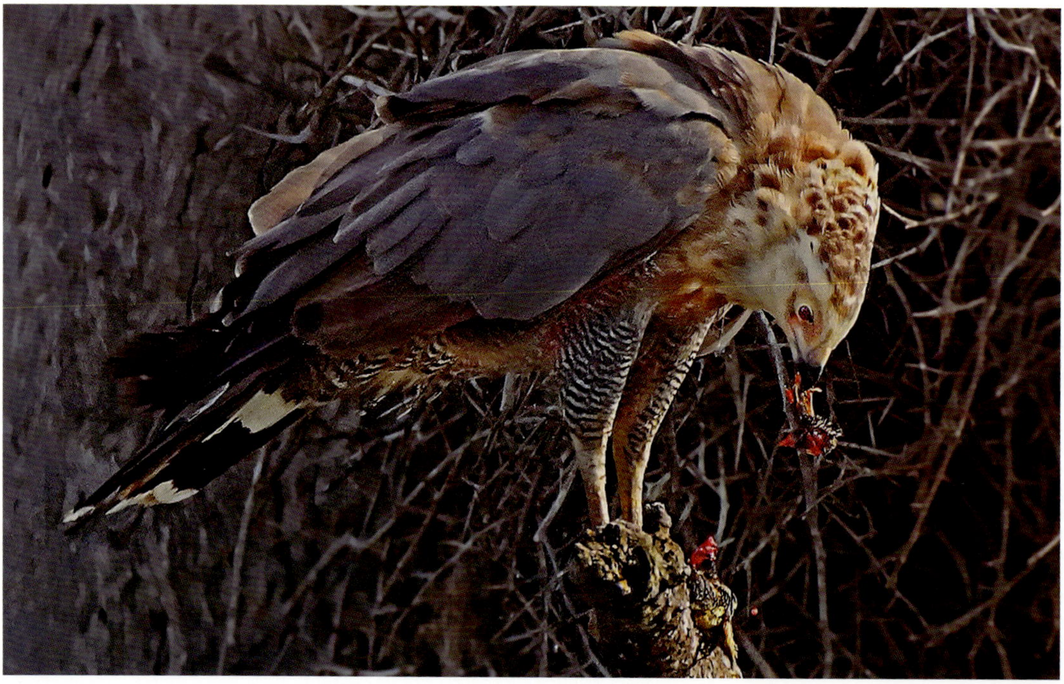

Bravery

JEAN DU PLESSIS

In the Seronera area in the western side of the Serengeti near the Barafu Kopjes, this tawny eagle was feasting on the eggs of a blacksmith lapwing when he was attacked from all directions by adult lapwings. They were flying very low in an attempt to get him off the nest. Eventually black-winged stilts joined forces with the lapwings, going all out to get the eagle to leave. But the thief was not deterred by the smaller birds and ate all the eggs in the nest.

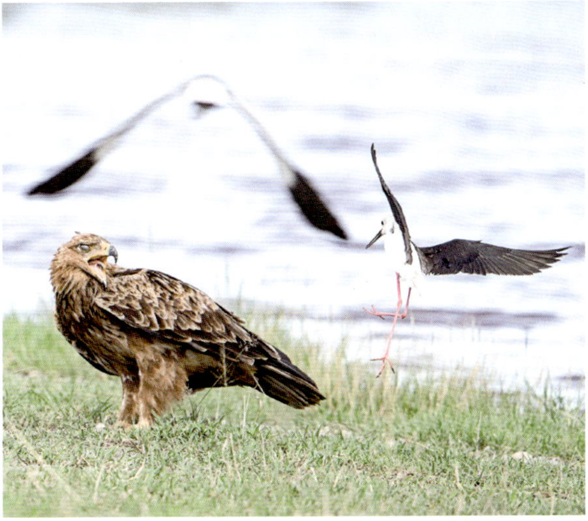

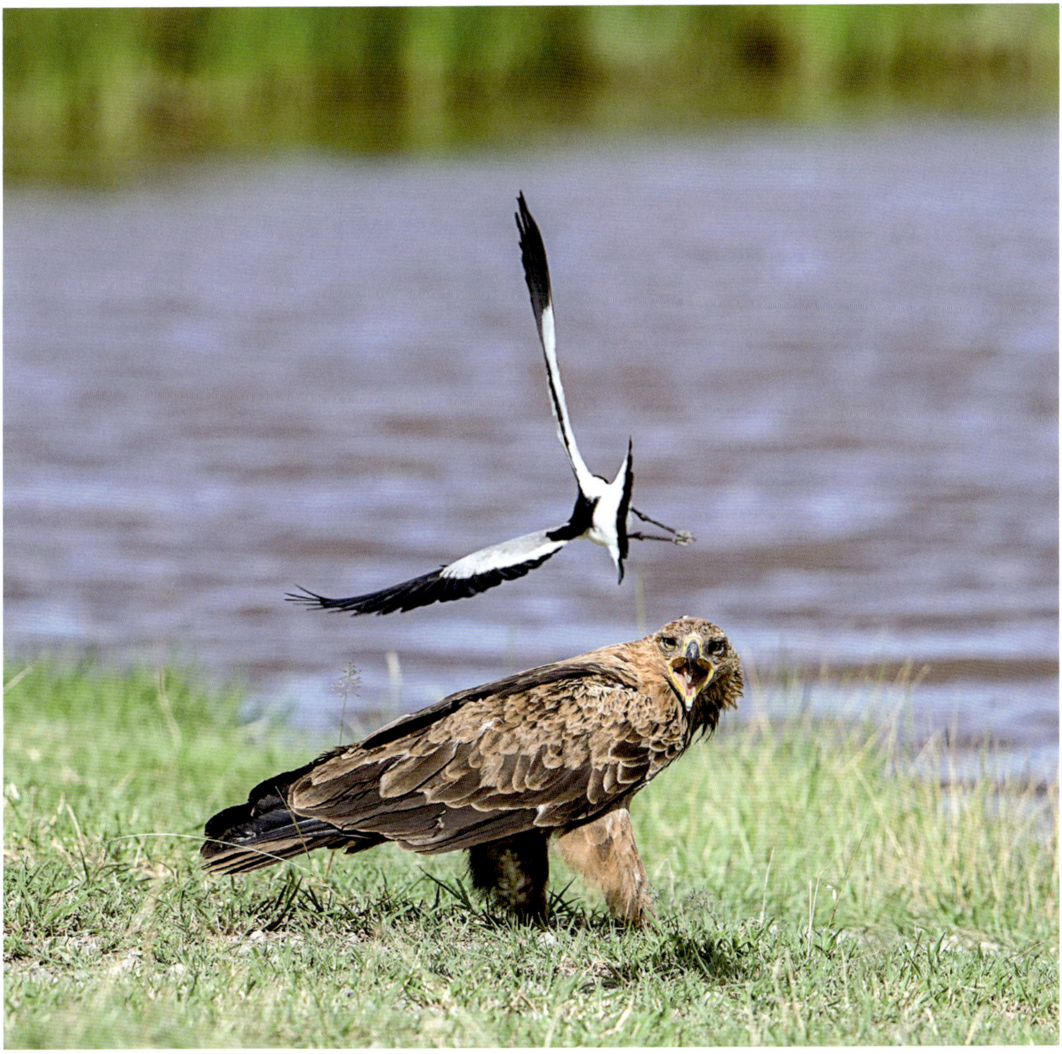

What to do with tricky food

LOUIS & INA TALJAARD

During a game drive in the Kruger National Park in 2017, travelling along the Mphongola River near Sirheni Camp, we spotted a Goliath heron stepping out of a large pool in the river with a wriggling catch in its beak. It had caught a rock-catfish. The bird climbed onto a small rocky outcrop adjacent to the river, dropped the fish onto the ground and proceeded to stab its prey with its long beak. After a number of stabs, it took the fish which was now covered in sand in its beak, climbed down the outcrop, walked back into the shallows of the big pool and rinsed it thoroughly in the water. This process of stabbing the prey on the outcrop followed by rinsing it in the shallow water of the pool was repeated at least a dozen or more times. Towards the end the bird would hold the prey by its tail and if it still wriggled it would continue with the stabbing.

About 15 minutes from the time the catch took place, the heron stepped back into the pool with the fish in its beak. Suddenly the feathers on its head, neck and body were raised in alarm and the bird performed a few awkward dance steps in the water. A fish eagle, which we had previously noticed in a tree further up the pool, swooped in with open beak in an attempt to steal the heron's catch. At the last moment the heron dropped the fish into the water and deployed its sharp beak on the intruder. The eagle veered off and flew away. The photographs taken confirm the heron's annoyance and it certainly gave the would-be thief a piece of its mind as it flew off. It's perhaps just as well we couldn't understand 'heron speak'.

The heron recovered the fish from the water, rinsed it thoroughly and flicked it into the air before catching and swallowing it head first. Twenty-one minutes had elapsed from the time the fish was caught until it was swallowed. The heron then took a long, leisurely drink from the pool and afterwards thoroughly rinsed its beak by shaking it in the water a couple of times. It strolled up the outcrop and sat down on its haunches to enjoy an after-lunch nap in the sun.

We saw a repeat performance at the adjacent pool later that afternoon. The Goliath heron went through the same ritual of repeated stabbing and rinsing of the rock-catfish before swallowing it. The time lapse between catching and swallowing was 18 minutes, this time without any disturbance from other predators. This was again followed by a drink from the pool and a thorough cleansing of the beak.

The next morning we witnessed the ritual once again. This time we didn't observe the initial catch so couldn't determine the duration. However, the prey and the process were identical, including the drink of water followed by the cleaning of the beak. The downside to this rather lengthy process is that it affords other predators, like the fish eagle, time to spot the opportunity for a potential theft.

A couple of days later we slept over in the Shipandani Hide and saw a Goliath heron catching a kurper (a member of the tilapia family). The fish was larger in size than the rock-catfish which we'd witnessed a few days before. This time the heron swallowed the wriggling fish without any stabbing. The fish never left the bird's beak. It was a matter of catch-and-swallow. It took about 30 seconds so we had no chance to take a photograph.

Freshwater anglers know the rock-catfish is a particularly resilient species, with a tough, leathery skin and the ability to stay alive out of the water for a significant period of time. The pectoral and dorsal fins are attached to razor-sharp spines with serrated edges which are covered with a slimy substance. The fish has a very strong wriggling action and can inflict quite deep stab wounds when handled. The wounds are painful, probably caused by the slime on the spines.

The Goliath heron must instinctively know about the dangers associated with swallowing a rock-catfish alive, hence the precautions taken to ensure the fish is dead before it is swallowed. We supposed the vigorous mouthwash was to clear the slime and sand from its mouth. The heron also seems to know by instinct that these precautions are not required for swallowing kurper.

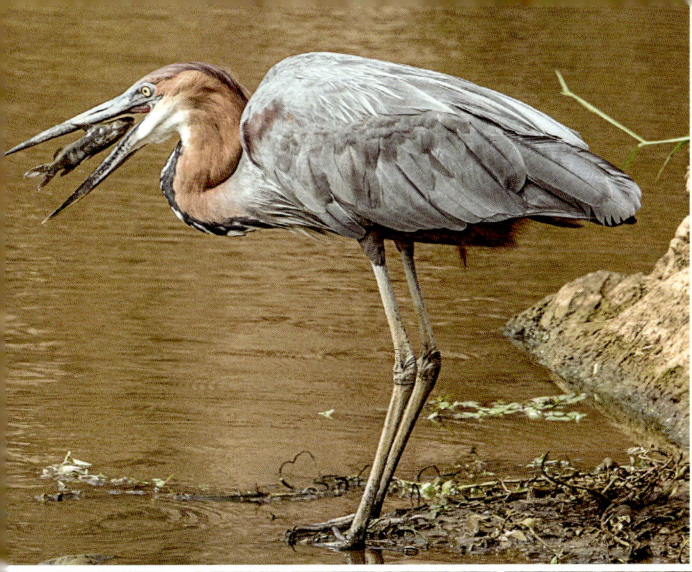
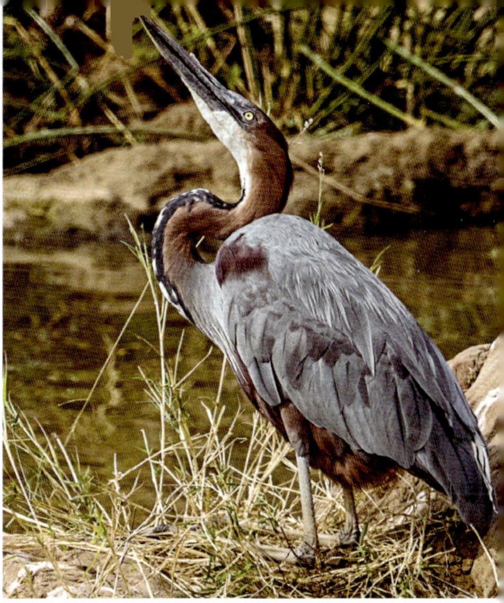
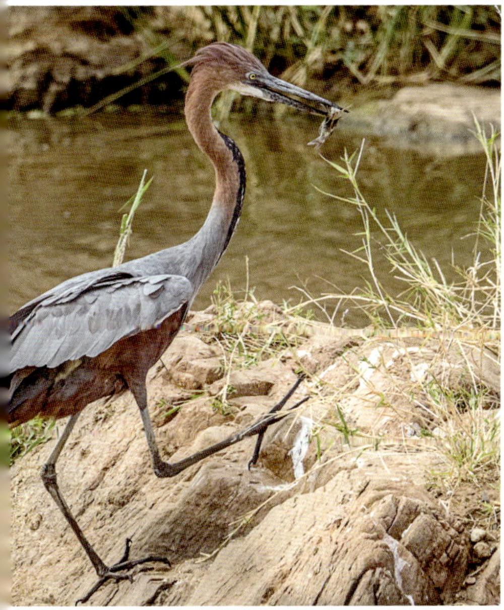
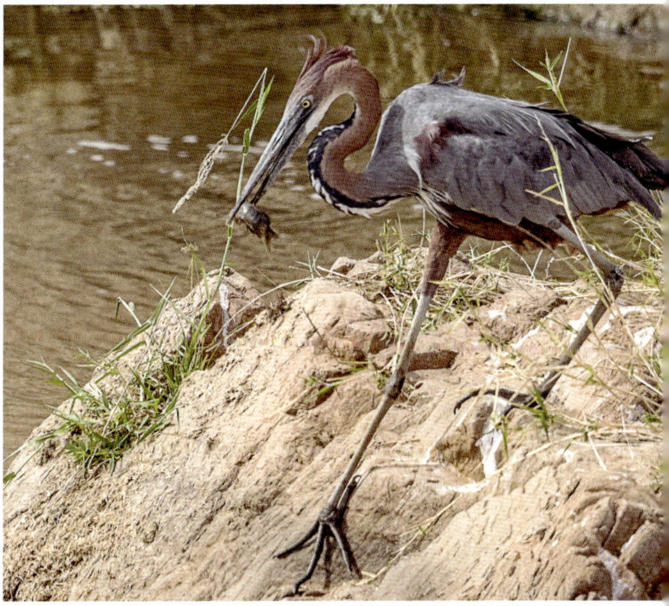
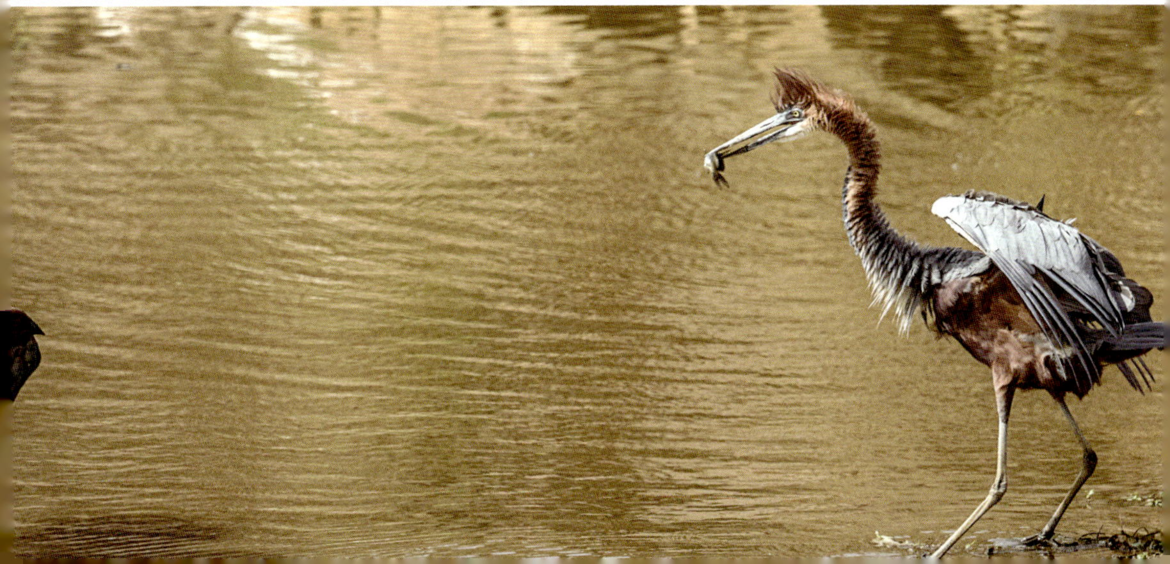

A big surprise

KATHY KAY

My husband and I were at a waterhole, watching a herd of elephants drinking. After a while, a game-drive vehicle arrived and parked about 10 metres away from us. Out of the corner of my eye I noticed another elephant on our left moving towards the water. He was moving parallel to the game-drive vehicle but turned and walked towards the tracker sitting on an elevated seat. I trained my camera on them as I heard the ranger quietly telling the guests not to move at all and not to speak. In the deathly silence the huge bull came towards the tracker, wound its trunk around his neck, played about his head with its trunk and then, after some time, quietly moved off.

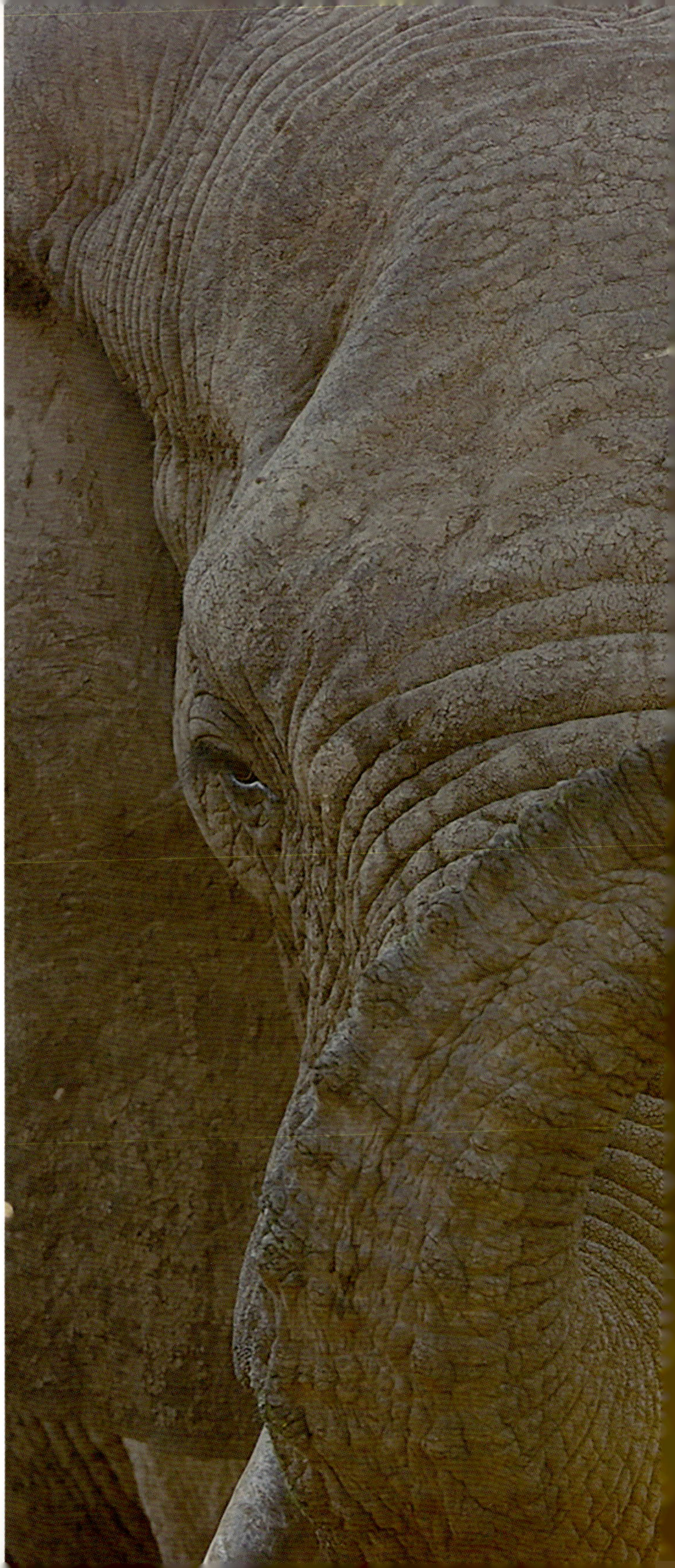

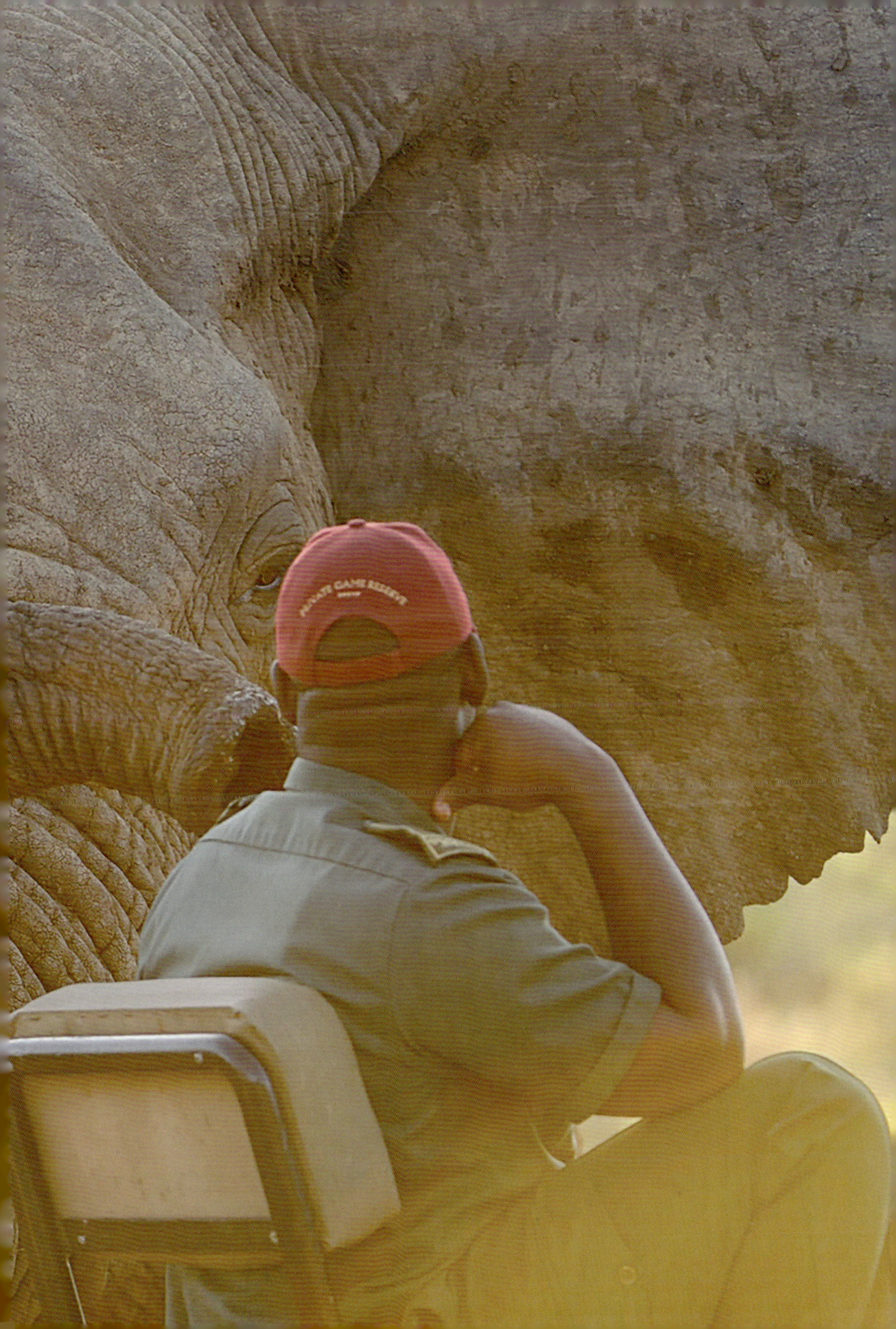

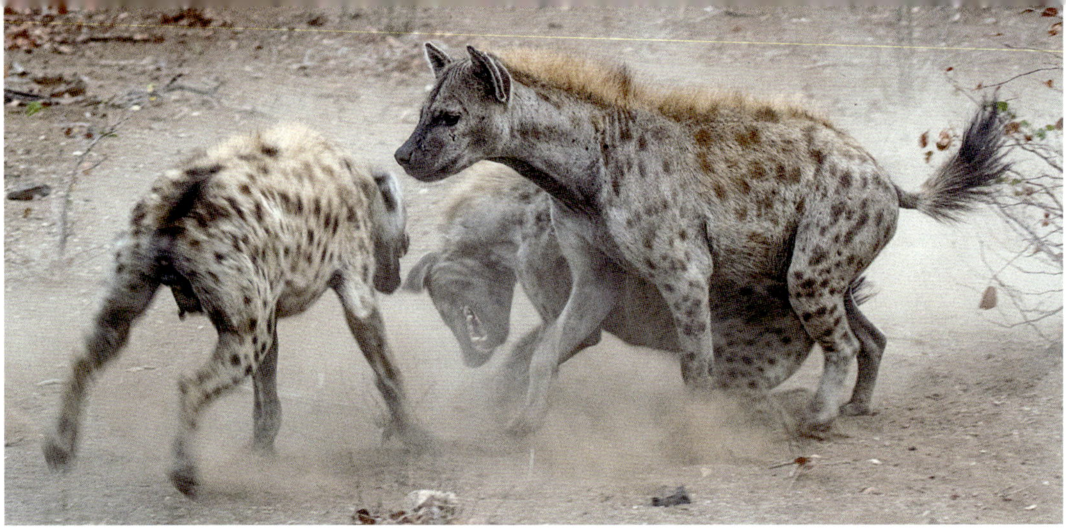

An altercation

LOUIS & INA TALJAARD

One late afternoon just before the Kruger gates closed, we were driving back to Letaba Camp when we spotted a male and female hyena next to the road. They were involved either in a friendly greeting or courting ritual. A third hyena appeared from nowhere and immediately attacked the male who was lying on the ground. The victim spun around to protect his exposed belly while the female attacked the newcomer. In a flash it was a free-for-all, with yelping and howling and dust flying in all directions. After about 10 seconds the female withdrew from the fight while the other two continued. The male broke free and ran into the bush, limping badly. The altercation was very brief. The aggressor kept snarling and baring its teeth but the female seemed to change her attitude and displayed some keenness, or even affection, towards the victor. It was not possible to determine the sex of the attacker. It should be noted that the female hyena has a fake genital organ which resembles the male penis and can therefore often be mistaken for a male. Was this a case of misplaced jealousy or sexual interest?

We estimated the whole encounter lasted about 20 seconds which shows how quickly the female of the species can change her mind. We never saw the outcome of the exchange because we had to leave but we couldn't help imagining the possible outcomes that might arise from this new liaison.

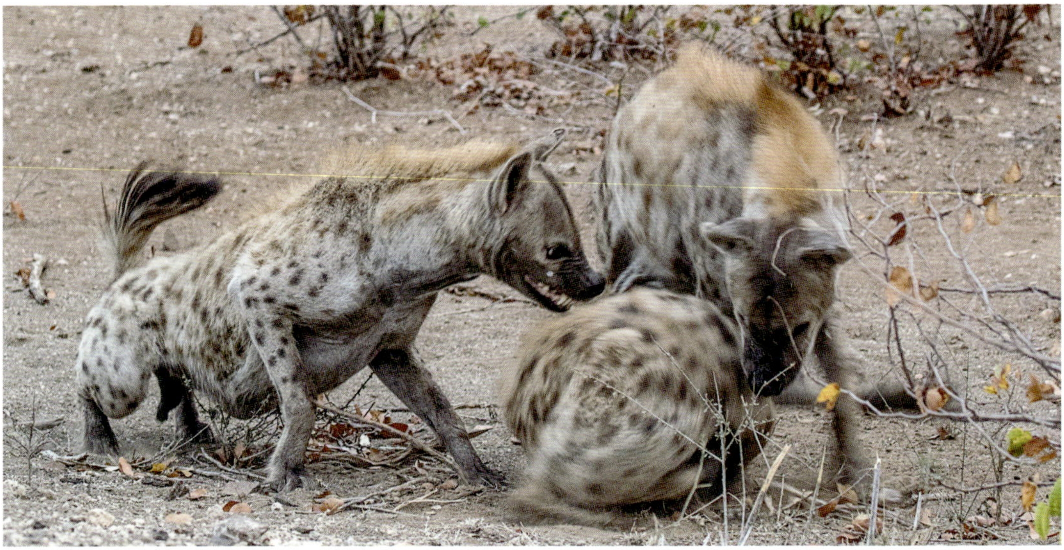

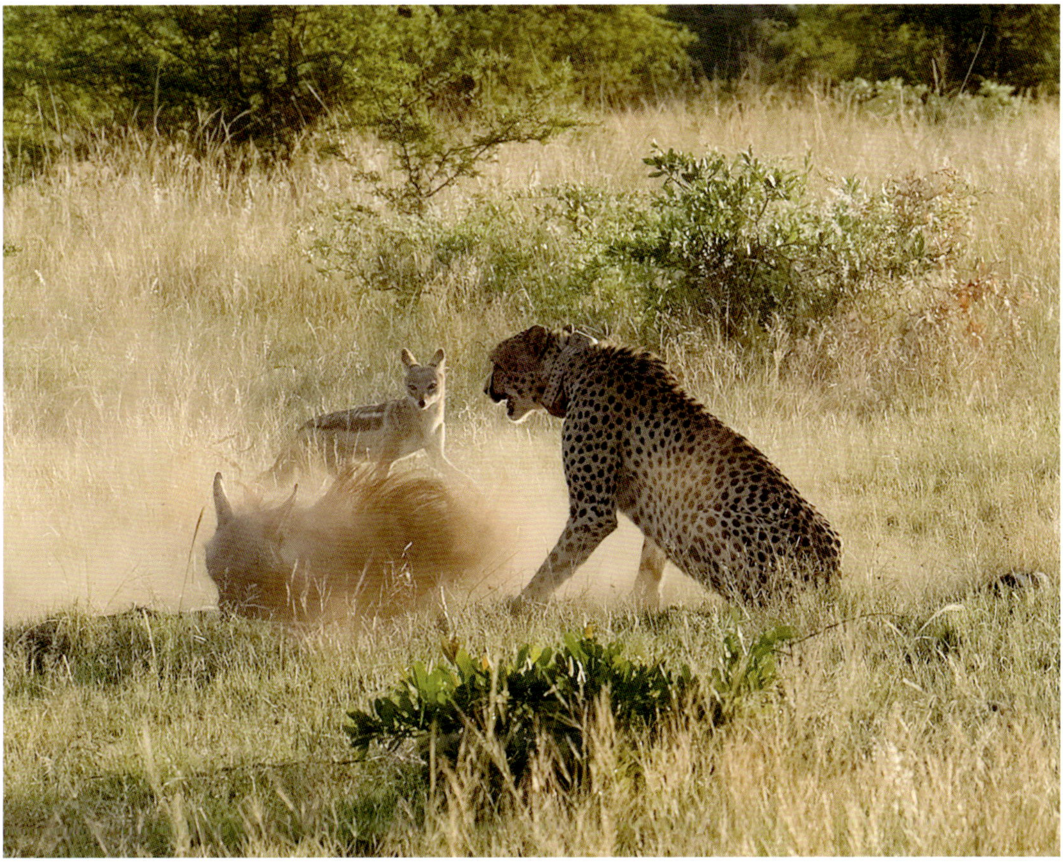

The thieving brown hyena

RICHARD RANDALL

As tour director, I was accompanying an overseas group of tourists on a visit to Mabula Game Reserve in Limpopo, and we were heading out on a morning game drive. I was in the first of three vehicles. Our driver/guide decided to go to an area known as Whole Owner's Plain to look for cheetah. His instinct was spot on because we soon came across two cheetahs with a kill. The driver took us as close as he was allowed to, so we could observe and photograph the two animals. He was giving the guests information about the cheetahs when I spotted a brown hyena running towards them and their kill. The hyena rushed in, intent on grabbing whatever it could. At first, one of the cheetahs fought back to protect their food but gave up when the hyena continued to snatch at the kill. The second cheetah then attacked the hyena but in a half-hearted manner. Eventually both cheetahs just looked on as the hyena took a large part of the carcass and left.

By the time the other two vehicles arrived at the scene it was all over, the hyena had disappeared and the cheetahs were looking forlorn at having lost their meal. Even the jackals, which had been in the background, had gone on their way. The whole episode had taken less than a minute.

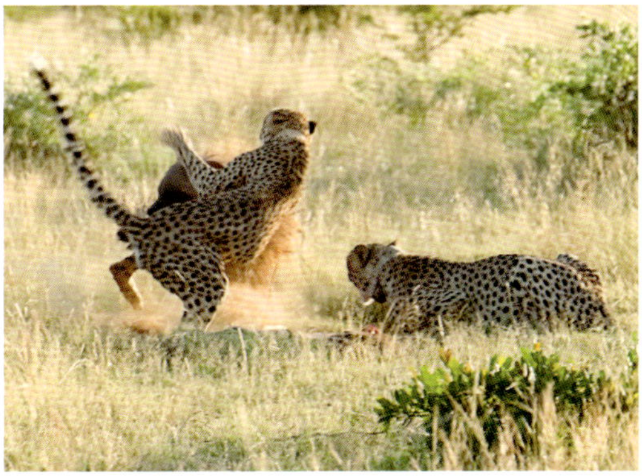

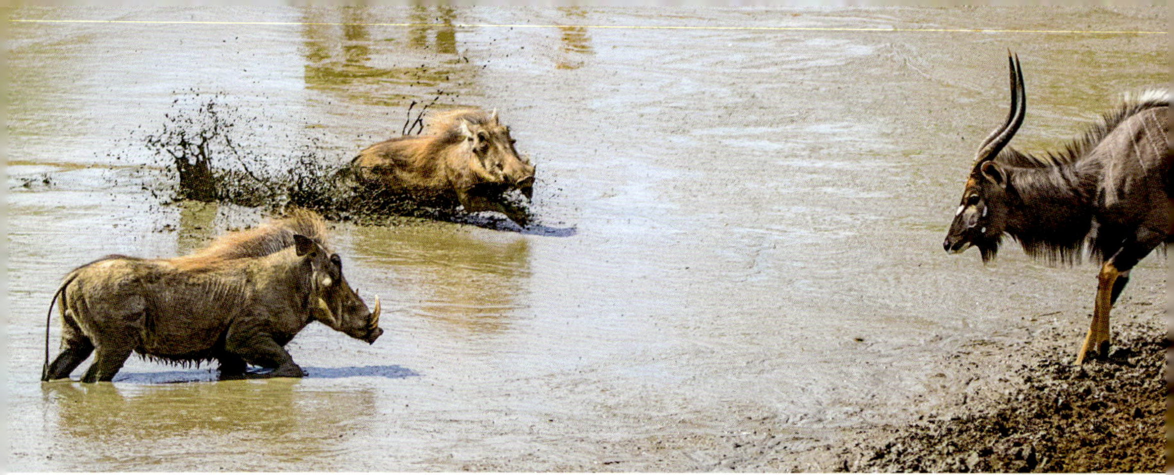

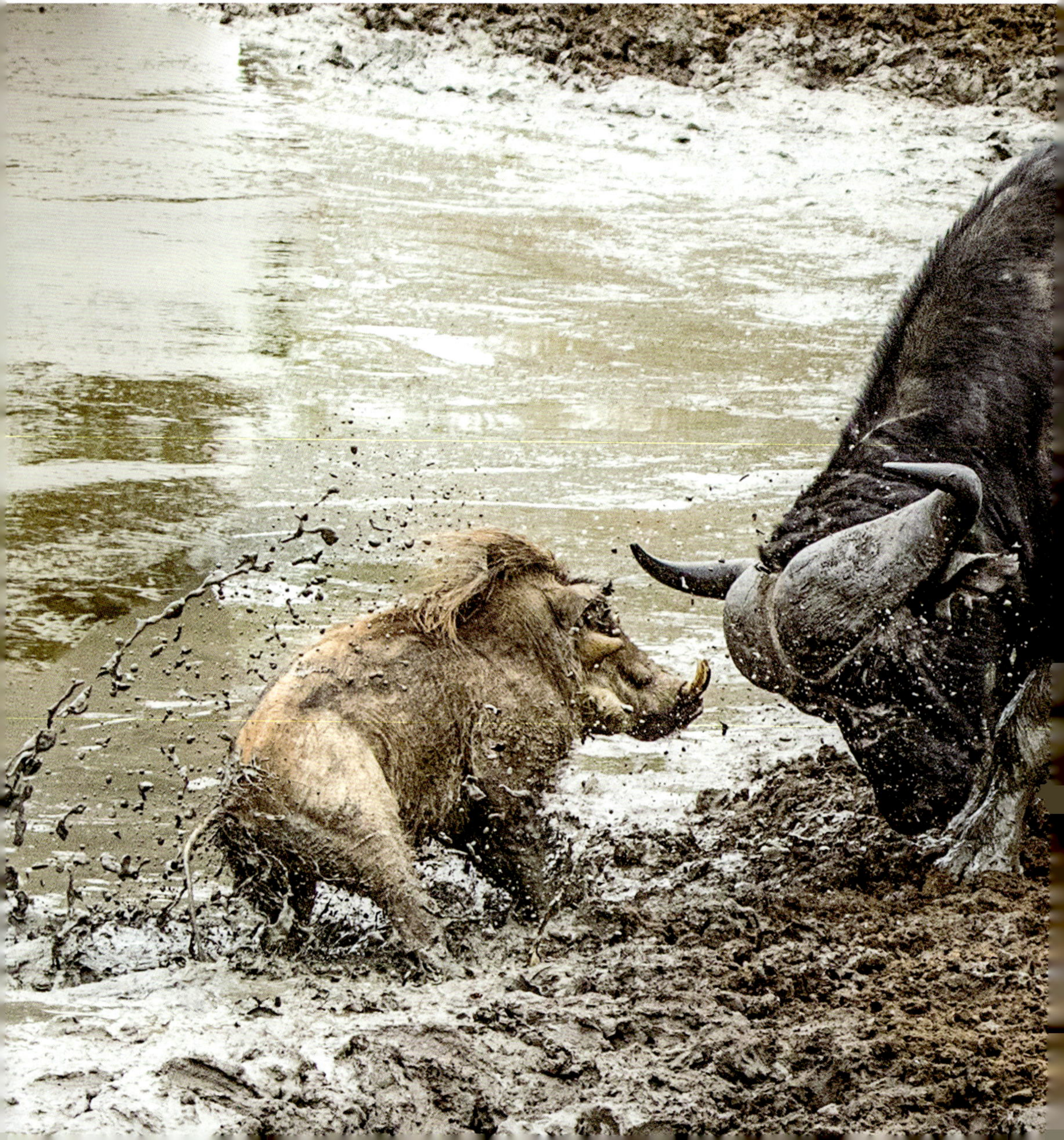

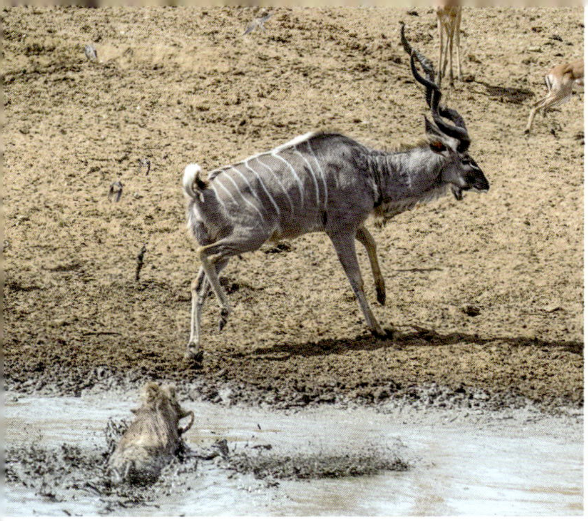

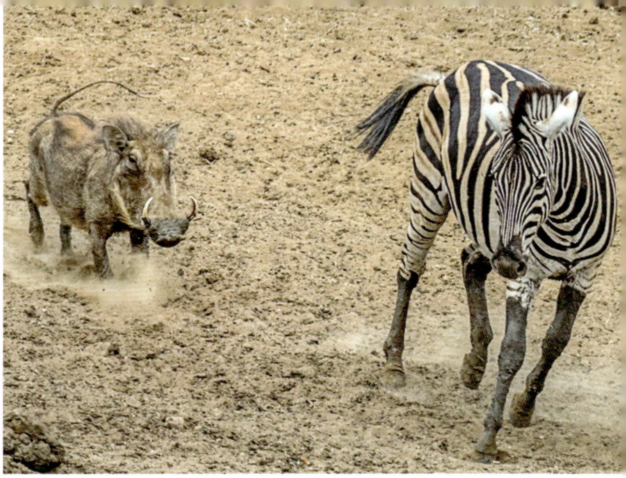

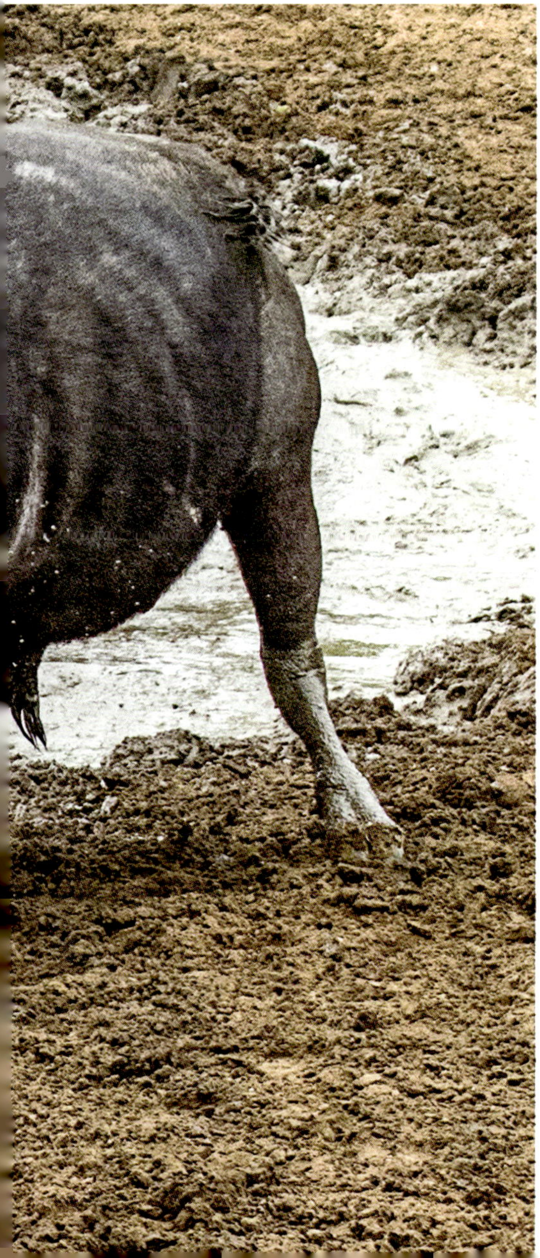

The Jack Russell of the Kruger

LOUIS & INA TALJAARD

It was during a trip to the Kruger National Park when we visited a waterhole located between Sirheni and Punda Maria. As a result of the severe drought in the region the dam had turned into a mud bath. A large variety of animals frequented this spot seeking to quench their thirst. Some ventured into the dam while others tried to extract a bit of water from the surface of the mud around the edges of the pool.

We spotted a warthog that behaved as if the pool belonged to him. He was chasing all and sundry away from the water. He didn't care who he faced up to. Size simply didn't matter to him.

We kept him in our sights and before long we saw him squaring up to a buffalo bull. The two were eye-balling each other for quite some time, each with a yellow-billed oxpecker perched on its back as a second for the duel to follow. The warthog moved forward in a flash, gave his opponent a whack against its horn that sounded like a pistol shot from where we sat, and then took off as fast as it could. The buffalo was so surprised that it hardly moved before the attacker took flight.

In light of his determination and fearlessness, my wife named him the Jack Russell of the Kruger.

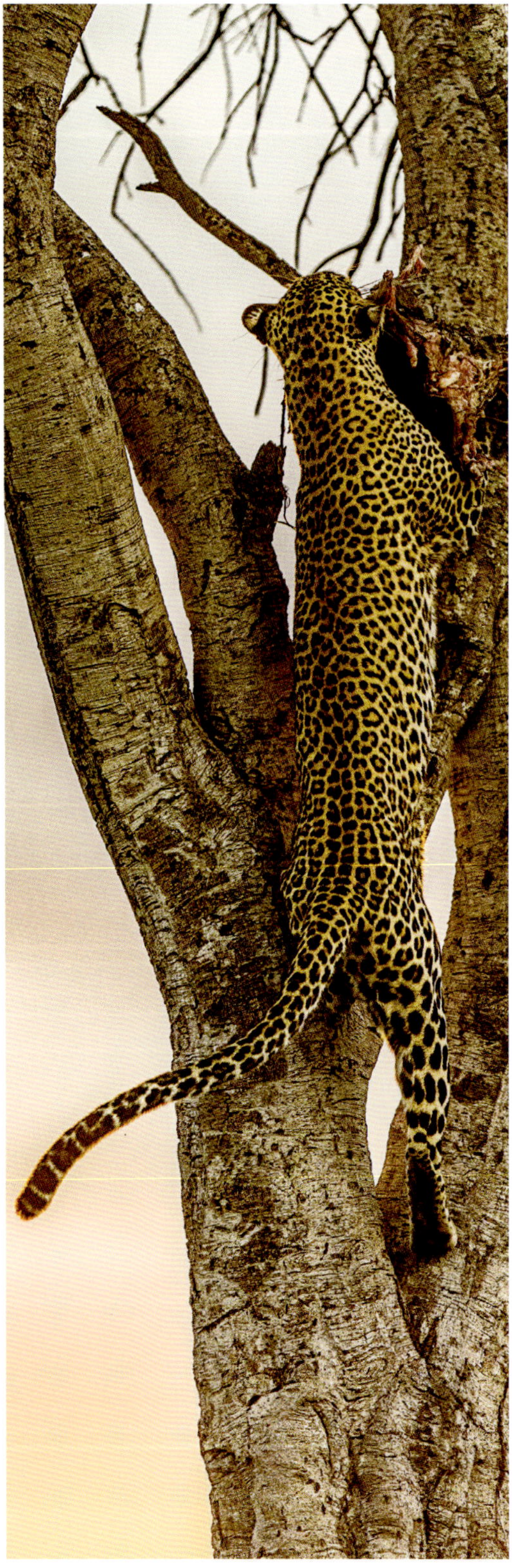

The tables are turned

PAUL VORSTER

We are often tempted to make sense of the complexity of the animal kingdom by sorting it into neat categories, or over-simplifying using stereotypes: some animals are predators, some scavengers and others prey, for example. All too often, we have it wrong.

We had spent hours looking for the female leopard, Luluka when the radio crackled, telling us this member of leopard royalty has been spotted. The race was on to get to the sighting before the light faded. When we did set eyes on her, she was on the lookout for her evening meal. To get a better view of what was happening in the vicinity, she sat upright on her haunches, resembling a meerkat. When she was on the prowl again, we saw that her route through the long grass towards a thicket would lead her straight to where some hyenas were munching the remains of a carcass. I feared these scavengers would be her undoing because the hyenas had numerical superiority and raw aggression. Luluka, however, had her cunning and determination.

Sammy, our photographic guide assured us she had seen them and predicted that she was going to steal their prey and run up a nearby tree. "Never!" I thought. "She's a predator and will keep hunting." But Sammy was confident she was planning to rob the hyenas for an easy meal. We raced ahead and waited at the foot of the tree knowing we would either get a great shot or miss out on the action completely. And there she went! What a sight to see Luluka catching the scavengers unaware, grabbing the carcass and racing towards us to scale the tree, leaving the hyenas open-mouthed in both senses. To get a clear view of Luluka's climb, we had to shoot directly into the setting sun which was painting the sky bright orange with tints of blue.

Of all the special sightings in the Mara, Luluka's audacious out-foxing of the hyenas was one of the very special ones. So, there went another stereotype, shattered for good. The hunter found it expedient to turn scavenger, and that's exactly what she did.

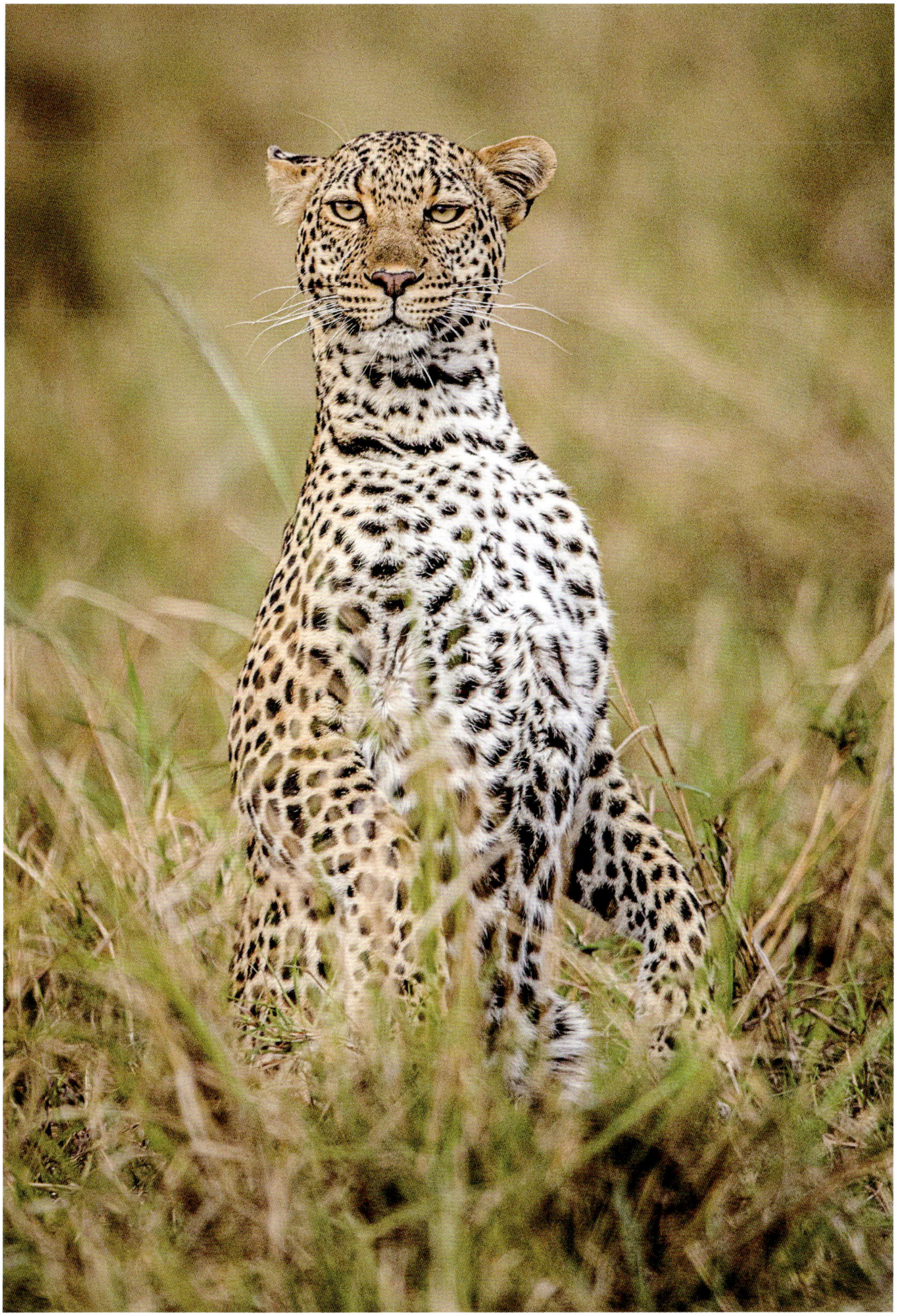

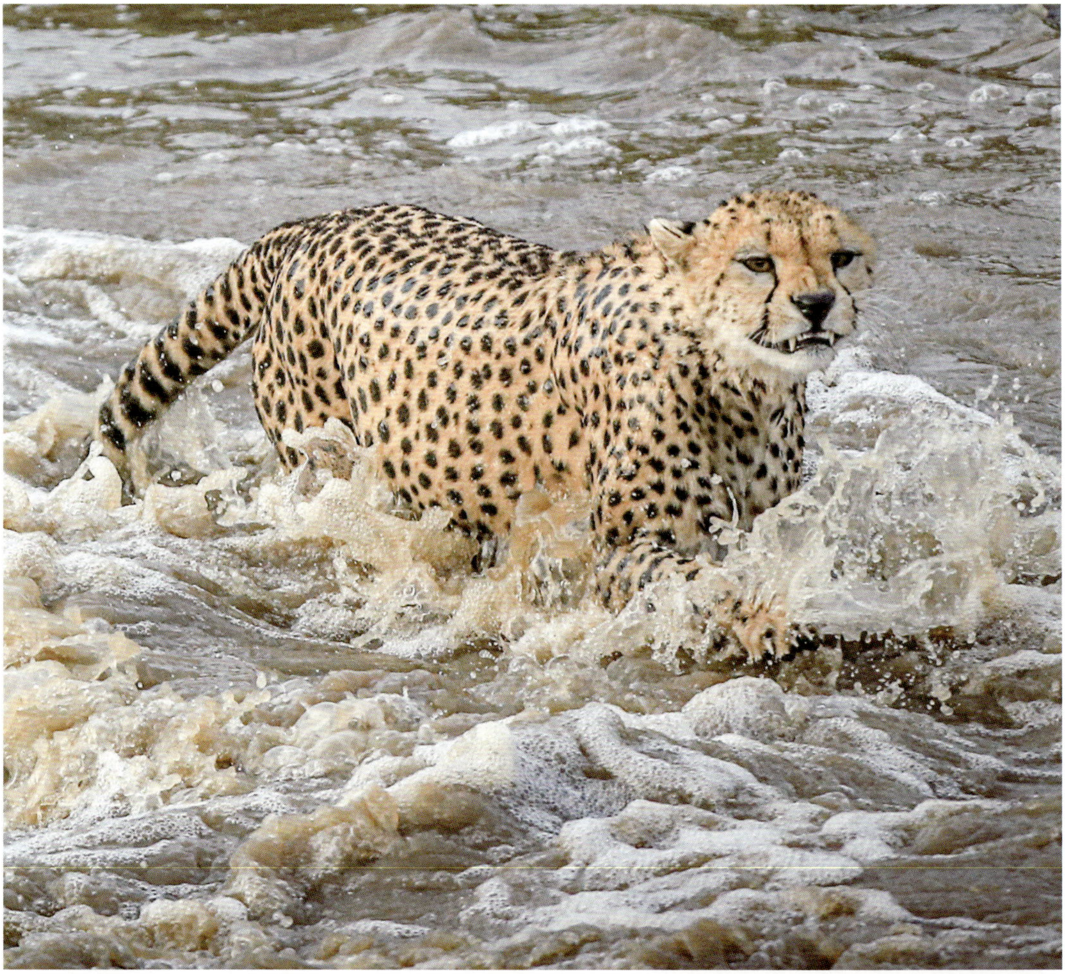

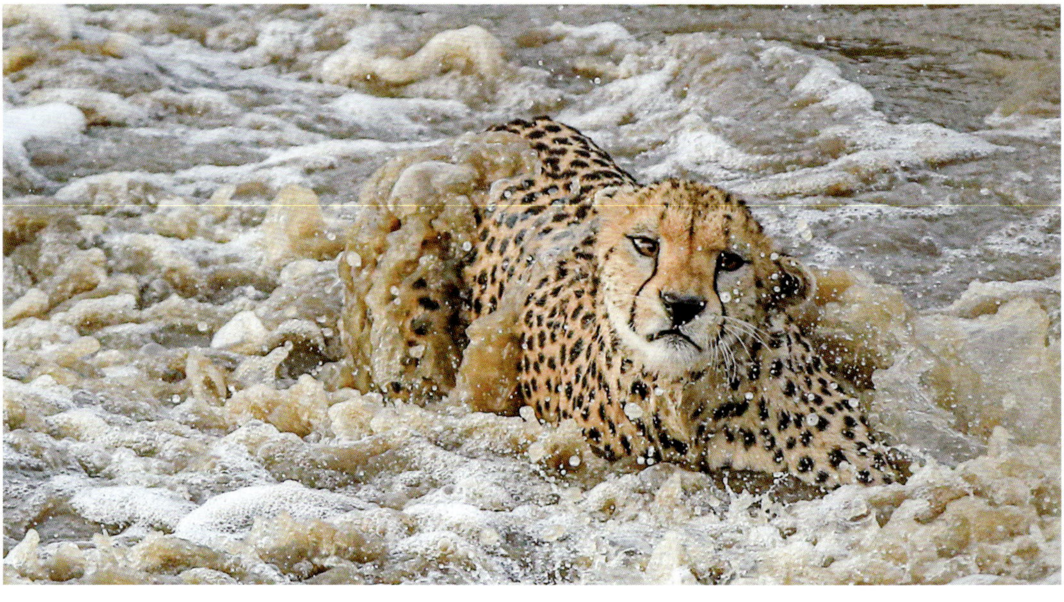

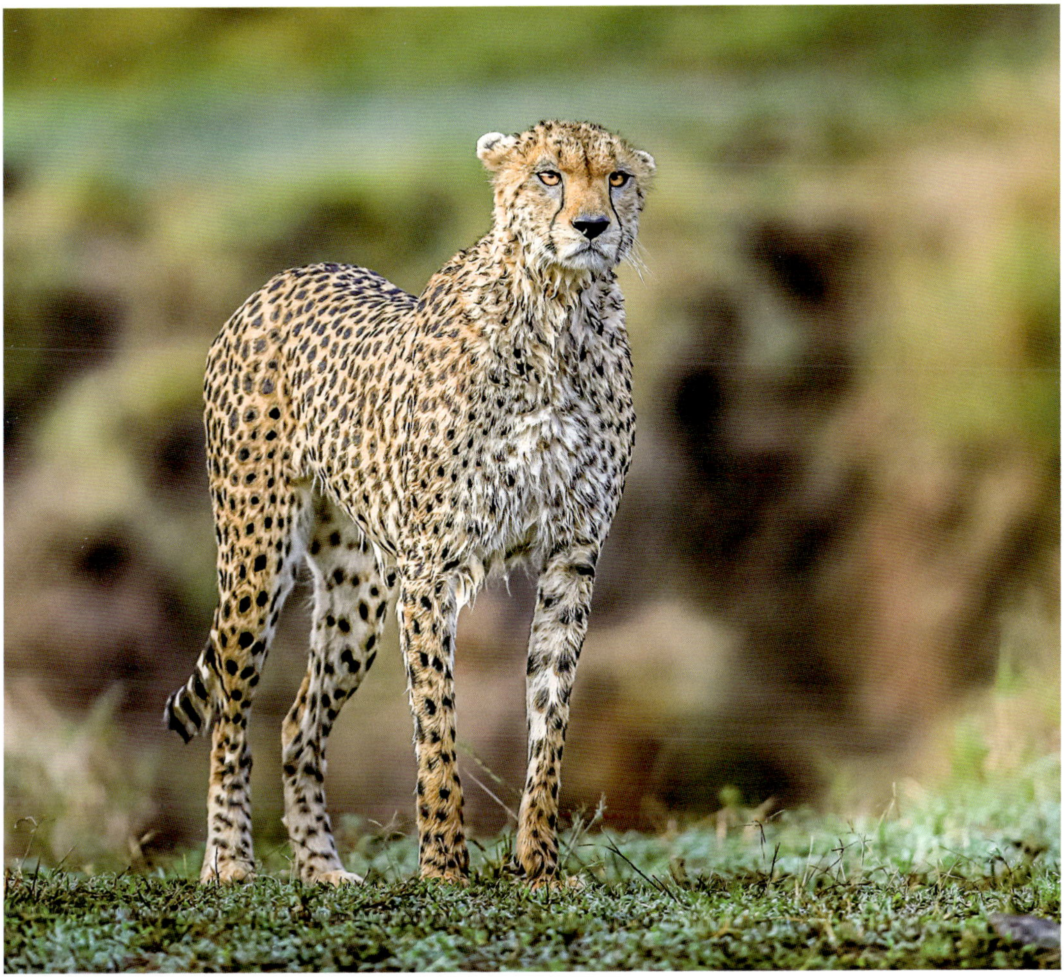

Crossing her own Alps

PAUL VORSTER

Seeing a cheetah running at full speed is pure poetry in motion: it's genetic engineering at its best! Able to accelerate from 0–75 kilometres per hour in three seconds, the cheetah is the fastest land animal on the planet. But having to cross a water obstacle is as daunting to a cheetah as crossing the Alps was for Hannibal and his army. Cheetahs can swim but clearly it is not their favourite pastime.

We came across Neema in the early morning during a visit to Kenya as she stood on the bank of the fast-flowing Talek River after good rains, intent on getting to the other side. Our hearts contracted, remembering the sad episode of our favourite cheetah, Malaika's drowning. Neema's approach was, to put it mildly, very unsure, and her facial expression made her dislike for the water evident. She approached and stepped back a few times. Then, with a determination that would make Hannibal leading his army across the Alps towards Italy seem hesitant, she committed to the raging waters. Struggling, she fought against the powerful sweep of the river but she kept going, even though she went under a couple of times. Then, with a flurry and a typical flick of the tail, Neema stood triumphant on the opposite bank, shook the water off her coat and prepared to begin her hunt.

Cheetah crossing

LYNN VAN TONDER

It was May 2016 in the Kruger National Park – my first camping visit to a national park – and I was fortunate to see a cheetah with her four cubs crossing the Letaba River. I was waiting for a vehicle coming from the front to cross the small bridge over the river when I saw the five felines. The mother first made sure the water was not too deep and that everything was in order and safe. She crossed the river and waited on the other side for the cubs to follow. They were hesitant at first but then crossed over one by one. The last cub, however, seemed afraid to follow suit. The adult cheetah gave him one look and turned around with the other three cubs in tow. The little fellow realised he was going to be all alone and then bravely followed his family members. They then went up the hill and later disappeared over the top. What an experience! My first encounter with a cheetah family will always remain special to me.

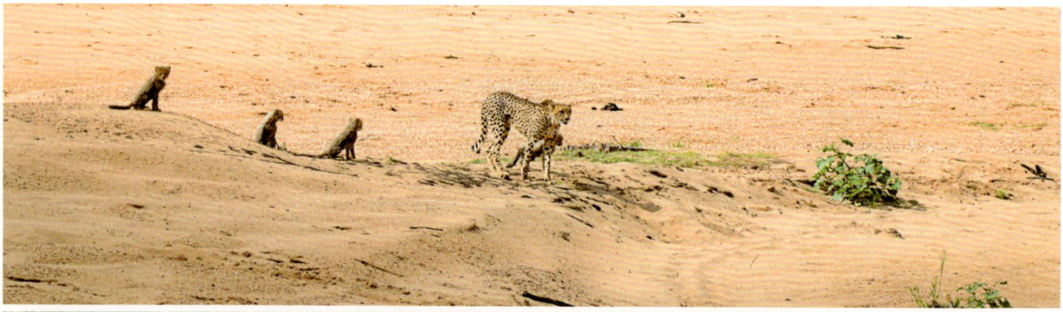

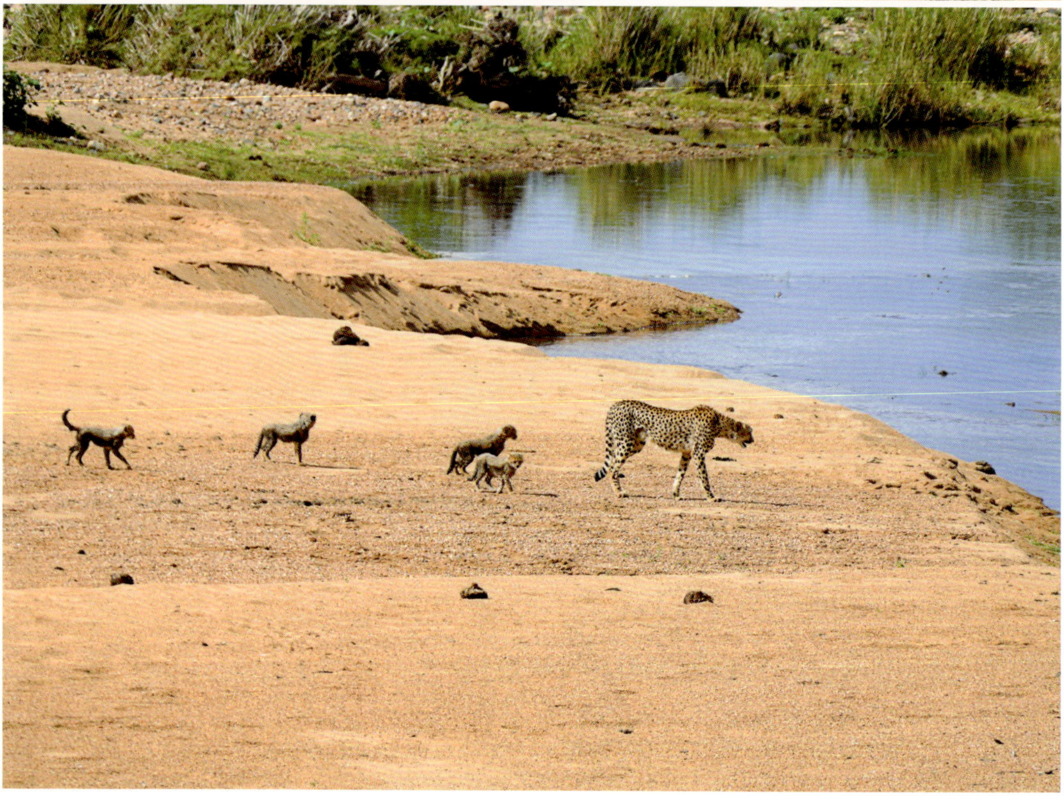

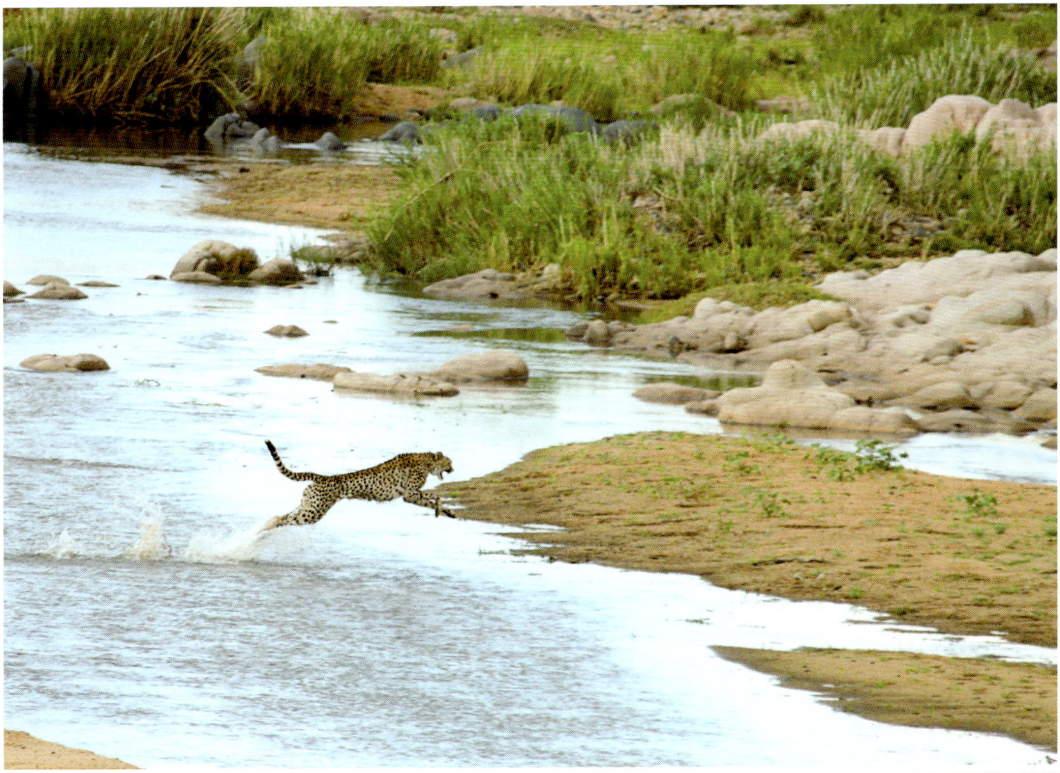

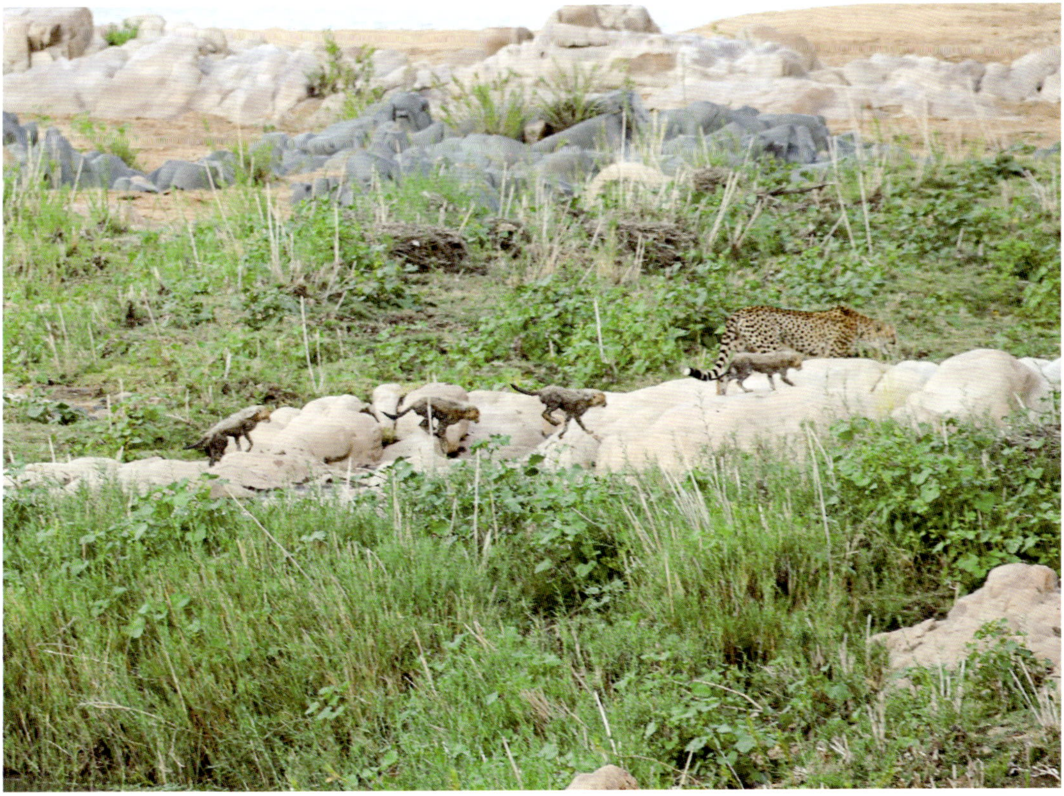

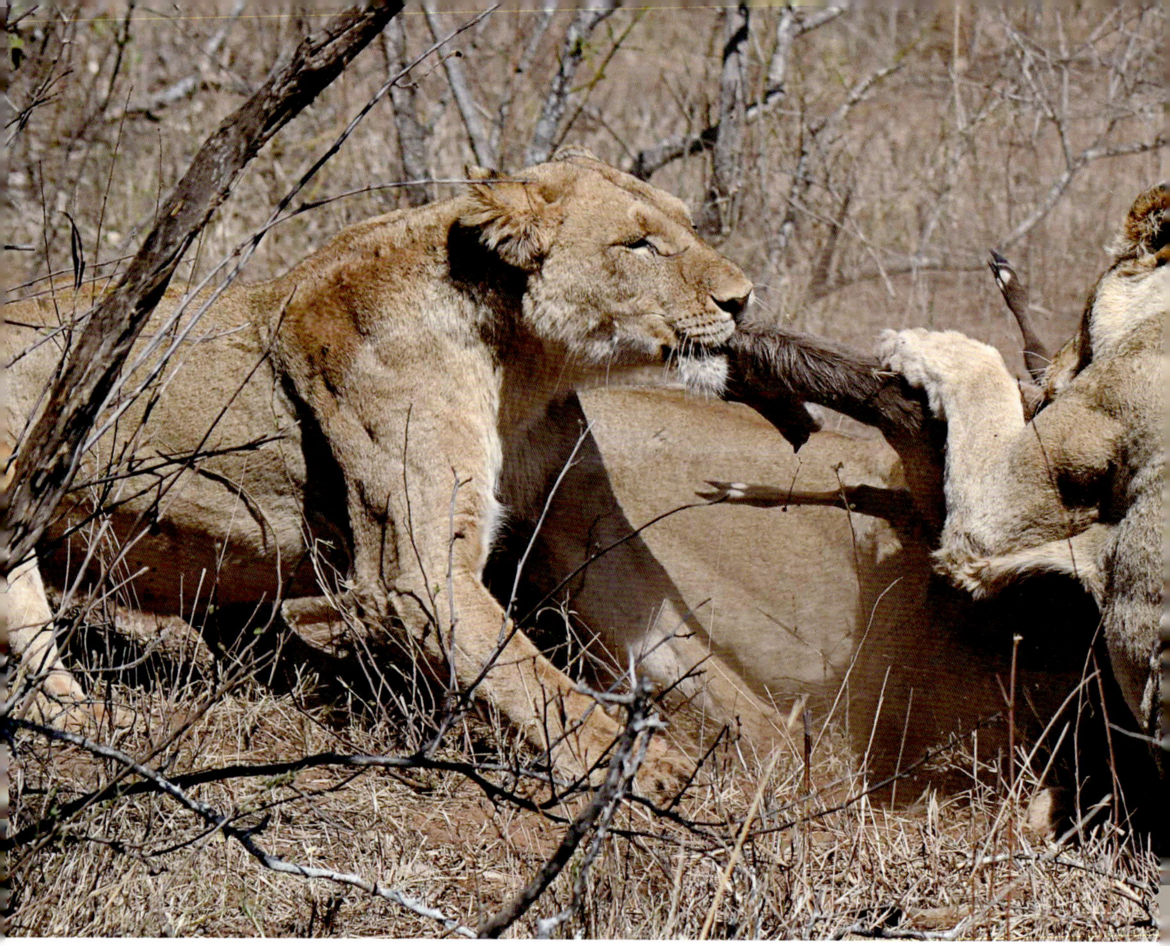

Modern family

REVASH SINGH

We'd been watching a couple of older, single male buffaloes at Sunset Dam in the Kruger National Park but decided to move along as it was becoming quite uncomfortable under the midday sun. As we left, we noticed a lioness walking along aimlessly. She was approximately 150 metres away and walking towards the buffaloes. At the time I found it strange when she decided to make her way towards my vehicle, but in hindsight her strategy made sense.

When she was close, her facial expression changed dramatically and her attention was zoomed in on something specific. Seemingly out of nowhere, a young male bushbuck appeared. Rapidly, she had him in a stranglehold. On hearing the noises of distress from this animal, lion after lion quickly materialised. Within seconds, there were eight lions, all tugging at any bushbuck portion they could sink their teeth into. It was quite gruesome as the poor bushbuck was still alive. But not for long because they pulled so hard the prey was literally ripped apart.

A couple of the lionesses made off with their prizes, while a young male lion got a firm grip on another portion. This didn't please the females which had other ideas and grabbed onto the same piece. He tried to keep his bounty by making his way towards a tree, with the two lionesses being dragged along with him. Working together in tag-team fashion, the one lioness fed while the other lioness held the piece of meat so the young lion could not get away.

In the end, the females outsmarted him and stole the prize. Before long the entire antelope was devoured. Replete, the lions lounged under a tree.

While they were resting, the savanna clean-up crew showed up. Within seconds numerous hooded vultures, along with a couple of marabou storks, arrived to see if they could pick up any scraps. Then a barrage of white-backed vultures

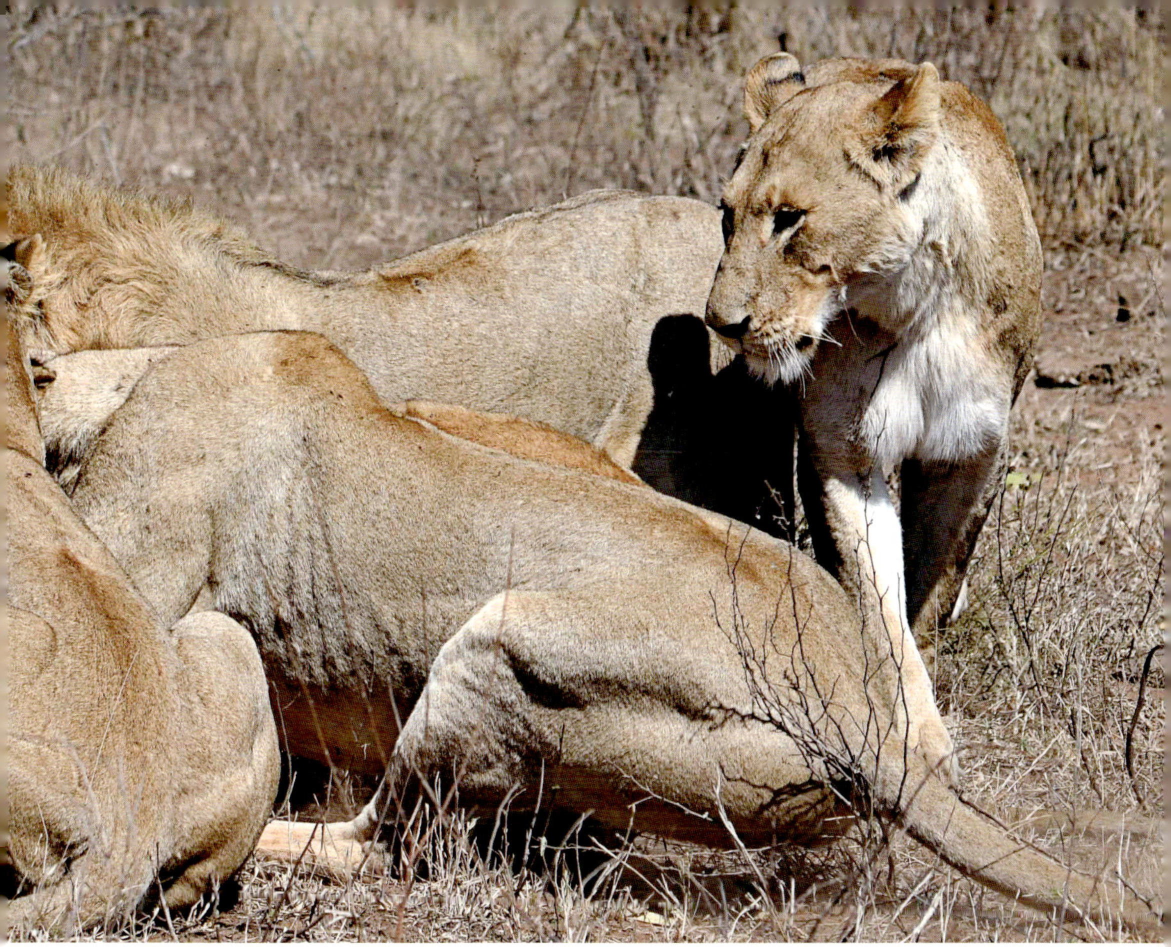

flapped down to bully the others away from the kill site. Not that they even got a bite, as the lions had consumed the lot.

By this time there must have been more than 40 vehicles piled up at this sighting. Presumably irritated by the traffic and the vultures, the pride made their way down to the Sabie River where, somewhat to our surprise, they played in the water for a while. The lions eventually crossed the river and disappeared in the bushes, leaving us feeling as if the whole drama had been a figment of our imagination.

It still gives me goosebumps thinking about how the lions strategised this kill, and the sound of them growling when they sunk their teeth into their prey.

I have read about and heard numerous stories of lions in the Kruger using vehicles to conceal themselves when hunting, but I never imagined my vehicle would be used in that way. Old tactics… new props. I guess modern families have to adapt with the times.

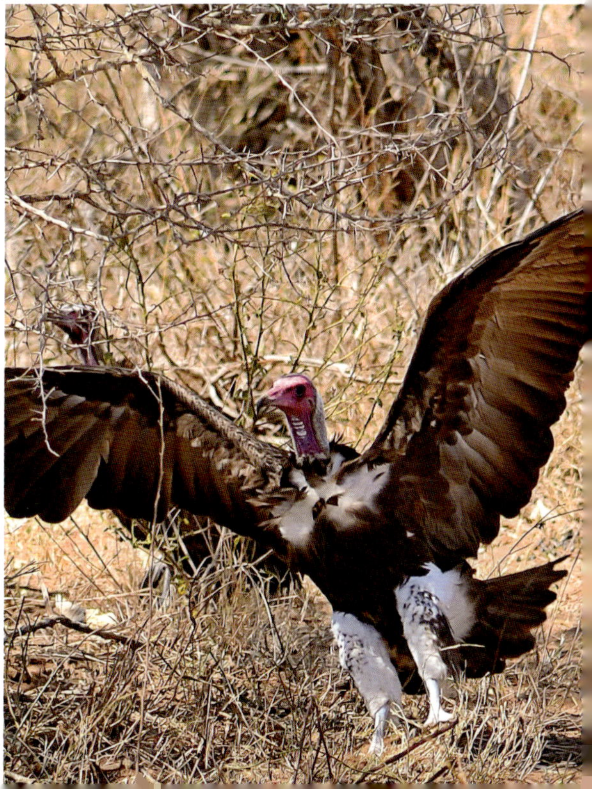

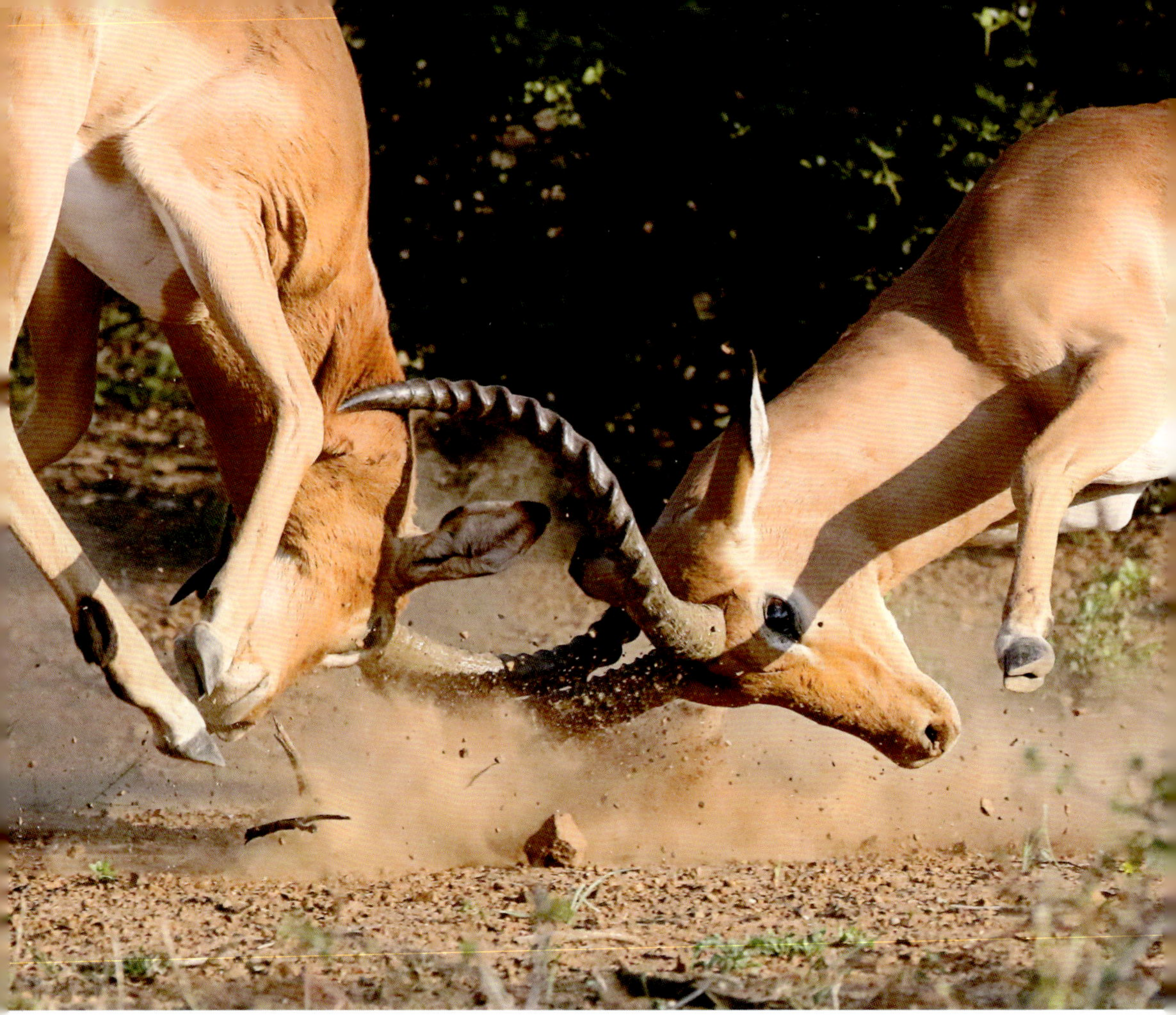

Fighting for supremacy

SHAWN CATTERALL

From the end of summer to the beginning of winter most antelope species go into rut. This is when the males get the chance to propagate and extend their family, though this might only happen once in their lifetime. So when the males fight for the right to mate, it can become very serious sometimes even lethal.

Out with guests in the Pilanesberg Nature Reserve one afternoon, we came across a beautiful herd of impala and opted to watch a male try to take over ownership of the herd from the present dominant male. The two rams slammed into each other with immense force. They put their heads down and cracked their horns against each other, using their back legs for momentum.

This continued for a while, backwards and forwards, through and over the bushes, into the road and back into the grass. All you could hear was the clashing of the horns. Then it intensified: the bigger male was getting really fed up with the younger one, and becoming more aggressive.

Suddenly the whole herd came to view the fight. They ran up to the two fighting males and then darted away and back again, all the while making a strange noise in their throats, as if cheering on the fighters. The members of the herd continued to dance and jump around the males, in particular the youngsters born that same year.

Fifteen minutes of ferocious activity ensued before the younger impala got his foot caught in the horn of the bigger one. The dominant impala took his chance and, pushing with all his might, tossed the contender to the ground. The young male fell on his back into a ditch with the victor on top of him, dust and stones flying. By now the rest of the herd had danced off, still making their strange noises, while the winner chased off the loser.

Once the victor had made sure the would-be usurper was well and truly gone, he came back to his herd making his conventional roar (the one all contenders make when in rut) proclaiming his win to the ladies.

Ownership of the herd changes continually during the rut until the final winner claims his position and mates with all the females. He will stay with the herd until the next rutting season, protecting his females and offspring.

As a field guide I'd seen many males fighting and being vocal but never before witnessed the herd reacting to a fight with dancing, 'cheering' and supporting the opponents. There is always something new to learn out in the bush, and our guests had the pleasure of an unusual sighting of those animals we tend to dismiss as unexciting: tho impala.

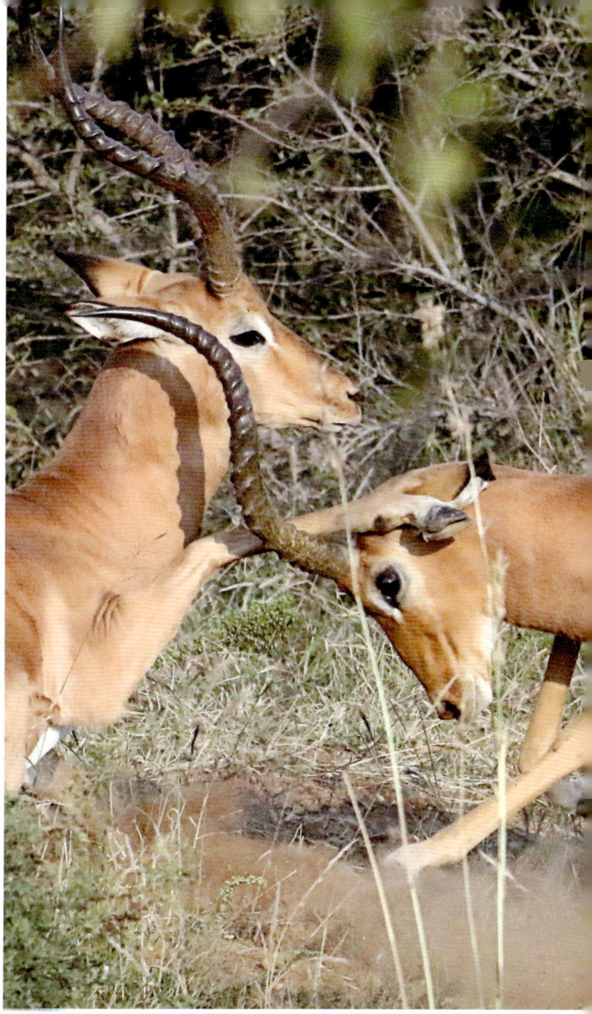

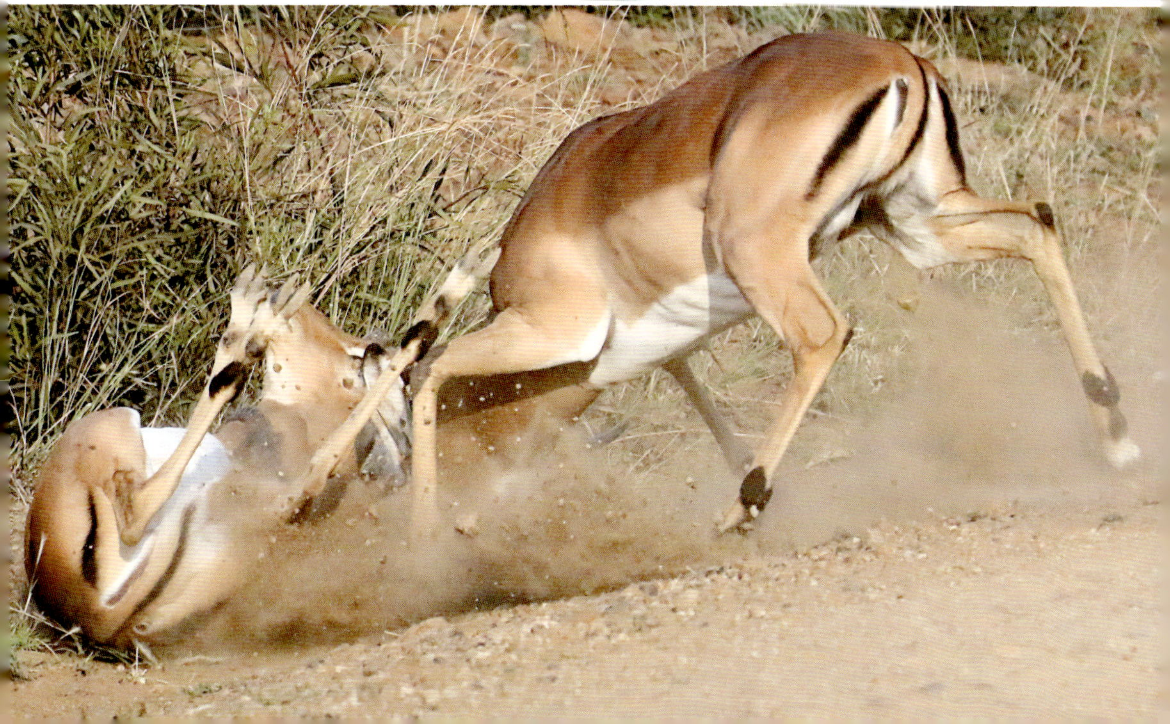

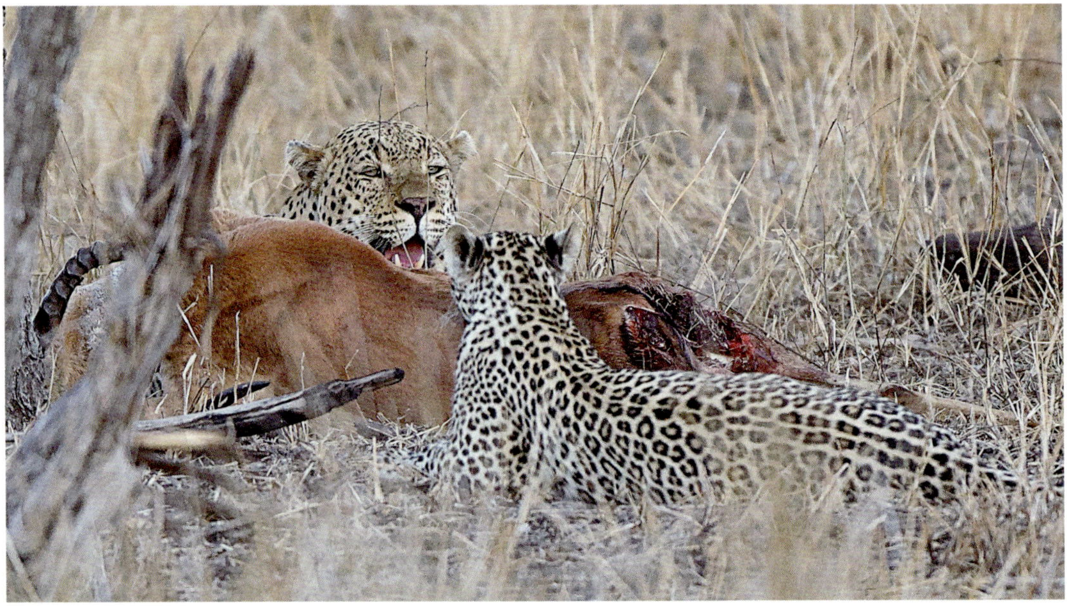

The winner takes all

SILVAIN BOURG

"What would you like to see today?" the ranger in charge of the game-drive vehicle asked.

"Leopard," I eagerly replied. I had spent the whole day keeping watch at the known location of a leopard family around the Satara area in the Kruger National Park, waiting for them to move into sight. When it was time for the gates to close, I realised my only chance was to join a night drive, knowing they would become active once the sun set. I told the ranger what I knew about the leopard location and we set off. About an hour into our drive, the ranger abruptly stopped and pointed in the direction of a big marula tree.

"There!"

I stretched my neck and grabbed my camera. I could not believe my eyes. There he was – a big male leopard. It wasn't just my dream sighting, but we were in for some real action too, as he managed to kill an impala right in front of our eyes. The leopard dragged the impala to the nearby marula tree where he started feeding. Fifteen minutes later, a female leopard arrived with her one-year-old daughter. One would have expected this solitary predator to show aggression towards the sub-adult in particular, but strangely, he allowed the females to join his feast.

Before long, a hyena turned up and attempted to share the leopards' meal. The mother tried to scare the hyena away but the male simply looked on. More strange behaviour on his part but perhaps he had already had his fill. The female leopards resumed eating, while the male climbed up the tree and vanished in the canopy. I can't be sure whether he was merely done with the meal or perhaps he had seen trouble in the making... Next, the sub-adult grabbed the prey and tried to carry it up the marula tree, but the impala carcass dropped to the ground.

The plot thickened as another hyena joined the first one. After an unsuccessful attempt to ward them off, the female leopard duo unexpectedly gave up, leaving team hyena winner of the booty.

It was an incredible exchange: three leopards giving up the impala with so little resistance. In addition, I was fascinated to see that it was the youngest leopard who worked hardest to defend the prey. It is possible the older female was on heat, resulting in the male's failure to fight for his meal.

The next day I spotted a new impala kill near Satara, but sadly, there were no leopards around this time.

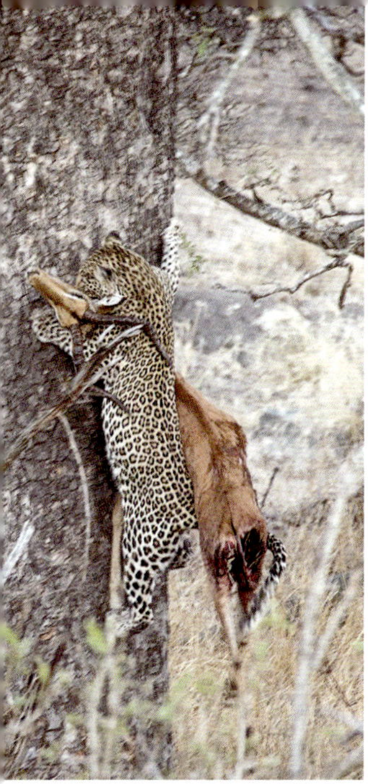
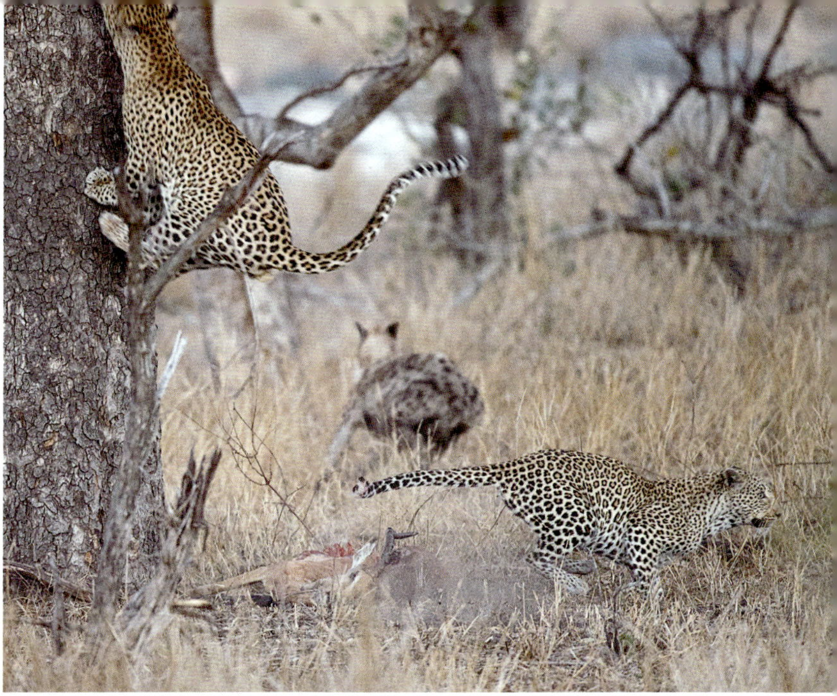
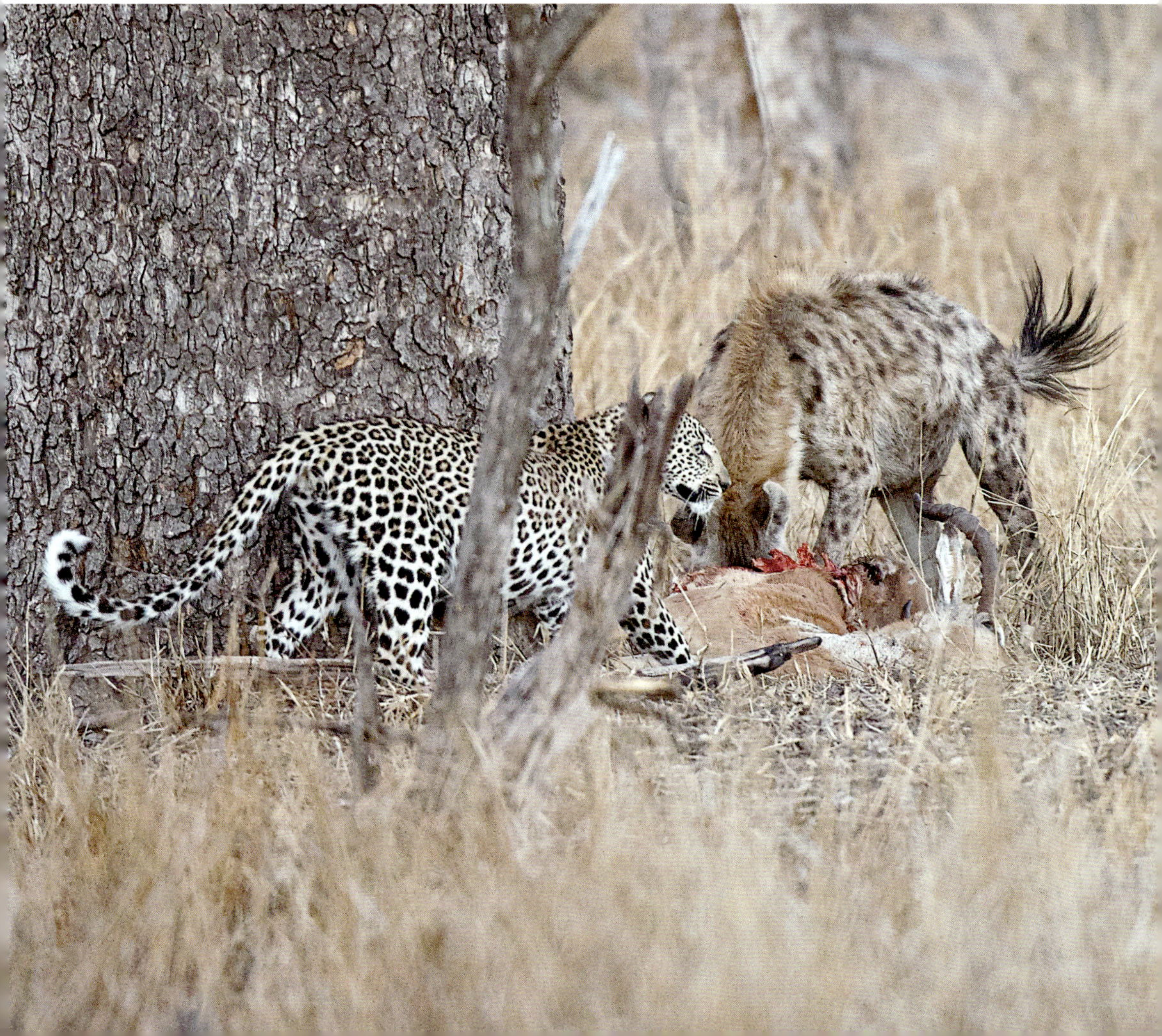

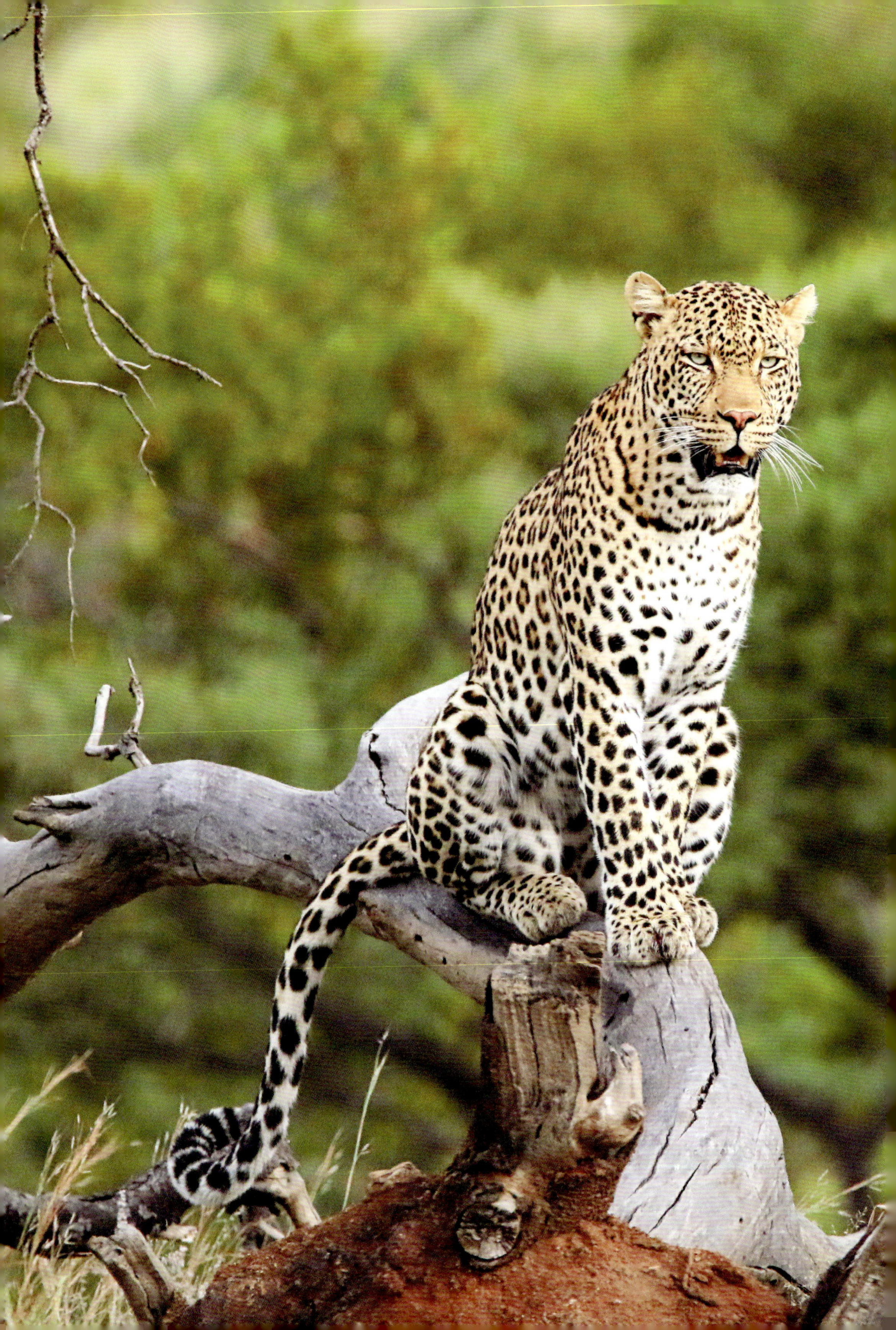

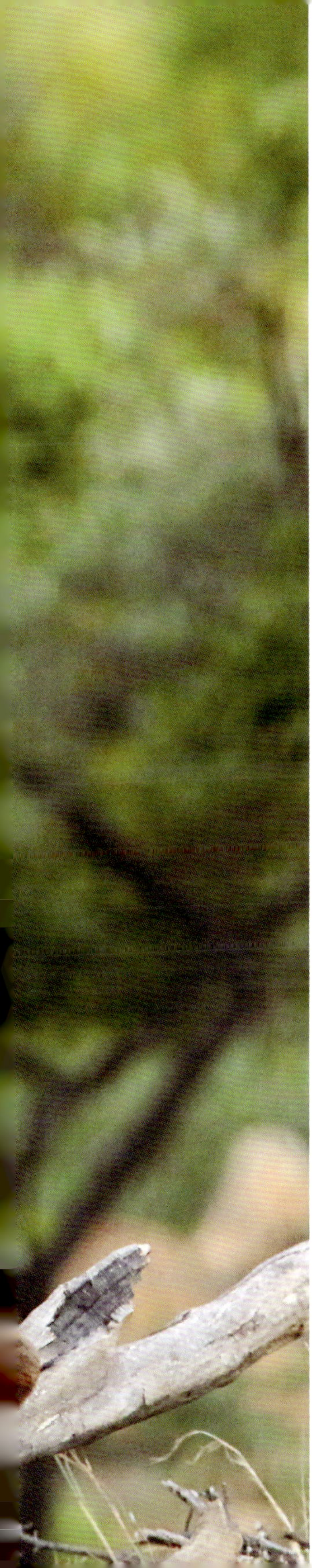

Watching him watching us

SHAWN CATTERALL

The wildebeest were all standing to attention, staring intently in one direction, which means one thing: a predator of some kind. Our guests were watching them from the main deck of the Tshukudu Bush Lodge in the Pilanesberg Nature Reserve during high tea. We got the binoculars and viewing scope out to see if we could locate the cause but the trees were in the way.

I suggested we move closer and didn't need to ask twice. Our guests rushed to jump into the vehicles and we were off, the visitors speculating about what it could be.

By the time we got there, the wildebeest were relaxed again with some even lying down and although we searched, we found nothing to explain their earlier alertness. I couldn't believe I had misread the situation so badly. Perhaps whatever had caused that reaction had gone up into the mountains. We decided to head out on a drive anyway and as we came down the access road, I glanced up towards the mountain.

And then I saw it – a tail – a white-tipped tail. I pointed excitedly. The guests' heads whipped to the right and then there was mayhem as they spotted the male leopard, walking on top of the ridge.

This was a phenomenal sighting because we'd never seen leopard in the daytime at the lodge before. I knew the guests would want to take some good photographs, so we followed the leopard but he kept slipping out of sight. I called the other vehicles to the scene. With extreme patience we waited on the downhill and then I think the leopard decided he wasn't going to get away with hiding in the rocks because he came down and jumped over the road in front of our vehicle. There was breathless silence apart from the clicking of cameras. I was so excited I couldn't have uttered a word even if I'd wanted to.

We followed the leopard up the opposite side of the hill. He was very shy and didn't show himself, so again we waited patiently. He reappeared. In our sight line there was a huge, dead tree pushed over by an elephant long ago. The leopard climbed onto the bare tree and there he posed for about 10 minutes, while in deathly silence, we watched him watching us.

After granting us this opportunity to capture him digitally in all his regal magnificence, he came down and climbed into another tree a little further away and fell asleep. Our guests' faces were full of emotion, which is the ultimate sight for a guide. We spent about 10 more minutes in photographic awe before leaving him in peace to sleep.

Perhaps three times in the last 11 years we've seen leopards close to the lodge at night but all we glimpsed was the flash of their spots. So this was a gift, a treat beyond words. On the drive back the guests were quiet, reflecting on this special sighting and musing on the mystery of leopards which are so secretive and elusive and yet can evoke such deep emotions in those who see them.

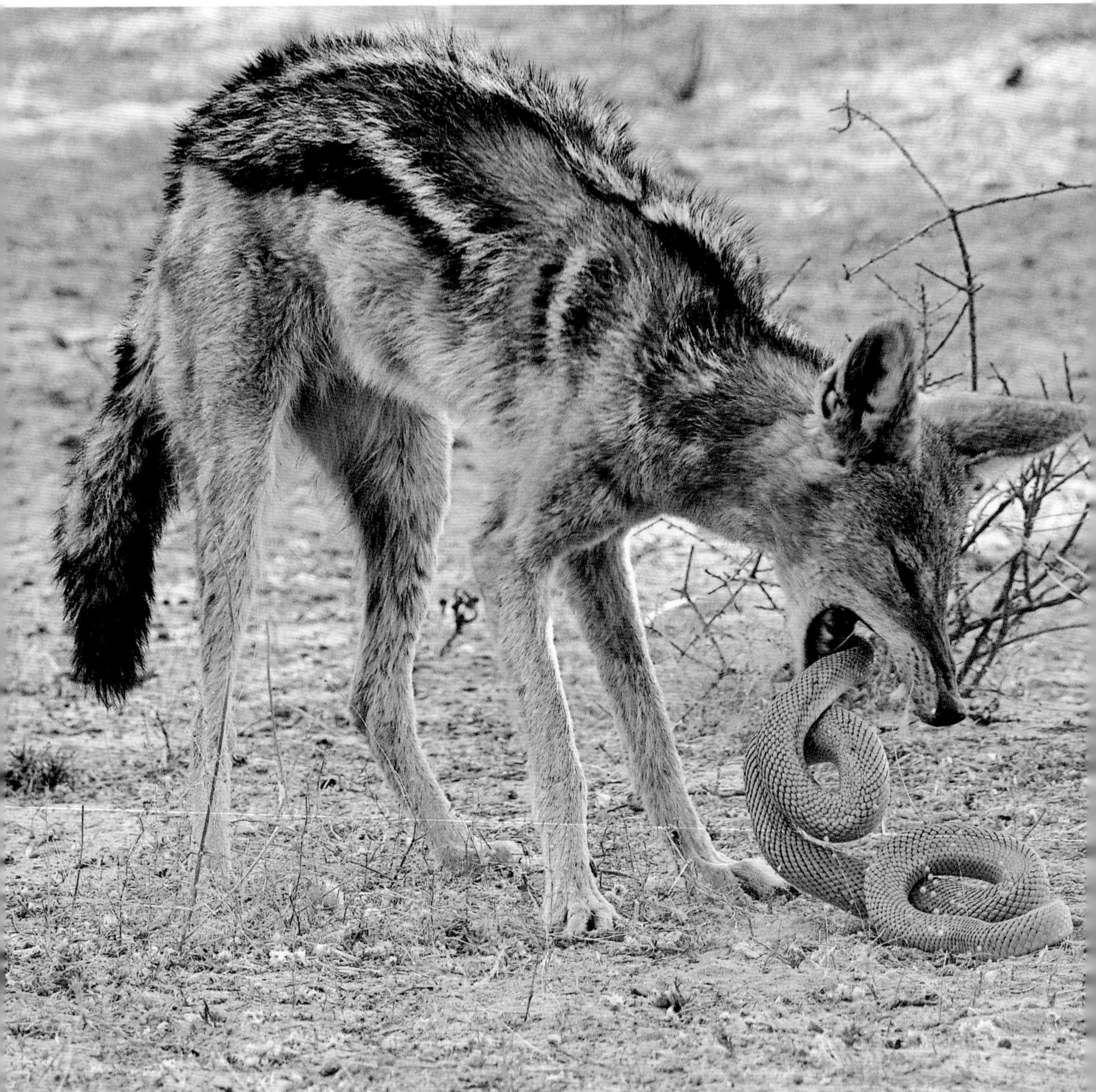

Give me whatever's on the menu

TRACY FICK

On a trip in October 2015 to the Kgalagadi Transfrontier Park, we had left Nossob to travel south to Twee Rivieren. It was about 8:00 when we came across a skinny and hungry-looking jackal staring down at what looked like an old car spring. When we looked more carefully, we realised it was a mole snake.

The jackal was not going to be fussy about what was on the breakfast menu and began to eat the snake. Although it fought back valiantly, twisting itself around the jackal's legs and nose, the snake had no real chance and it lost the fight. The jackal eviscerated the snake and devoured its meal.

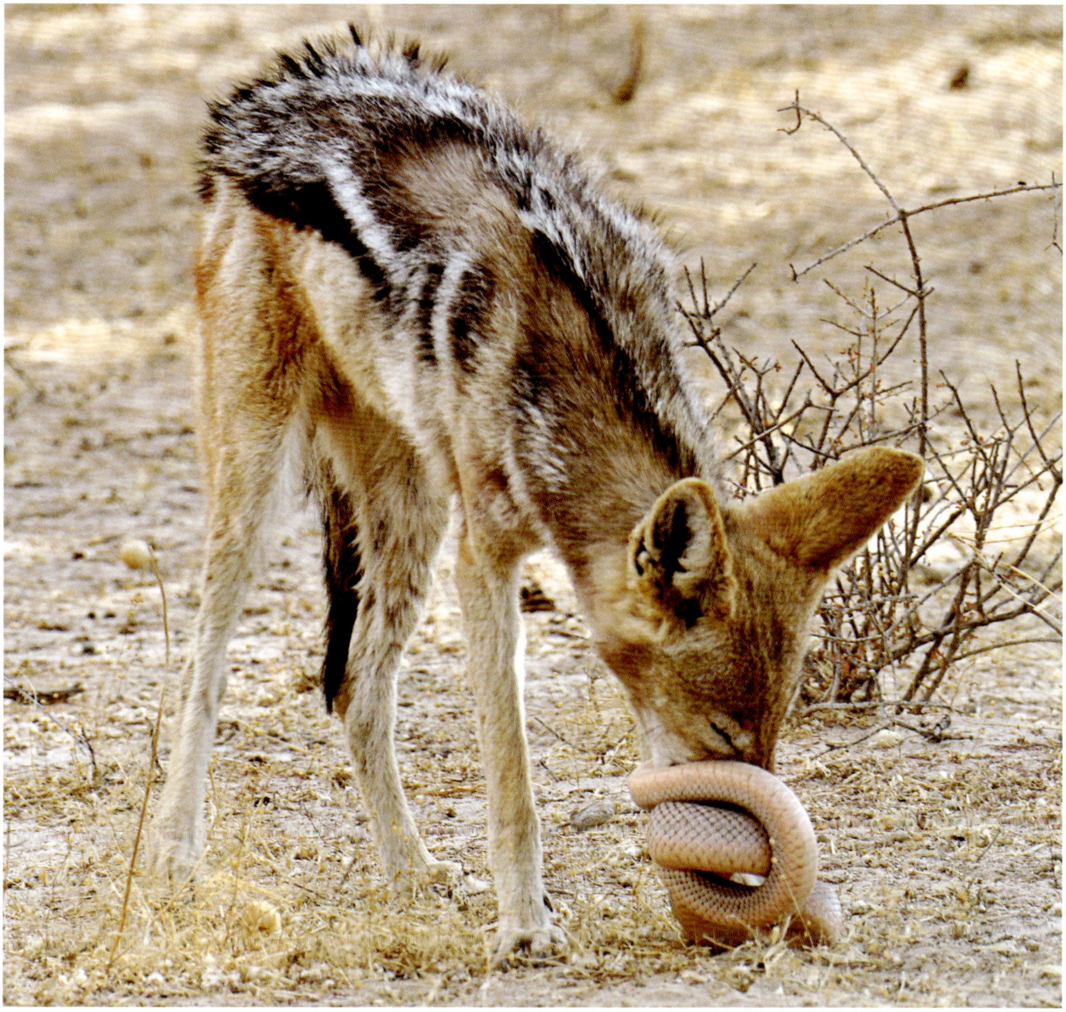

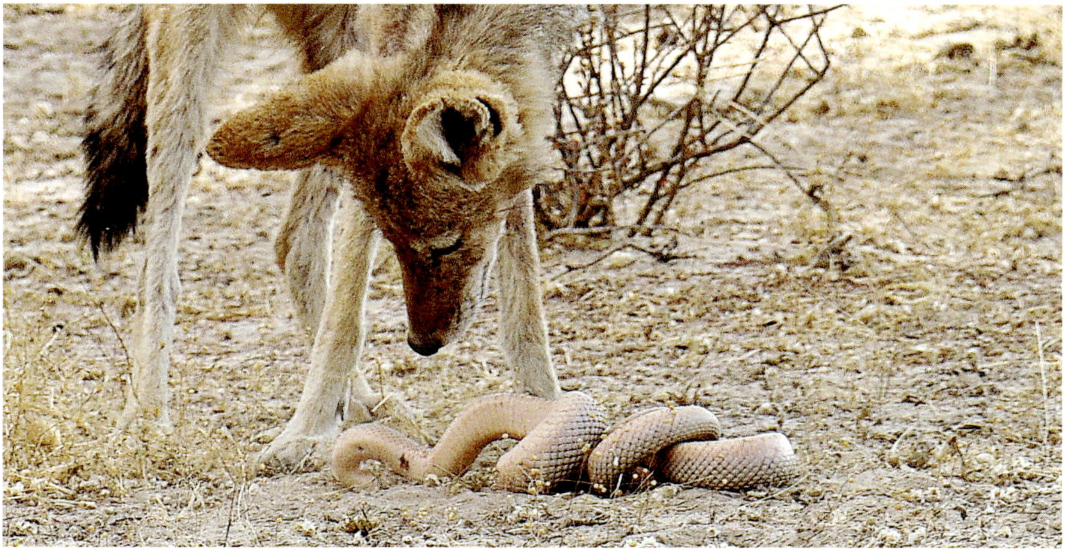

A dream come true

CALLUM EVANS

We got up at 5:15 in the morning at Third Bridge Campsite in the Moremi Game Reserve, situated on the edge of the Okavango Delta in Botswana, on a mission to find wild dogs. I had never seen wild dogs in their natural environment before and I was dead set on finding a pack here. I knew that quite possibly we wouldn't see any but I had high hopes.

Driving through the forest, we saw nothing at first. The only signs of life were the calls of woodland kingfishers and Senegal coucals. The Cruiser screeched to a halt and I looked up to see Stewart (who was driving) pointing to the road ahead, where about 10 wild dogs were standing. And then 10 became 30 as the entire pack, including 12 half-grown pups, trotted down the road towards us and walked right past the car. I was so thrilled by my dream coming true that I wanted to cry. A whole pack of my favourite animals was right in front of me and the reality was better than any pictures. They had to be some of the most beautiful creatures I have ever seen.

We spent about 45 minutes following them and watching them as they moved about. Some members of the pack rested while the pups played tug-of-war with dead palm fronds, and they even attempted to hunt four lechwe bulls. But the most interesting part of the sighting was when the entire pack gathered around the old carcass of a sub-adult giraffe. They were transfixed by the remains, sniffing every inch of it. Now and then, one dog would jump back as if it had received an electric shock. Our theory was that the giraffe had been killed by lions and the smell of lion caused the reaction, though I've never witnessed such behaviour before in person or heard of it via media of any kind, so the jury's still out on that one.

After a while, the pack slowly lost interest and trotted in single file back into the forest. I'd had my dream realised and I couldn't have been happier.

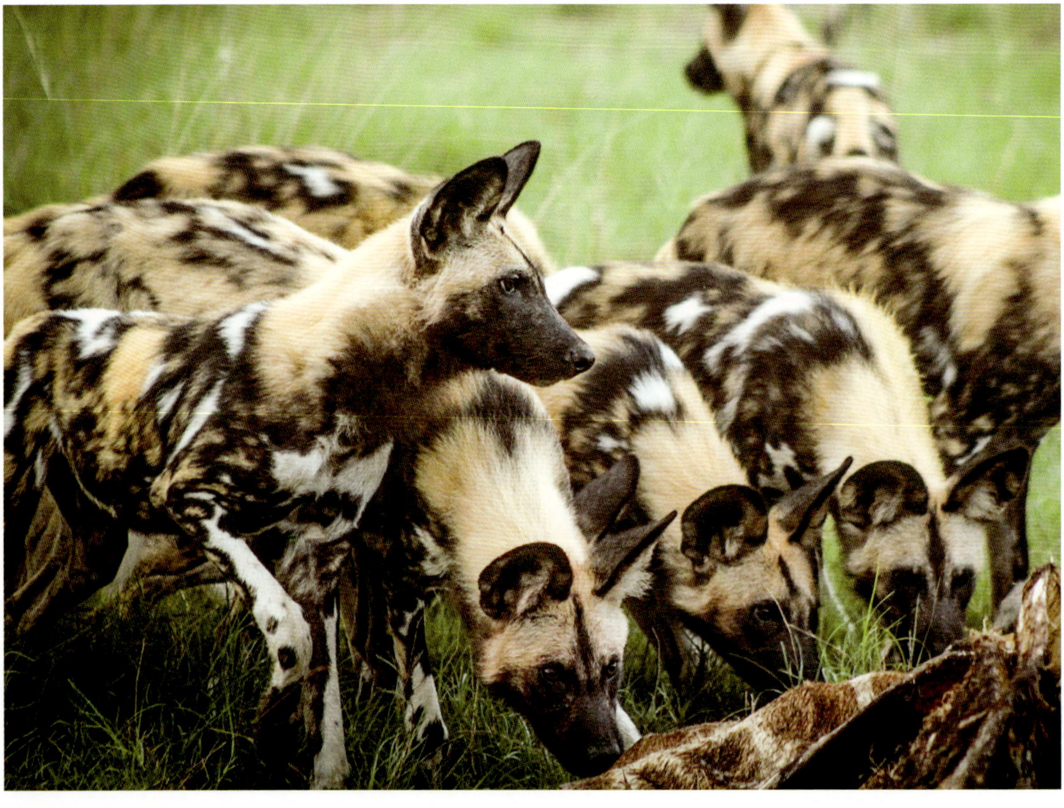

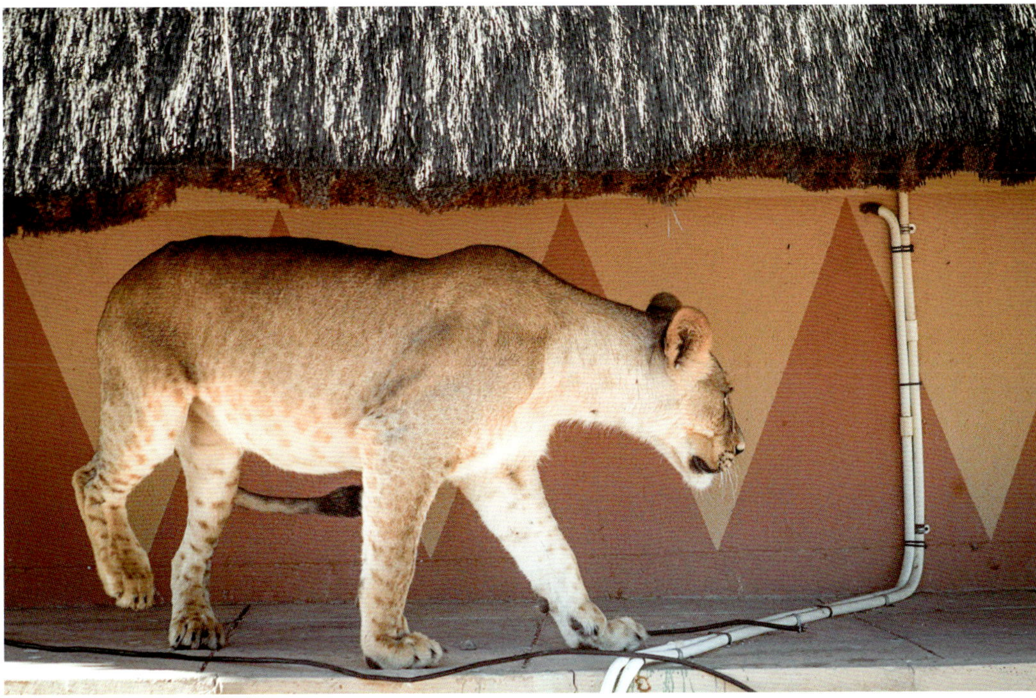

Welcome to the Kgalagadi!

CALLUM EVANS

It was my first time in the Kgalagadi Transfrontier Park and we were spending the night at the Entrance Gate Camp at Mabuasehube. We'd spent the afternoon driving around in search of lions but with no success and by 19:00 we were unpacking our things and beginning to set up our tents and camp chairs.

I went to look at the lion tracks which had been left in the camp the night before but when I was walking back to our own campsite, I heard the sound of something being tipped over to my left. I turned to see a massive lioness in the campsite next to us. This was enough to send all of us straight back to the Land Cruiser. As we watched, one lioness became two lionesses, followed by their seven adolescent cubs. They finished causing havoc in the neighbours' campsite and were moving towards ours. The sub-adults came incredibly close to the Cruiser and stared at us while their mothers glared at us from a more comfortable (for us) distance. We watched with some alarm as two of the males began chewing on one of the camping beds. This was too much, so we drove the vehicle towards them to stop this destruction of our property. But this strategy backfired since one of the males ran off into the bushes with it! And that was the last we saw of that camping bed.

We spent the next three hours trying to drive them away from our possessions and simultaneously trying to stuff our things back into the car. Eventually we got everything in and the rangers arrived to escort us to the fenced staff camp just across the road because the lions showed no sign of moving along.

Funnily enough, when we entered the staff camp, we obviously didn't shut the gate properly because one of the young lionesses managed to get in and she stayed in the camp until the rangers drove her out just as we woke up. When we left to drive around the reserve, the pride was lying around the entrance, their inactivity a stark contrast to a few hours earlier. Now that's what I call a Kalahari welcome. Oh, and to crown it all, that night we had a leopard sleeping 10 metres from us in the next camp we stayed at.

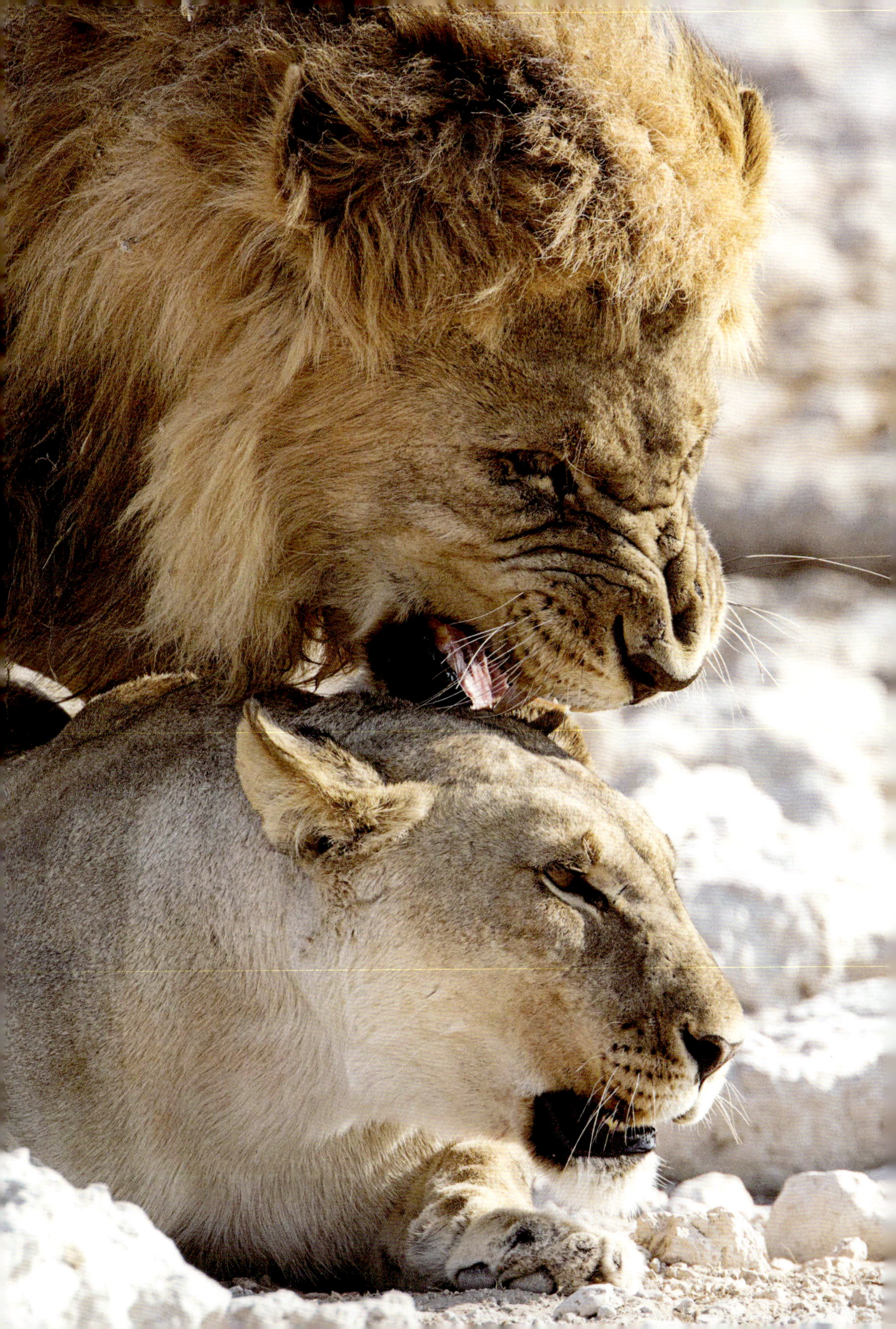

Lions in lust

CAROL POLICH

The roars and snarls were tumultuous. My stomach churned as though it were in a spin dryer and practically vibrated from the deafening sound. The facial expressions were right out of a horror movie. Lions in a state of lust take no heed of anyone or anything else around them. The area they claimed for their sensuous acts are off-limits, and herds of zebras, springbok and other ungulates wait impatiently on the periphery to quench their thirst. Lions can mate for a period of three to four days. The rhythm of the mounting occasions during a 24-hour period is absolutely precise, as I found out.

With my heavy 500 millimetre lens perched on a beanbag on my car window sill, I was at the ready for their romantic liaison when the lioness got up from a restful lying position to approach the patiently awaiting suitor. Coyly, she rubbed up against him. It was time for more of the vociferous and wild theatrics as she crouched, and he mounted. This manoeuvre only took a couple of minutes. I had to manoeuvre my own car position to shoot their expressions and then get full body shots with another camera and lens. After toothy, gaping mouth-to-mouth engagements and a harmless bite to the neck (common in mating cats), she told him to buzz off for a while.

I began timing their passive interludes and realised I could take a break and rest my hands, arms and mental focus for 17 minutes. When 15 minutes had passed, I lifted the equipment onto my beanbag and sure enough, the lioness was once again ready for her suitor to approach. She beguiled and teased him. With his face to hers, he gave her a gentle, starry-eyed look. She rebuffed him by looking away. Attempting to charm her, he licked her and begged her on his knees. A 'gentle' roar erupted and he opened his mouth, showing his canines. She succumbed to his blandishments and was enticed into his massive paws. All the same, I wasn't deceived that he was totally in charge because before long the balance of power shifted again. After she had been seduced, it was time for her to reclaim her independence, roll onto her back and to ignore his impertinent paw nudges. A lioness will take her own sweet time before allowing the foreplay to begin again.

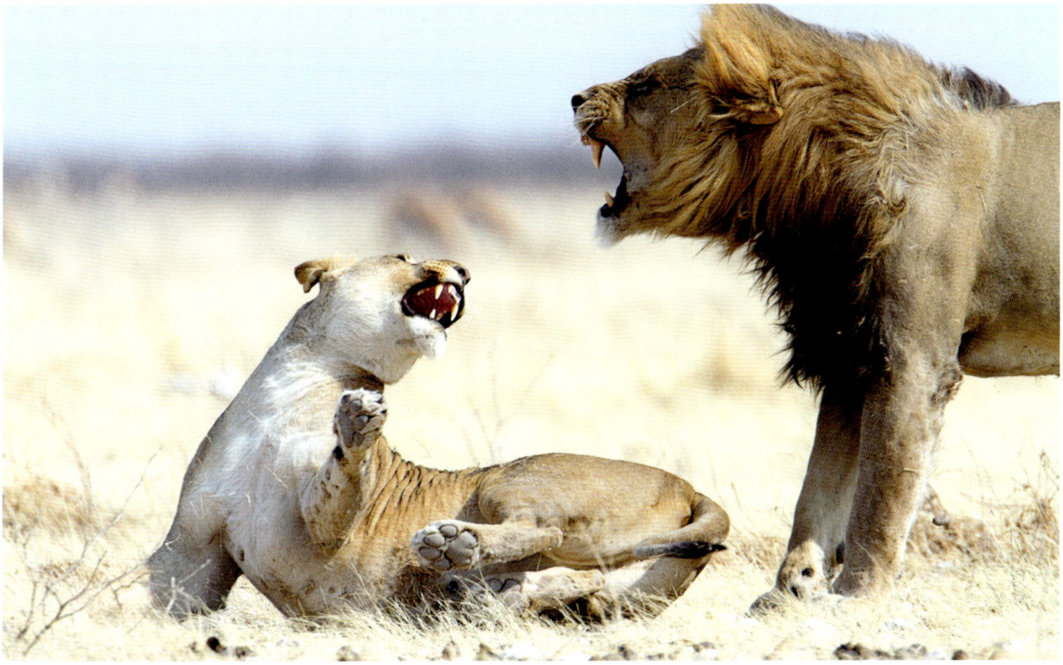

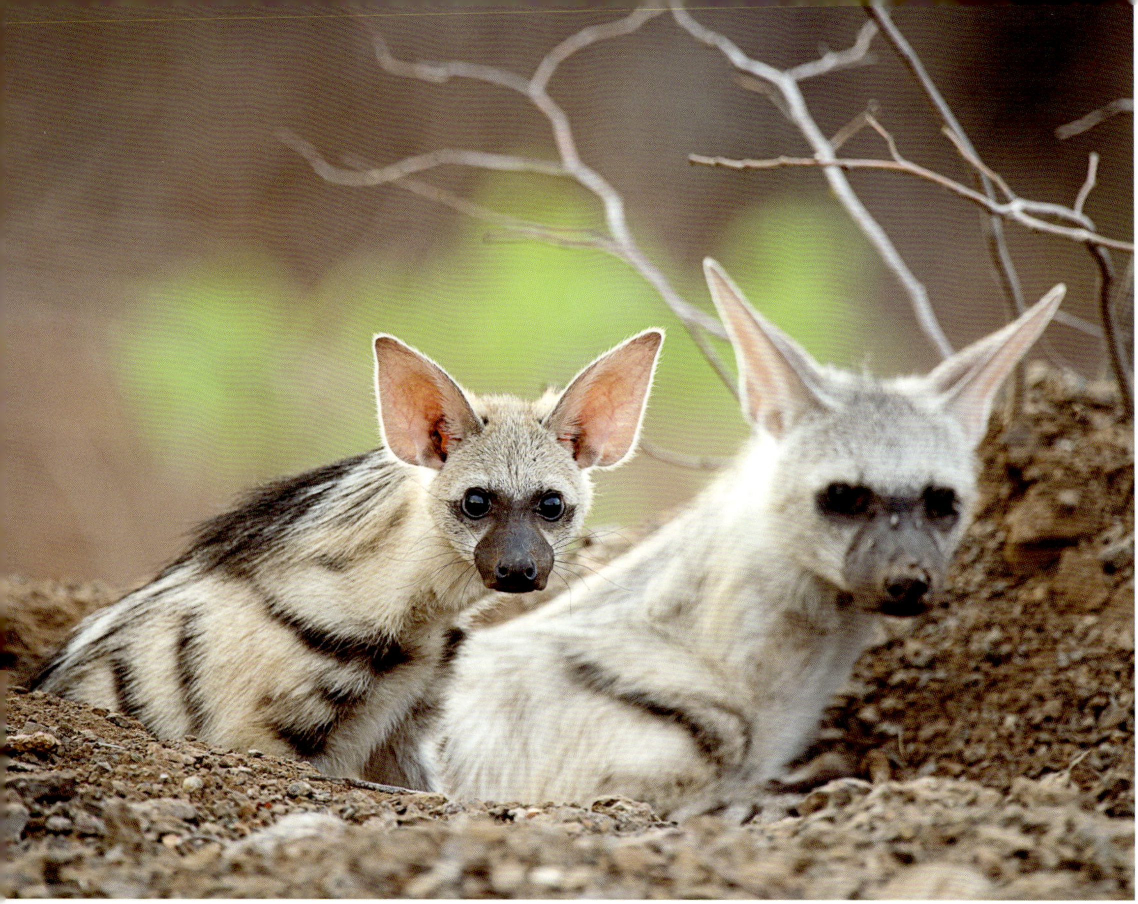

A tale of an aardwolf, jackals and a hare

LIZ HART

I often wonder why we keep getting up so early in the morning to go on a game drive. What keeps us so committed to that drive, especially in winter when we can hardly move because we have so many layers of clothing on? I suppose the simple answer is no day is the same and every game drive provides a new chapter and story, full of adventure and special experiences. Sometimes the moments are difficult to capture in photographs and instead remain only as extraordinary memories.

One exceptional game drive occurred while we were on safari in the Mashatu Game Reserve in the southeastern corner of Botswana. We had heard of an aardwolf den near camp and had arranged to leave extra-early in the morning, hoping to catch a glimpse of the mother aardwolf and her pups. When we arrived, we were in luck because we found her lying at the entrance of the den with her young. Needless to say, the camera shutters went into frantic action at such a rare sight. What made this sighting so remarkable was that she was not in the least concerned about the vehicle and merely lifted her head slightly to survey our whereabouts and then continued dozing. Aardwolves tend to be shy and often run away when they see a vehicle, yet this one was totally relaxed. We continued to photograph them as it was such a wonderful opportunity to be near an aardwolf den with an unperturbed mother and her offspring.

A short while later black-backed jackals began calling, startling the mother aardwolf who became agitated. She immediately alerted her pups to the imminent threat and they promptly vanished into the underground den. The mother aardwolf then ran out to fend off the jackals who had just discovered a scrub hare and were determined to catch it for their morning meal. The aardwolf bristled, making herself twice the size in order to scare off the jackals; something we had never seen before and gave us some insight into aardwolf territorial behaviour.

In the meantime, the jackals were so intent on catching the hare that they didn't see the mother aardwolf until they were almost at the den. She immediately gave chase to scare them away.

Aardwolves do not eat other mammals but feed primarily on termites. We knew, therefore, that she was not set on killing the jackals, but merely intent on deflecting and chasing them far from her den to protect her babies.

It was like a theatrical farce: the aardwolf chasing the jackals, who were chasing the hare. But in the commotion the hare spotted a safe haven in the form of the aardwolf den, where the pups were sheltering. It bolted into the den, vanishing underground. The mother aardwolf continued to chase tho jackals further away from the den. When she was eventually satisfied they were far enough away, she returned to the den and her family to relax.

As for the hare, we didn't spot It again. Could it have stayed in the underground den, having made a home with a new and unorthodox family?

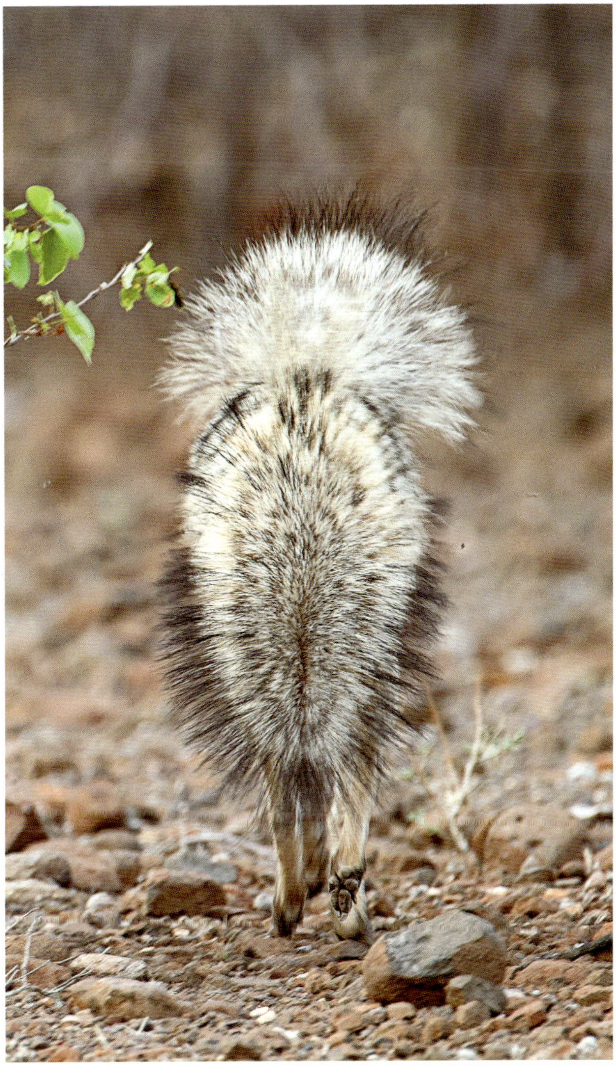

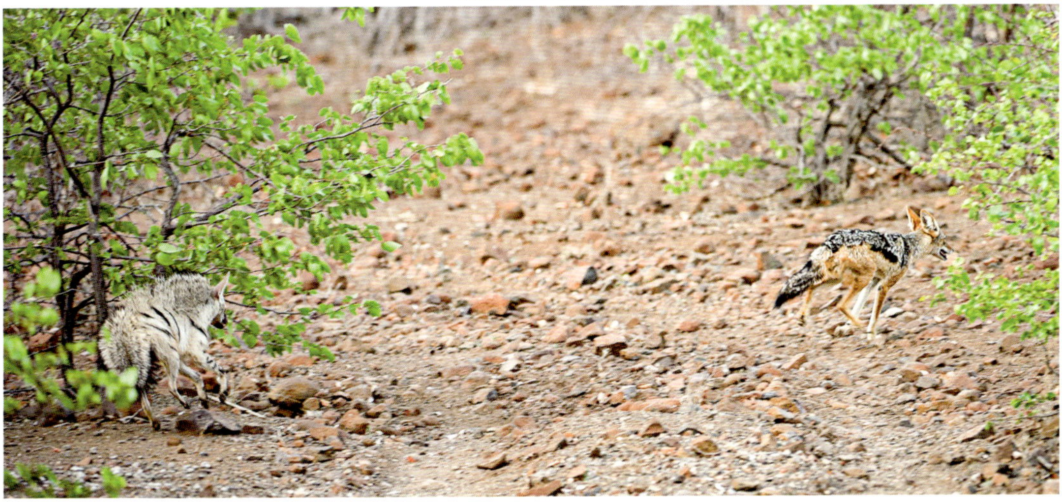

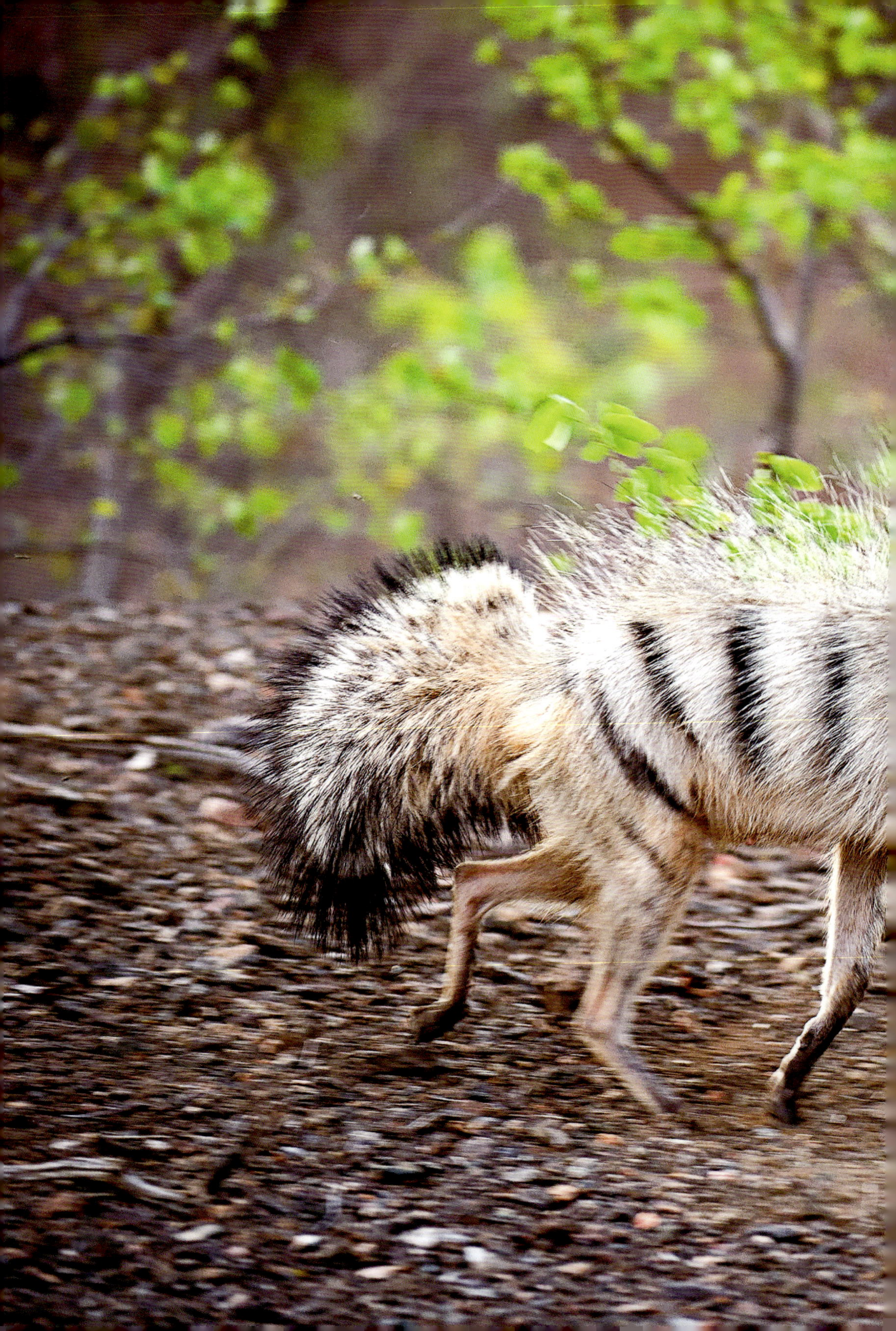

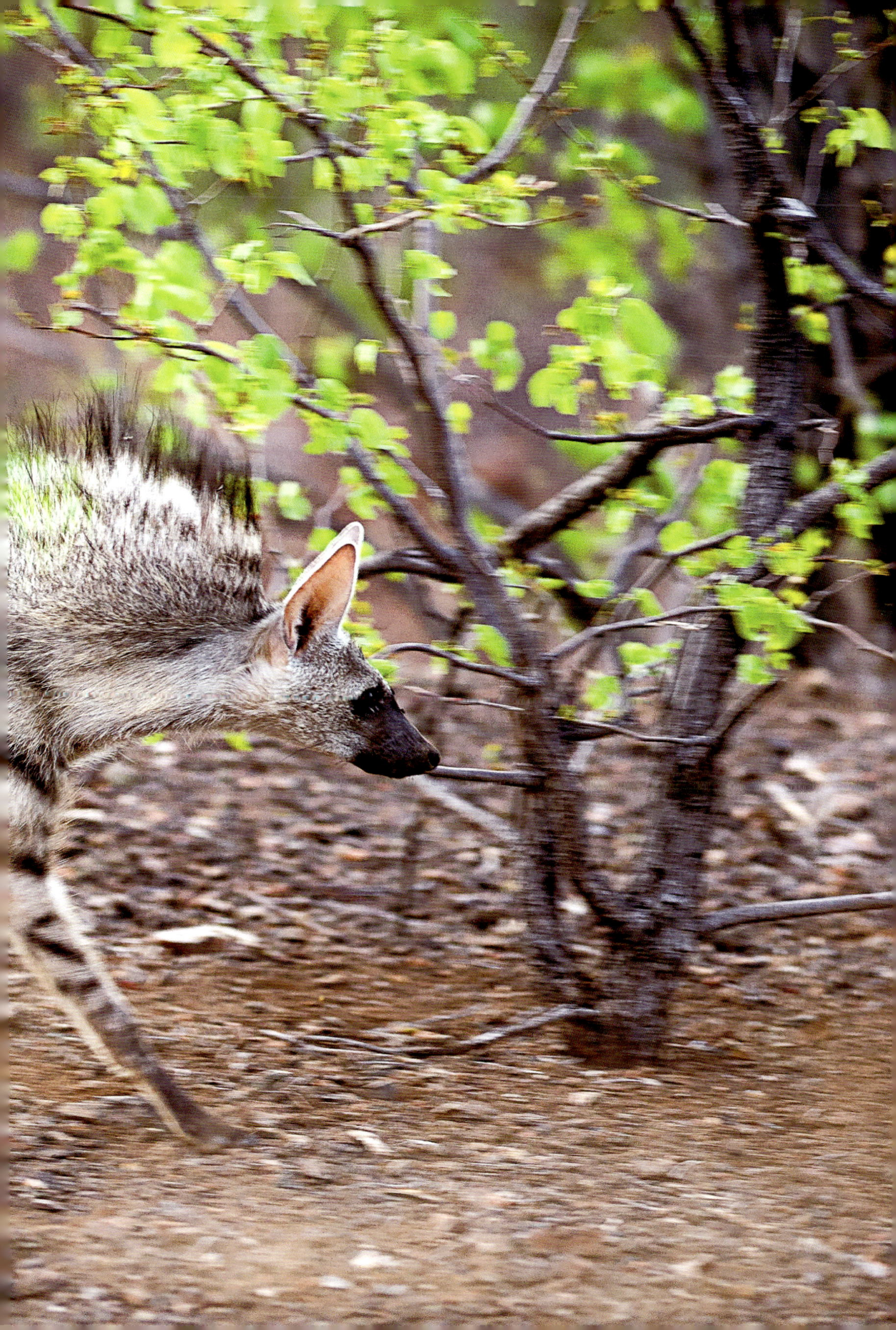

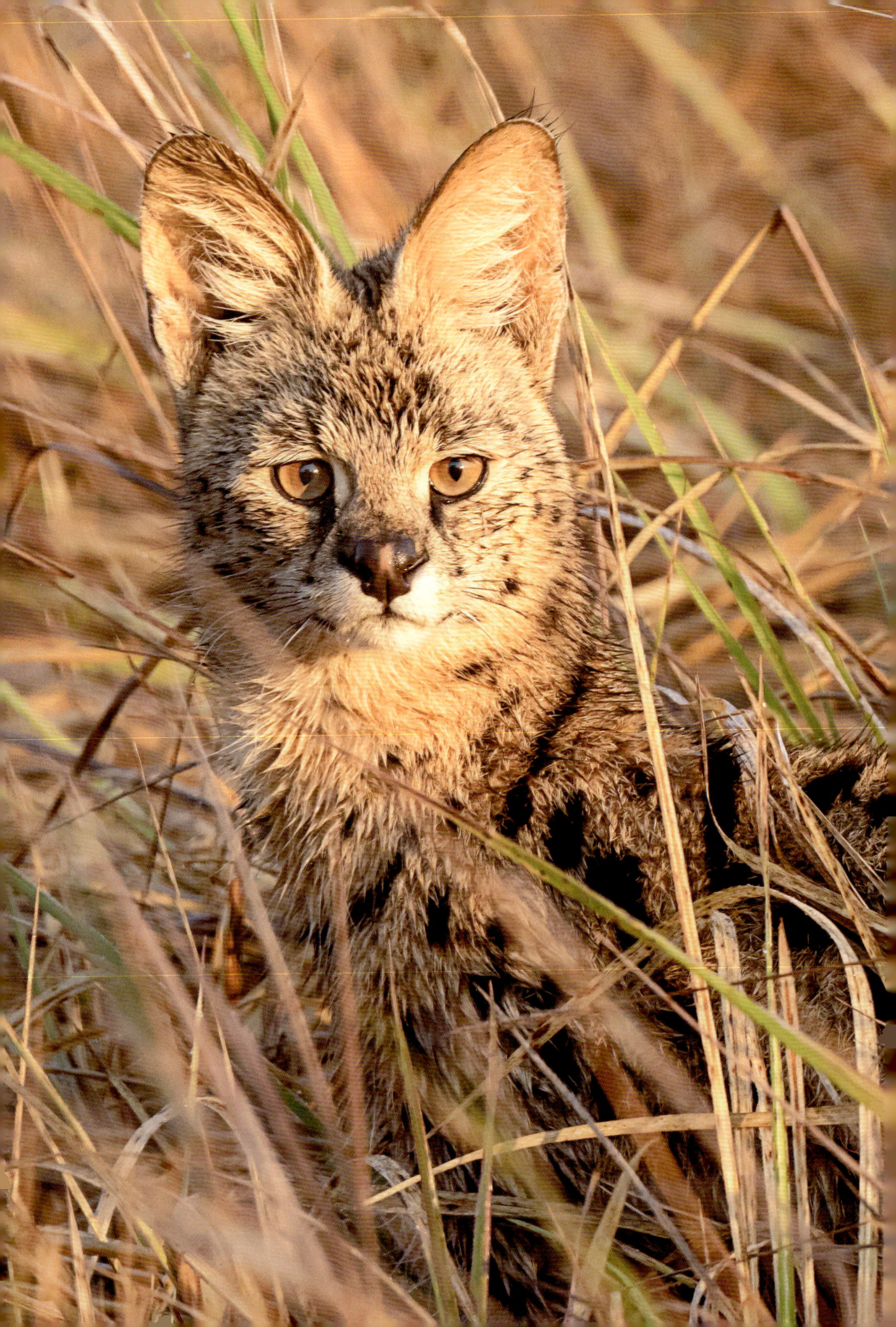

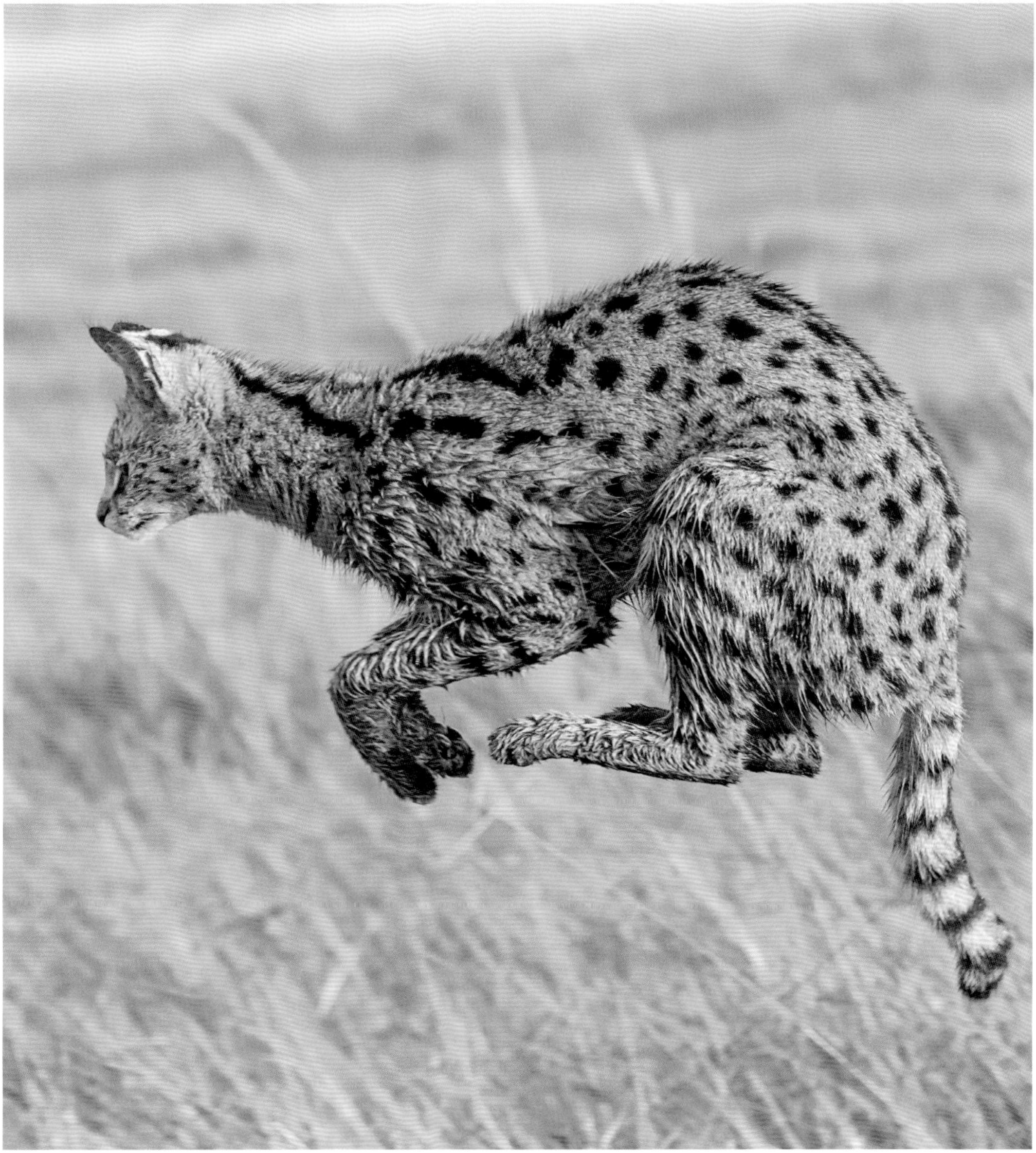

Small-time hunting in Kafue National Park

EDUARDO GARCÍA DEL ÁLAMO

This episode occurred when I was staying in Nanzhila Plains Safari Camp in southern Kafue, Zambia. I was driving along early one morning when suddenly I saw a serval jumping in the grass, close to my car. It stopped and watched me for a few seconds before the imperative of food took over and it continued hunting. This was a lucky moment for me because I could take a few good photographs.

In fact, this was not the only serval I saw during my stay at Nanzhila Plains. I was fortunate enough to see three different servals. The pictures in my mind, and my photographs, serve to remind me of what an amazing reserve Kafue National Park is.

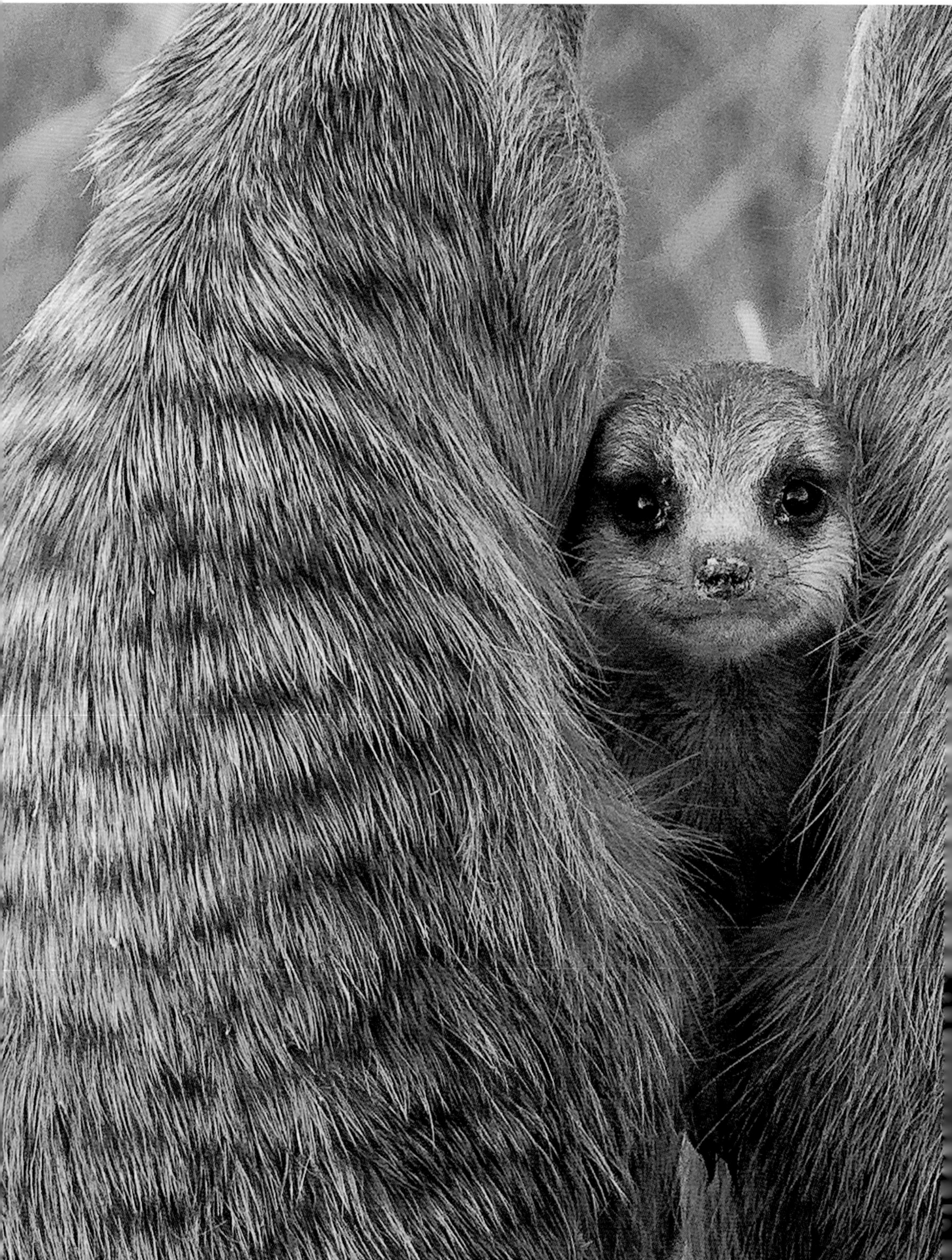

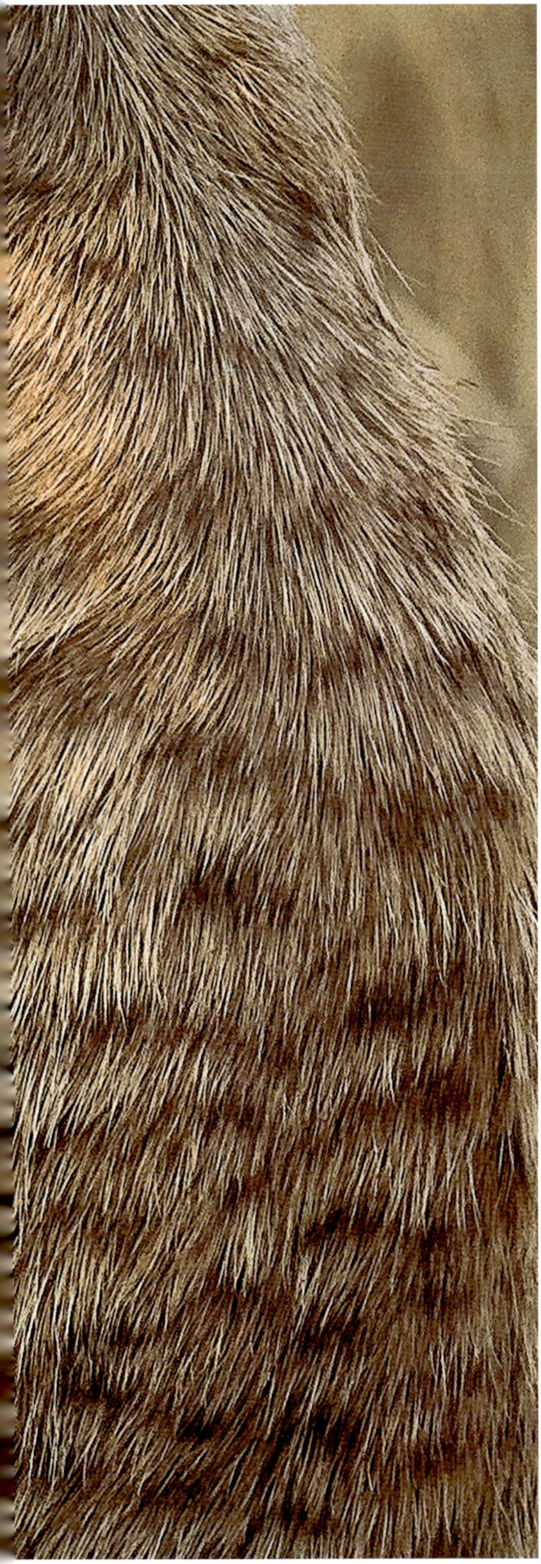

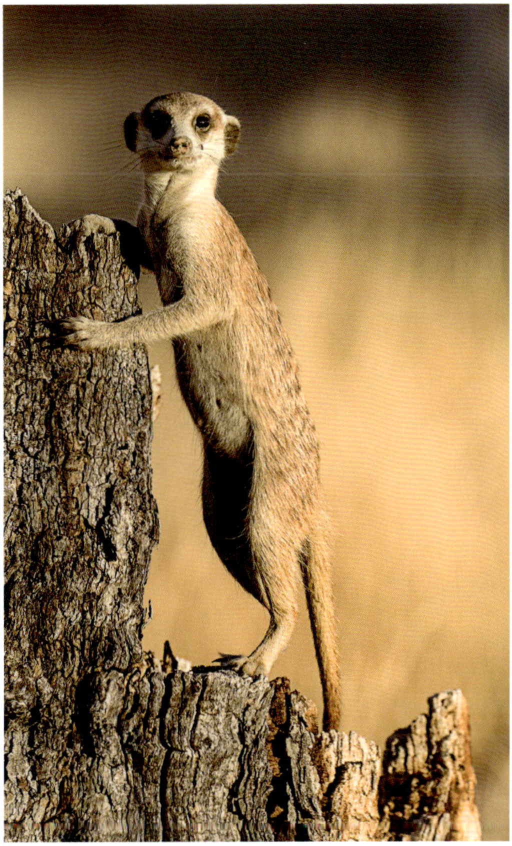

Life in a meerkat family

EDMUND AYLMER

On a trip to Mata-Mata Camp in the Kgalagadi Transfrontier Park, we had the privilege of photographing the daily comings and goings of a family of meerkats that had taken up residence in a burrow behind the chalets. In the morning the family, including the pups, would emerge from the burrow to warm and groom themselves before setting off on their foraging activities. It was fascinating to watch as the sentinels kept watch over the family from a suitable vantage point, sending out 'all clear' or alarm calls.

After the morning grooming session, the adults moved off leaving the babysitters to attend to the pups. In the late afternoon, the foraging members returned to the burrow to connect with the rest of the family for grooming and feeding before retiring for the night. The golden light provided superb photographic opportunities.

The scorpion king

BILAL MOSAM & SAFIYYA LAHER

Our last days spent in a reserve always have a bitter-sweet feeling to them. On the one hand, there's regret that the adventure is coming to an end. On the other, there's excitement because you never know whether Mother Nature has a last surprise in store for you.

And boy, did she have a treat for us! We headed from the Kalahari Tented Camp to Twee Rivieren in the Kgalagadi Transfrontier Park and enjoyed a few special sightings along the way: a cheetah in beautiful morning light calling for his brothers, two male Kori bustards fighting for dominance, a honey badger foraging for food in the riverbed and a leopard and cub walking along the calcrete ridges in the distance. Yet our next sighting was one we'd often hoped for but never thought we'd be close enough to enjoy.

We had come across a colony of meerkats searching for food along the riverbed, and even though it was quite late and the light was harsh, we decided to take some photos since they were so close to us. They were actively foraging and we spent some time with them. After about five minutes or so, one of the meerkats came within two metres of us to search on the top of the bank.

As we locked onto it, it was already up to its middle down a burrow. It quickly emerged with a slender-tailed scorpion in its mouth. This was the moment we had hoped for and it was happening right in front of us. We watched in silence, a silence broken only by the crunch of the scorpion's exoskeleton as the meerkat's needle-like canines pierced through it. Within seconds the scorpion was totally devoured. As soon as the first meerkat was done, a second one pulled out another scorpion. Our attention switched to that one and we watched again in awe as it efficiently devoured its meal.

During our stay, we met a man who said to us, "The Kalahari reveals itself to those who come to it with a pure heart." Well, the Kalahari certainly revealed itself to us in the last few hours we spent in the park on that occasion. I'd like to think this was indeed due to the purity of our hearts while we watched, humbled by one of nature's small wonders.

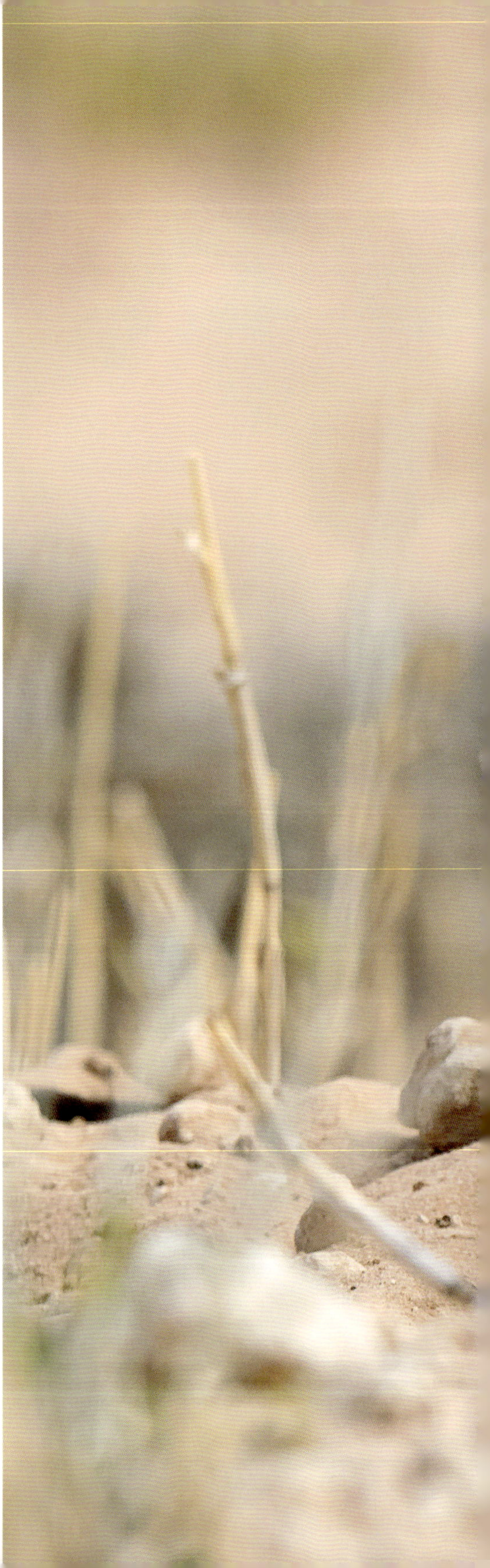

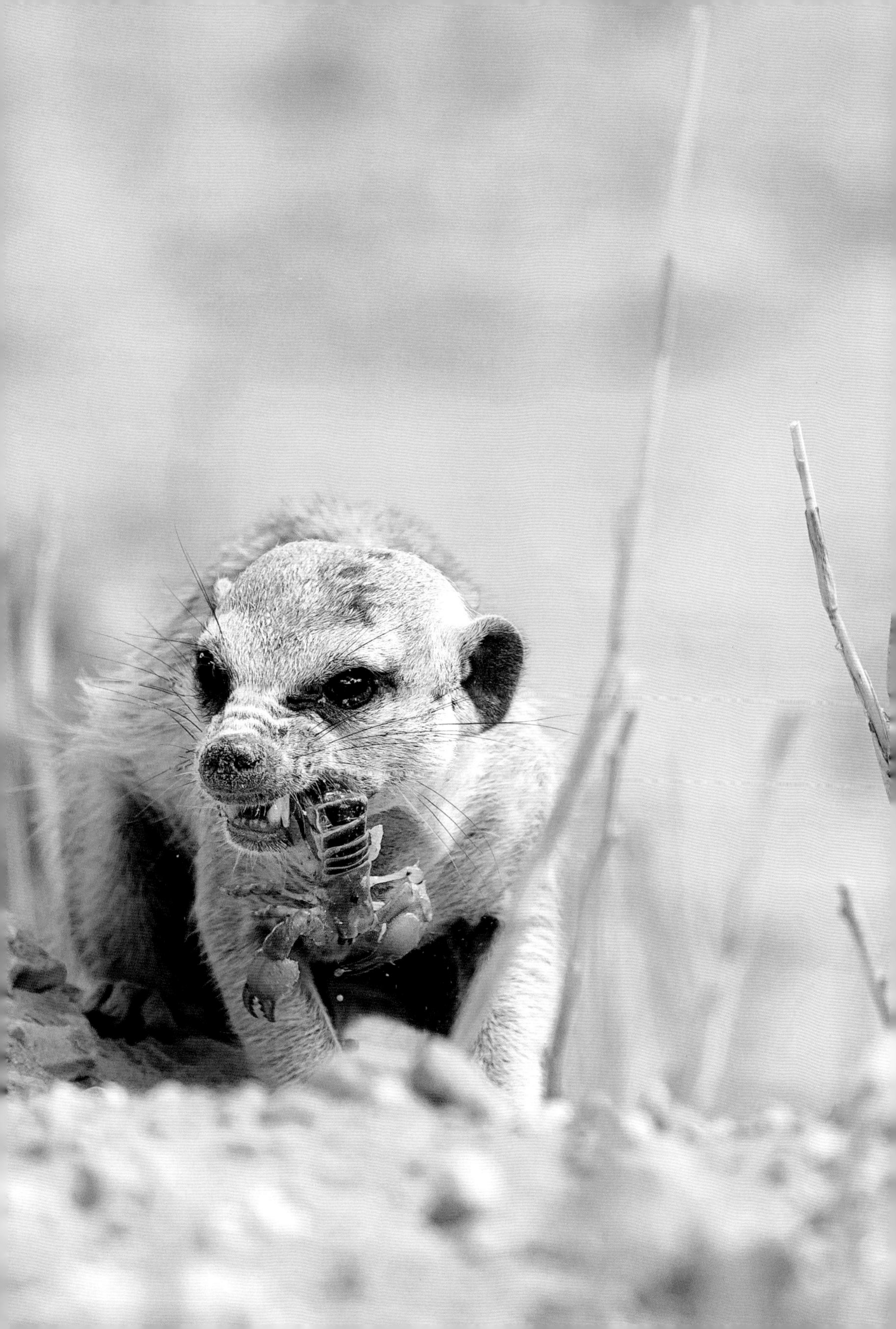

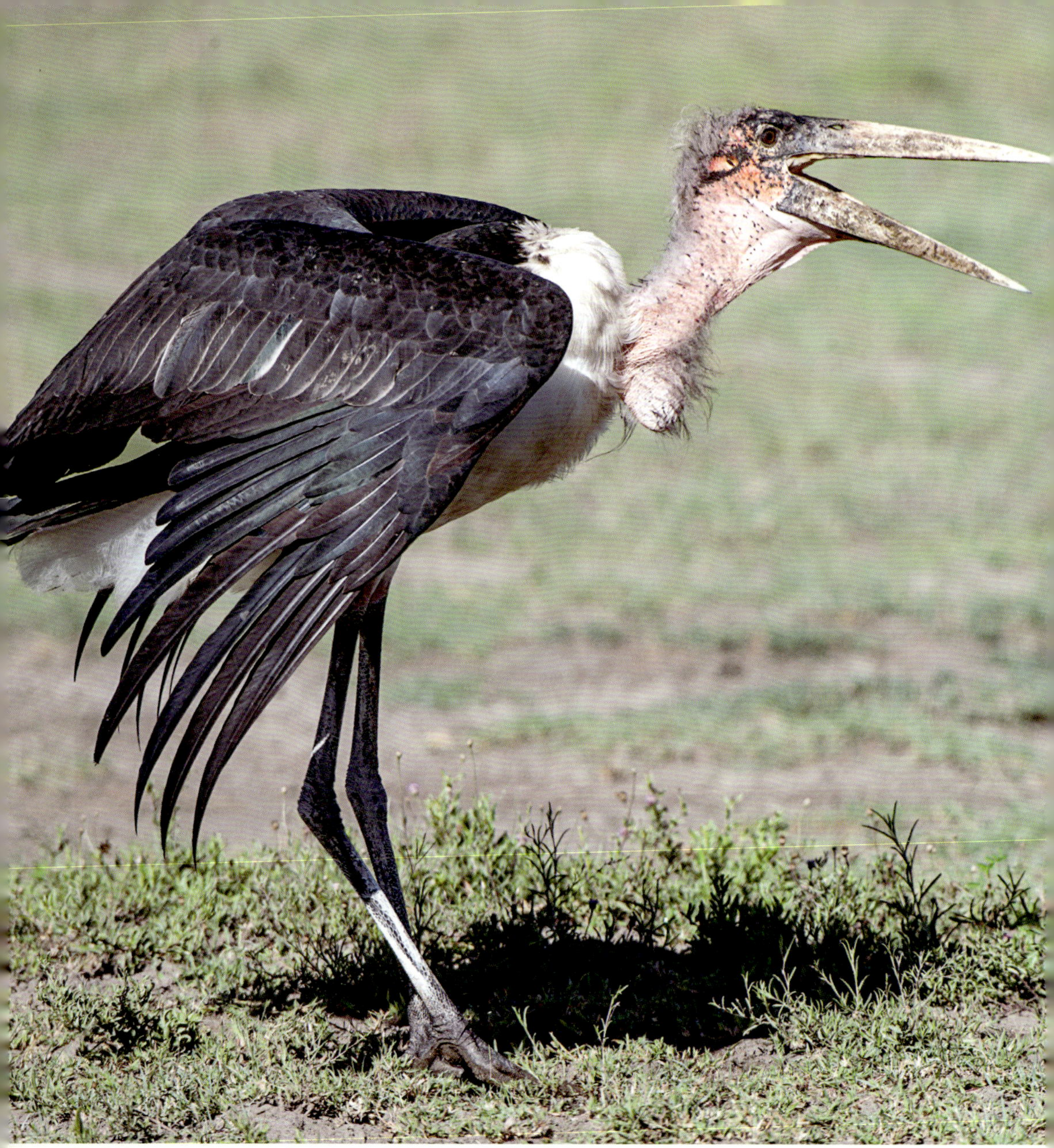
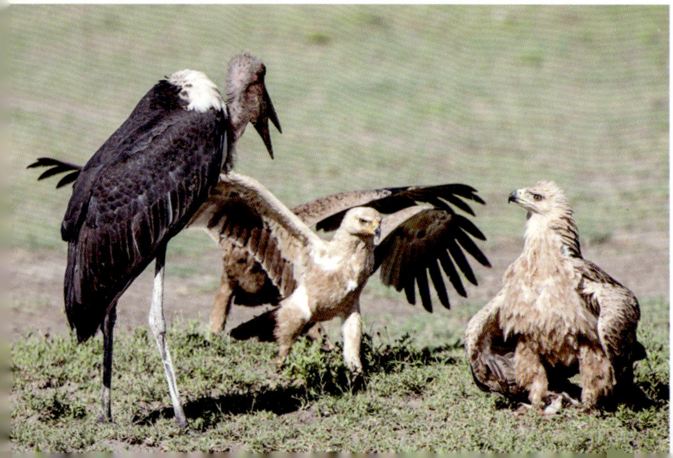
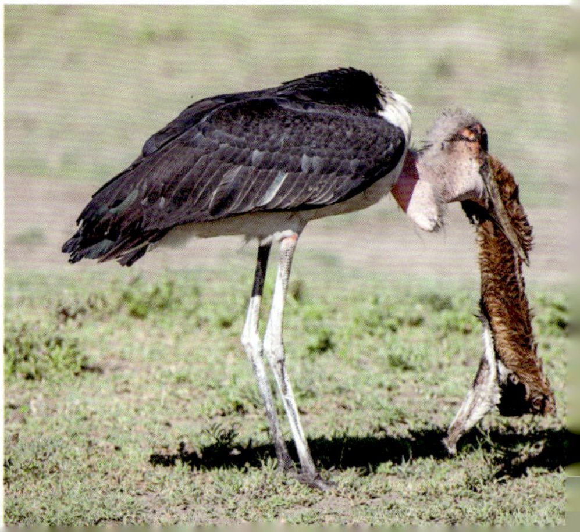

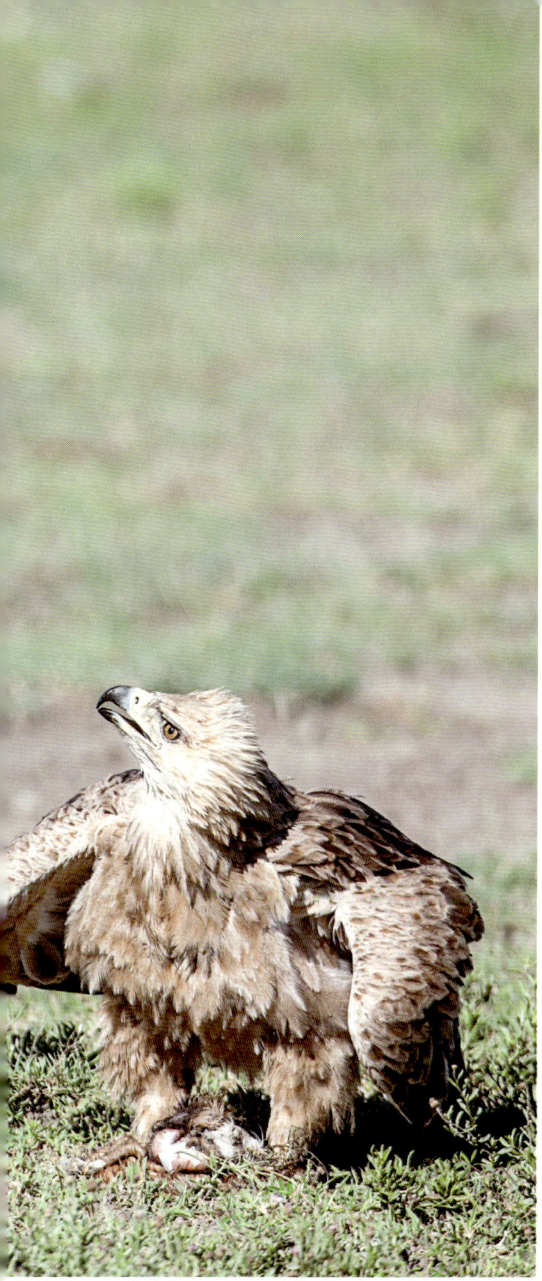

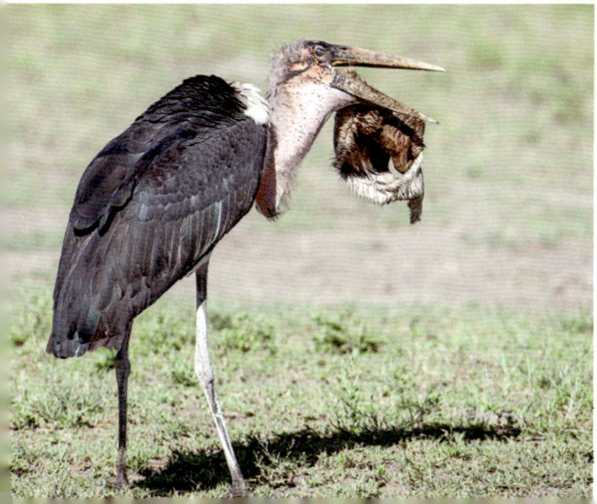

Greed

JEAN DU PLESSIS

On a trip to the Serengeti in the Ndutu region, which lies in the Ngorongoro Crater Conservation Area, we unexpectedly came across a tawny eagle tearing away at his rabbit catch. A marabou stork arrived on the scene and made a grab for the rabbit. Then two more tawny eagles appeared to help the first one, it seemed. But they were no match for the determined marabou stork which evaded the eagles, snatched the limp body of the rabbit and gulped it down, skin and all. The tawny eagles looked as if they were utterly shocked and more offended at the greediness of the stork than at the theft of the prey.

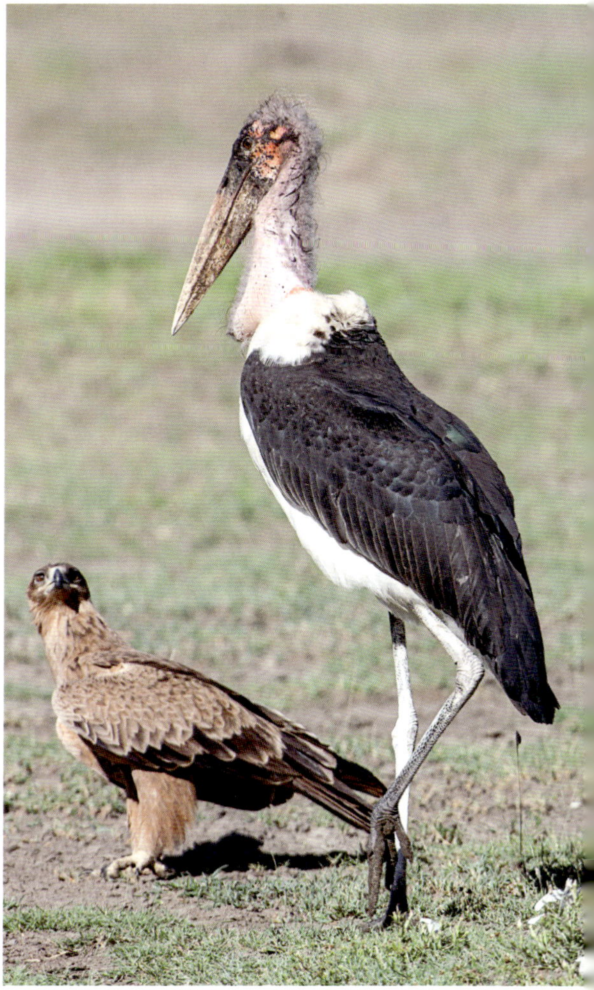

A three-sided battle

JEAN DU PLESSIS

We were out on a safari drive east of Seronera, in the western part of the Serengeti, when we saw a tawny eagle attacking a secretarybird. The secretarybird had a rabbit and the tawny eagle was trying to claim it. The eagle grabbed the rabbit but hadn't reckoned on the secretarybird's tenacity. The bird attacked the eagle with its long powerful legs and pinned it to the ground. Eventually the eagle managed to grab the prey but in the meantime, a third contender had turned up – a jackal approached at speed and tried to snatch the rabbit from the eagle.

At the end of the battle it was the eagle that triumphed. Almost mockingly, it soared above the other two with its booty in its claws.

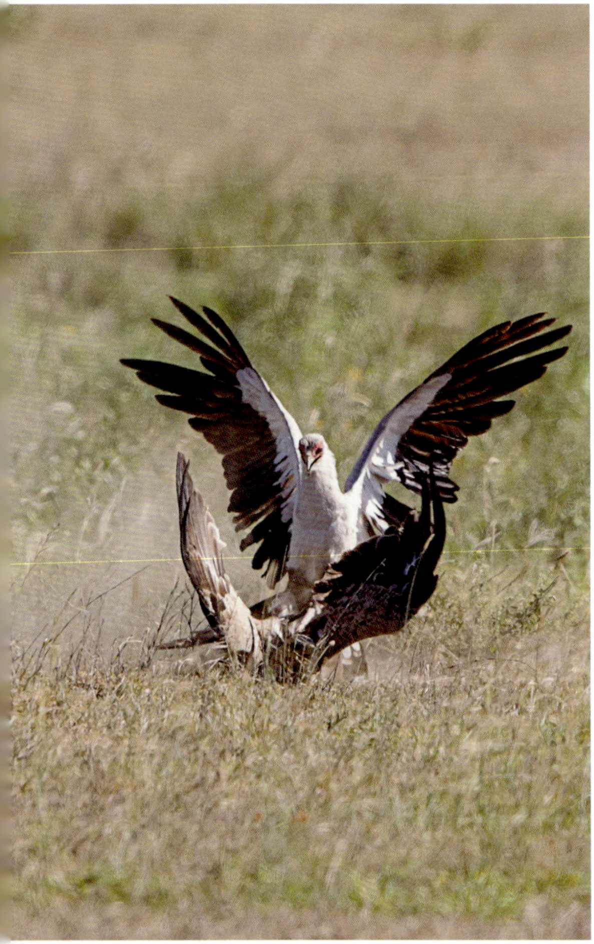

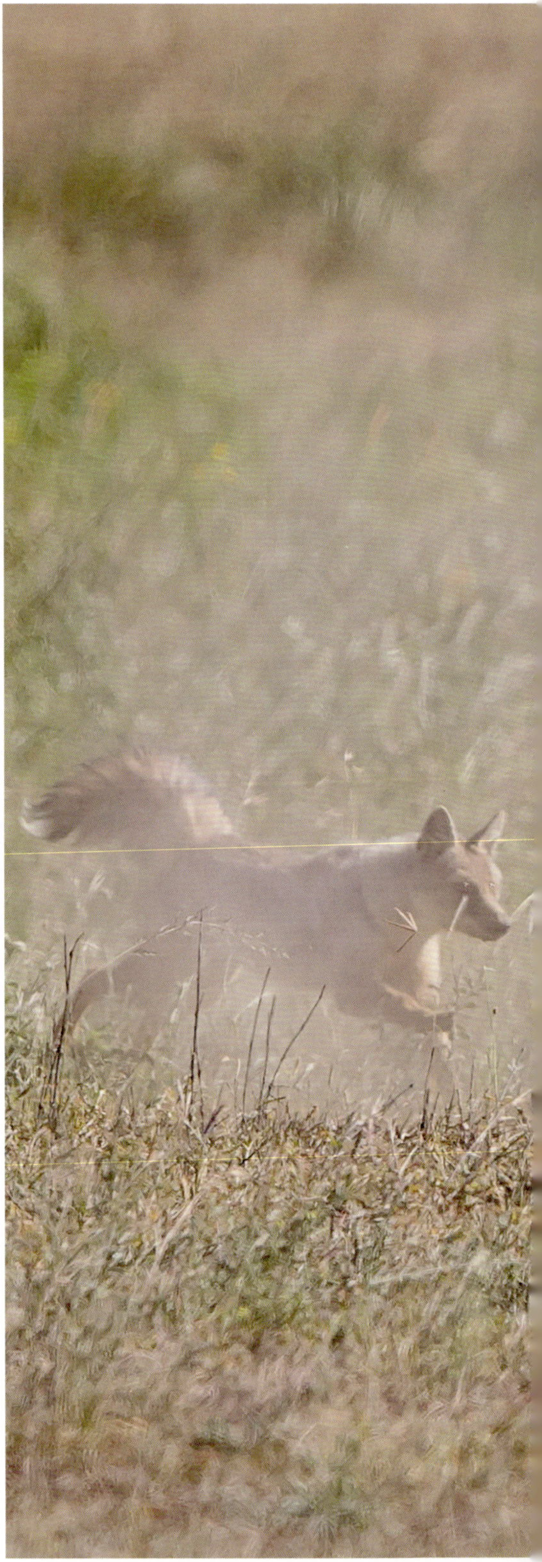

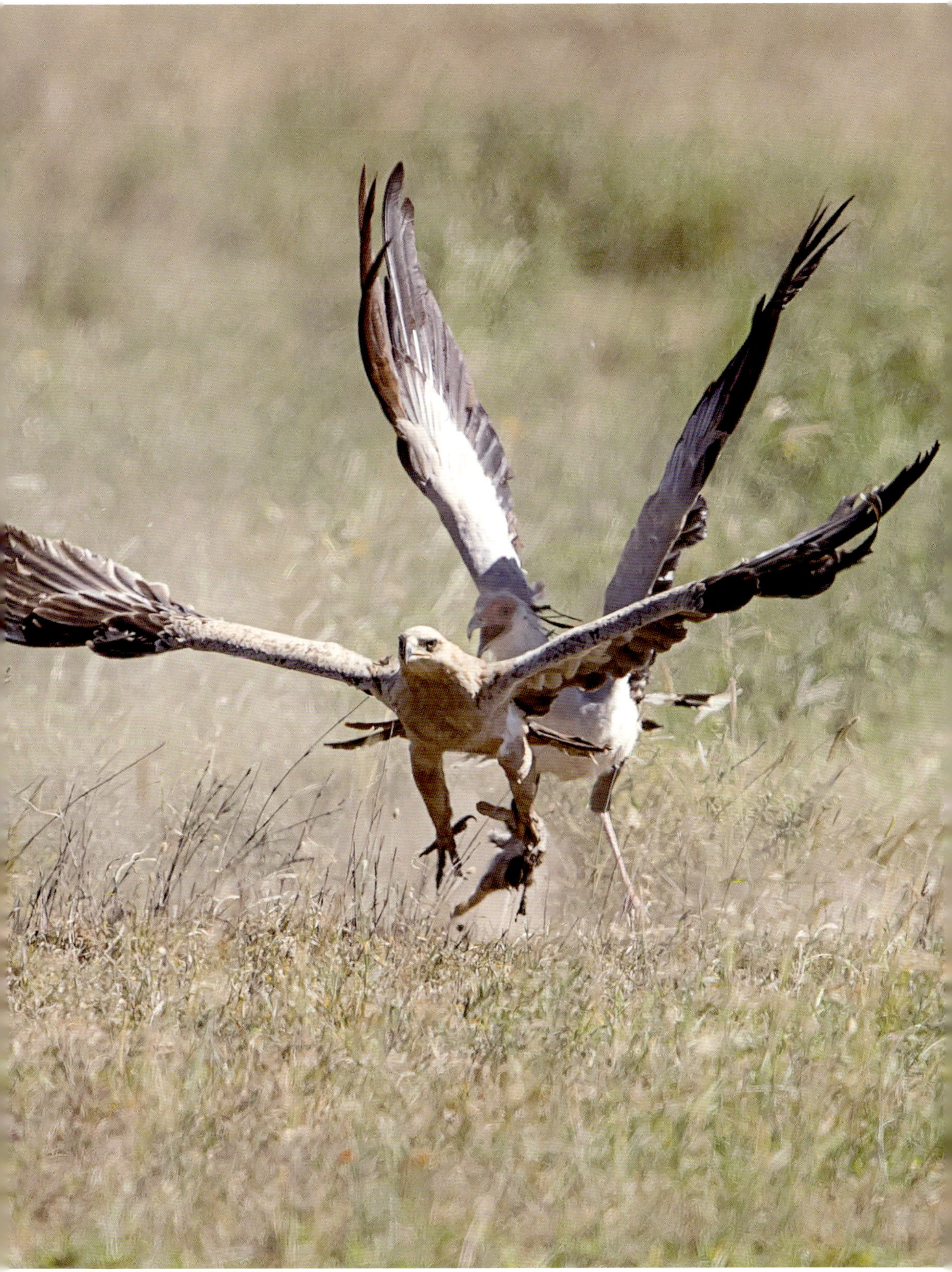

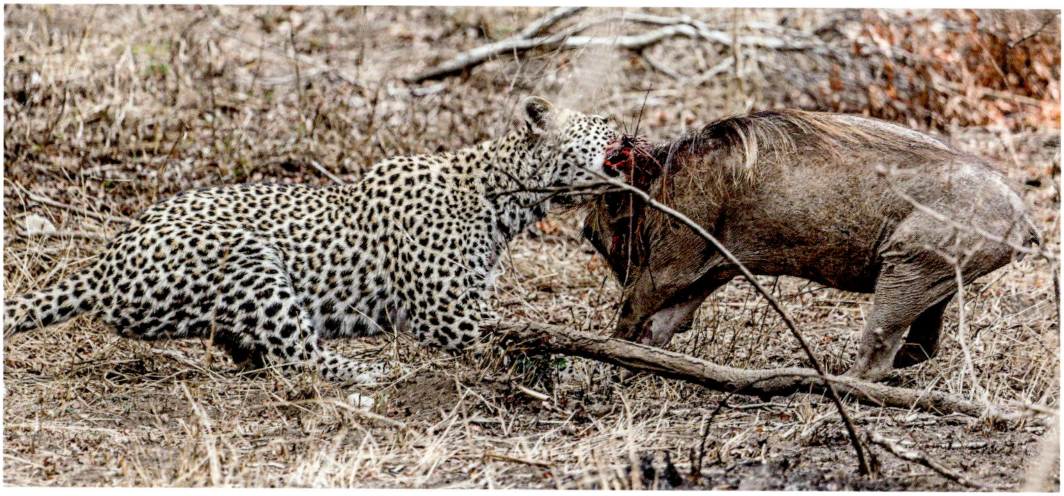

Nature gives with one hand and takes away with the other

HENDRIK DU PLESSIS

It was late afternoon when we were on our way back to Crocodile Bridge Camp, although we were not keen for the day to end yet. Suddenly we heard the terror-stricken squeal of a warthog and were lucky to find the source quickly. A leopard had caught the warthog and the battle for its life was in progress. The warthog was not going to surrender easily. The struggle went on and on. At one point both were so exhausted they just lay there. In a last desperate effort, the warthog jumped up but this time the leopard got hold of its throat and cut off its airway. The death throes must have lasted at least 10 minutes.

Even though the leopard had finally overcome its victim, it jumped up, abandoned its meal and ran past us. We understood why when a lioness burst onto the scene. The unfortunate leopard could only ascend the nearest tree to safety while the lions took over and squabbled over the carcass in the last light of the day. We agreed this rated as one of the highlights of our visits to the Kruger National Park.

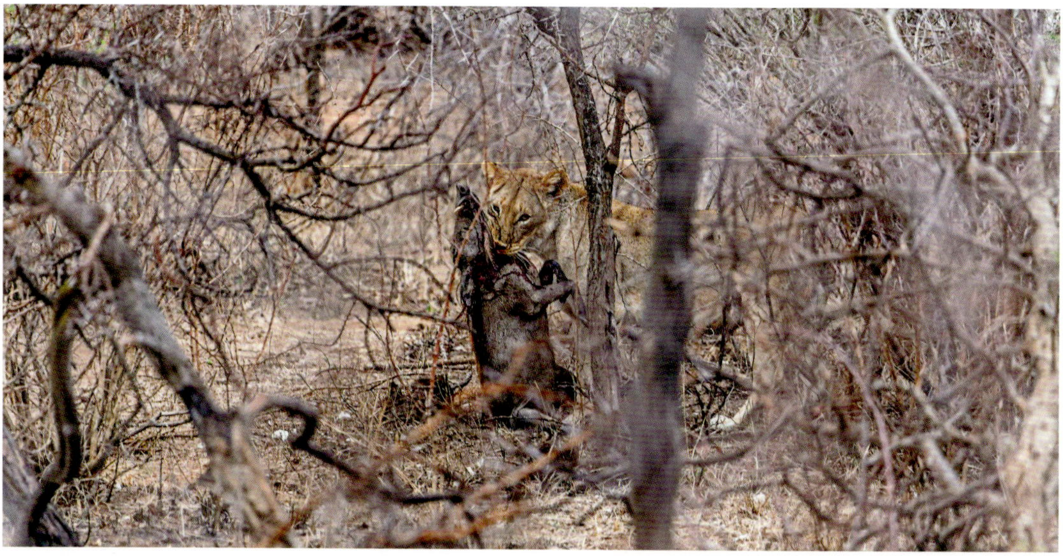

An epic encounter

THOKOZANI PHAKATHI

It was an early Saturday morning a few years back. We were around 300 metres from Skukuza Camp in the Kruger National Park when we came across about a dozen buffalo bulls lazily resting next to the road chewing the cud. We were busy taking shots of their faces and horns when we noticed some nervousness and unusual restlessness among them. Those standing started sniffing the air, running around with their tails up and nudging those resting as if to say, "Get up, fellows, danger is looming."

When we looked further into the bush through the thickets, we saw three majestic male lions emerging, intent on ambushing the herd. We instantly realised the inevitable was about to occur. The predators attacked, forcing the herd across the road. The hefty buffalo soldiers galloped across the tarred road. But one slid on the smooth surface because his hooves couldn't grip. The lions capitalised on this slip-up and within seconds they were all over him.

It was a dreadful yet thrilling sight as we had never witnessed a predator killing anything before, despite our frequent visits to game parks. With a desperate desire to live, the buffalo fought very hard to escape. But lions must kill to survive. Prompted by empty bellies, the lion trio took their due with open claws and sharp teeth.

After approximately 25 gripping minutes the buffalo warrior uttered his final groan. The lions, exhausted, rested for a few minutes before feeding. Then, irritated by the traffic, they dragged their breakfast into the bush and started gorging. We could hear the tearing of skin and the crushing of bones while they indulged in their feeding frenzy.

Seeing the entire episode from the stalking, the chase, the catch, through to the kill and the feeding made the experience extra-special. And observing how the lions struggled to rip apart the tough buffalo skin was particularly fascinating. What a memorable adventure.

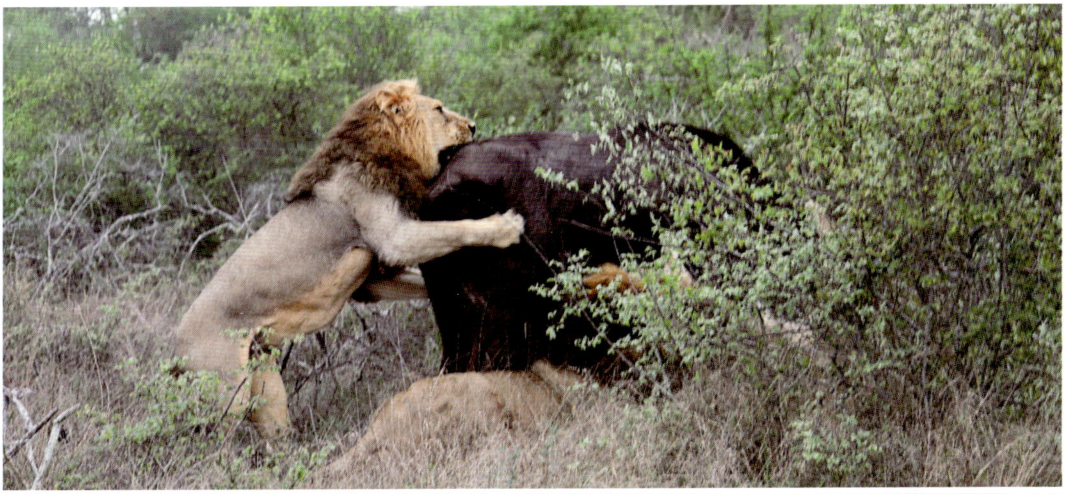

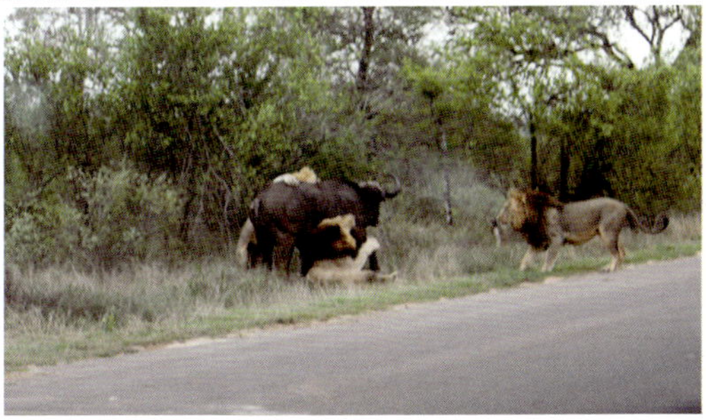

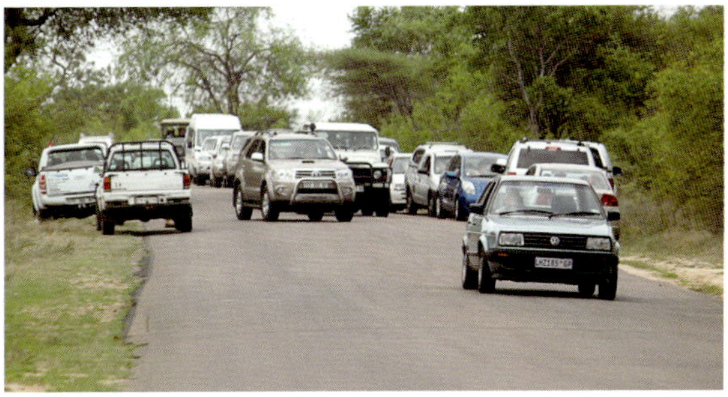

The dune hunter

BILAL MOSAM & SAFIYYA LAHER

When we booked our first Kgalagadi trip for December 2018, we had no idea what to expect. We dreamt of possible sightings. One was definitely a cheetah hunt.

On our second day in the park, we came across a lone female on the hunt. There was a herd of springbok less than 200 metres away and we were convinced this was it. Together with a few other visitors, we waited patiently for a few hours until they disappeared off her radar, and she decided to rest as the Kalahari sun turned up the heat. We did the same. Later that afternoon, we met the Wessels couple who were at the cheetah sighting earlier that morning.

The next day, we made our way slowly to Nossob Camp. As we approached Melkvlei, we found the Wessels parked facing the riverbed with the dune to their backs. They mentioned the female cheetah had eventually caught some prey the afternoon before. They also told us they had been keeping an eye on an injured springbok in the area and knew of a cheetah that was somewhere beyond the dunes behind them. They were hoping to observe a hunt.

Not having the luxury of playing the waiting game, we decided to head off. Just as we did, Safiyya spotted the cheetah coming over the dune,

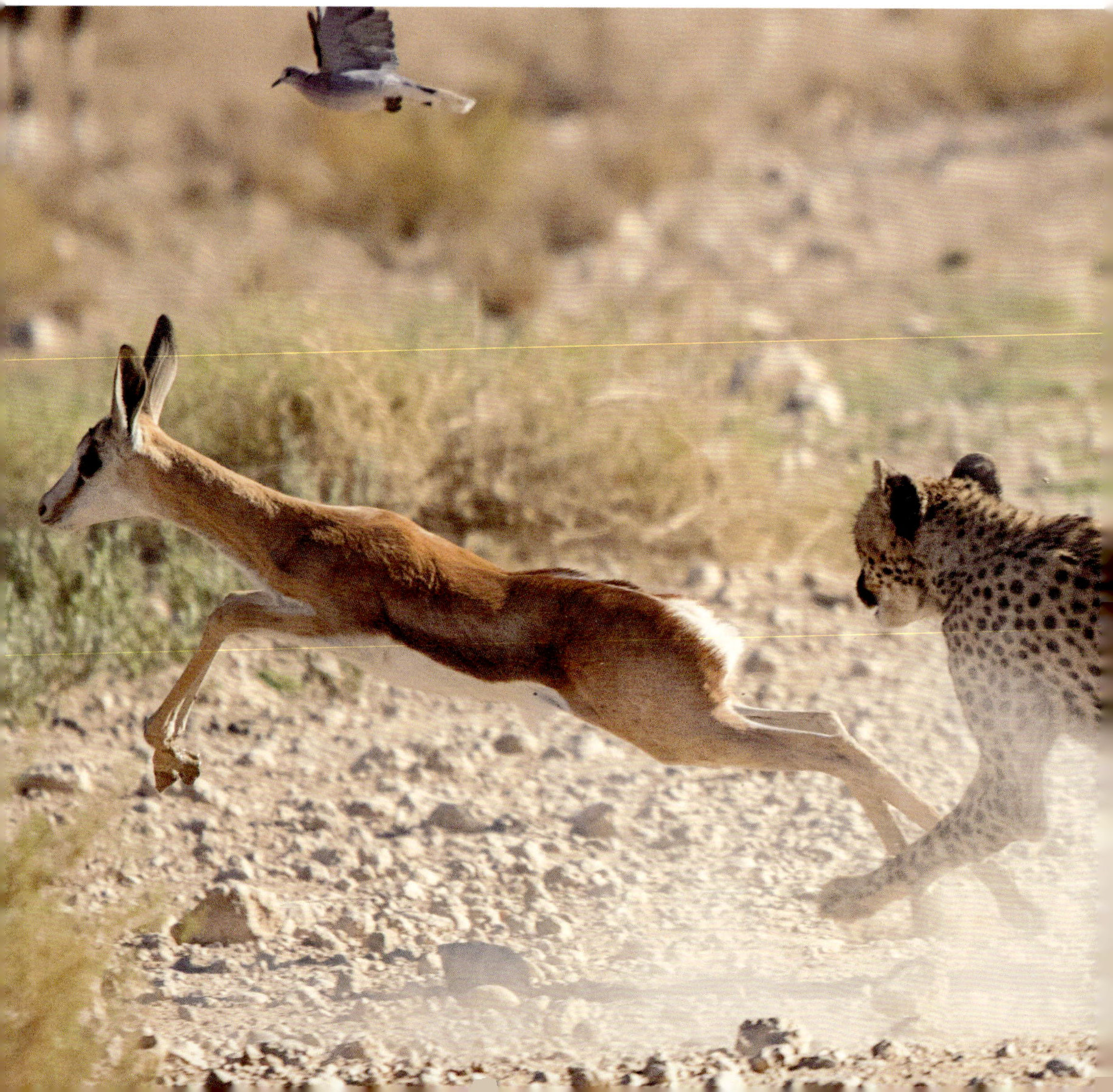

its eyes locked onto the injured springbok drinking from a puddle in the road, oblivious to danger.

Every time the springbok put its head down to drink, the cheetah closed the gap. Once it was close enough, it waited for the buck to put its head down to the water again before shooting like a bullet out from behind the dune. The cheetah had to make a 180-degree turn as the springbok ran almost towards it and then chased its prey into the bush where it managed to overcome the buck.

It dragged the buck to a nearby tree to feed as we watched, shocked and thrilled in equal measure. We had witnessed our first cheetah hunt and although it had taken only seconds, the memory of it will remain forever.

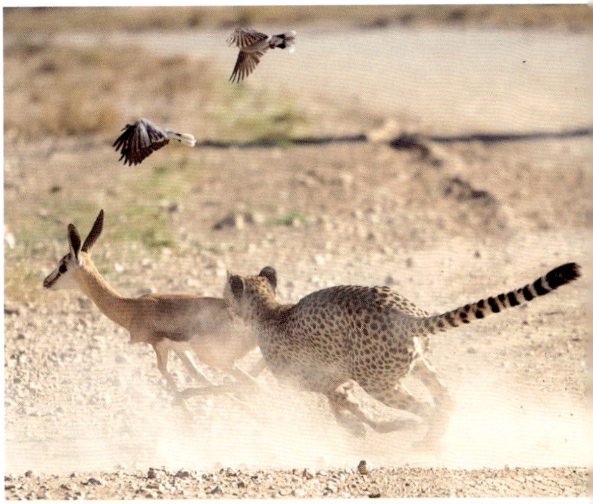

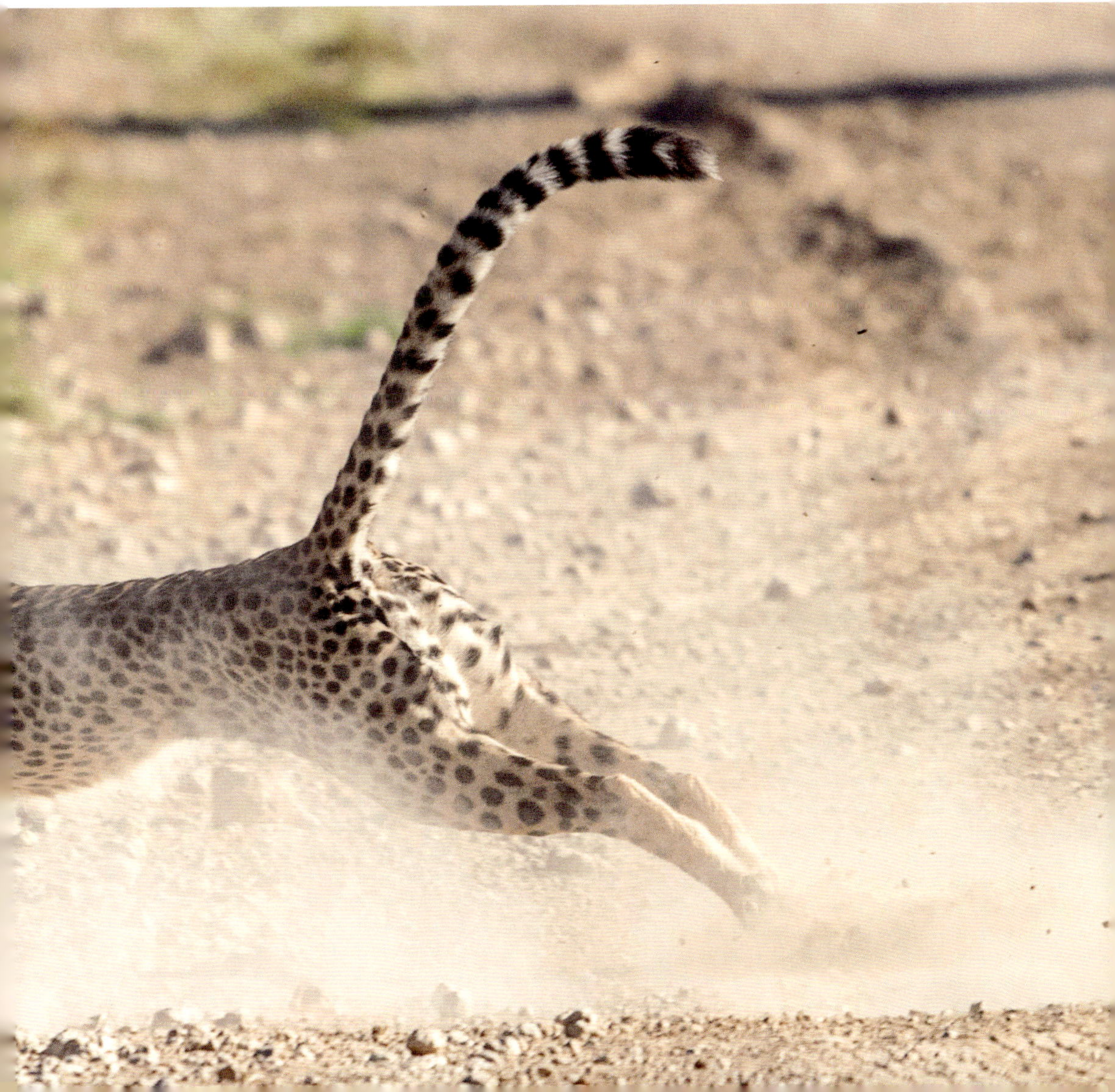

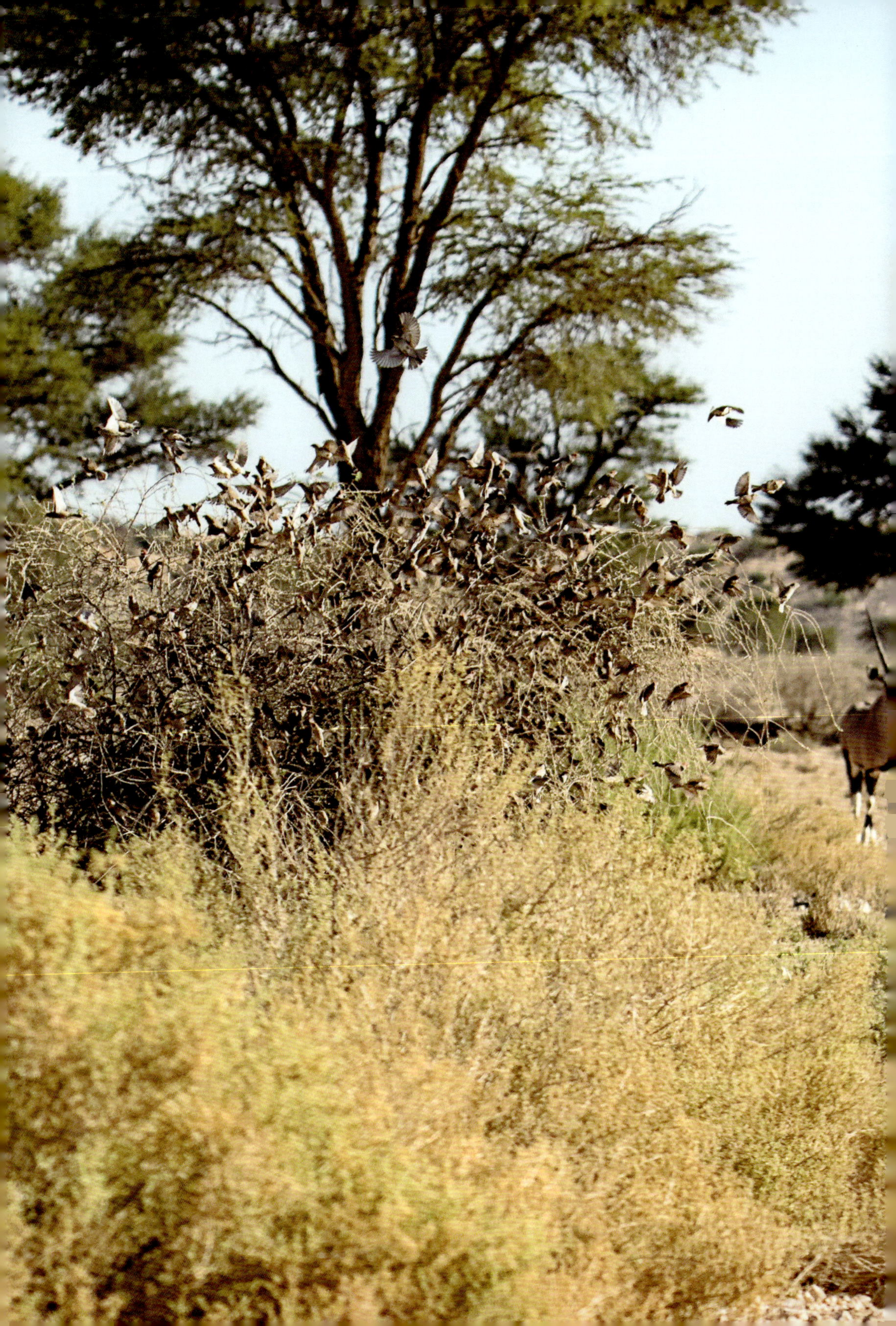

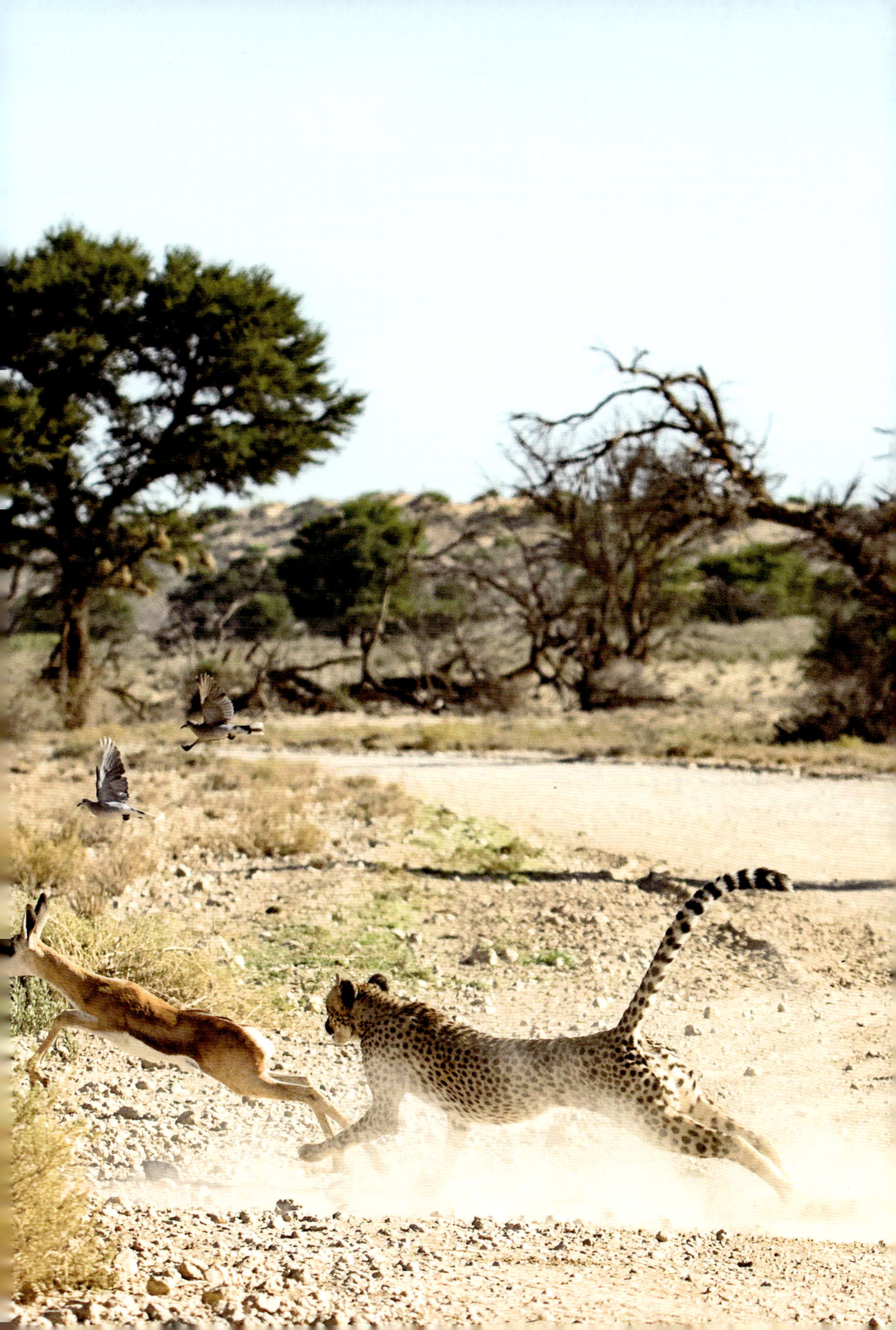

Dust – the photographer's dream

CAROL POLICH

Dust is everywhere. We clean it out of our homes and – 'poof!' – it reappears as a stealthy menace whether we are at home or away. We can't seal it from our lives or our photographic equipment. We human beings simply have to put up with it. In nature, however, it's a vital substance for body maintenance. Birds, for example, dust bathe to maintain plumage, keeping feathers in top condition, and wildlife use it as a drying property to help protect their bodies from insect bites and to deflect harsh sunlight.

I find that capturing a dusty scene has its challenges, particularly in getting the correct exposures. Galloping zebras disappear and reappear in a ghostly fashion. Elephant herds march through dust as it sweeps around their colossal forms. Once they find their favourite dust bathing areas, they become a part of an animated fantasy. They toss the gritty soil over their bodies in a precise tempo from side to side. After this routine, they throw a spray of dust over their heads, forming a rhythmic arc like gymnastics in motion. The powdery substance possesses its own magic, providing something glorious and wonderful to both the wildlife and the photographer. On sweltering hot days, on the Etosha dry plains, dust devils gather and sweep along, building momentum as they create a cloud over the wildlife at the waterholes. Everything turns its back and races away trying to escape this 'devil.' Fortunately, it doesn't last long, and animals and birds return to quench their thirst. Dispersed light from this insubstantial element creates brilliant sunrises and sunsets. Thorny, silhouetted bushes encapsulated in a thick blanket of dust take on a desolate, uncanny appearance. The sky and air and entire habitat exist within an aura of diffused light.

As photographers, we relish this magical effect of dispersed lighting upon our subjects. The brilliance and mystical qualities of dust add a dreamlike overlay to our photographic endeavours.

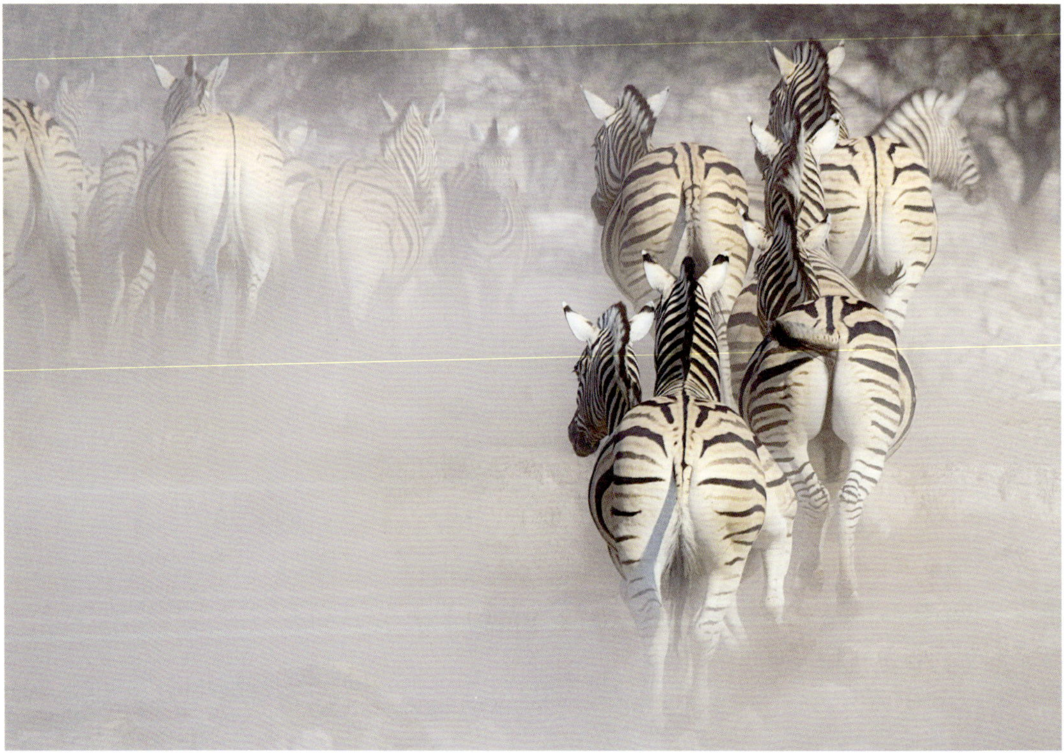

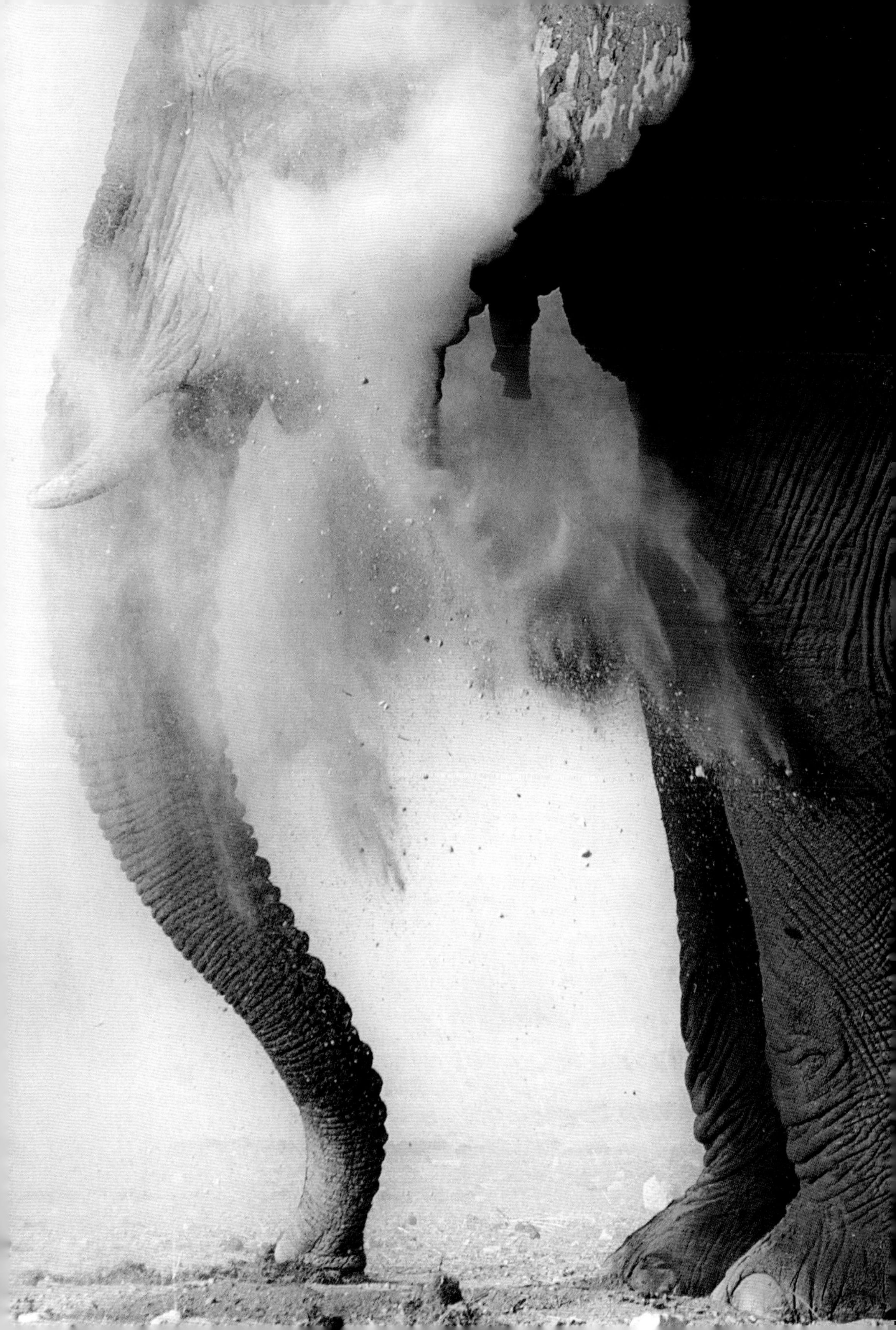

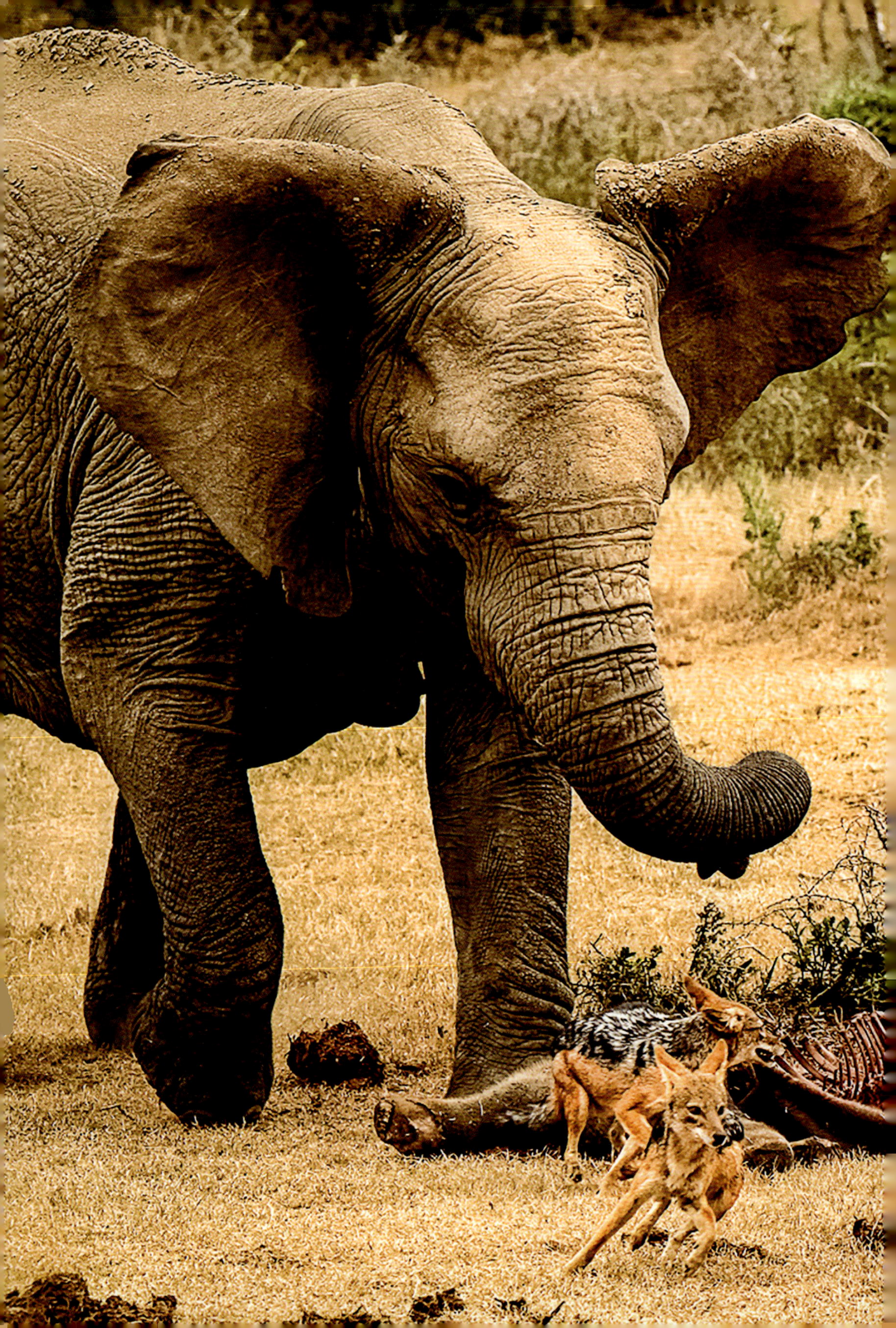

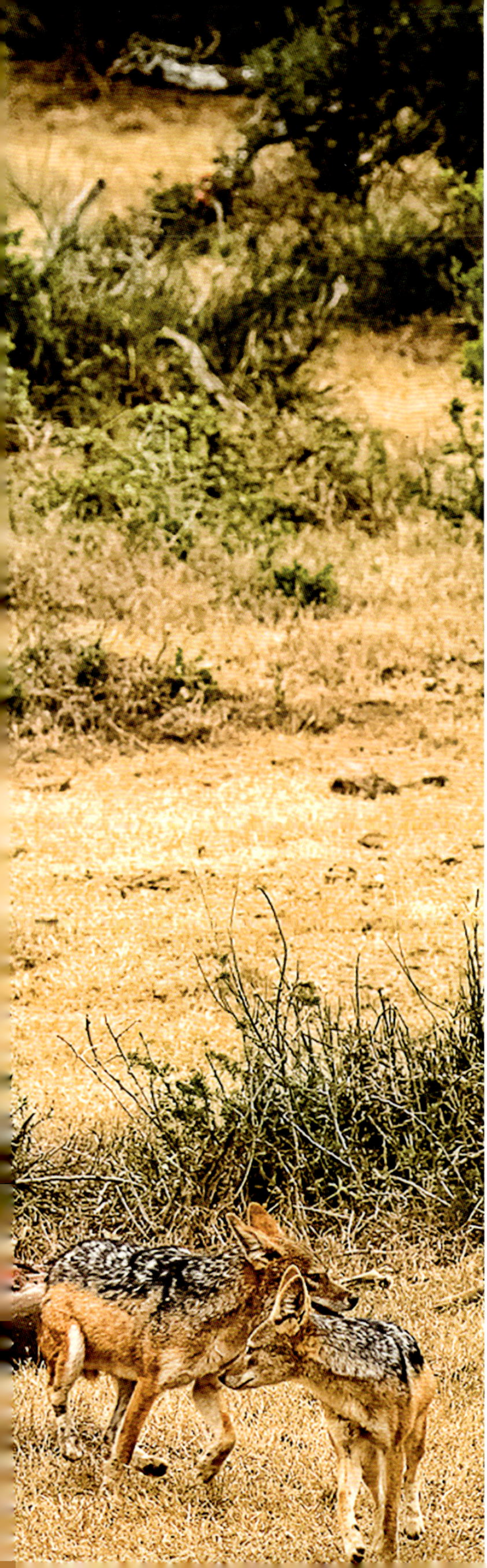

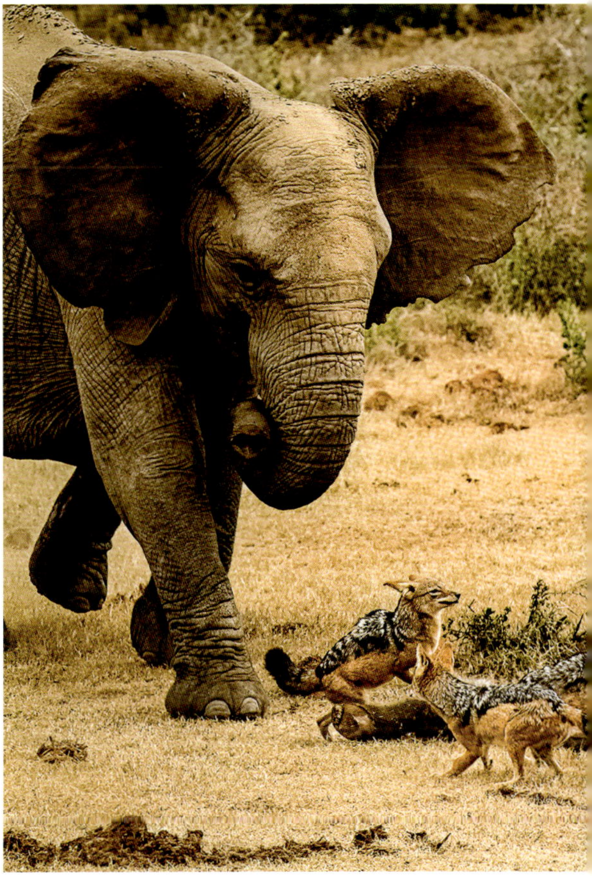

A mother's devotion

MARONEL STEYN

One Friday at Addo Elephant National Park we came to a waterhole where we noticed an elephant calf had died and the mother elephant was standing over it. All the other elephants that came to drink would first stand with her for a moment as if sympathising, and only then go on to drink.

On the Sunday we observed a hyena and 14 jackals trying to steal the calf's remains from her. She reacted with fury, keeping them away as much as she could.

By the Monday morning only the hide was left but she was still obviously reluctant to abandon it. It was heart-breaking, but also inspiring, to see that a mother's love and protection go beyond her offspring's death.

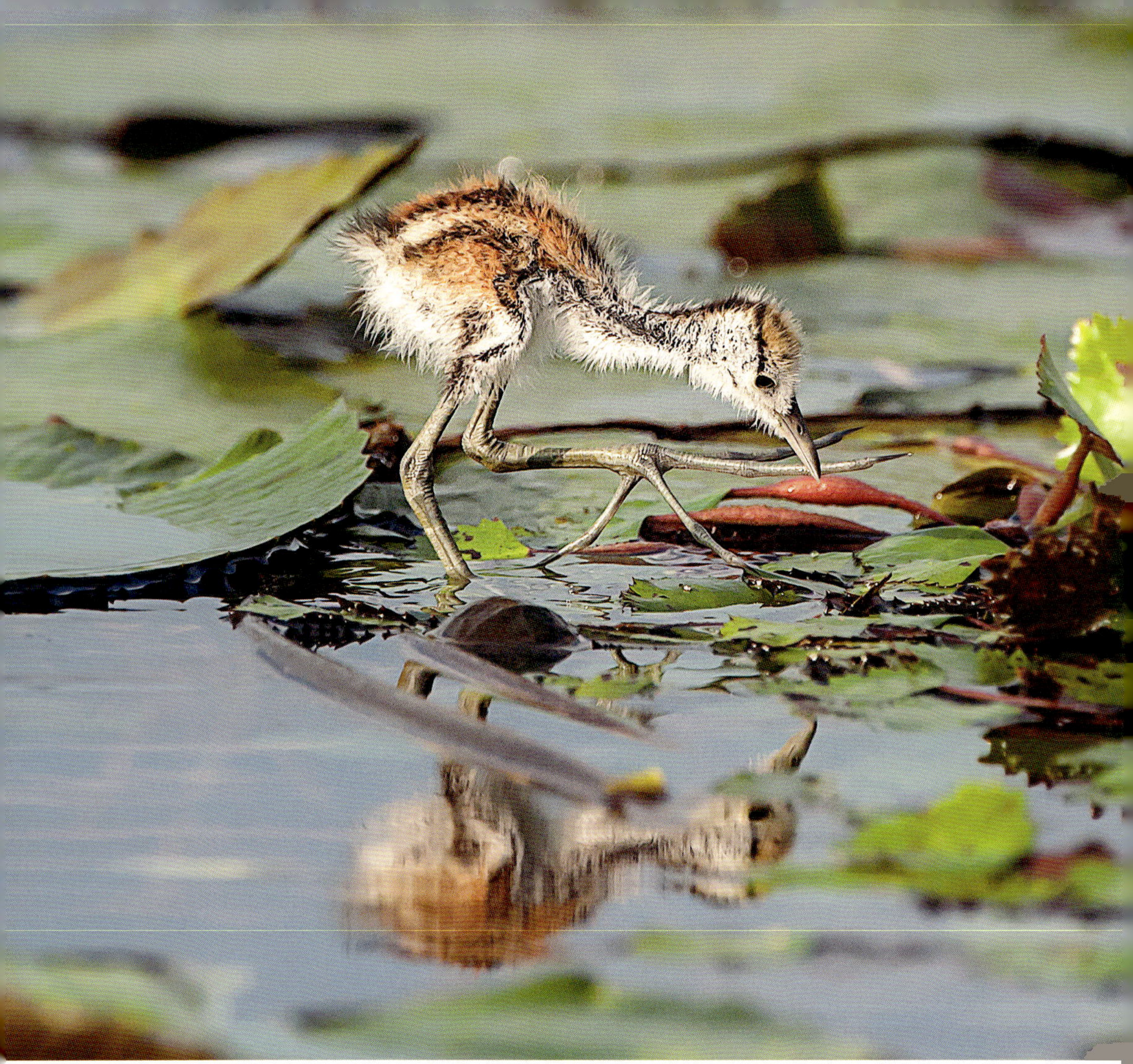
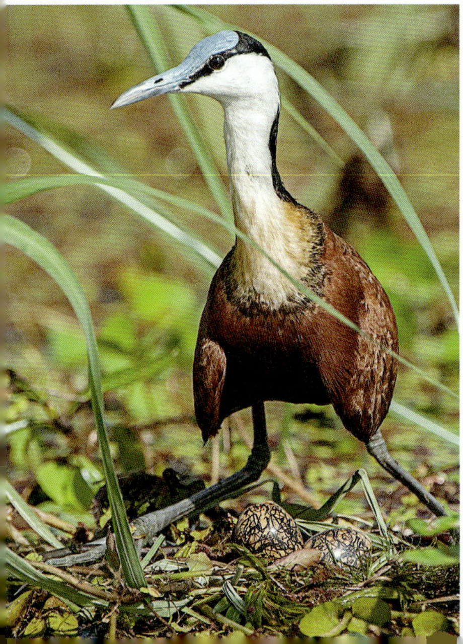
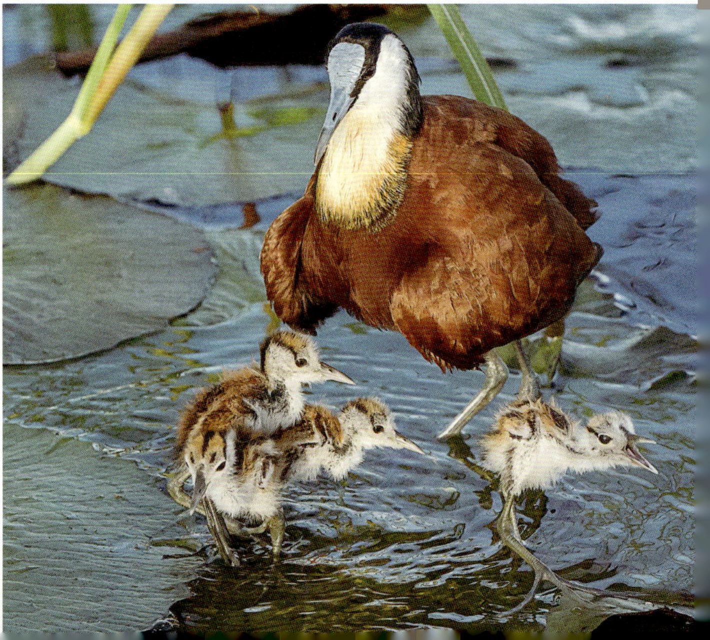

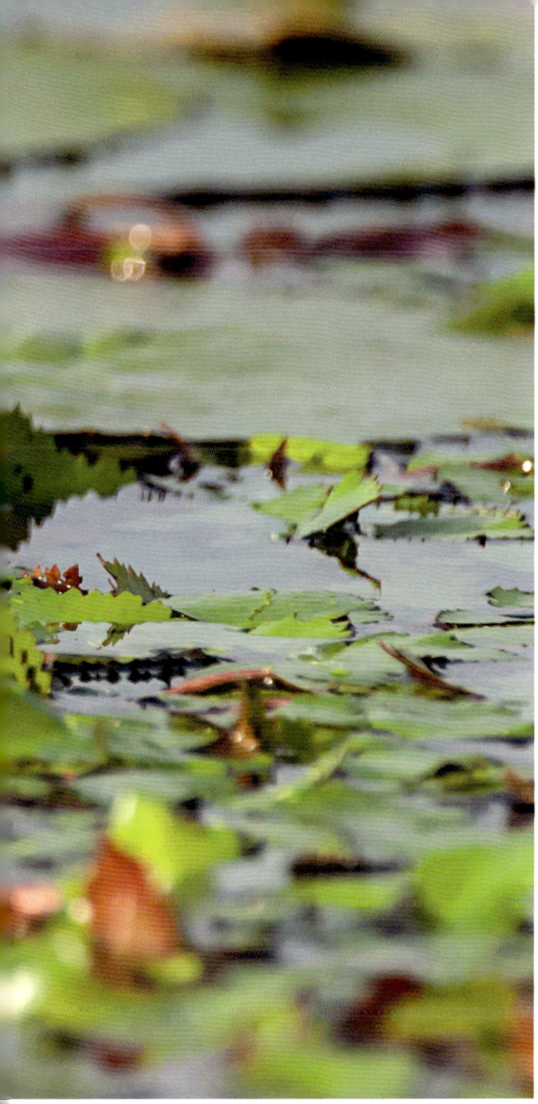

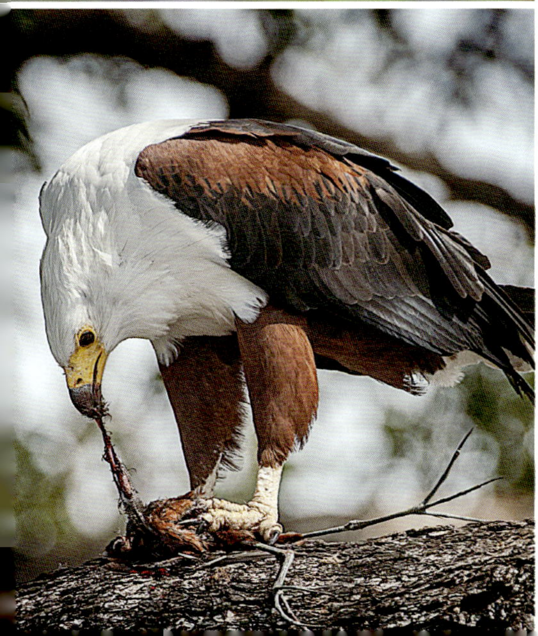

The life cycle of a jacana

PAT SCOTT

A waterbird endemic to sub-Saharan Africa, the jacana is found in the tropical wetlands of this area. The images presented here were taken from a river boat on the confluence of the Chobe River where Botswana, Zambia and Zimbabwe meet. Jacanas are small, light birds and have long thin legs with very long toes; this results in a good size-to-weight ratio, enabling them to walk on the surface leaves of water lilies. These birds are able to run around on the leaves with ease and from a distance they look as if they are walking on water, leading to their local names of 'Jesus birds' or 'lily trotters'.

The female jacana lays her eggs – usually four – on a pad of aquatic vegetation where the male will have made a raft-like nest. Thereafter, the male bird does the brooding for the two to three weeks until incubation and he is the primary caretaker of the offspring. Once the chicks are hatched, the parent bird is able to lift and carry them under his wings, generally two on each side, where he keeps them warm, dry and safe. The ease with which he moves on the leaves with the four chicks under his wings is fascinating to watch.

This initial phase lasts about two weeks. As they grow, the chicks learn to fend for themselves, eating insects, larvae and even small fish found on and under the lily leaves. However, if there is any sign of danger the male jacana calls the young ones to climb to safety under his wings. If one gets lost he will tuck his wings in tightly over the other three and go off looking. He makes a loud chirping sound which is his call for the stray chick. Once danger has passed he lifts his wings and the young ones tumble out and wander around exploring their environment and looking for food.

After about two months they are fairly independent, but being so small they must be vigilant for predators always on the lookout for a tasty morsel. A common predator on the Chobe River is the African fish eagle which swoops in, grabs a jacana in his deadly claws and flies up into a tree. The last image illustrates the sad end of the story, an all-too-common conclusion to a jacana's life cycle.

Family life

CALLUM EVANS

I'd been seeing posts on Facebook groups about a Cape batis pair nesting in a banana tree in Kirstenbosch Gardens but I'd never been able to locate the nest myself, despite extensive searching and asking around. Then one day, my friend Robyn and I were walking along the Boomslang Canopy Walkway in the gardens and there, in a banana tree right next to the walkway at eye-level, was a female Cape batis perched on a tiny, cup-like nest. Two small chicks peeked over the lichen-fringed rim of the nest. We stood a safe distance from the nest to watch the comings and goings of the parents and we were completely blown away by what we saw of their devotion to their offspring. At the beginning, the parents would fly in separately at 10-minute intervals, either to bring food or to remove the chicks' faecal sacs. Then, after 20 minutes, the female sat on the nest for about five minutes until the male arrived with an insect, which he gave to the

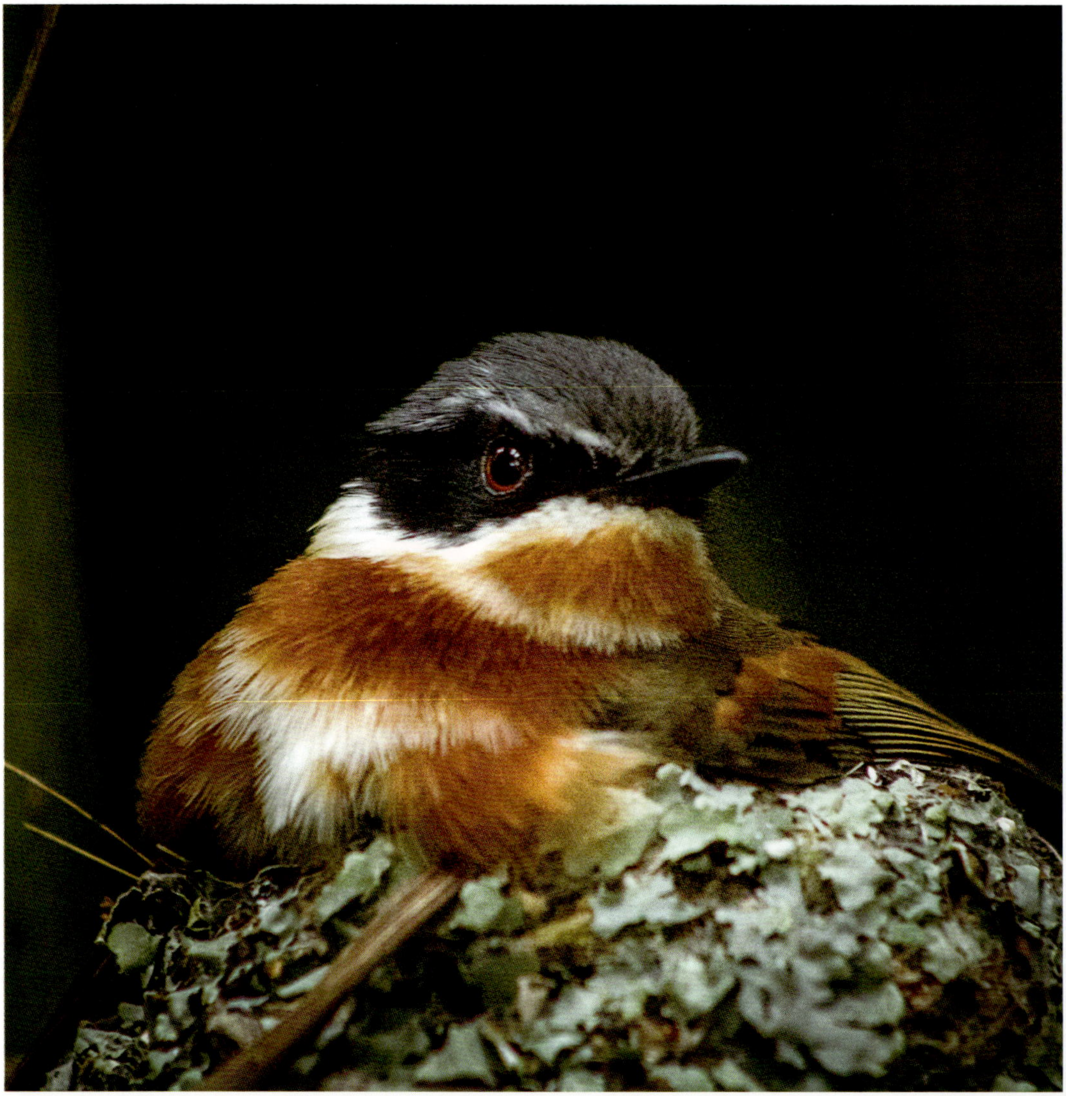

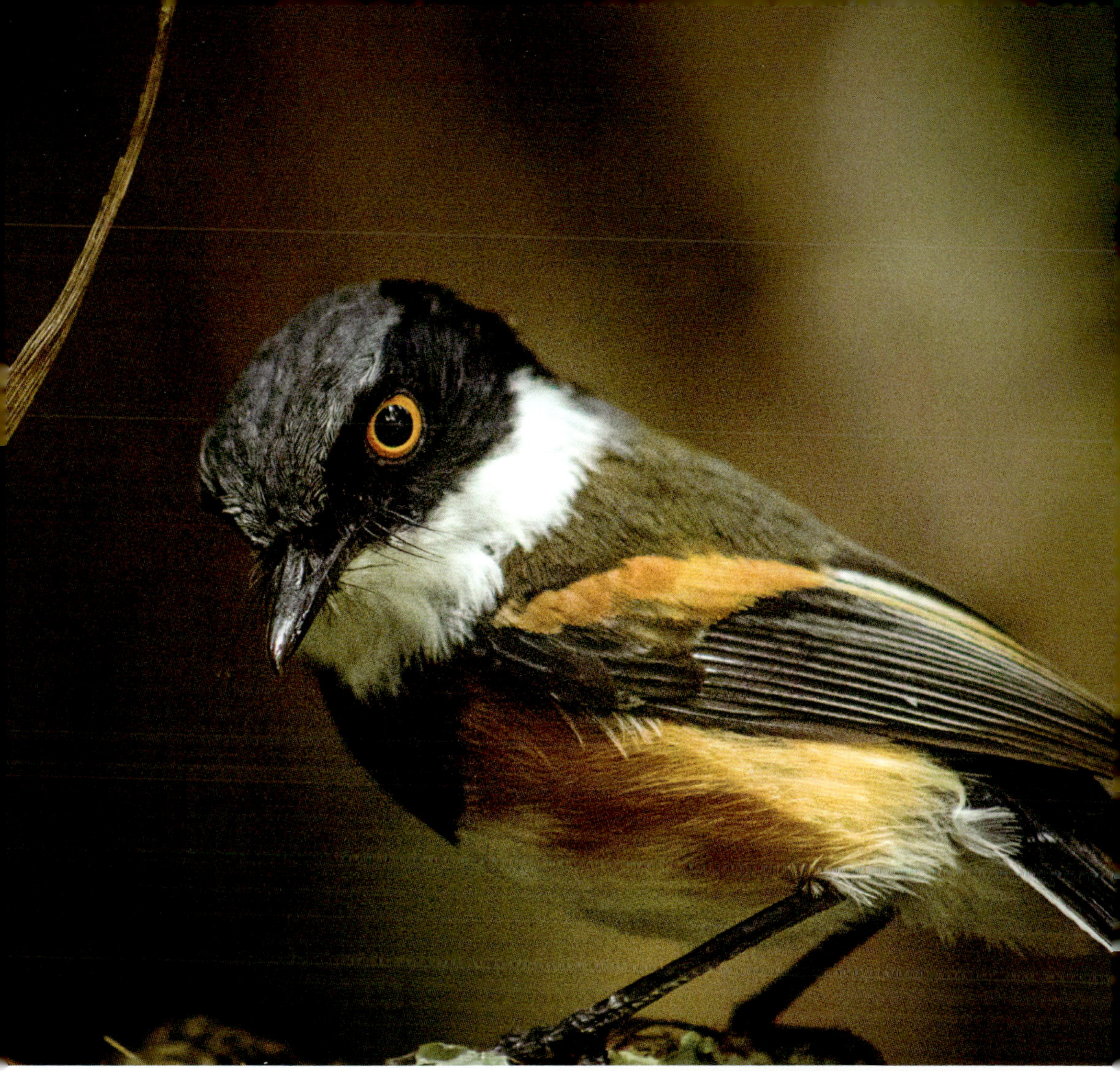

female which promptly fed it to her chicks before both parents flew off again.

We spent about an hour at the nest that day and I returned the next day to get more photographs. I was rewarded with an incredible sighting of the male bringing a large cicada to the female sitting on the nest, which both parents struggled to fit into their chicks' beaks. Eventually, after about five minutes, one chick swallowed the prize.

While the Cape batis may not be the rarest bird, it is still one I don't get to photograph very often. To have such an intimate and precious opportunity as this, not to mention a chance to observe their behaviour closely in one of my favourite places on Earth, made it a most memorable birding experience.

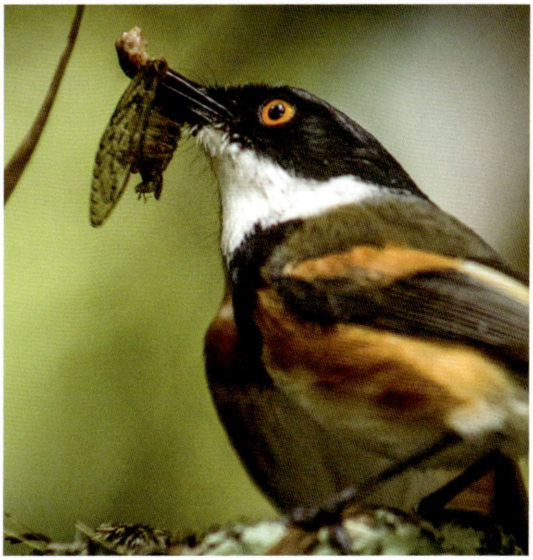

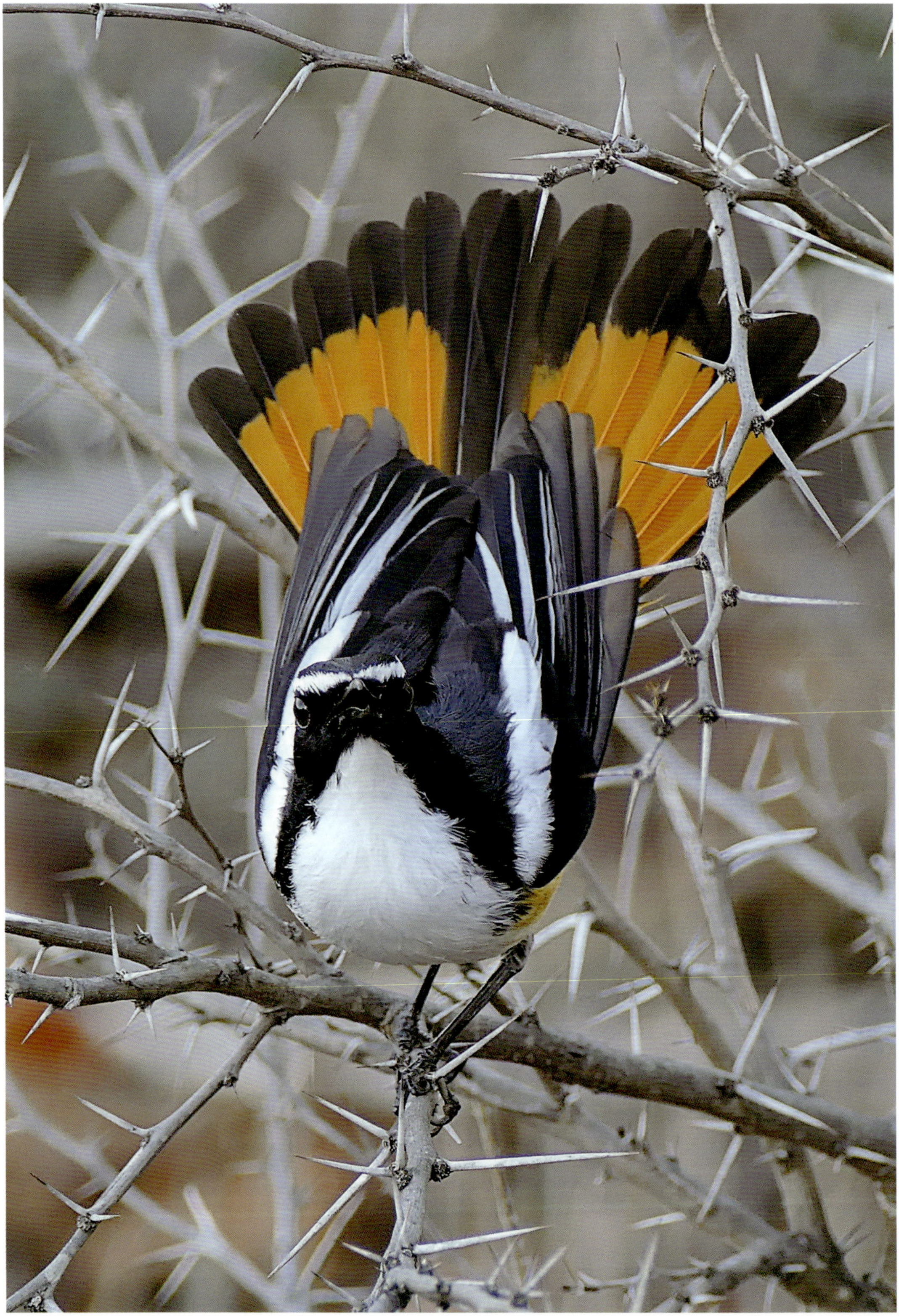

Robin-chat delight

JOHAN SLABBERT

My interest in birds and bird photography lends an extra dimension to the multitude of natural charms of the Kruger National Park, making it a favourite holiday and photography destination. Just after sunrise one July morning, in Olifants Camp I was skulking around the perimeter on the lookout for birds or anything else to photograph. The early-morning light imposes limitations even on the bridge camera (with one-inch sensor) that I use, so I've learnt the hard way not to expect too much from it.

Soon I heard the call of the white-throated robin-chat nearby, and tried to entice it by mimicking its call. It responded and came to the thorny shrubs close to me, frantically calling and looking around for the bird that had dared intrude on its territory. The robin-chat is not a spectacular bird, but this one in its agitated state had gone into territorial display, fanning its tail wide, which made it quite a sight to behold. It was magnificent. Of course, I had no way of knowing its sex, or what I had conveyed in robin-chat language with my mimicking, so the bird could have been demonstrating territorial aggression or mating behaviour – I'll never know!

Though the shots didn't turn out as sharp as I would have liked, the exceptional action more than made up for it. The stark contrast between the vivid colour of the robin-chat's fanned tail and its drab surroundings also lent additional visual impact to the shots.

The setting of natural photographs can make or break an image and in this case, thankfully, the visual appeal is substantially enhanced by the bird being depicted in its typical habitat (thorny shrub) without any unwelcome or intrusive background features. The shots also show beyond doubt that the bird was acutely aware of my presence, fixing me with a challenging, in-your-face stare. The aggression of the bird was almost palpable and this made a huge contribution to the impact of the images.

Time and time again, I have found that the best birding and bird photography in the Kruger National Park is to be had by trawling the rest camps on foot. Some of my best bird shots have been captured that way. This might be because of the unusually lush habitats found in rest camps, including water points (Punda Maria's little bird bath next to the barbequing area opposite the bungalows comes to mind). But also because the birds are more habituated to people and don't fly off at the first sight of someone approaching or raising a camera. And again on this occasion, the rest camp came up trumps, delivering a great photographic opportunity. So my advice is: be there, be primed for action, with camera poised and ready to shoot.

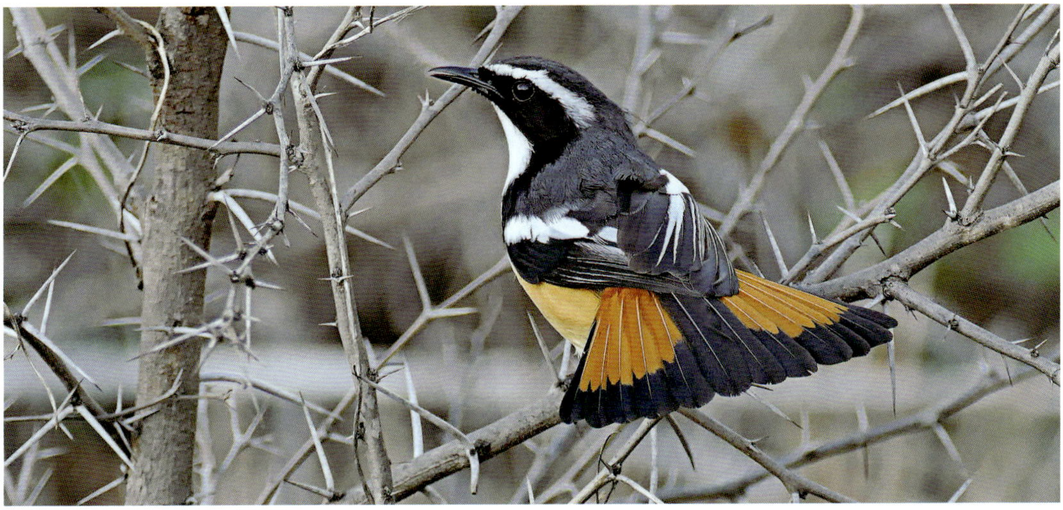

An age-old rivalry

LOUIS & INA TALJAARD

During a late-morning game drive in the Kruger National Park, we spotted a leopard cub eating from a carcass of an impala ram under a large bush about 20 metres from the road. The bush, shaped like an igloo, with branches touching the ground, had an opening facing towards us as well as a small opening on the opposite side.

The cub and carcass were just visible through the front opening but although we expected to spot the mother, she was nowhere to be seen. After a while the cub had eaten its fill and moved to a spot where it was clearly visible. It spent time cleaning its blood-stained face and paws before playing around in the shade.

We left the scene around lunch time and returned during the late afternoon. The carcass was still in the same place and we saw the mother and cub relaxing in the shadows of another bush some 30 metres away. It was a particularly tranquil scene with both leopards staring into space enjoying the golden hour.

A baboon barked close by. The female leopard and her cub, immediately on alert, sat up and stared in the direction of the noise. After a while the sounds made by the troop of baboons, moving in our direction, were clearly audible. The leopards' eyes were fixed in the direction of the approaching troop.

The mother leopard started to crawl in the direction of the igloo-shaped bush with her belly

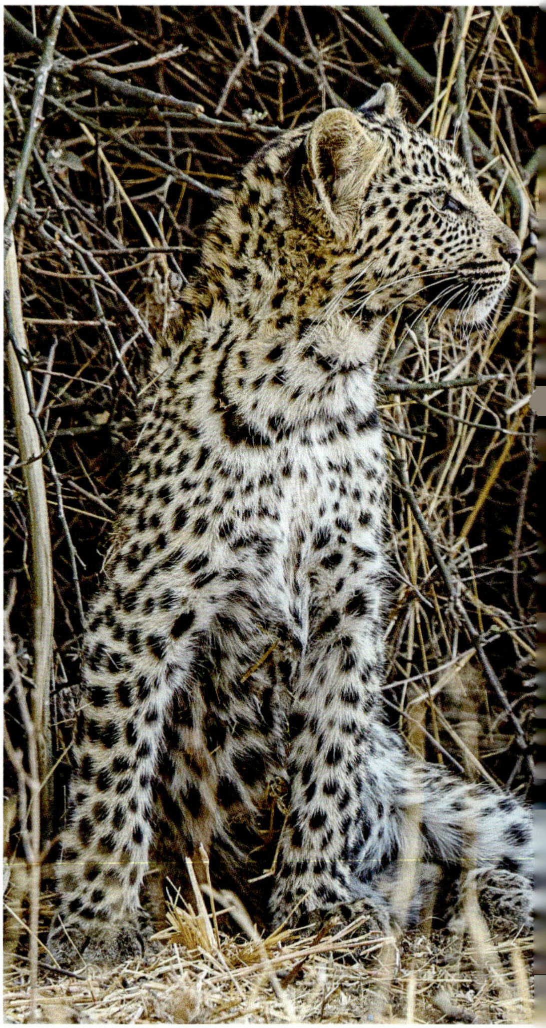

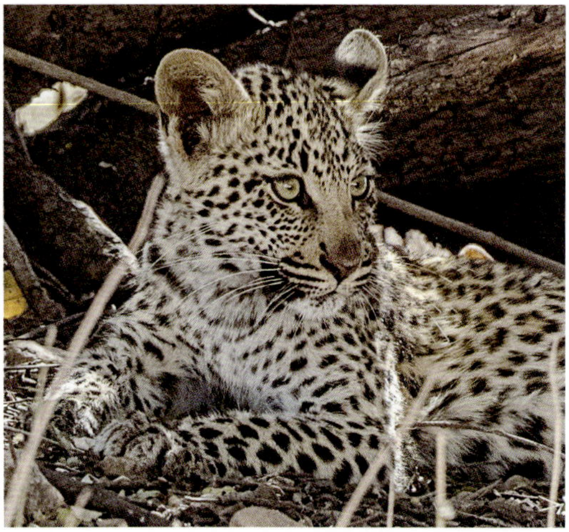

almost touching the ground. The cub followed the mother into the igloo and then disappeared through the rear opening. The mother sat inside the igloo next to the carcass for almost 20 minutes while the baboons were approaching. Eventually she decided to abandon the carcass and disappeared through the backdoor just before the first baboons came into sight. The troop passed within 10 metres of the igloo without paying any attention to the carcass.

We returned early the next morning to find the bush abandoned. Scouting around, we detected the remains of the carcass wedged into a fork high up in a nearby tree. The leopard must have returned to recover her prize after the baboons had passed through.

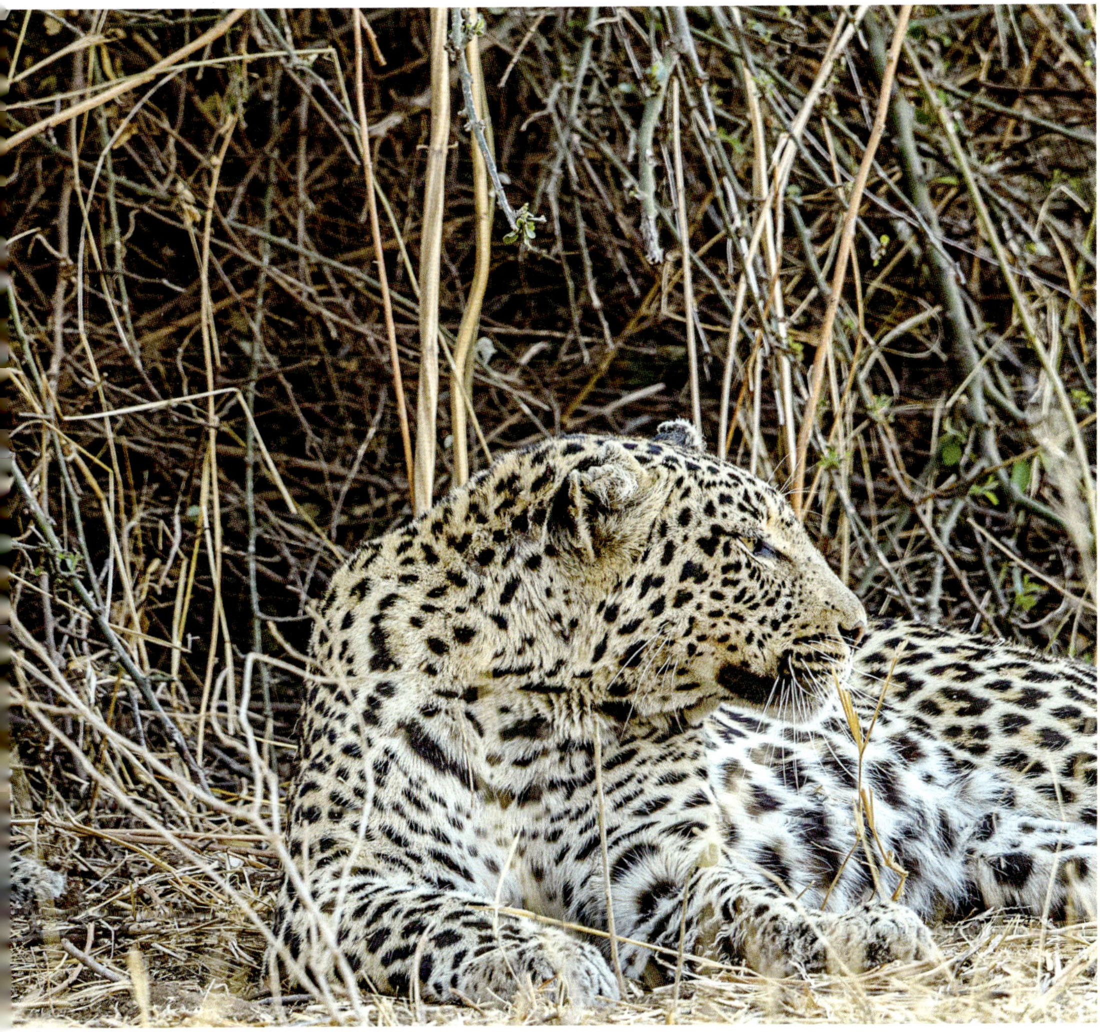

A little later, we spotted the mother and cub playing in the sun as if nothing had disturbed them the previous evening.

It is well known that baboon is a favourite prey of leopard, with attacks usually occurring during the hours of darkness. Baboons are terrified of leopard in the dark and a troop of baboons will never attempt to attack a leopard at night, even to rescue a victim from its claws. However, it appears that in spite of baboons' phenomenal eyesight, the camouflage of the spotted cat renders it invisible during low-light conditions prevailing at dusk or at night.

What is less well known is that it's a very different story in the daytime. A leopard is no match for the baboon males in a troop during the day. The cat that attacks a baboon straying from the troop in daylight must beware. One alarm call and the sentries will rush to its assistance. They are fearless and equipped with canines which match that of the leopard.

There are many instances on record where baboons have torn full-grown leopards apart during a rescue operation of that nature. Leopards usually avoid contact with baboons during the day and will surrender their prey without confronting the primates.

Usually, it is the interaction between animals that makes interesting photo tales. But in this instance, it was the avoidance of a confrontation that revealed so much to us and told its own intriguing story.

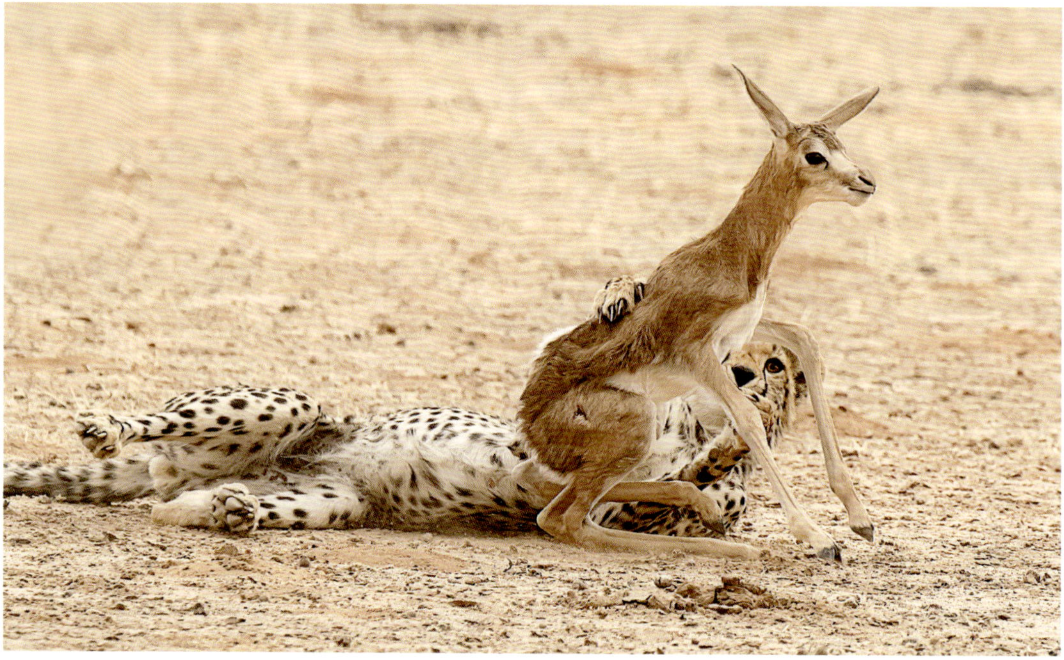

'Cat and Mouse': Kgalagadi style

PAT SCOTT

These photos illustrate the basic principles of the everyday 'cat and mouse' scenario played out in the Kgalagadi Transfrontier Park.

Cheetah mothers take their young cubs out for hunting lessons from an early age. To begin with, she is the sole hunter but as the cubs get older, they become more involved and start going for the prey themselves under a watchful maternal eye. During this learning process the cubs – usually two to four in a litter – operate as a team and they really do play with the prey, which initially are small or young creatures of the veld. Gradually they become more efficient and more independent. The cubs tend to stay with the mother for two to three years as they develop their agility and speed to chase and bring down their own prey. Once they have become proficient hunters, they go off with a sibling or on their own.

As we were driving along the Aoub River Road, we became aware of a commotion among a herd of springbok and when we rounded the corner we saw two young cheetah cubs chasing one of the herd. There was no apparent urgency about the chase, as clearly the cheetahs were playing with their victim. While it was obvious the springbok was trying to get away, it was just as clear that the cheetahs were working as a coalition and playing catch-and-release with the poor bleating animal, with mother cheetah observing from close by. It was heart-breaking to watch the young springbok repeatedly get up and try to escape, and at times the cheetahs seemed to let the buck go for some distance on purpose before one of them ran to bring it down again. At one stage both predators and prey appeared to run out of steam and the three lay down together as if for a team photo.

In some of the images the cheetahs' tails are very evident; the tail being similar to a rudder in that it helps the animal retain balance while running at speed or when it is required to change direction at top speed.

This cat and mouse hunt went on for over 30 minutes before the adult cheetah intervened and went for the throat of the springbok, putting it out of its misery. The family of three settled down and in about 10 minutes had devoured all but the head of the buck.

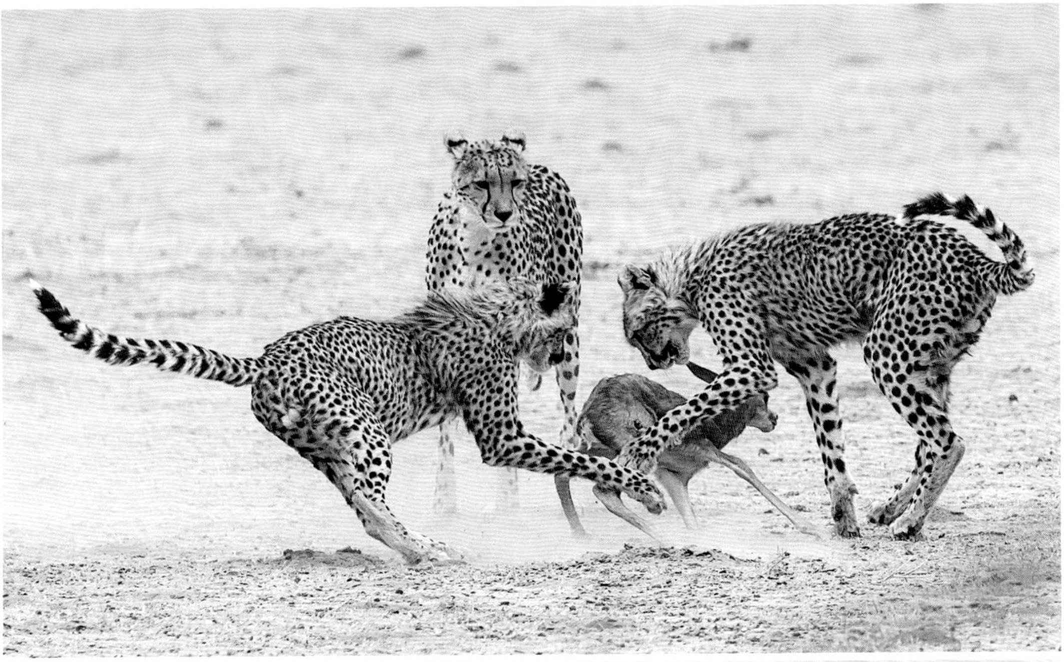

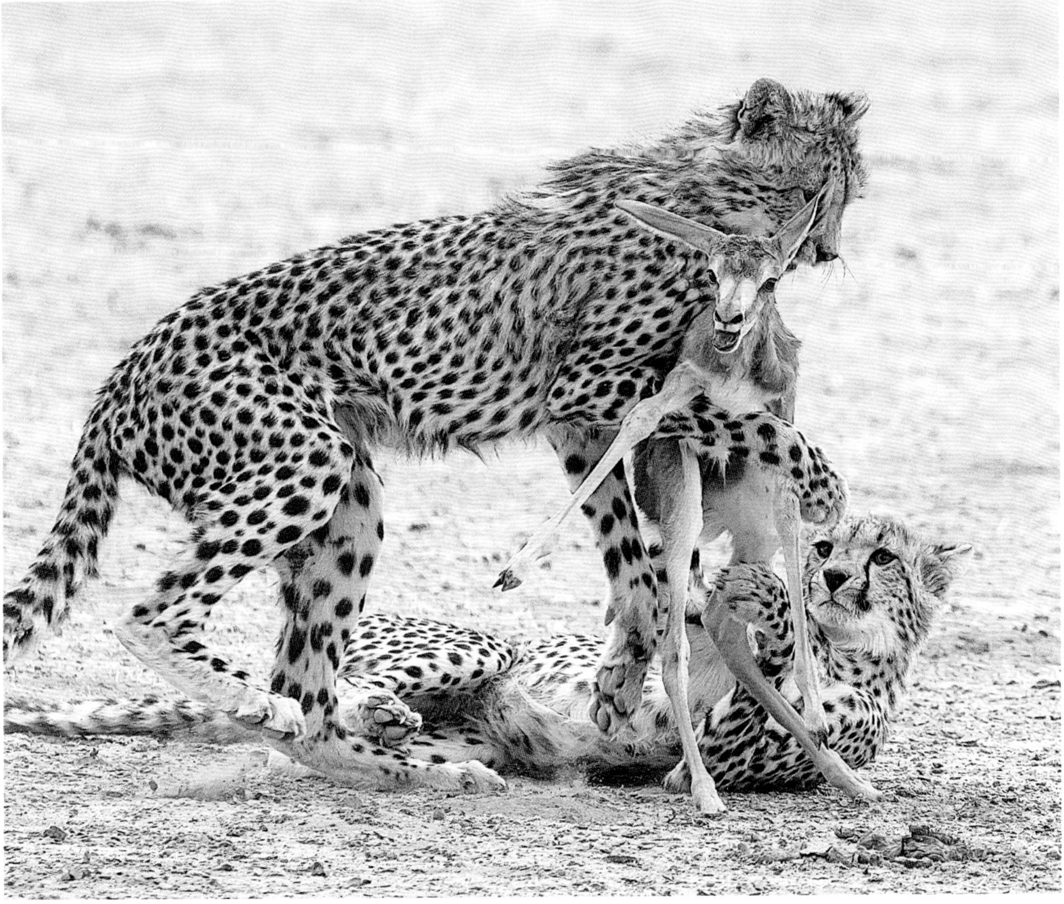

The three sittings

ASHLEA TODD

We were on a game drive and had just had a lion sighting, when two cheetahs crossed the road in front of us. Little did we know how exciting the next 50 minutes would be. The cheetahs went into thick bush, heading for the main road so we drove up there quickly to locate them again.

Having the trained eyes of a ranger in the car definitely helped because I know I would have missed them. As the cats came over a small rise we watched as they spotted some ostriches. The first cheetah quickly went into stalking mode, cautiously moving forward, crossing the main road through a now-growing number of vehicles, and continued to stalk. The second cheetah hung back nearly the entire time, seeming a little daunted by the vehicles and the intended target. He was so still that I think only a couple of people in the many cars present knew he was there: he was our secret cheetah.

The first cheetah crept closer to its prey until it suddenly took off and flew at the back end of an ostrich. Chaos broke out! All we could see was the cheetah being dragged through the bush but hanging on regardless. They came at speed into an open area where, out of nowhere, the second cheetah (the seemingly nervous one) took the lead and grabbed the ostrich from the front. Now we realised his behaviour was in fact a skilled hunting tactic. Both of them tackled it, there were ostrich feathers flying, ostrich and cheetahs spinning in a blur, reactions from us in the car and cheetahs biting at its legs, until they got it down on the ground and could finish it off.

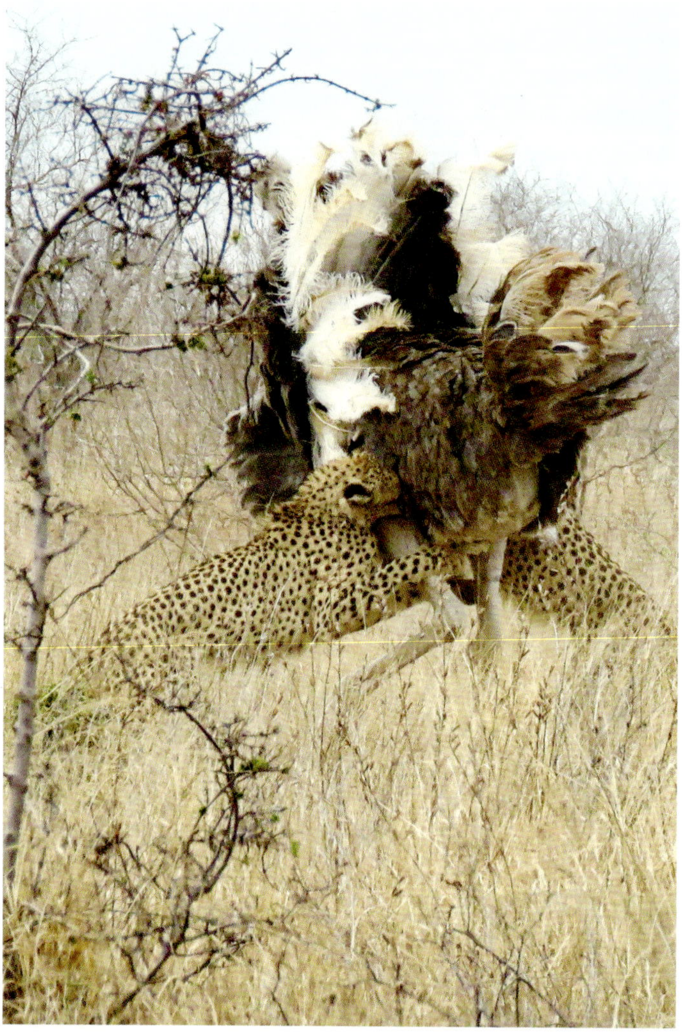

Once it was all over, they both sat up and rested, panting heavily and on the lookout for any potential threats to their success. They began to recover from this fight to the death and settled down to eat. At this point, reluctantly, we had to leave to pack up camp. We heard later that the lions we'd seen earlier moved in soon afterwards and stole the kill. When we passed by after some time, the cheetahs were further down the road, the lions were apparently sleeping off their feast and some vultures – the next sitting! – had moved in. An unforgettable sighting and one which demonstrates just how interconnected the elements in nature are.

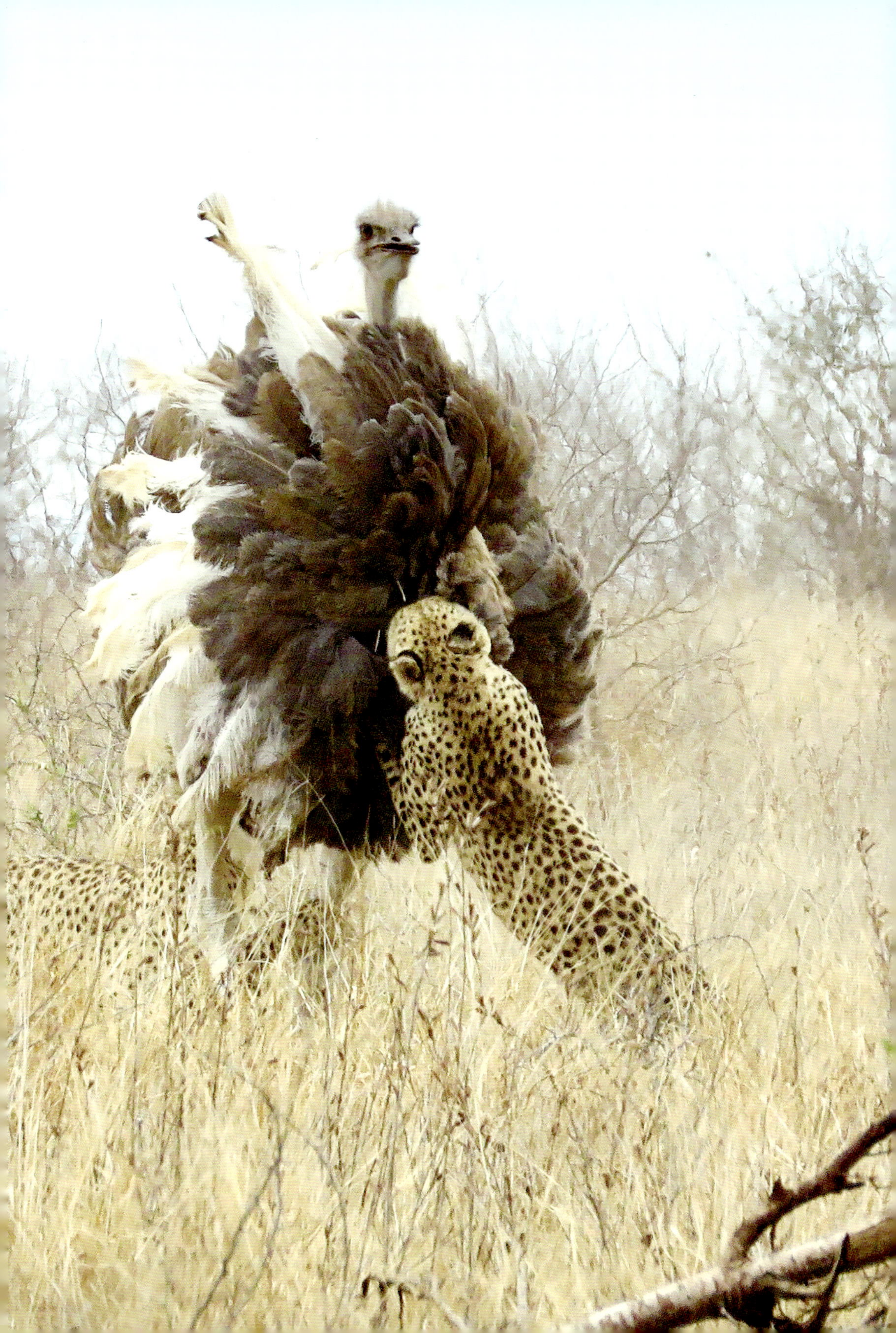

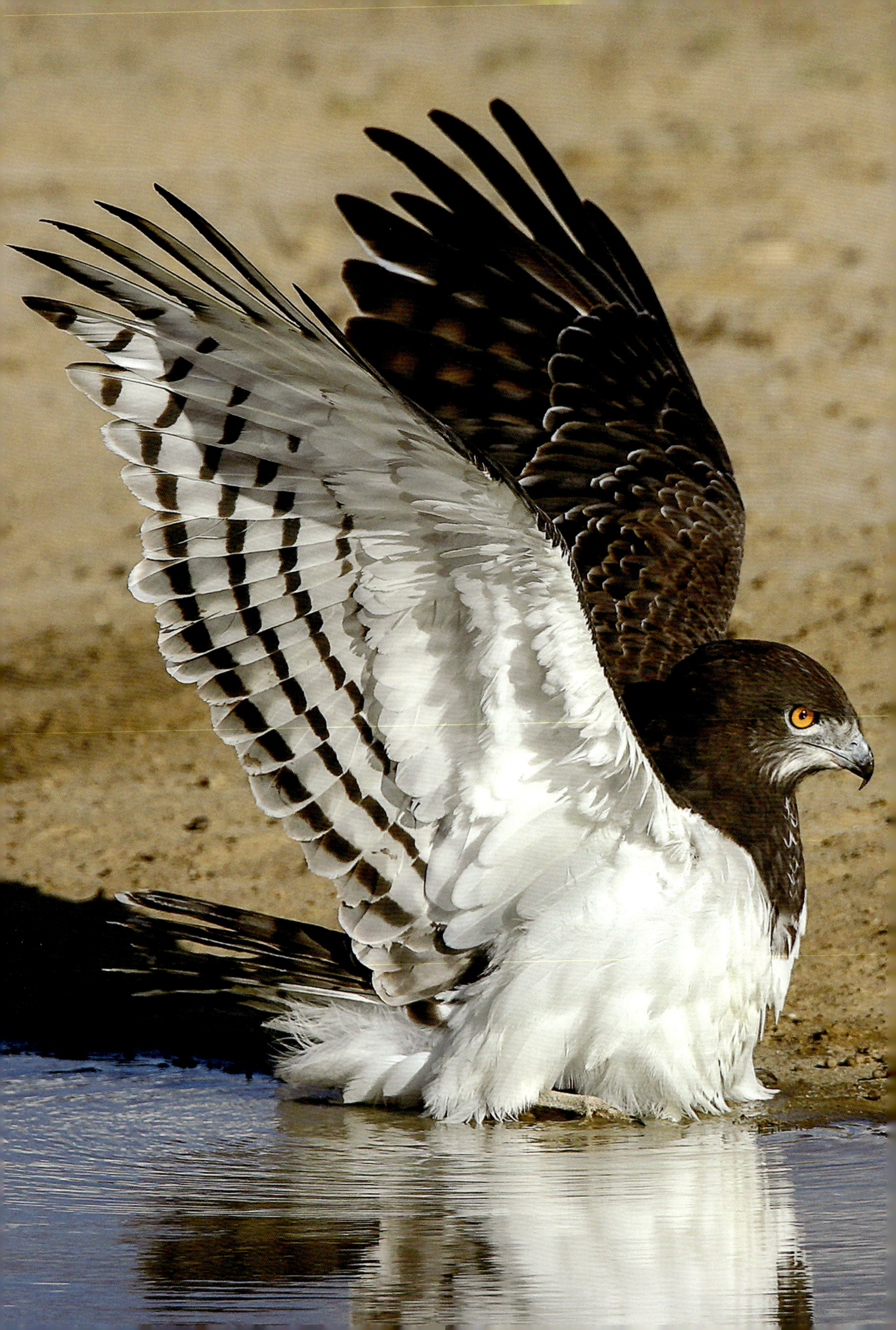

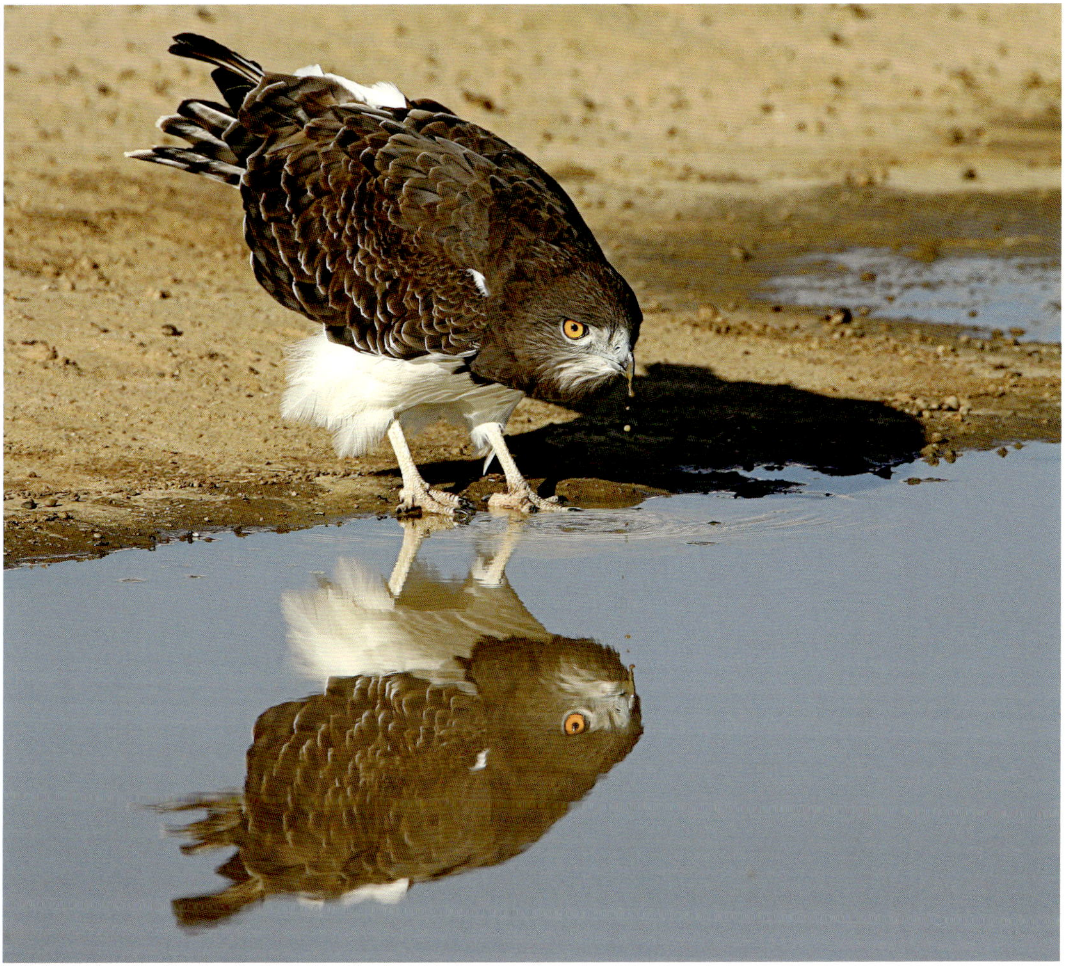

The black-chested snake-eagle in all its glory

EDMUND AYLMER

During one of our trips to the Kgalagadi Transfrontier Park, we had a wonderful opportunity to photograph the behaviour of a black-chested snake-eagle at the Nossob Camp waterhole. Following a few days of good rain, a large puddle of water had collected around the man-made waterhole which provided perfect photographic opportunities. The bird initially landed at the waterhole and walked up and down surveying the surroundings. It then approached the water and started drinking. Its reflection in the water added another dimension to the already impressive scene before us. After a display of opening and closing its wings, it walked into the water and sat down with its belly submerged. We felt privileged to see this magnificent raptor at close quarters, but to view it while it displayed unusual behaviour was a particularly special experience.

Once the eagle had finished drinking and bathing, it flew to a nearby dead camel thorn tree and started preening itself. Before long, a fork-tailed drongo appeared and started dive-bombing it. The eagle was clearly annoyed with the drongo and kept trying to avoid the onslaught. Eventually, the drongo gave up and with peace restored, the eagle continued preening and shaking its feathers. The out-of-focus background provided a superb backdrop for taking photographs.

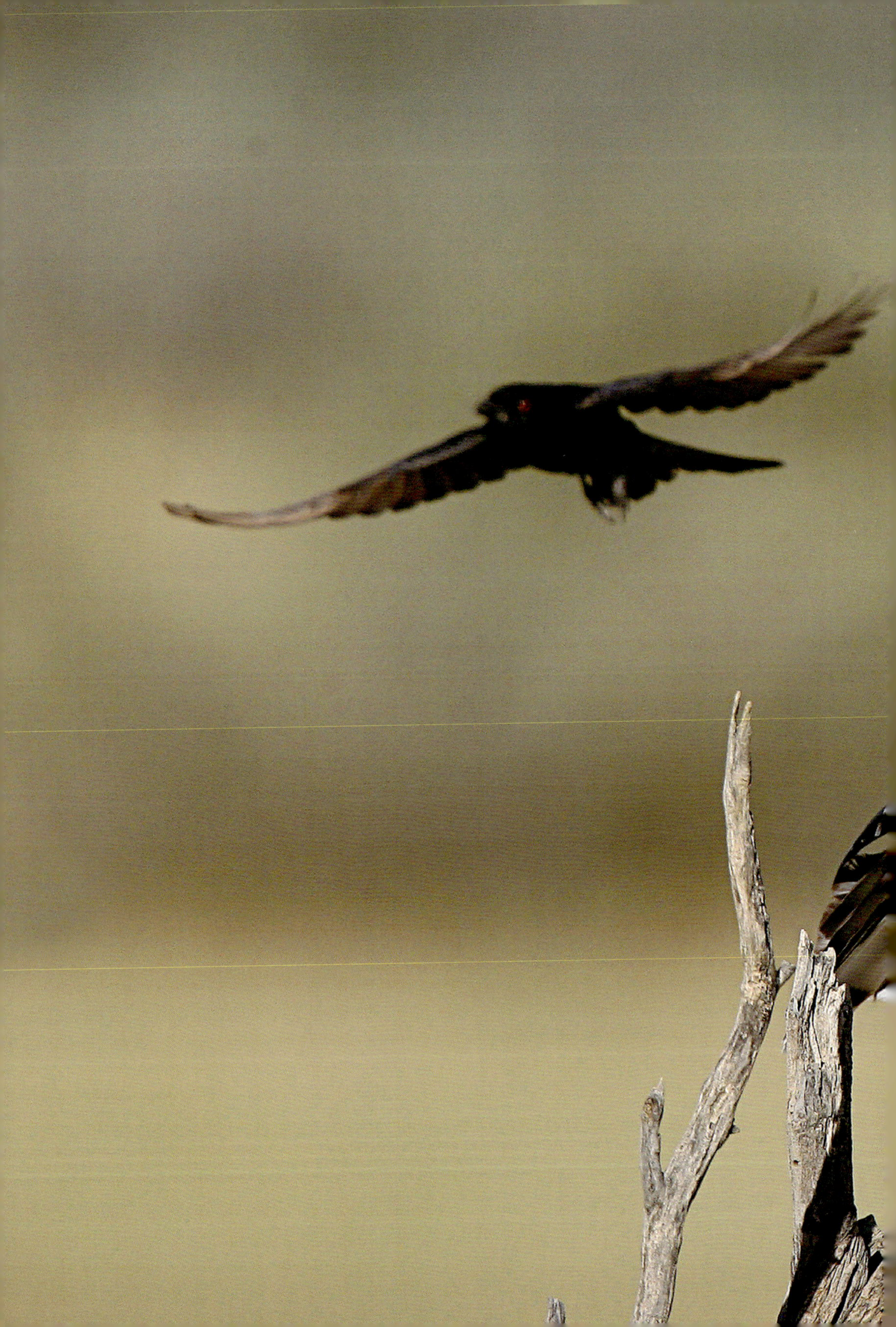

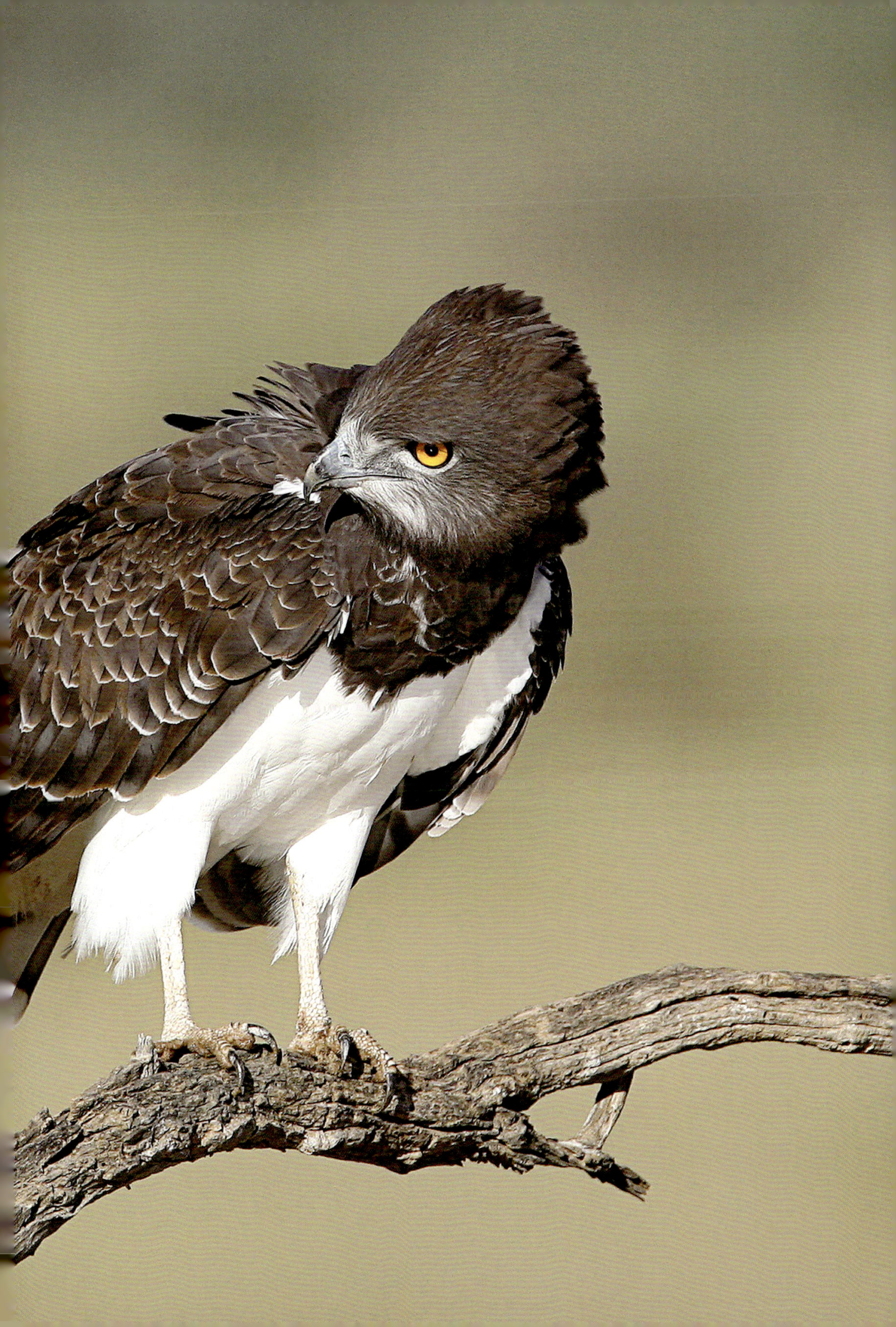

One of life's nasty little surprises

KATHY KAY

Kruger National Park is one of my favourite game parks, particularly for viewing baboons.

During a morning game drive we came across a troop of them and when I spotted this youngster I focused on him. He put what looked like a prickly worm into his mouth. It must have hurt or scared him because he suddenly jumped back in horror, falling over backwards. I was fortunate to capture the action. Life doesn't always deliver what you expect it to…

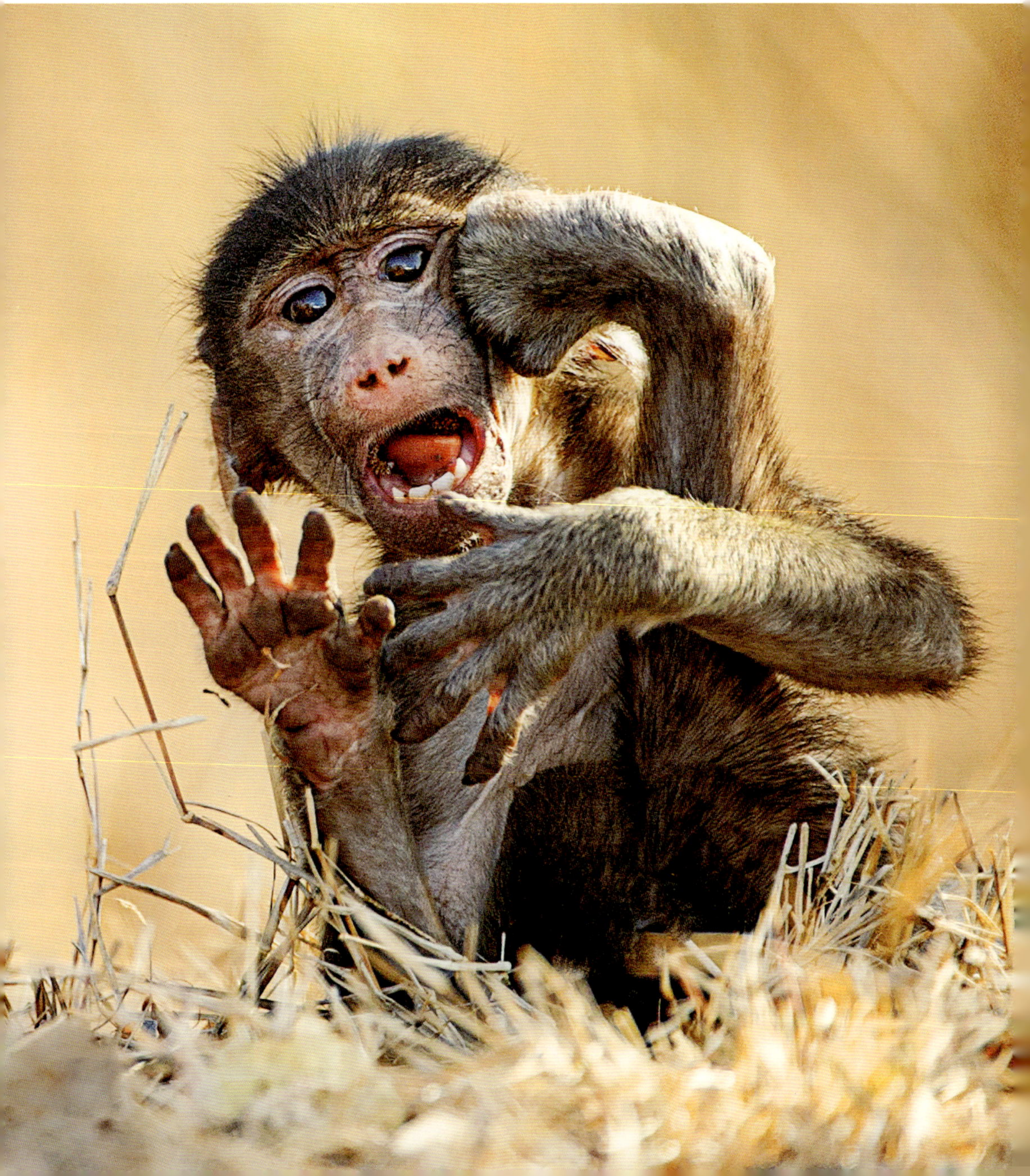

Never underestimate a hyena

MARIUS KRITZINGER

While staying in Grootkolk Wilderness Camp in the Kgalagadi Transfrontier Park we were driving past Kannagauss Waterhole in a southerly direction to see what was left of a kill from the previous afternoon, when we noticed a lone red hartebeest at the waterhole. We were amazed when we returned about an hour later to find this same hartebeest had been killed by a pack of six hyenas, that presumably surprised the buck while it was drinking at the waterhole.

After taking out all the innards and eating only the lungs, heart and liver of the animal, the hyenas had obviously had enough (perhaps they had eaten the night before at the earlier kill), and one of them started dragging the hartebeest towards the waterhole. We couldn't work out the method in its madness but then it became clear. The hyena continued to drag the hartebeest towards the waterhole and then, eventually, over the wall and into the water. When it was done, the pack of six regrouped and trotted away over a dune.

Back at Grootkolk Camp we found a park ranger who told us this is one of the ways hyenas will preserve the food they can't eat immediately for later consumption. Storing the hartebeest underwater is their way of 'preserving' it from jackals and vultures.

Late that same afternoon we watched the hyenas return to the waterhole, drag the submerged hartebeest out of the water and begin to feed on it again. Unfortunately, we couldn't photograph this very last episode of the unlucky hartebeest's existence because the water reservoir was in the way and spoilt our view. But what we witnessed that day is yet more proof hyenas are highly intelligent and always fascinating.

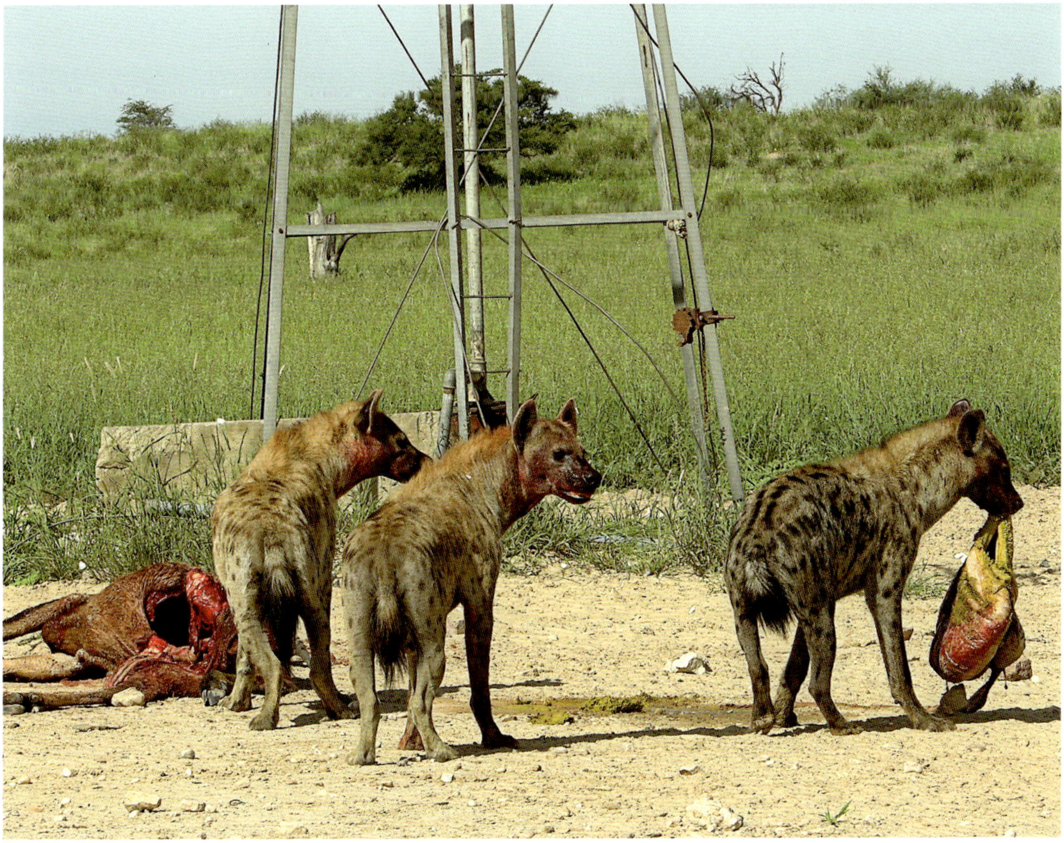

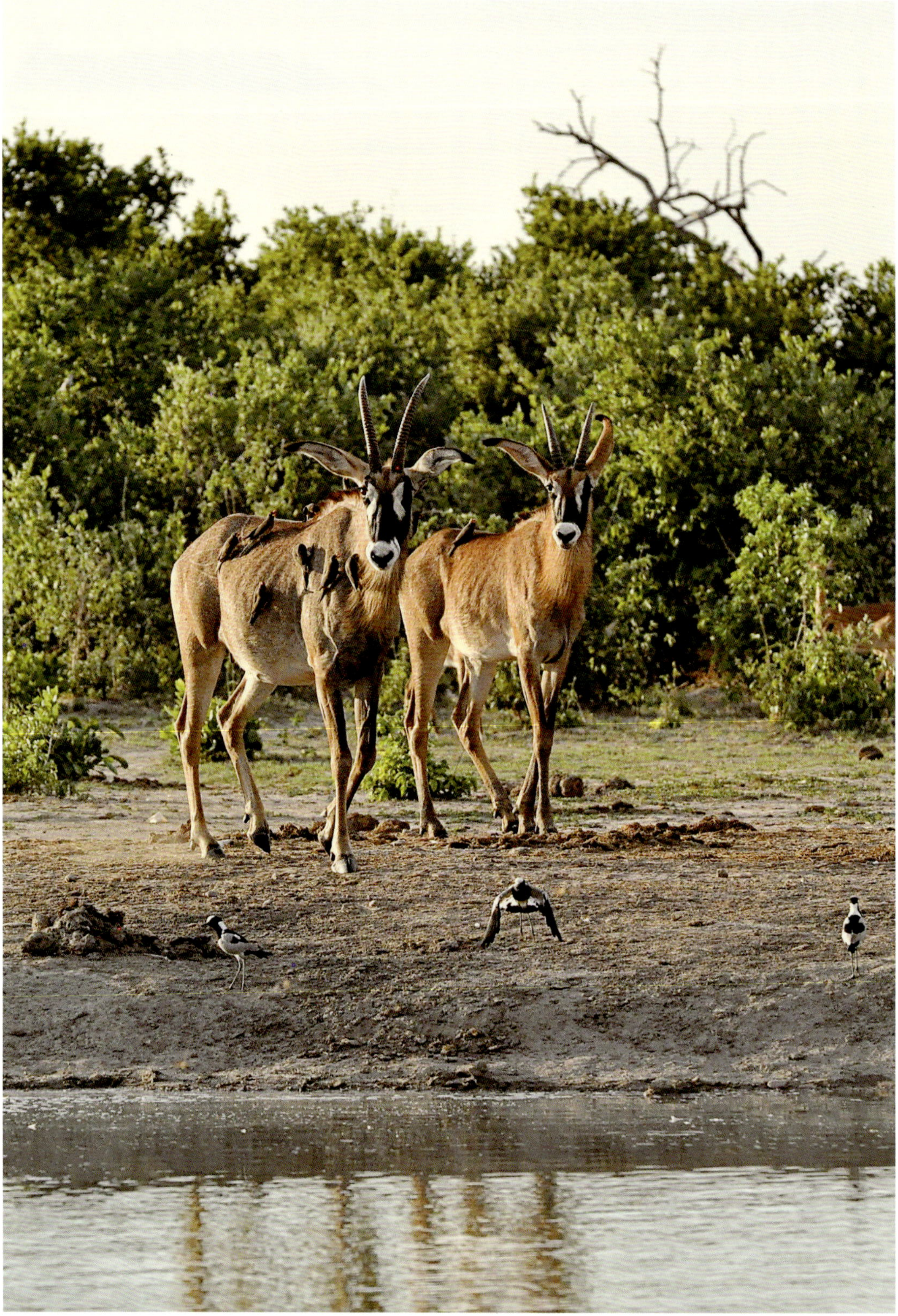

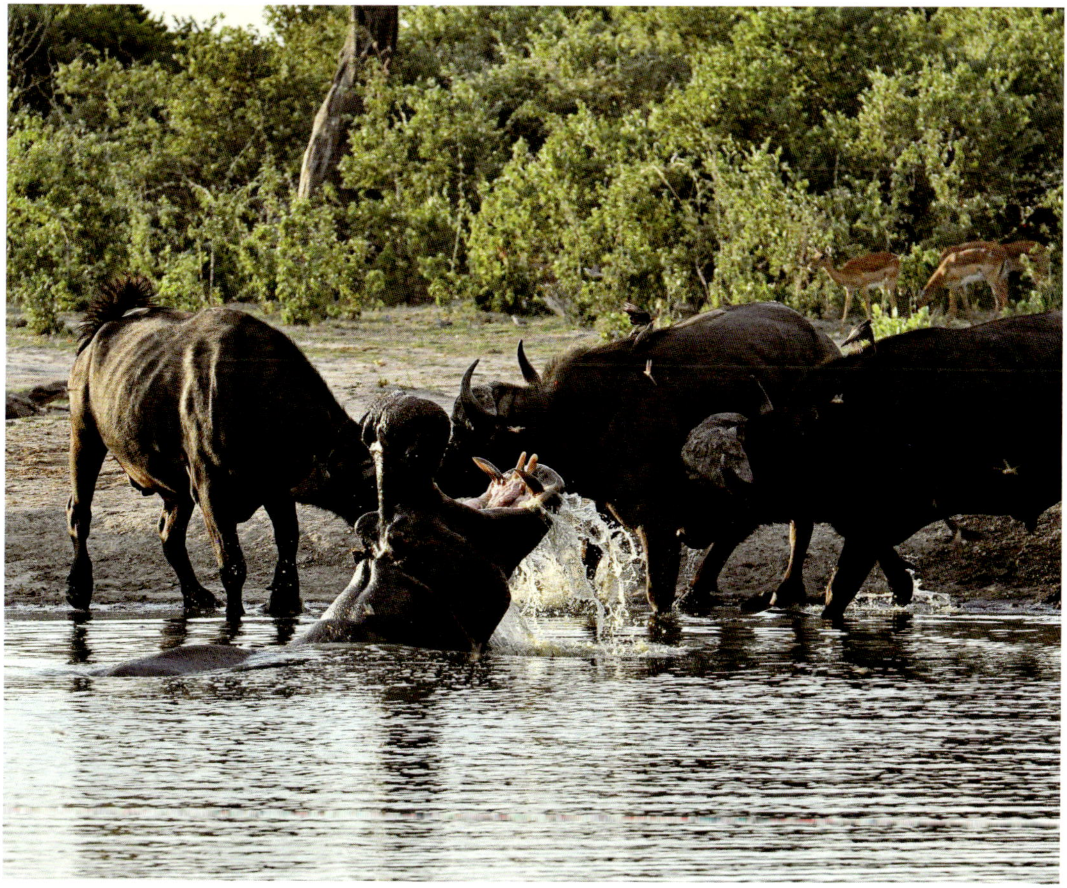

This is my waterhole!

HILTON SCHIPHOLT

It was 23 December 2018 and the Savuti Game Reserve was baking under the summer sun. At around 18:15 we went out for a short 'sundowner drive'. The park was parched so we stopped at a small waterhole a few kilometres from the camp to see what would come down for a last drink. There were a few blacksmith plovers darting about energetically, a few lethargic impala grazing on the fringes and one lonely hippo in the centre of the waterhole.

Out of the mopani thicket a thirsty pair of roan antelope appeared. A great and rare sighting for us but it seemed to be an unwelcome sight for the hippo in the centre of the oasis which moved uneasily and watched their every move. Sensing the unwelcoming stare and reception, the two paused. They glanced at the hippo and looked longingly at the refreshing water and then reluctantly walked away. We wondered if they'd met this grumpy inhabitant on a previous occasion.

Shortly after a few tired-looking buffalo ambled up to quench their thirst. The hippo twitched edgily, uncomfortable with the new visitors once more. As we all know, there's not much that scares a buffalo, so a few braved the evil eye watching them and edged closer for a drink. The hippo put up with this but when the couple of buffalo became several, we could almost hear our grumpy resident thinking, "Enough is enough – these big-hooved beasts are going to empty my waterhole!" So with his mouth wide open and a heave or two in the water, he showed them who owned this patch of water, and banished them to the lower reaches of his waterhole.

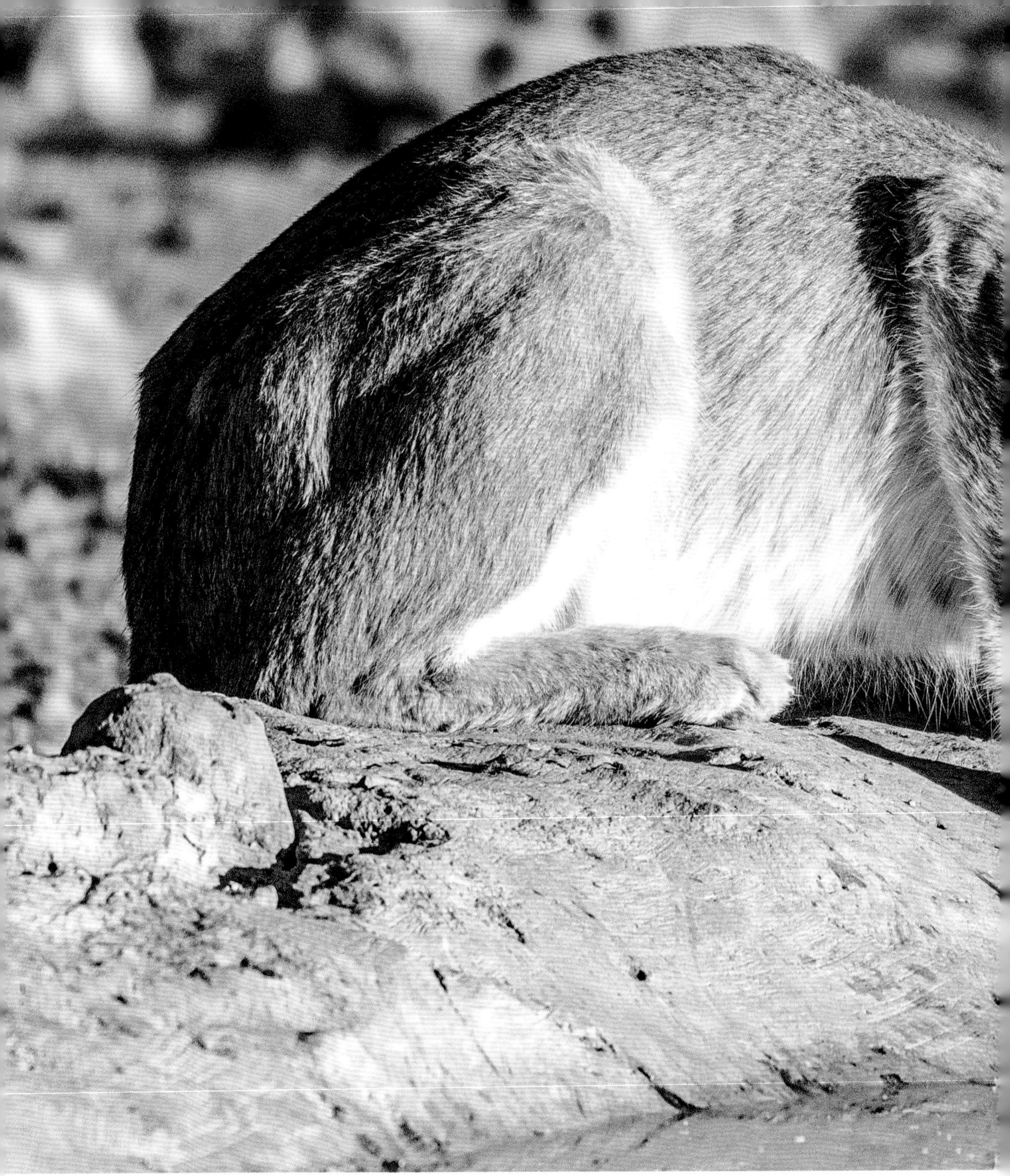

Six forty magic at Kij Kij

GERHARDT THERON

For three consecutive days Kij Kij Waterhole in the Kgalagadi Transfrontier Park presented me with amazing photographic opportunities at precisely six forty in the morning. On the first day, which fell on 6 January 2019, it was a brown hyena, the second day another brown hyena and on the third day a caracal.

The day before, I was parked a short distance from Kij Kij Waterhole on Nossob Road watching several black-backed jackal. From where I was parked I noticed nervous gemsbok scattering in all directions as they approached the water. Lion had

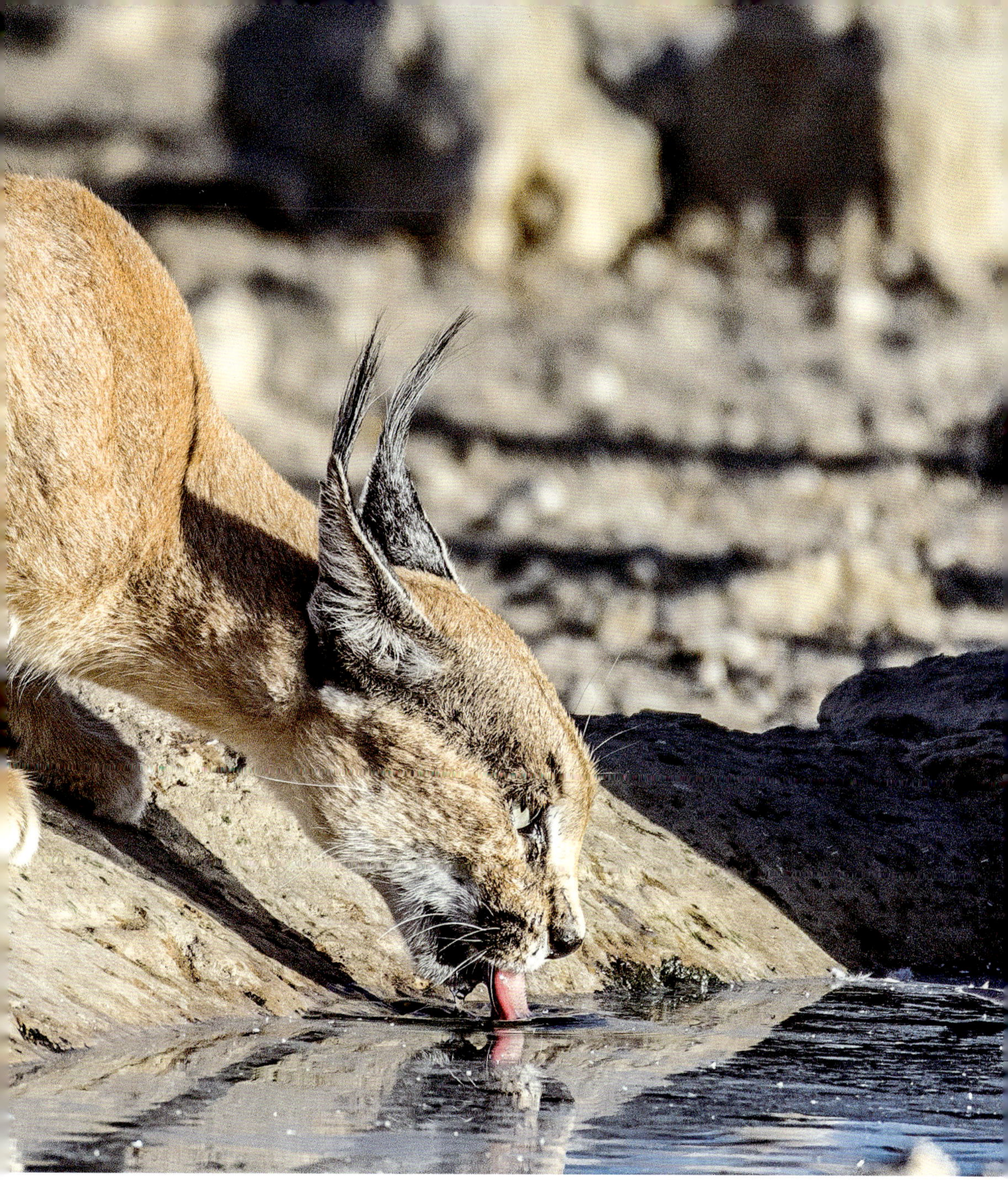

been seen there the previous day and I wondered if they were still around and putting off other game. I could see nothing and so I moved on at around 8:30. That evening my campsite neighbours at Twee Rivieren told me about an amazing sighting of a leopard soon after I'd left. I decided to return early the next morning in the hope that I might be in luck. I was, but instead of a leopard, I spotted a brown hyena at 6:40. I was there again the next morning and at exactly 6:40, I saw the brown hyena once more. When I told fellow campers about the magic of 6:40 at Kij Kij, they laughed, and said it was pure coincidence. But their scepticism meant they lost out on a magnificent sighting of a caracal at Kij Kij Waterhole the next day at – yes, you've guessed it – 6:40 sharp.

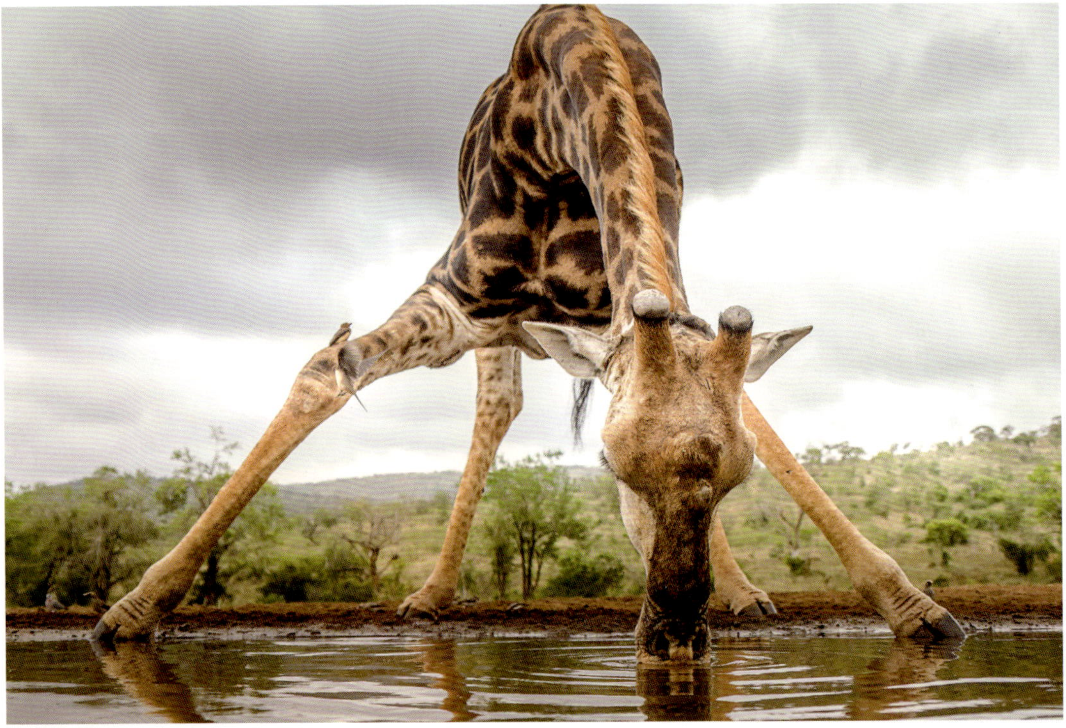

Birthday gifts

DARRYLL BENECKE

My wife and I were visiting Zimanga Private Game Reserve in KwaZulu-Natal to celebrate her birthday, where we had the privilege of a wonderful wildlife experience with an emphasis on wildlife photography. I had kept our destination secret from her, so she was very excited when we arrived.

Our three days there were spent revelling in the majesty and wildlife diversity of this estate.

The pinnacle of the visit was our sleep-over in the waterhole hide. The game-viewing area provides sturdy tripods, comfortable adjustable chairs and is curtained off from the rest of the apartment to ensure no light shines through towards the wildlife. Observing the comings and goings of the birds and animals from late afternoon until well into the evening was like watching the commuters in a busy underground train system.

We had passed a large elephant bull with huge tusks on our way to the hide and within minutes of settling in, we received a visit from him. He started drinking two metres from our camera lenses. My wife's compact camera caught him, but with my 24–70 millimetre lens all I could get was a partial view of his head and eye, with a couple of centimetres of his tusks. When he finished drinking, he started to spray himself with water and mud which landed on our viewing glass, spoiling our outlook. After he'd left us, it took about 30 minutes to clean up before we could view the game again.

There were many visiting buffalo in the night, with one bull in particular that seemed to pose deliberately to give us all the shots we wanted.

In the early hours of the morning there were few visitors, but as dawn approached the commuters began arriving until the activity became frenetic. A woolly-necked stork patrolled one metre away, and we had notable sightings of guinea-fowl, warthogs, zebra, nyala and many others before the special sighting of an enormous male giraffe bending down in front of us to drink. I just managed to get him into the frame.

If only all birthdays could be celebrated in this spectacular way…

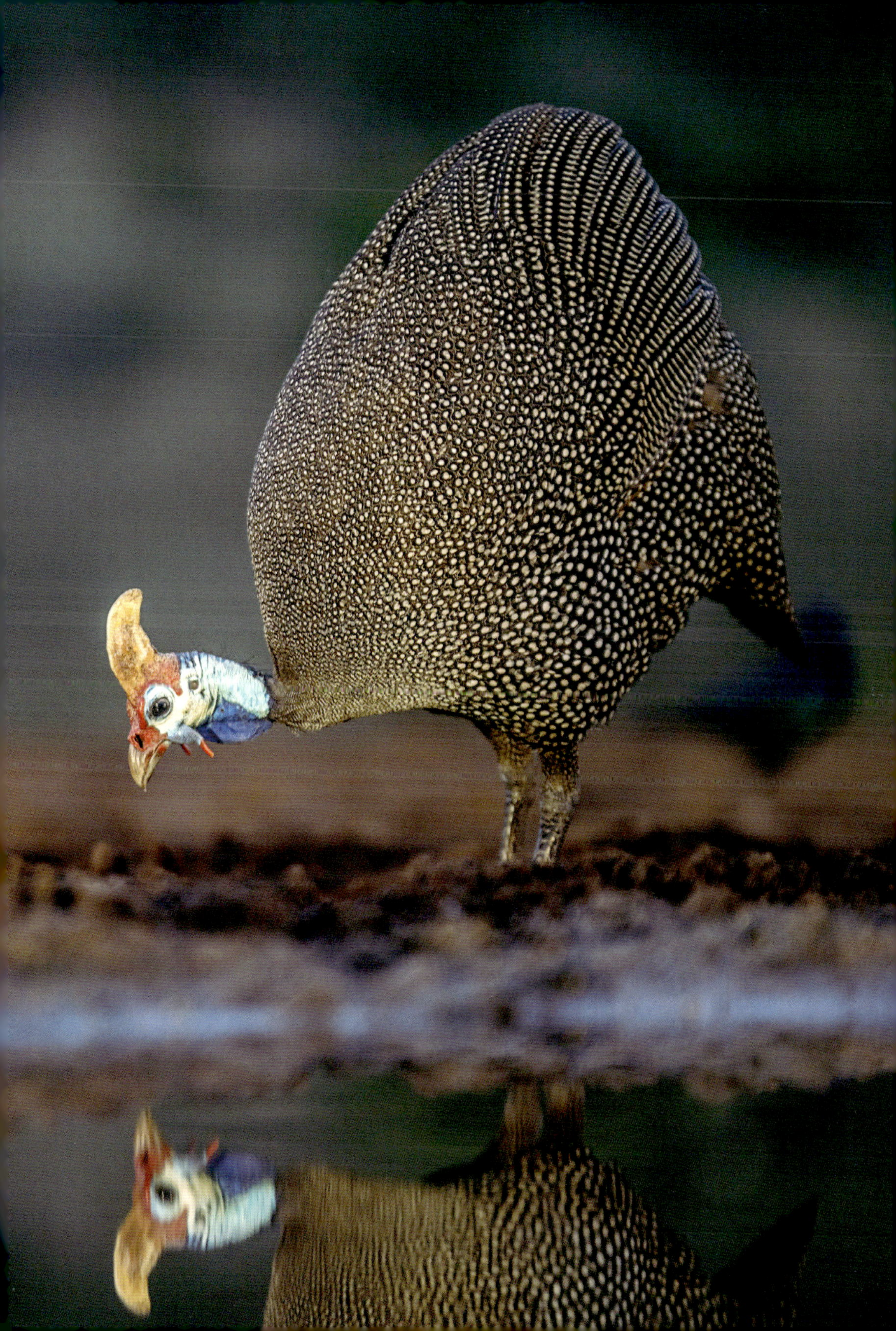

Wildlife studies in the garden

TOM PRINS

As pensioners living in a retirement village with limited space, my wife and I share the same study/ art workshop. This serves as my dry lab where my editing is done. A while ago I was doing some editing on sport images and noticed the busy bird life in the bottlebrush just outside my garden on the pavement. I thought this might be an opportunity for me, despite my limited equipment, to take some 'wild' garden bird photos.

First I had to make some preparations. In the wild, these birds flock together at natural feeding spots such as grasslands or where there is fresh water. If I was going to photograph the ones that came to my vicinity, I needed to line up what I called the 'landing space', with my hide (my study) where the camera would be. I had to create an acceptable background as well.

For the landing space, I fixed a thick branch to my portable braai near the grass on the pavement, with fresh water about a metre away. Much to my delight, this piece of wood did eventually become the landing spot and point of departure for many birds. Against the opposite wall I fixed a grey backdrop which was in line with this landing spot and the camera. Of course, there was a lot of action which took place outside the coverage area but I was still fortunate enough to enjoy many pleasant moments, both observing and capturing images.

I found, somewhat to my surprise, that the birds displayed wild bird characteristics, perhaps because many of these birds began to assert ownership of the landing spot. Some enjoyed it as an inspection point before they took on the challenge of eating or drinking. Some interacted with, or confronted and challenged other birds, and often they tried to defend their territory.

Taken in all, it has been a wonderful experience. It gave me great satisfaction that they accepted the background within a few days and became accustomed to it. I observed extraordinary behaviour as well as a great variety of species. Some birds, like the Indian myna, Cape turtle-dove and laughing dove favoured the landing spot, though they didn't interact much. There were the dominant birds which claimed ownership of the landing spot. Some of them even dictated the flow (arrivals as well as departures). These were mostly the weavers, sparrows and occasionally the red-eyed bulbul. Aggressive confrontations between these dominant birds were the highlights of my photo sessions.

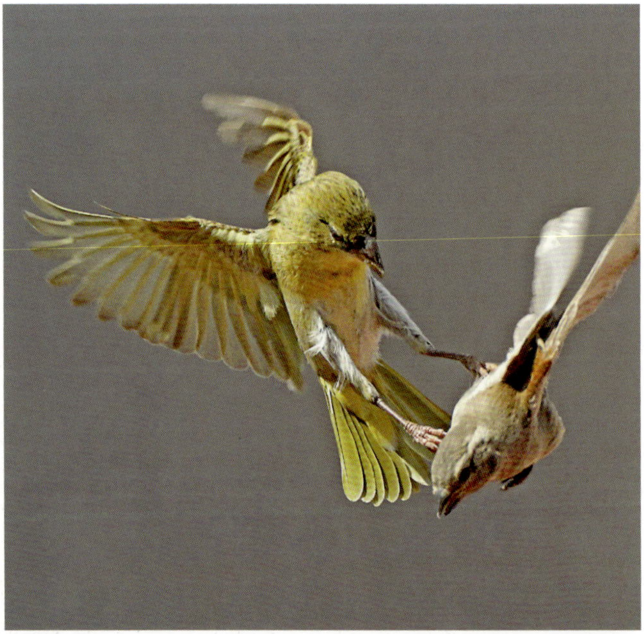

The sudden noise of a motorcar passing by often caused all the birds to flutter to safety in the bottlebrush. They would settle down within five to 10 minutes.

I noted and captured their actions and interactions and came to realise just how wide a study of bird behaviour I'd created for myself. I'm looking forward to enjoying more of this for many a sunny morning to come.

Necessity is the mother of invention, as the old adage goes, and this was definitely the case with me. Having used some ingenuity, I'm able to enjoy wildlife sightings (even if on a small scale) and to record images that have value for me and – who knows – maybe for others as well.

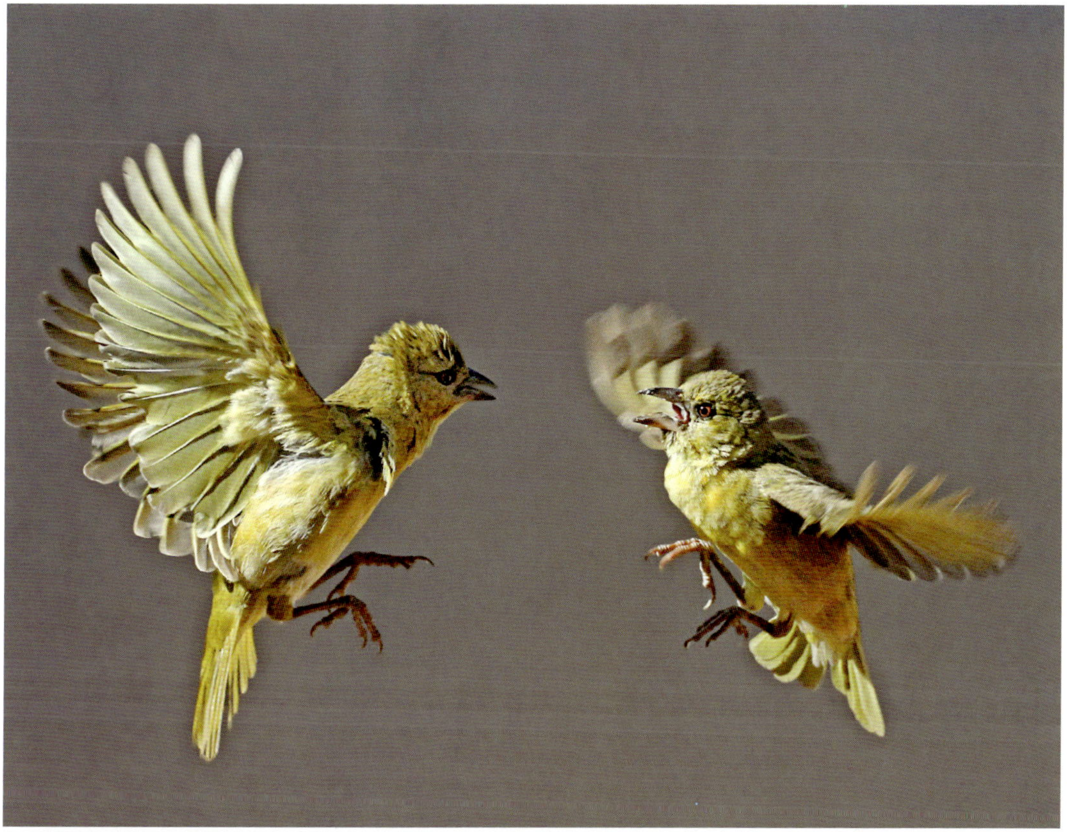

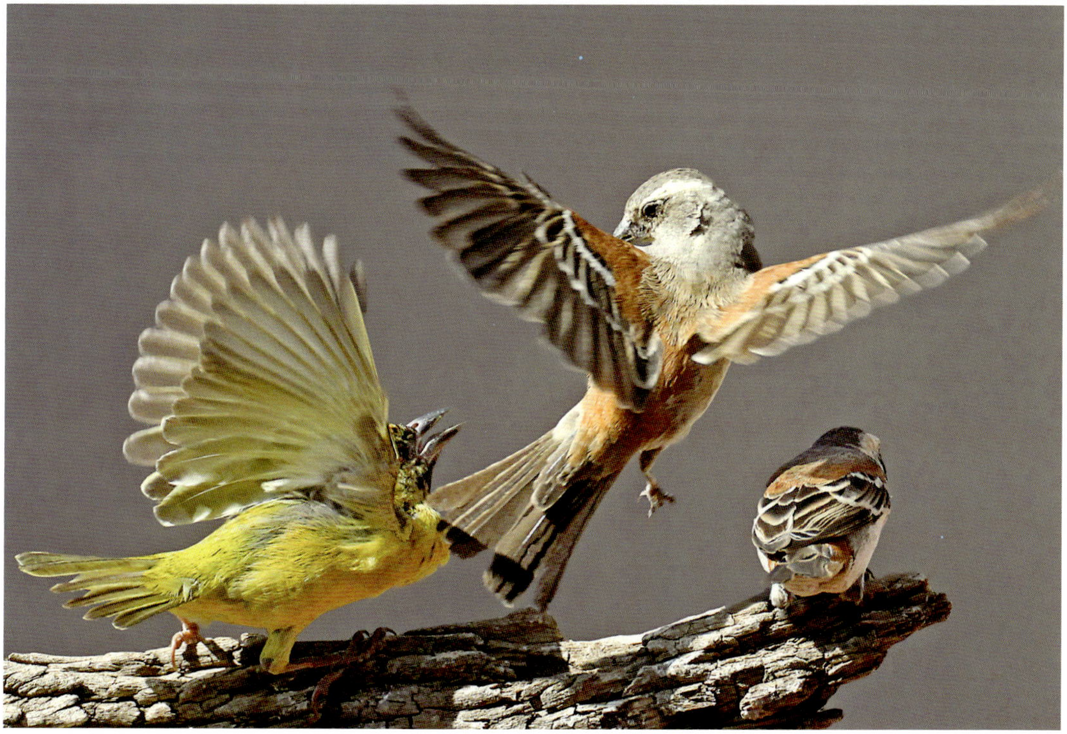

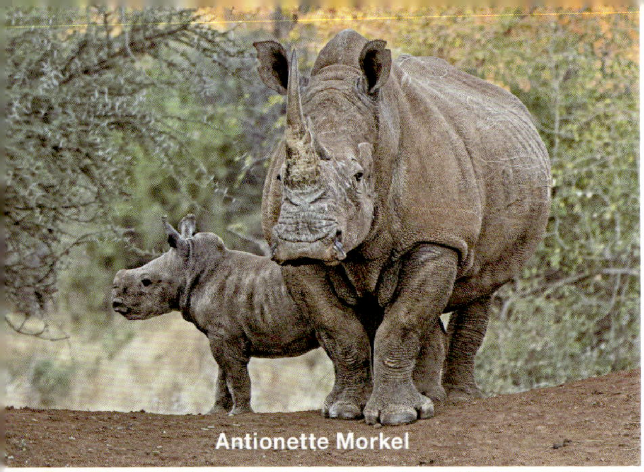
Antionette Morkel

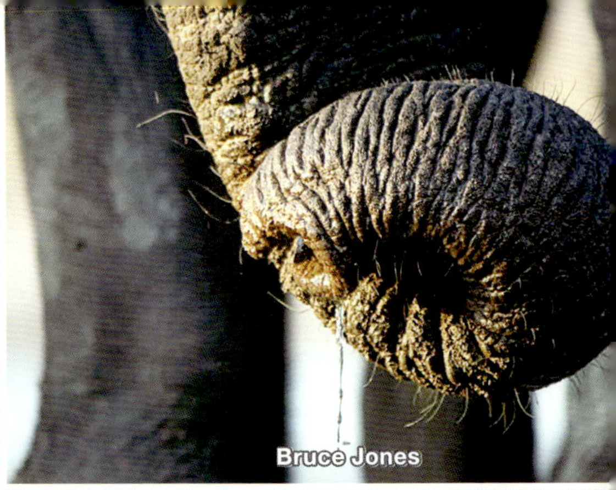
Bruce Jones

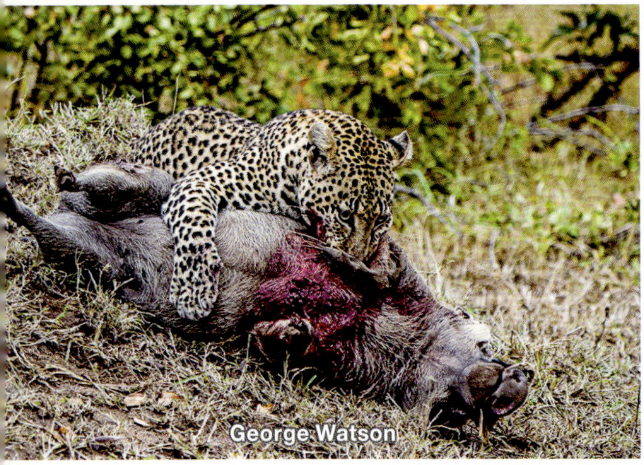
George Watson

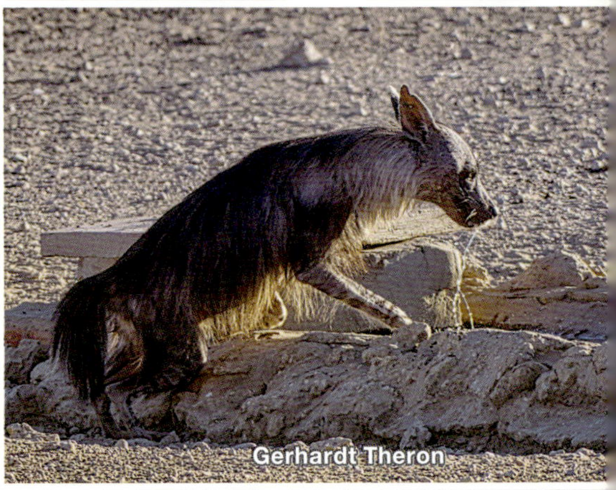
Gerhardt Theron

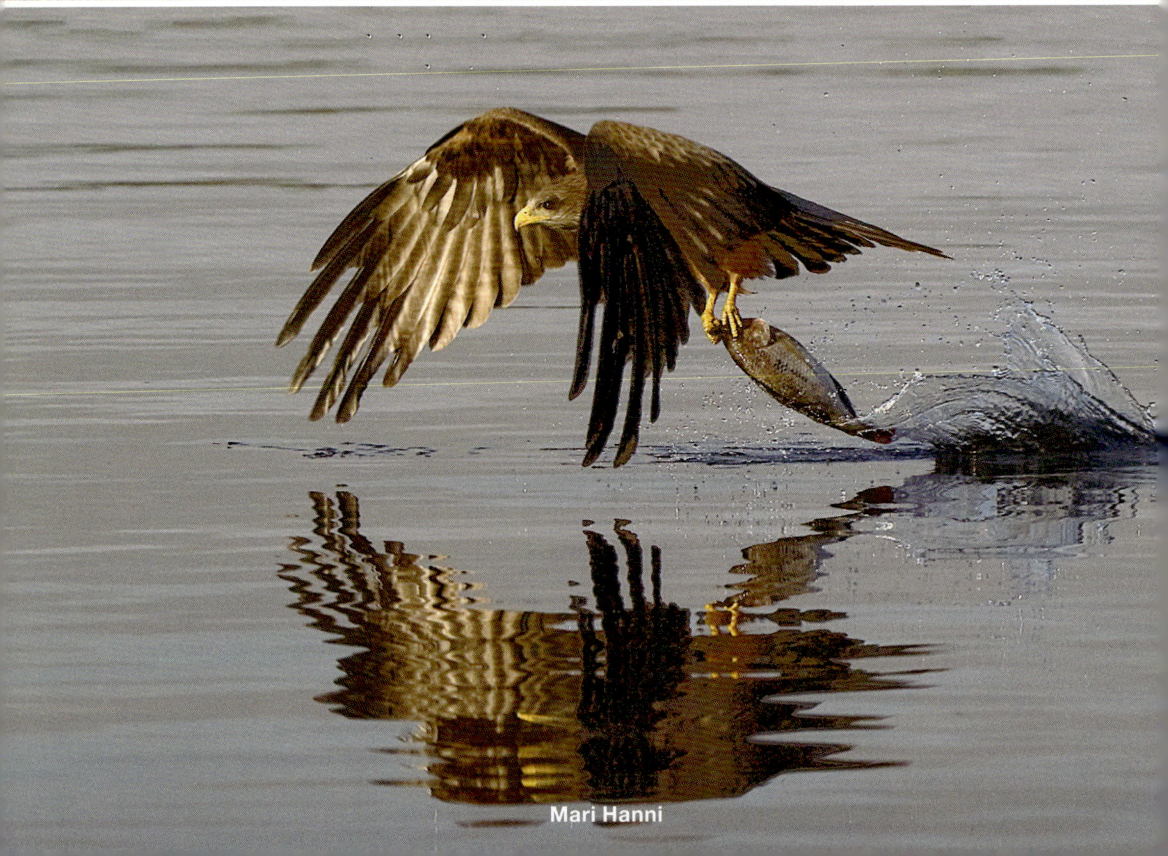
Mari Hanni

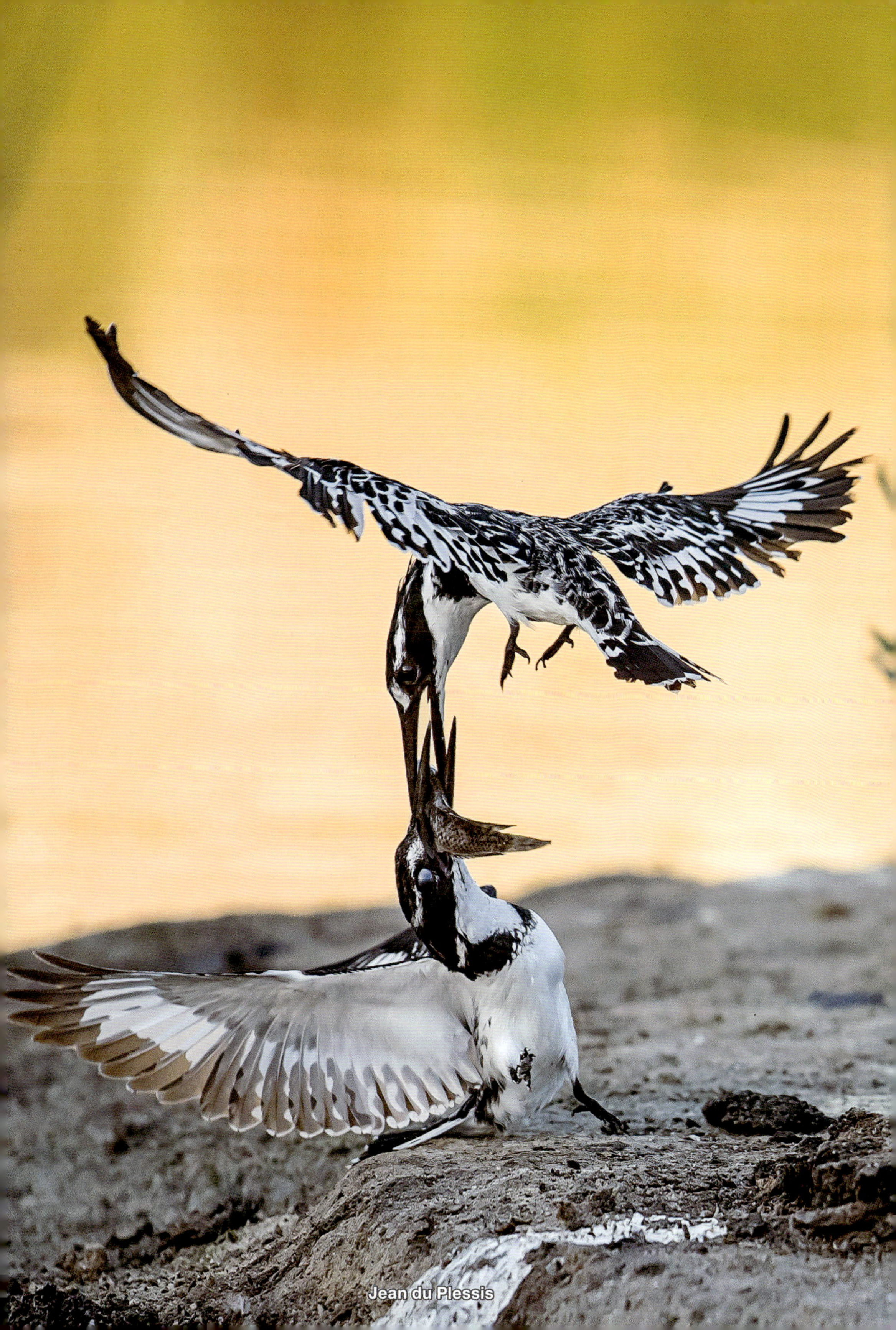

Jean du Plessis

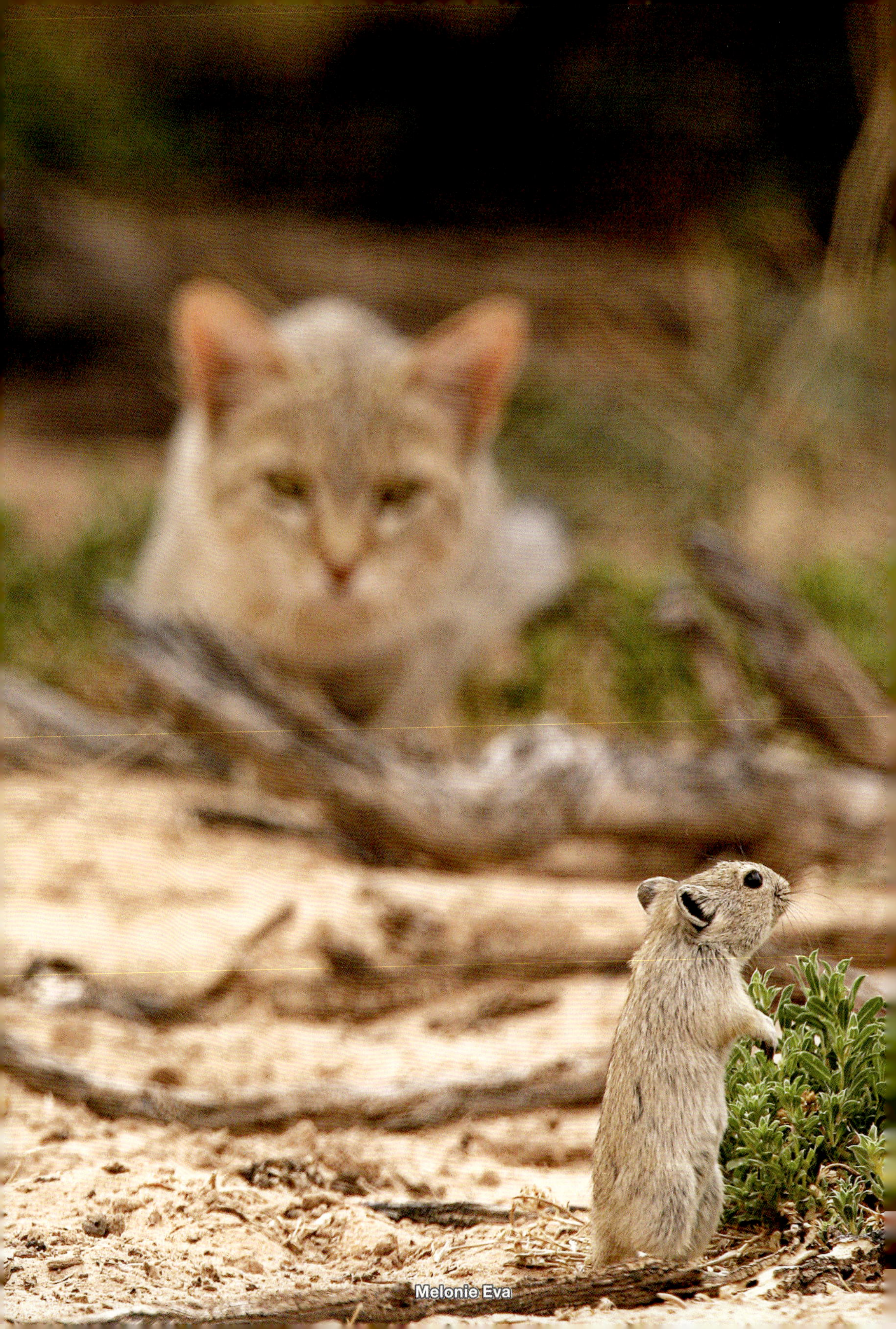
Melonie Eva

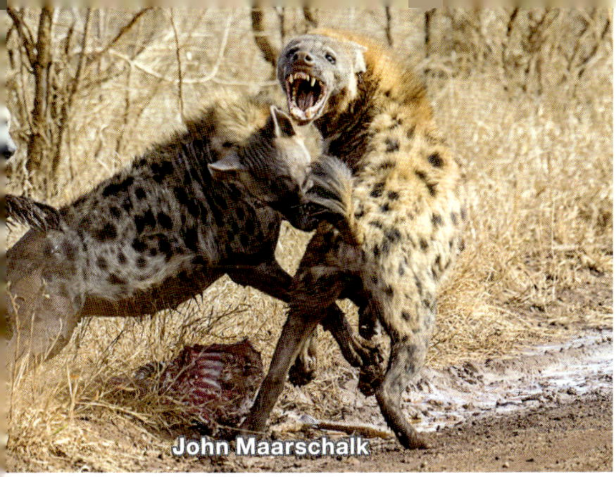
John Maarschalk

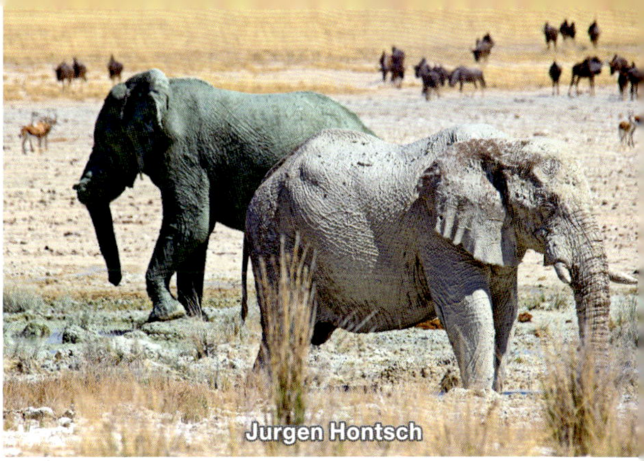
Jurgen Hontsch

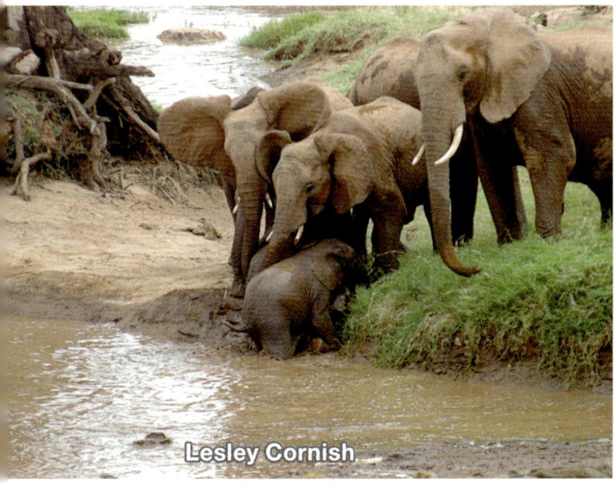
Lesley Cornish

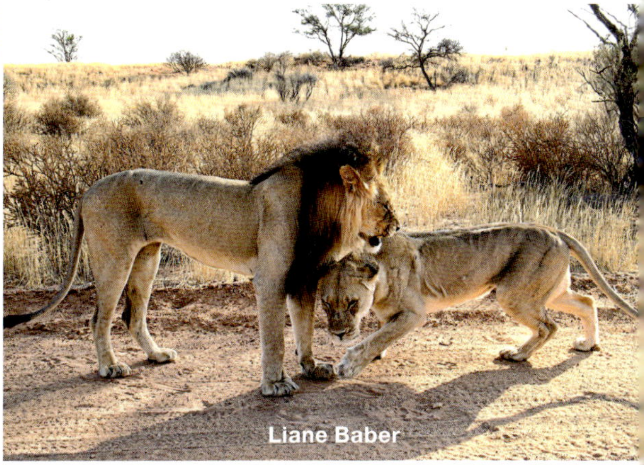
Liane Baber

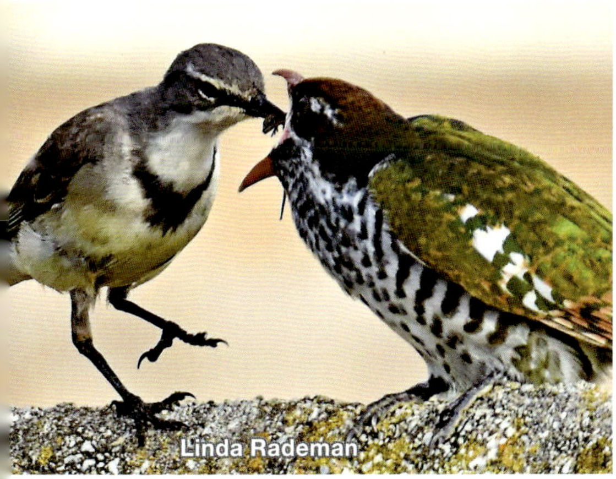
Linda Rademan

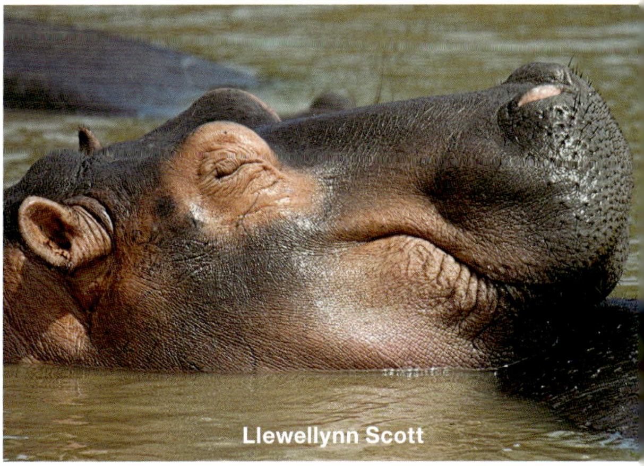
Llewellynn Scott

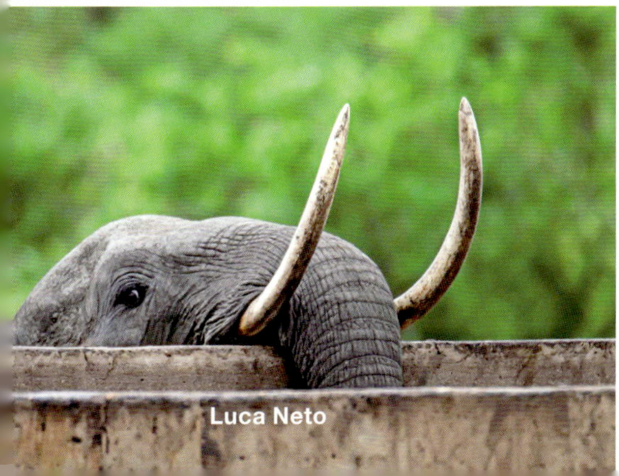
Luca Neto

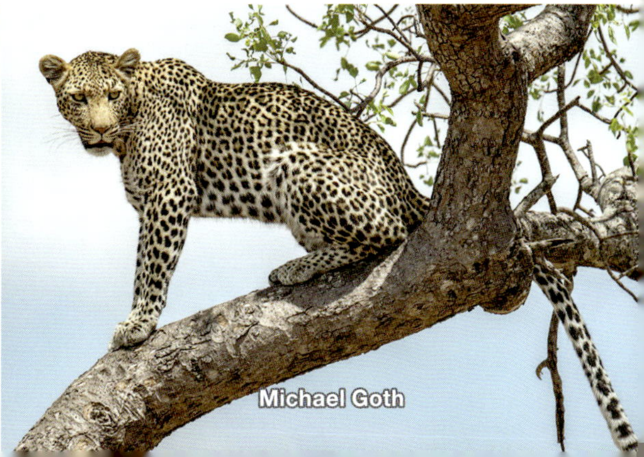
Michael Goth

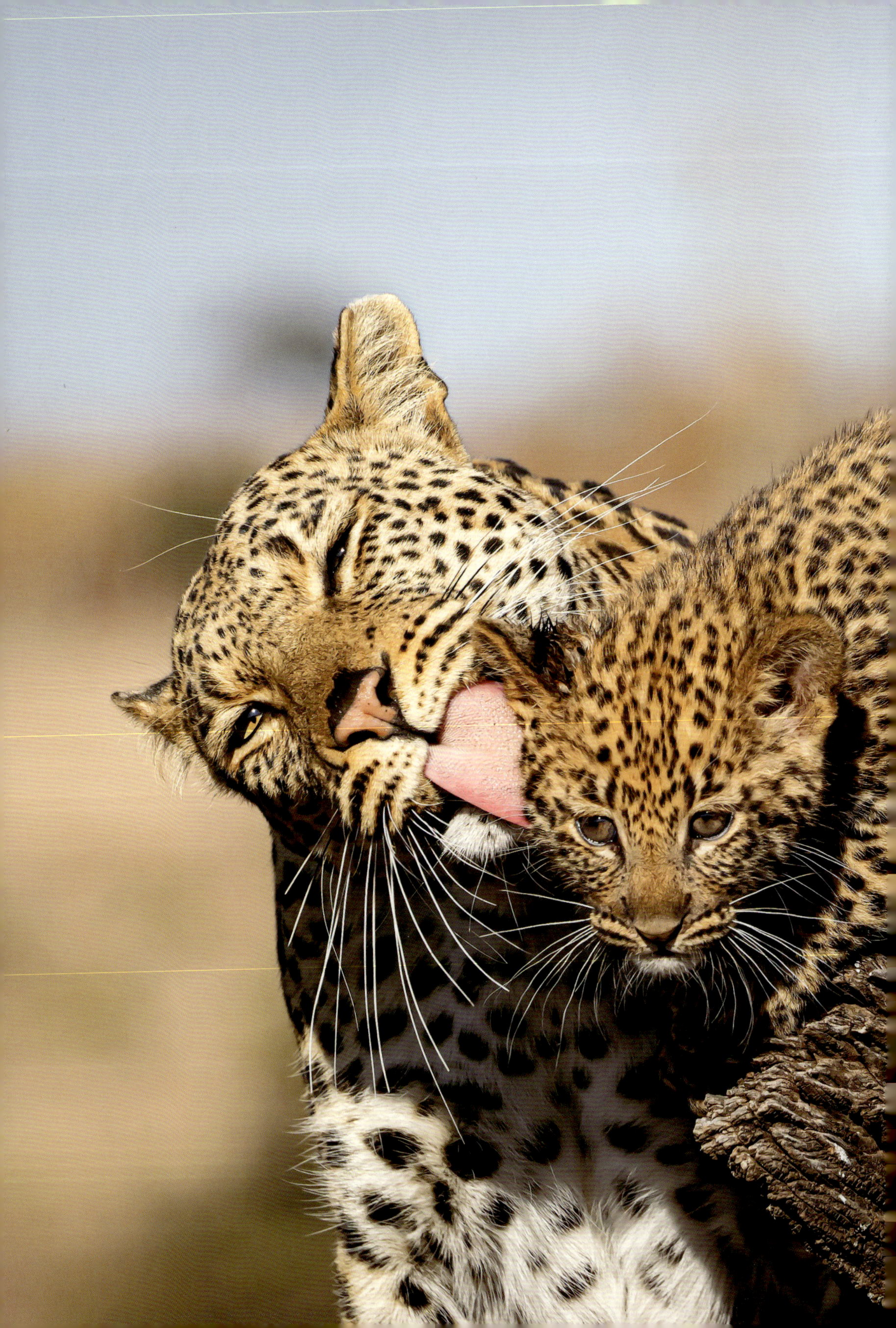

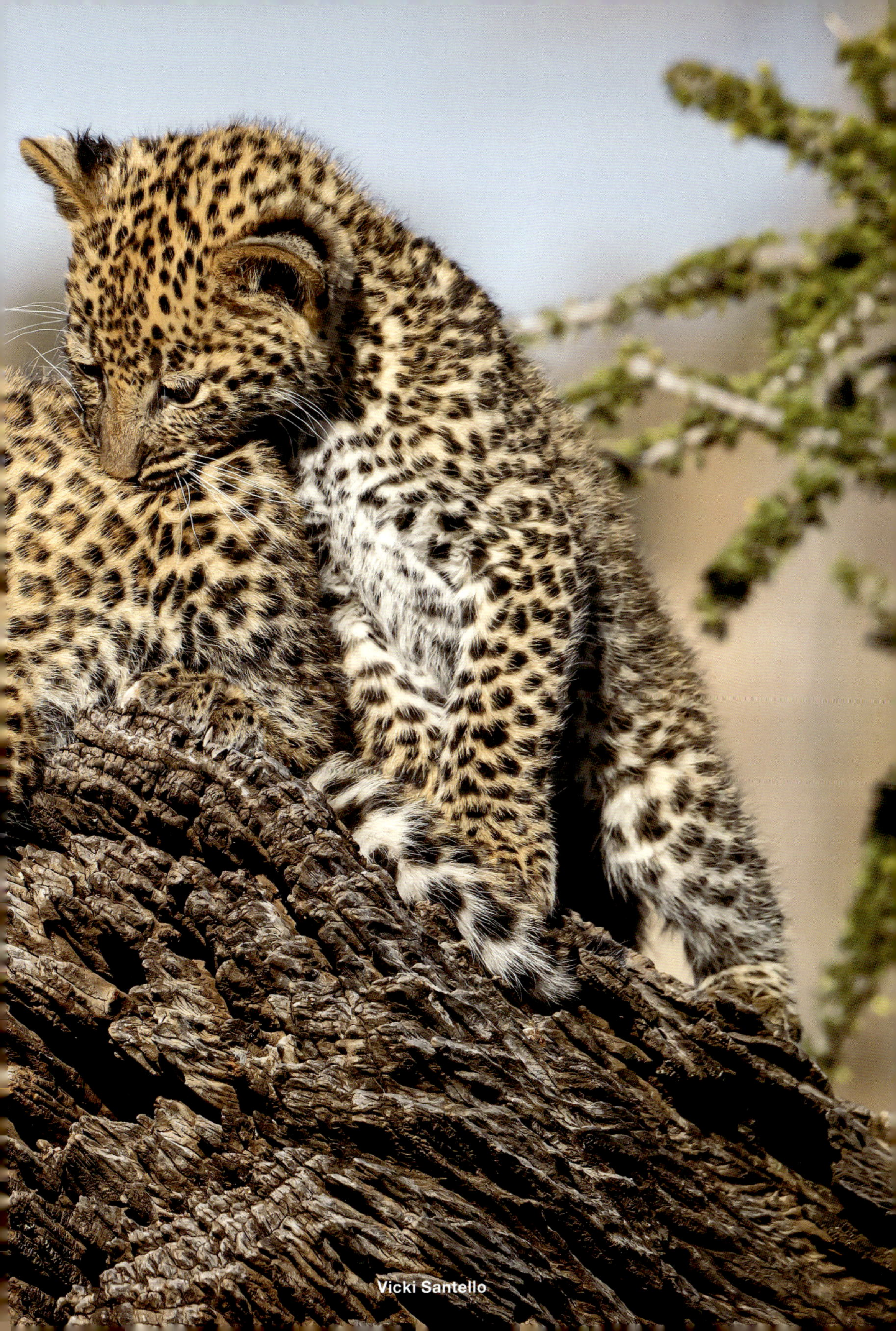

Vicki Santello

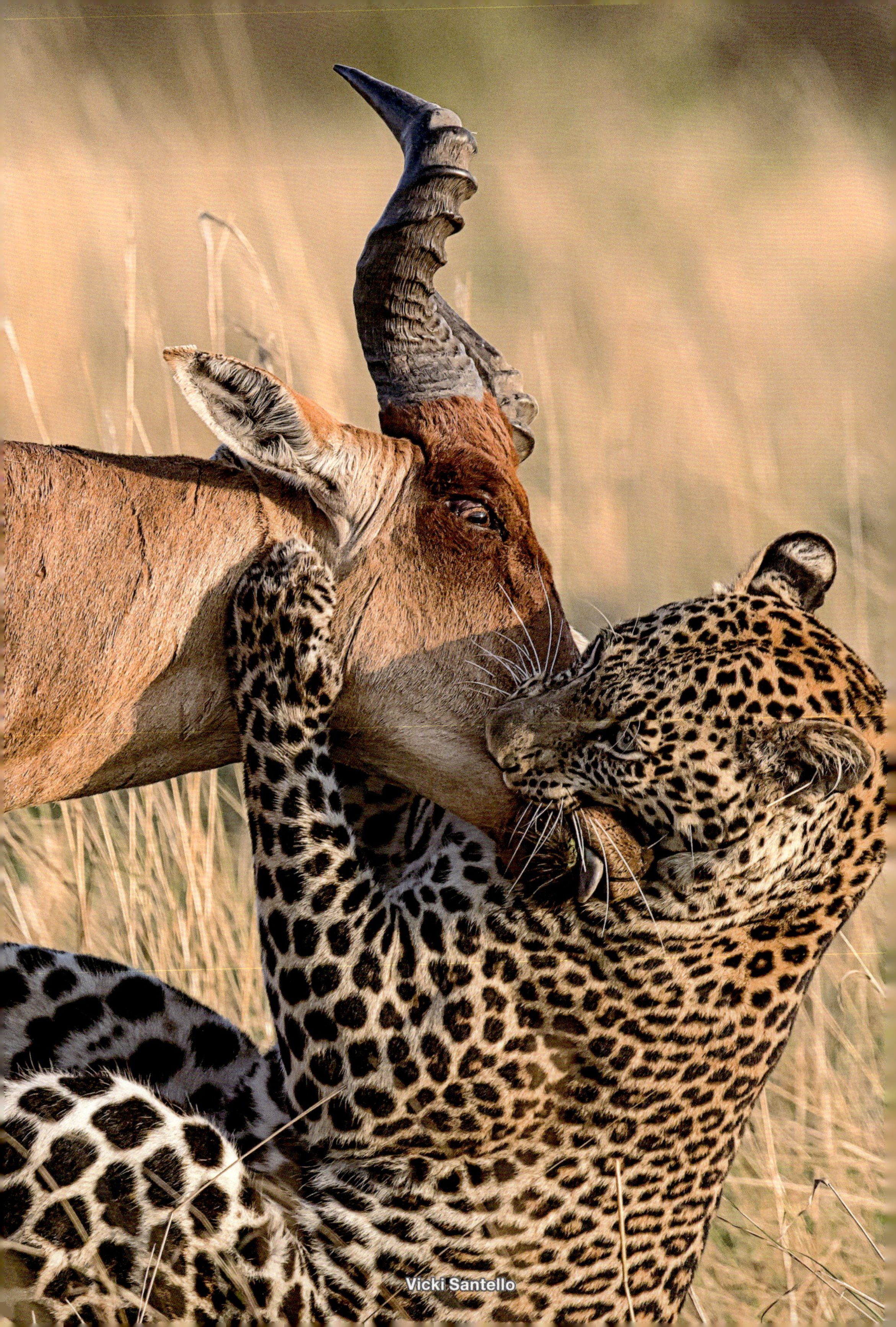

Vicki Santello

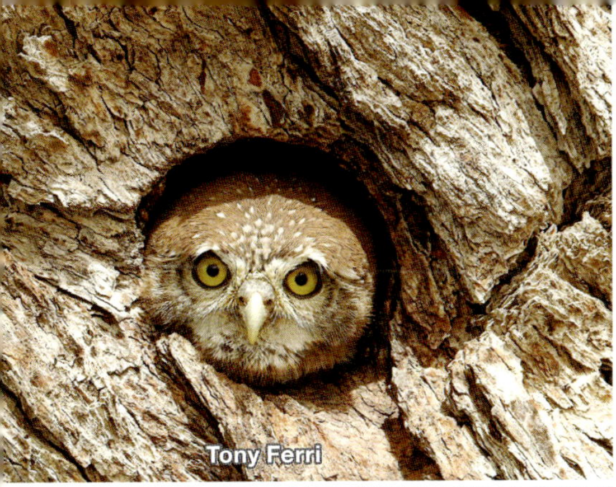
Tony Ferri

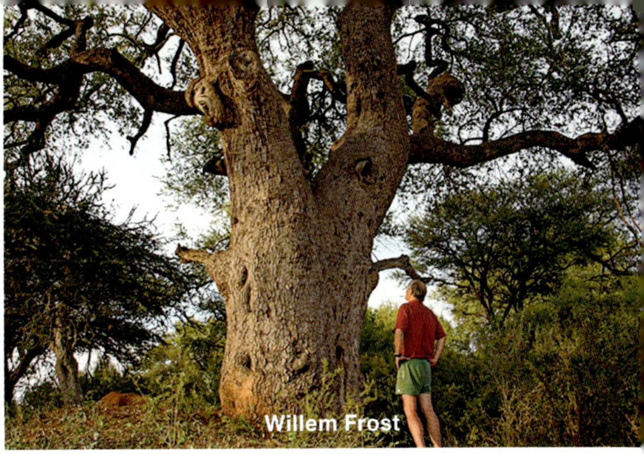
Willem Frost

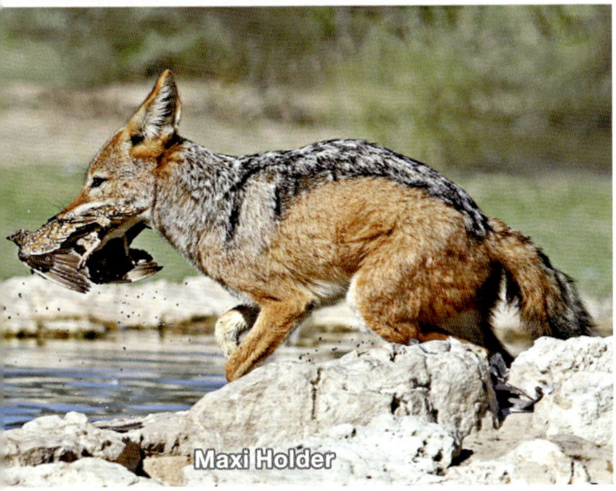
Maxi Holder

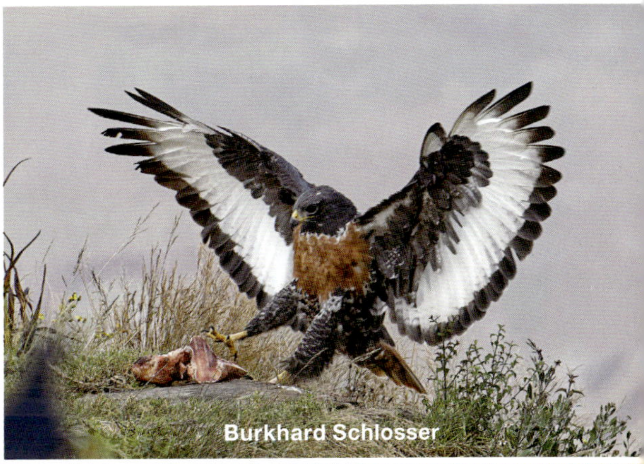
Burkhard Schlosser

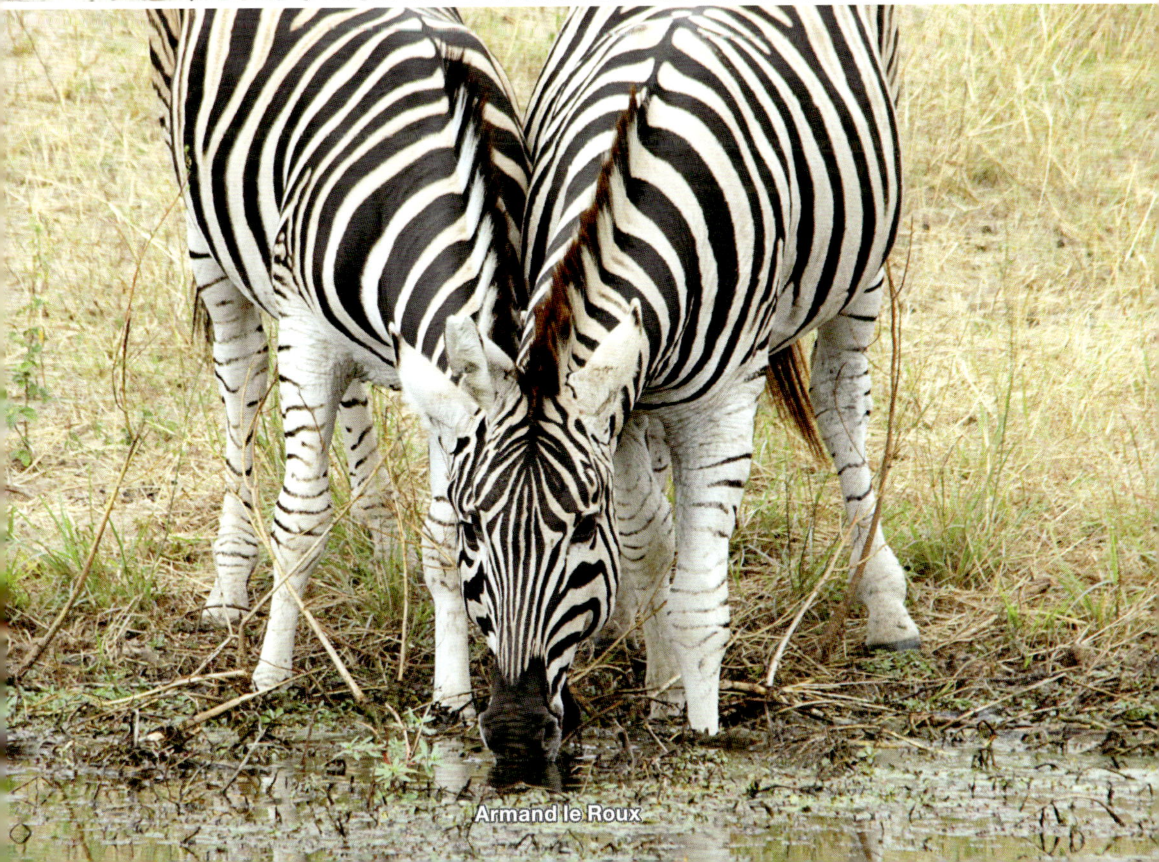
Armand le Roux

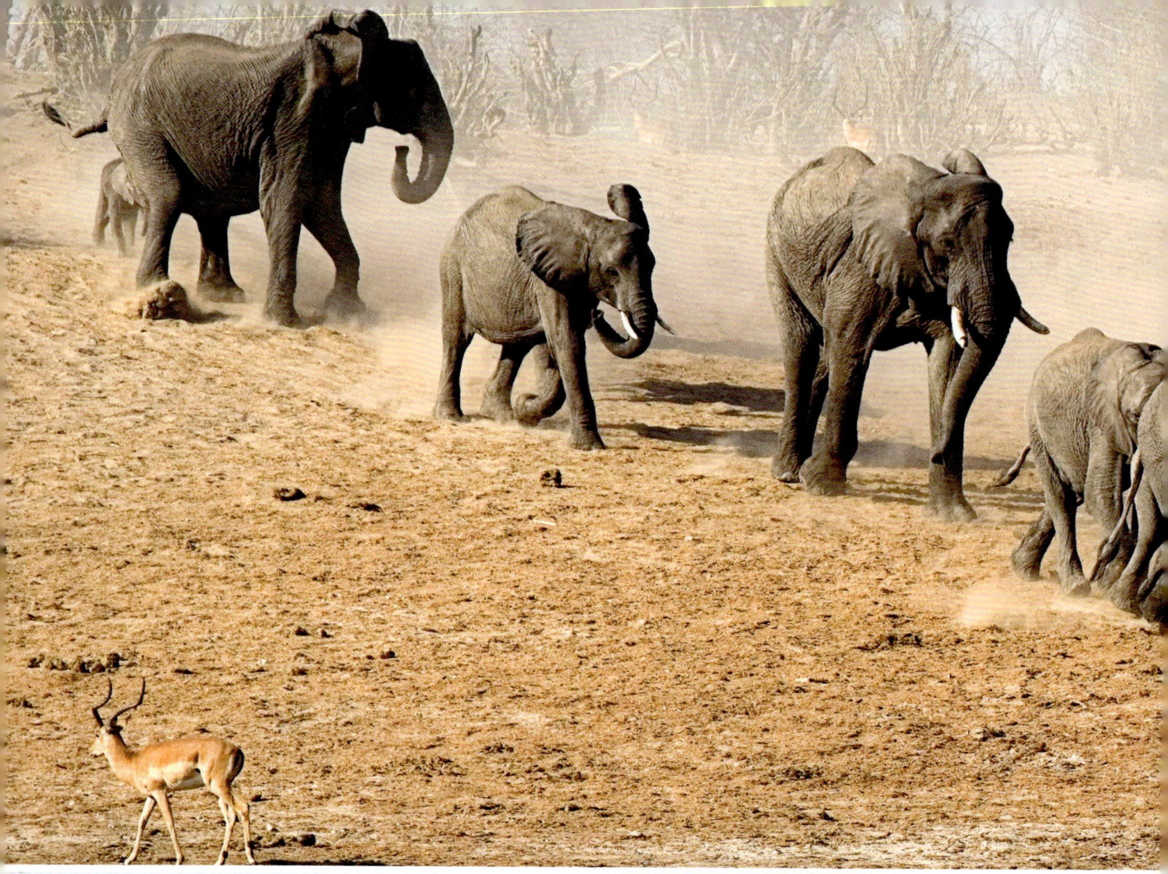

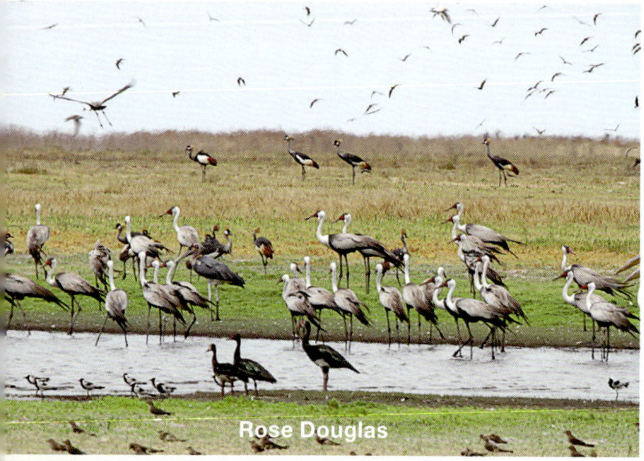

Rose Douglas

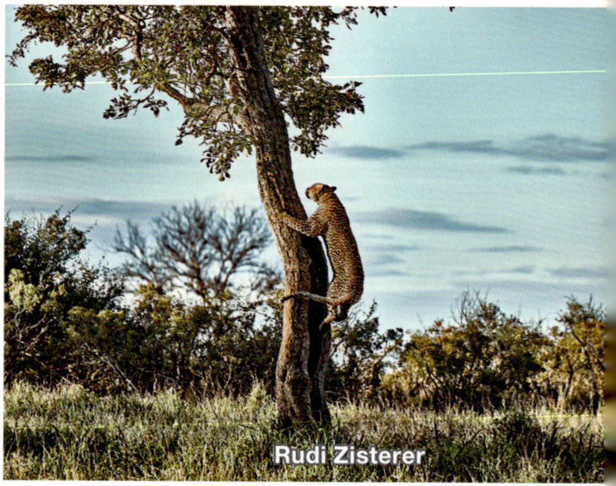

Rudi Zisterer

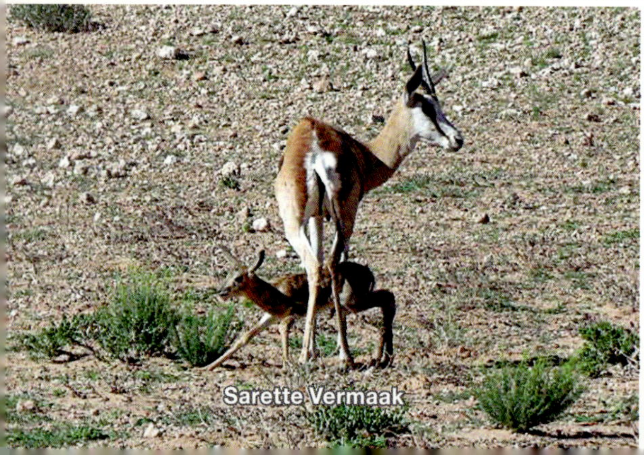

Sarette Vermaak

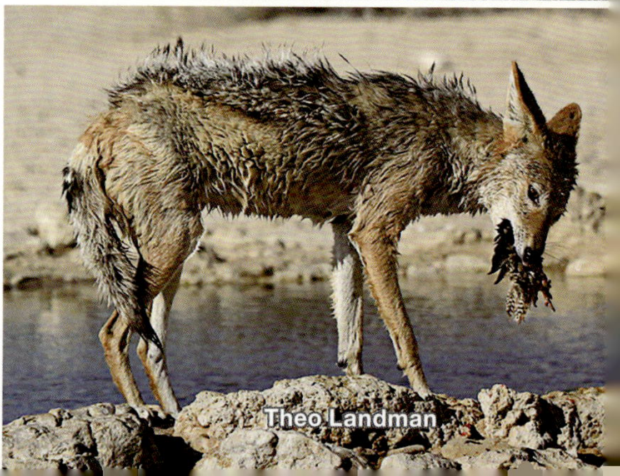

Theo Landman

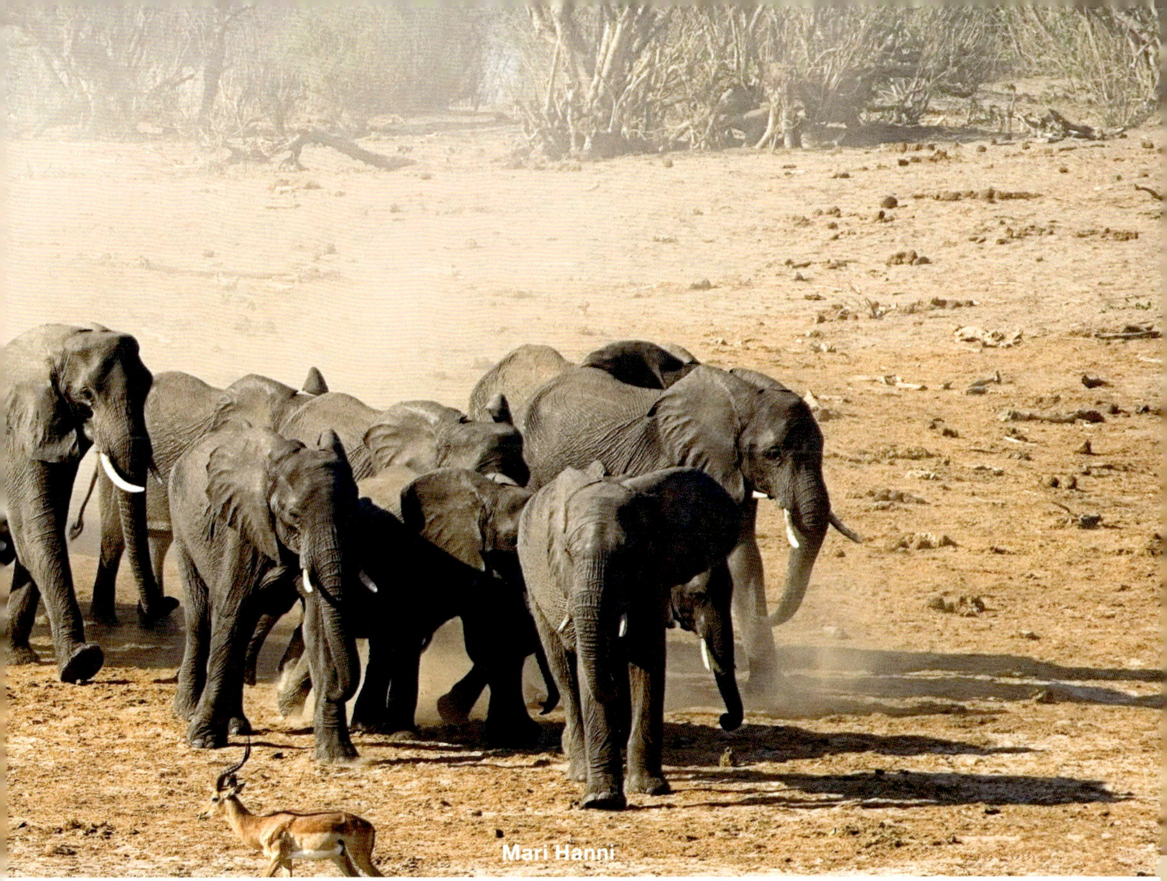
Mari Hanni

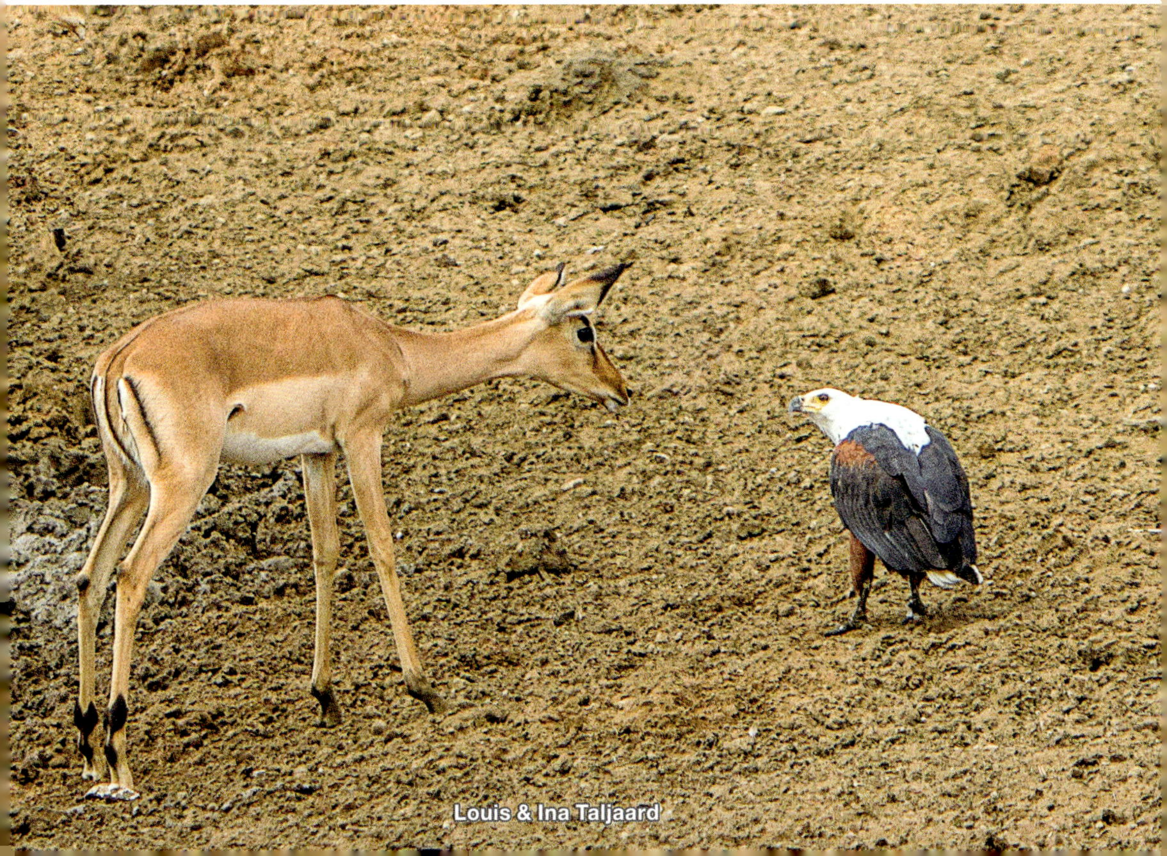
Louis & Ina Taljaard

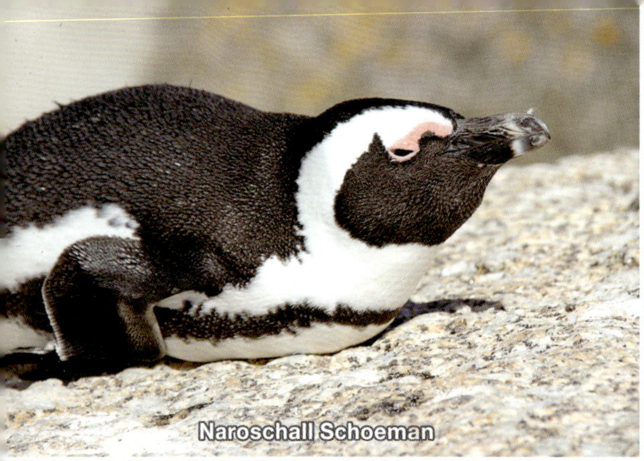
Naroschall Schoeman

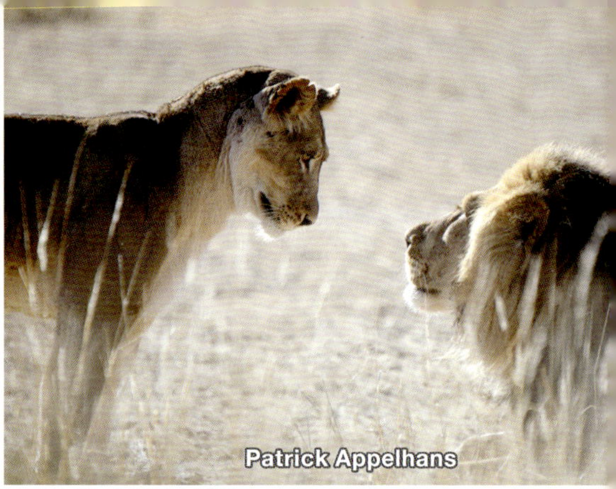
Patrick Appelhans

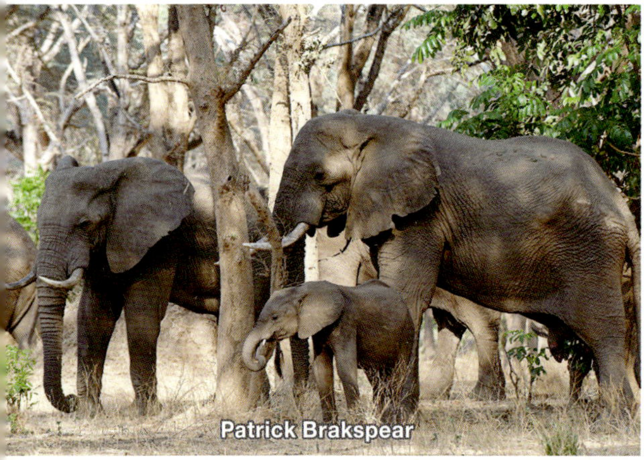
Patrick Brakspear

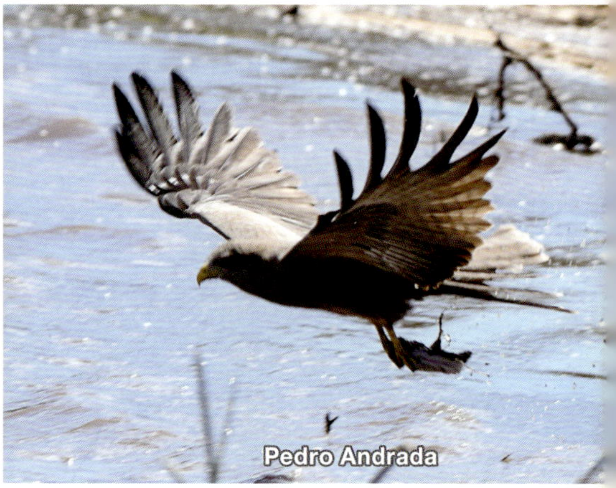
Pedro Andrada

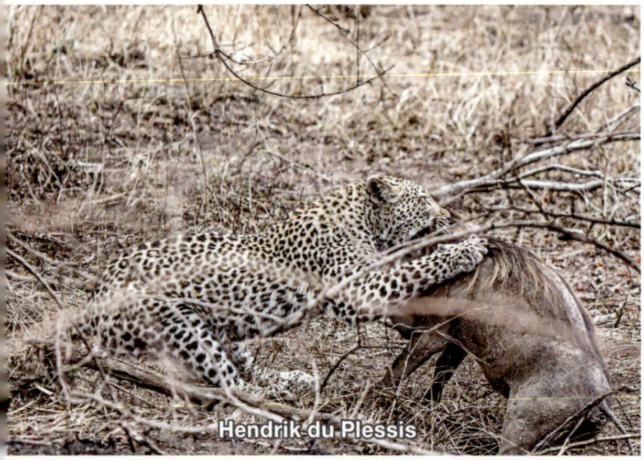
Hendrik du Plessis

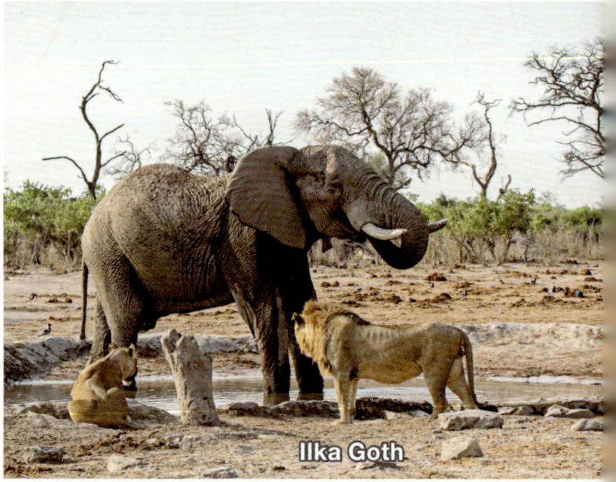
Ilka Goth

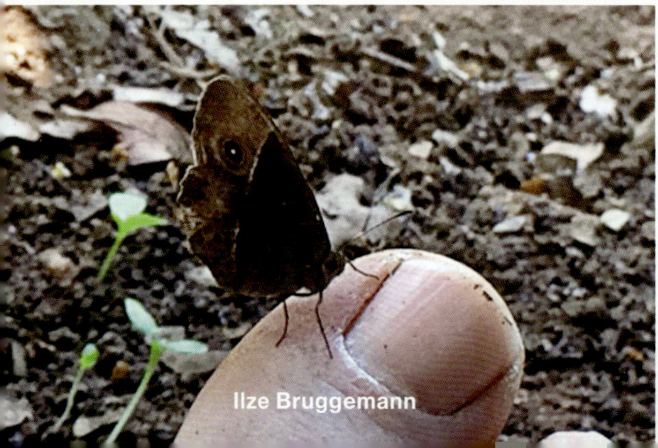
Ilze Bruggemann

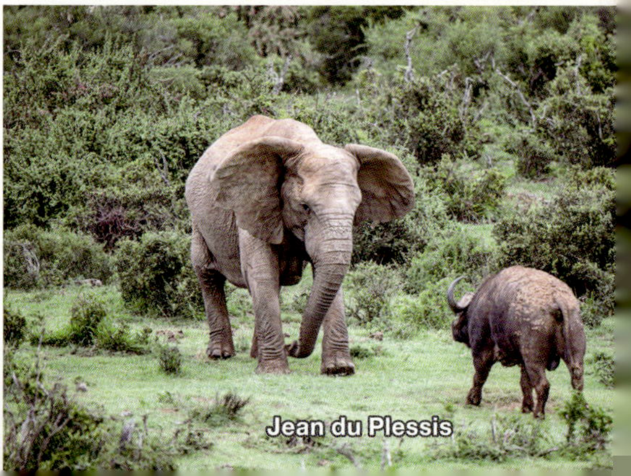
Jean du Plessis

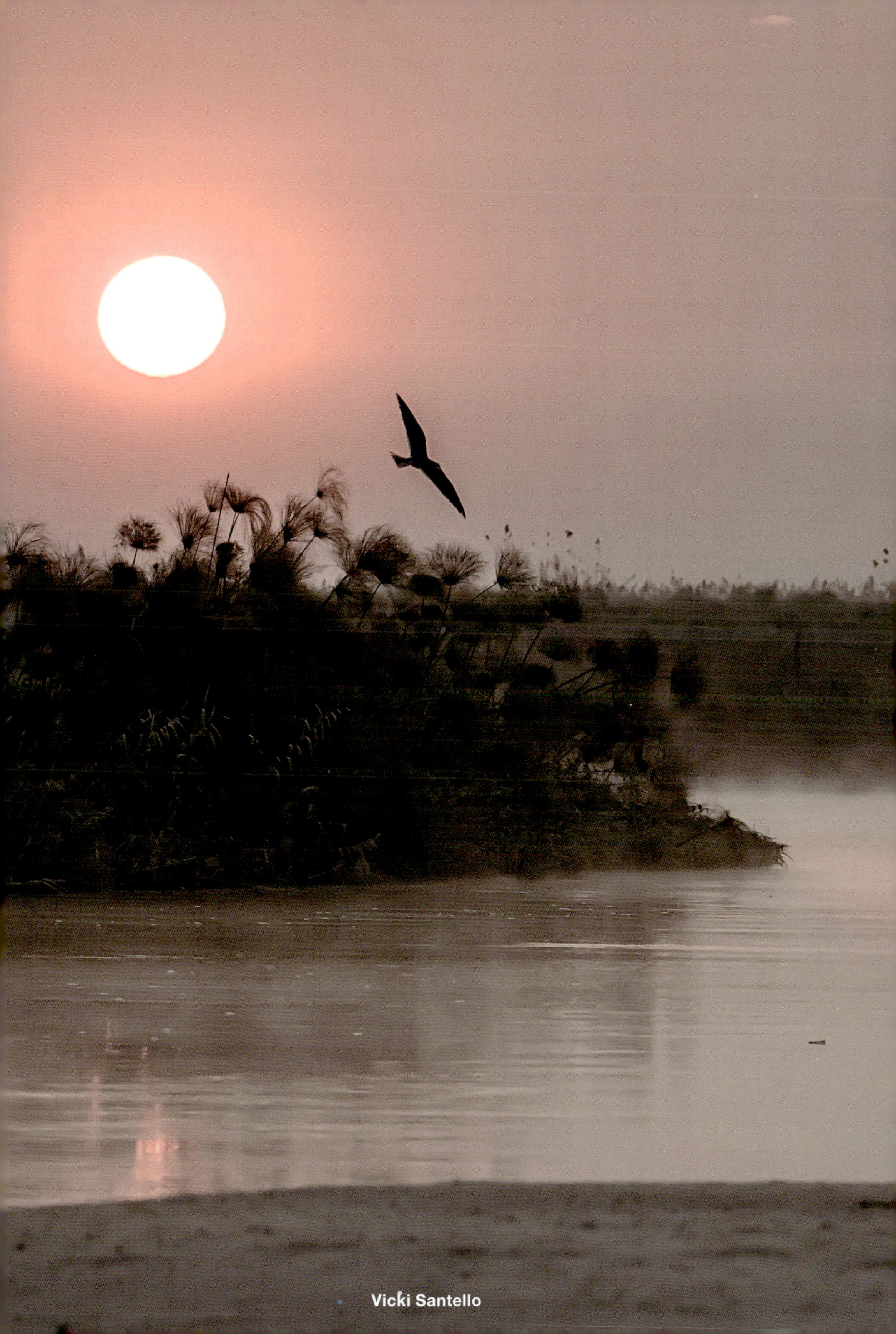

Vicki Santello

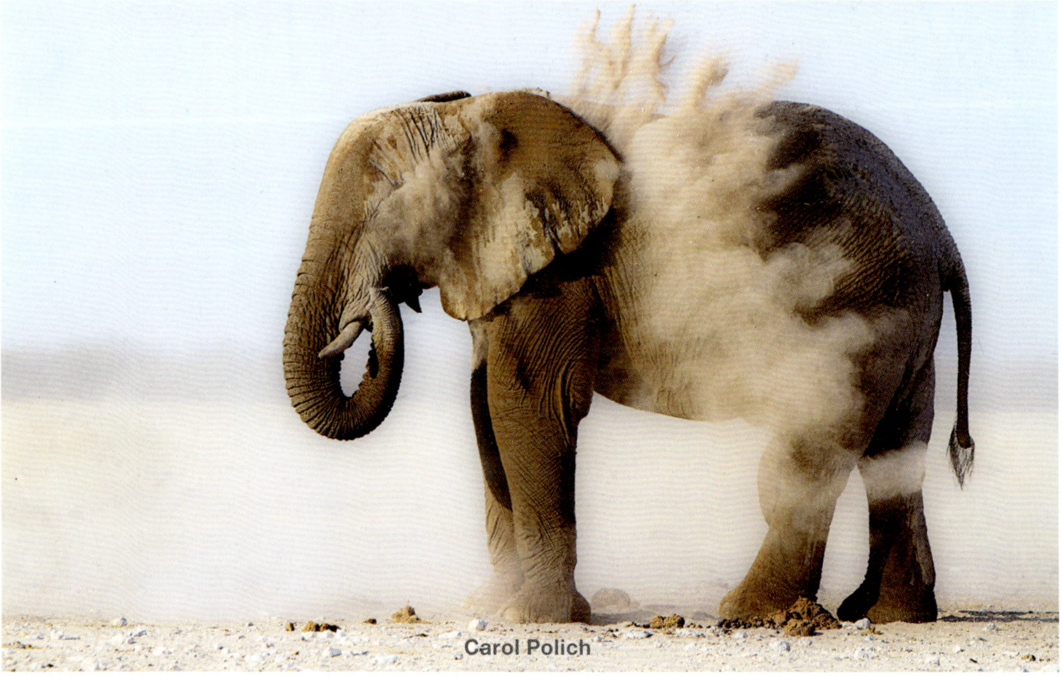
Carol Polich

First Edition
ISBN 978-0-6399473-7-2
Text by various writers
Photography by various photographers
Compiled by Heinrich, Philip and Ingrid van den Berg
and Ronél Bouwer
Publisher: Heinrich van den Berg
Edited by Diane Mullen
Project management by Ronél Bouwer
Proofread by Ronél Bouwer and Margy Beves-Gibson
Design, typesetting and reproduction by
Heinrich van den Berg and Nicky Wenhold
Printed and bound in China

First edition, first impression 2019
Published by **HPH Publishing**
50A Sixth Street, Linden, Johannesburg, 2195, South Africa
www.hphpublishing.co.za
info@hphpublishing.co.za